The Gilmartin Report

The Gilmartin Report

by Dr. Brian G. Gilmartin

The Citadel Press   Secaucus, N. J.

Published by Citadel Press
A division of Lyle Stuart Inc.
120 Enterprise Ave., Secaucus, N.J. 07094
In Canada: George J. McLeod Limited, Toronto
Manufactured in the United States of America

Library of Congress Cataloging in Publication Data

Gilmartin, Brian G.
   The Gilmartin report.

   Bibliography: p. 474
   Includes index.
   1. Group sex — United States. 2. Family — United
States. 3. Adultery — United States. I. Title.
HQ18.U5G555   301.41'53   78-14289

Acknowledgments

Ten years were required to complete the research effort upon which this book is based. The project was immense in scope, and there is no way I could have successfully completed it without the generous help, encouragement and moral support of many dedicated colleagues and friends.

The research was financially funded by the National Science Foundation (Grant #GS-3047). I am especially grateful for having received this grant, as without it this book simply would not have been possible.

I am immensely grateful to Dr. Hallowell Pope, chairman of University of Iowa's sociology department, for his scores of very helpful criticisms and suggestions. Special thanks must also go to Dr. Ira L. Reiss, director of University of Minnesota's Family Study Center and author of many books on sex and family life, for providing me with a great deal of inspiration and encouragement for empirically exploring within the largely unexplored sea of unconventional sexual behavior. This inspiration along with his many helpful comments and his storehouse of knowledge is gratefully acknowledged.

I am grateful also for the encouragement, cooperation and moral support supplied by many other academic colleagues. In particular I would like to thank Dr. Nancy Barclay, head of Virginia Tech University's family life department, Dr. Joseph Maxwell and Dr. George Houston also of Virginia Tech, Dr. Roger Libby of SUNY at Albany, Dr. Robert Whitehurst of Windsor University, Dr. Gordon Clanton and Dr. Lynn Smith of San Diego State University, Dr. James Carroll, chairman of the sociology department at California's Humboldt State University, and Dr. Howard J. Ruppel, Jr., of the University of Iowa. Special thanks must also go to Dr. Berkeley Rice, editor of *Psychology Today* magazine, and to the Rev. Paul Leon Masters of Los Angeles, whose warmth and true spirituality served as a profound inspiration to me during the final months of this project.

To the hundreds of people, particularly the sexual mate-sharing swingers and their children, who were willing to open up their personal lives to me, I feel especially indebted. For without their gracious help this research never could have even been launched. I learned a very great deal from all of these people, and I shall always fondly remember their kindness, enthusiasm, and gracious willingness to supply their time and fascinating conversation.

In order to conduct this research effectively it was also necessary to obtain the assistance of numerous owner-managers of clubs catering to a swinging clientele. The help I received from such people and from other recognized leaders of the California swinging community proved indispendable to the process of efficient and effective data gathering. The promise of anonymity precludes my mentioning the names of these generous and understanding people. However, they know who they are, and their help is gratefully acknowledged.

I am grateful too to the hundreds of students who have taken my "Deviance" and "Family" courses at California's Humboldt State University, Virginia Tech University, the University of Iowa, Cal Poly University, and California State University at Los Angeles. I have learned more from their unlimited flow of comments and reactions than I had ever dreamed possible. And more specifically, I shall always remember the cheerful, constantly friendly and compassionate encouragement of my HSU student Karen Rockwell.

Finally I would like to thank my incredibly practical, hard-headed businessman father, Mr. George V. Gilmartin, who worked as trust officer of the First National State Bank of Newark, New Jersey, from 1921 until his well deserved retirement in 1970—a total of 49 years with the same firm! He never could understand the reason behind studying "those damned crazy swingers." Yet, in his own way he contributed immeasurably to the successful completion of this project.

Brian G. Gilmartin, Ph.D.□

Los Angeles, California
August 11, 1977

Contents

Tables

"I am tempted to believe that what we call necessary institutions are often no more than institutions to which we have grown accustomed, and that in matters of social constitution the field of possibilities is much more extensive than men living in their various societies are ready to imagine."

ALEXANDER *de* TOCQUEVILLE

Chapter 1

Introduction

The behavior with which this book deals has been variously labeled comarital sex, wife-swapping, swinging, sexual mate sharing, and group sex. It is a form of deviance believed by many people to be becoming increasingly prevalent in areas of middle-class suburbia. And it represents one particular species of adultery or extramarital sex. It is a type of deviance which sociologists have classified as "not involving a victim" and as "nonconformist deviance," as opposed to "aberrant" or "criminal" deviance. But it also represents a form of nonconformity which most middle-class people continue to recognize as grossly outlandish, immoral and evil. This is especially true when they find out that it is going on right within their own immediate neighborhood.

Statistically, relatively few Americans are currently involved in sexual mate sharing. Most scholarly estimates place the figure at about 2 percent of all married couples. But this seemingly small percentage actually represents approximately 900,000 married couples, nearly all of whom are middle class and at least 80 percent of whom have children. In essence, a substantial minority of socially and financially well-off American couples are involved in swinging. And many of these people consider themselves to be in the vanguard of social and family change in America.

In this book I shall be dealing with middle and upper middle-class suburban families, most of whom had been involved in sexual mate sharing activities for at least three or more years at the time the data were collected. The majority of the husbands and wives had children, and many of the children were involved in adult-sponsored sexual activities of their own. This is the first book to devote any attention at all to the children in swinging families and to their relationships with their highly nonconformist parents and with their local communities and schools. Up to now, all of the books written on sexual mate sharing have focused almost exclusively on what swingers do at their parties and on how and why they initially involved themselves in such deviant sex practices. Even though this book will not ignore these matters, the prime focus will be on the past and present family life of swingers and how it differs from the past and present family life of non-swinging husbands and wives who live in the same immediate neighborhoods.

The second distinguishing characteristic of the research discussed in this book is that it made use of what scientists call a "control group." A control group for our purposes is simply a group of husbands and wives who are very similar to the swinging husbands and wives on all major social, demographic, and economic characteristics except one: namely, that they were not and had never been swingers. For example, the non-swinging husbands and wives were drawn from the same neighborhoods of residence as were the swinging husbands and wives. Neighborhood of residence is usually an excellent indicator of similarity of life style. In addition, the swinging husbands and wives were quite similar to the non-swinging couples on such personal attributes as education, annual income, age, and number of children in the home. All of the couples in both groups were legally married.

At first glance it may seem that the presence of a control group has little bearing on the quality and importance of a study. Some readers might even regard the idea of a control group as an unnecessary distraction. After all, the main objective in picking up a book such as this is to learn more about mate swapping, the people who practice it and their motives for having involved themselves and their spouses in it.

Hence, it is important for the reader to recognize at the outset that the presence of a control group will permit him or her to learn far more about swingers and their motivations than could ever be learned from reading a report about swingers that does not make use of a control group. For example, by comparing the childhood backgrounds of swinging and non-swinging husbands and wives it becomes possible to pinpoint certain factors that may have led to the swingers' initial interest in involving themselves in this nonconformist life style. Sometimes comparisons between the swingers and the non-swingers will reveal little or no difference between the two groups of couples. But in cases where a clear and strong difference between the swinging and the non-swinging couples becomes apparent, it is likely that an important factor *causing* the development of an initial need for and interest in sexual partner sharing has been isolated.

The study reported on in this book revealed many significant differences between the backgrounds of the swinging husbands and wives and those of the non-swinging husbands and wives. I believe that these differences have a very great deal to teach us about what causes sexual deviance in American society. As such, I believe that many of the findings to be presented in this book will eventually prove to be of immense social significance. Moralists, in particular, have long been baffled by the rapidly increasing popularity of sexual nonconformity within the institution of marriage. The material which follows should remove much of the mystery in people's minds as to why an increasing number of people seem to be attracted to such deviant practices as sexual spouse sharing.

Types of Adultery

It was not until the late 1960s that social scientists began suggesting that there are different forms of extramarital sex, and that the consequences of such behavior may vary with the forms that it takes as well as with the unique personalities of the people who engage in it. Because it has only been about two decades since sex emerged from "under the table" even in the academic world, the very limited attention given to the subject of adultery by social scientists cannot be considered surprising. In fact, it has only been within the past decade or so that research into the important subject of human sexuality has begun to enjoy a modicum of respectability among social scientists.

Various types of adultery can be identified. A distinction can be drawn between conventional adultery and consensual adultery. The former entails secrecy and deception, whereas the latter is marked by openness, by the knowledge and consent of the spouse. Consensual adultery may or may not also involve spousal encouragement, and it may be undertaken either as an individual or as a joint activity involving both husband and wife.

In the case of conventional adultery, the deception on the part of the adulterous partner may have a good, bad, or indifferent effect upon the marriage. Popular and psychiatric writers have tended to stress the negative consequences, and there is usually an implicit assumption in their writing that extramarital sex is *in and of itself* symptomatic of marital deterioration. Indeed, this is as true of these writers' approach to consensual adultery as it is in their approach to conventional adultery.

However, it is unlikely that a husband or a wife could successfully practice consensual adultery for very long unless the internalized values of his or her spouse on matters pertinent to the relationship between sex and marriage were reasonably similar to his or her own values. Indeed, the consequences of consensual adultery are also very likely to be directly affected by the relationship (and degree of similarity) between the internalized norms of a husband and those of his wife. A man who is highly satisfied and happy with his marriage and family life may still occasionally desire and actually experience extramarital sex so long as he does not regard sexual exclusiveness as lying at the very heart of his marriage. If that man knows that his wife would perceive his behavior as rank infidelity if she found out about it, then his careful plotting and deception would clearly be beneficial to his marriage.

There is basically only one form of conventional adultery, although its outcome can be considered a function of several factors such as (1) how good the marriage is; (2) how successful the deception is; (3) whether the person *un*consciously as well as consciously wants to deceive his or her spouse; (4) the number of extramarital partners involved; (5) ability of the adulterous spouse to intellectually *and emotionally* compartmentalize his feelings; and (6) length of friendship with the extramarital partner or partners.

Consensual adultery, sometimes referred to as "faithful adultery," is more complex. Three major conceptually distinct forms of it have emerged in our contemporary culture:

(1) *Adultery toleration.* This is the form that is most similar to conventional adultery. Spouses practicing this form simply extend to each other the freedom to engage in extramarital sex individually, usually according to a set of ground rules that they develop for themselves. Active encouragement may or may not be involved, and the extent of emotional (as opposed to intellectual) acceptance may not be entirely complete for every married couple practicing "adultery toleration." In their book *Sex and the Significant Americans*, John Cuber and Peggy Harroff (1965) fully discussed such adultery toleration pacts among

upper-middle-class suburbanites. Adultery toleration allows extramarital sex into the marriage relationship on very much the same basis as conventional adultery except that the partners are relieved of their commitment to sexual exclusiveness. The necessity for deception and secrecy is thus removed.

(2) *Group marriage*, which usually involves a common residence, is the second form of consensual adultery. Because it transcends the conventional dyadic marital relationship, it precipitates the emergence of a significantly altered form of marriage or marriage/family systems. Strictly speaking, it does not constitute "extramarital relations," because all of the parties consider themselves to be married to each other. Since the "marriages" are not legally recognized, group marriage constitutes an ambiguous analytic category. Most of the recent group marriage experiments involving communal living have been short lived. But during the time such groups remained intact, many of the members were able to function under the assumption that everyone was "married" to everyone, and that so long as there was mutual desire and consent sexual intercourse between any particular man and woman could take place and would be considered perfectly acceptable in the eyes of the group as a whole.

(3) *Comarital sex* or "swinging" is the third form of consensual adultery, and it is the form with which this book is concerned. Despite the numerous differences in behavioral style and in sexual philosophy among comarital sex participants, the following definition comes close to covering all the contingencies: *Comarital sex (or swinging) is that form of extramarital sexual behavior which involves legally married couples sharing coitus and other sexual behaviors with other legally married couples in a social context defined by all participants as constituting a kind of recreation-convivial play.*

This definition is not intended to imply that *all* participants unconsciously *as well as* consciously, or emotionally *as well as* intellectually, define the comarital social situation as convivial play. What it *does* mean is that all participants will understand each other to define it in this manner. In short, when a person is involved in the sexual mate sharing scene, he or she is expected to adapt to the normative prescriptions and proscriptions of the swinger role. Whether or not most swingers of both sexes are presently capable of adapting to the demands and expectations of their role is an interesting and important question in and of itself. This is one of the issues upon which this book will attempt to shed some light.

In studying a group of San Diego area swingers Charles Varni (1970) suggested the following as a typology of swingers. This typology appropriately amplifies and clarifies the above definition:

Egotistical swingers are sexual mate sharers who do not seek any emotional involvement with their partners. But they nevertheless tend to be quite selective in their partner selection. They want purely sexual experiences and they seek to gratify their own needs and desires, which usually involve feeling attracted to and desired by other persons. Swinging is viewed as a distinct and separate part of the lives of these people and they have no social relationships or friendships with their swinging partners outside the context of the swinging parties. They enjoy party and one-couple situations and may be members of a fairly stable sexual partner sharing group.

Recreational swingers tend to emphasize the social aspects of swinging. They are usually members of fairly stable groups, enjoy both party and one-couple situations and engage in non-swinging activities with one another. These couples tend to view swinging as a recreational and social activity in which significant emotional involvement with the sexual partners (to whom they are not married) is neither needed nor desired. The emphasis of the recreational swinger tends to be on the sociability and sexuality of the swinging experience.

Interpersonal swingers desire and emphasize close emotional relationships with their partners. They tend to seek intimate and viable long-term friendships with couples with whom they can share themselves both emotionally and sexually. The sexual aspect of an extramarital relationship is not felt by interpersonal swingers to be of primary importance, and they do expect to engage in social and recreational activities with their partners. Most interpersonal swingers emphasize openness and honesty as basic values. They also always prefer one-couple situations. Most of their friends also tend to be swingers.

Not all swinging couples can be easily classified into one of the foregoing three categories. There are many couples who seem to fall somewhere on a continuum between two of the categories. Nevertheless, the descriptions should provide a general indication of the range of variation that can be found among couples who call themselves swingers. There are probably very few married American mate-sharing couples who fall outside the purview of these three categories.

Most of the people who engage in comarital sexual activities refer to themselves as swingers. Such terms as "swinger" and "swinging" serve a number of special purposes. A very small minority of comarital sex enthusiasts shun these terms because they stir up connotations of a type of sexual mate exchange which they very strongly dislike. But most spouse sharers find in the label "swinger" a kind of nebulous ambiguity which enables them to use the term publicly without having to worry about hostile reactions. For example, they can ask a passing acquaintance whether or not he likes to swing. If the acquaintance turns out to be "square" all they need do is specify that they meant "have a great time at fun parties." Because of their convenience and popularity the terms "swinger" and "swinging" will be used throughout this book, although the other major synonyms cited earlier for comarital sex will also be used occasionally.

In sum, swinging differs from the majority of extramarital sexual activity in five major regards:

1. *Both* the husband and the wife practice it *together;*

they do so *simultaneously*, i.e., at one and the same time along with one or more other couples.

2. The participating spouses at a swinging party understand each other to view sex as *play* and *recreation* which is devoid of deep emotional feelings of romance and attachment of the possessive conjugal variety. The party situation is *not* defined as "impersonal," however. All guests at a party are expected not only to like, but also to feel some degree of personal affection, concern and respect for fellow group members. And very often they are expected to feel a sense of unity and oneness with all fellow swingers.

3. Feelings of jealousy and possessiveness are always defined as normatively inappropriate as well as downright dangerous within the context of a sex party. However, defining something as obligatory does not always make it so in practice. One of the purposes of this book will be to shed some light on the extent to which swinging husbands and wives are able to comfortably internalize the normative prescriptions and proscriptions of their role.

4. Sexual mate sharing, in sharp contrast to the more conventional forms of adultery, is allowed to occur only at certain well-defined times and places which are agreed upon beforehand by all of the participants.

5. Swinging couples usually expect each other to enjoy happy, satisfying, well-adjusted marriages. Whether or not they actually do is an issue which will later be dealt with at length. Traditional psychiatry has always viewed *any* form of adultery as symptomatic of a weak or deteriorating marital relationship. Suffice it to say here that couples who appear to have problems very often find it quite difficult to obtain membership in a swinging group.

The Value Stretch Concept

In his analysis of common law quasi-marriages in Trinidad, sociologist Hyman Rodman (1963) introduced the concept of "value stretch." The idea grew out of his observation of a distinction people made between what is normatively *preferable* and what is normatively *acceptable* behavior. In order to adapt to the demands of certain occupational and cultural pressures, lower class Trinidadians usually enter into consensual unions. But unlike the cohabitation that is becoming increasingly popular among American young people, this cohabitation is not restricted to the childless years; in fact, it typically lasts well into a couple's parenthood years. The overwhelming majority of the Trinidadians involved in such sexual unions tend to view them as perfectly acceptable although *not* preferable to legal marriage.

The "value stretch" concept may also partially explain the behavior and self-legitimating ideology of American swingers. Even though most swingers reject any distinction between the normatively acceptable and the normatively preferred as far as their own sexual behavior is concerned, there can be no question about the fact that virtually all swingers reject the "hippie" and other escapist approaches to life. In short, swingers depart from the conventional only in the area of sex. Virtually all of them are strong capitalists; they do not reject affluence or the necessity for occasionally dishonest role-playing in order to sustain the appearance of community respectability. To be sure, swingers could hardly be expected to attain or to maintain an upper-middle-class station if they did reject affluence or the discipline of respectable career involvement, or if they failed to appropriately compartmentalize their deviant sexual recreation in a discreet manner. The swinger's rejection of society is thus *only partial*, and it is highly discriminating. It is never advertised in any conspicuous manner outside of the swinging social circles.

The highly selective, carefully guarded rejection of *some* of the conventional middle-class normative structure represents *one kind* of "value stretch." It represents one way of "having one's cake and eating it too." Further, it represents *one way* of freely adapting to some of life's stresses and strains (*and* basic human desires) that is not open to the bulk of the population at the same socioeconomic level.

Prior to the publication of this book practically no light had ever been shed on the question of how affluent people come to identify with the role of sexual mate-sharing swinger. But of this much we can be certain: it requires plenty of work, perseverance, and determination to become educated for and to successfully maintain oneself in an upper-middle-class occupation and career. A person of low "ego strength" or of poor self-discipline is not likely to "make it" either socially or occupationally among the affluent.

The fact that well-educated, financially well-off men and women are able to enjoy extremely active, highly nonconforming sexual lives casts serious doubt on the validity of the traditional position that *sexual liberality* and well-developed *internal controls* (self-discipline) are mutually at odds with one another. Evidently there are conditions under which occupational success and community respectability can be attained and enjoyed by married couples whose behavior in the sexual area of life is vastly different and far more active than that of most couples of the same society. The existence of swinging among well-educated groups suggests that key behavioral attributes widely believed to be mutually exclusive may actually not be so. The old cliché that "those who work hard play hard, and those who play hard work hard" may be basically valid.

Even today it is easy to make a strong case for the position that if a society is to arrive at and effectively maintain a civilized, highly cultured status, then the majority of that society's adult citizens must possess a well-developed set of internal controls. *But* there are *many* possibilities for socially patterning man's sexual drive in an orderly, predictable, well-structured way. *Some* of these structured patterns could conceivably allow for copious coital activity and erotic pleasure among people of all ages from pubescence onward. The traditional pattern of sexual norms is *only one of many possibilities,* even though deeply internalized idea systems supportive of this pattern could lead anyone to jump to the conclusion that it is the *only* workable pattern.

Plan of the Book

This book will focus on four basic issues: (1) how and why initially conventional middle-class people become attracted to and involved in sexual mate sharing; (2) the life style of minor children whose parents swing; (3) the quality of the marriages and of the family lives of swinging husbands and wives; and (4) a controversial but highly effective method of birth control popular among many younger swingers and their teenaged children. In discussing the first and third issues a great deal of use will be made of the data collected from the "control group" of *non*-swinging husbands and wives.

I have organized the book into fifteen chapters. Chapter 2 provides an historical and cross-cultural perspective on swinging, and it makes very clear the point that this form of sexual nonconformity did not suddenly and capriciously appear on the American scene in the late 1960s. Swinging in one form or another has been very much around for thousands of years.

Chapter 3 will present a brief discussion of the methods used in collecting and analyzing the data on which the substance of this book is based. However, I do want to make clear at the outset the point that this book was written for the general lay public. Social scientists and other scholarly readers should find the material both illuminating and provocative. But they should look to my other published articles for a discussion of the more technical aspects of data collection and methods of statistical analysis. A comprehensive bibliography is presented at the end of this book for the benefit of those wishing to read further.

Chapters 4 through 8 will deal with questions pertinent

to how and why middle-class people decide to become involved with swinging. Chapter 4 will focus on the past and present relations that swinging husbands and wives have had with their parents and kin. It will also deal with the quality of their childhood years while living in the homes of their parents.

Chapter 5 will deal with relationships with chosen friends as well as with neighbors. Recreational interests (not relating to eroticism) and club memberships will also be covered here. Chapter 6 will deal with political and religious background and present political and religious philosophy of the various husbands and wives studied.

Chapter 7 will discuss the premarital dating, courtship and sexual lives of the respondents. It will also cover matters pertinent to romantic interests, involvements, and psychological needs. Chapter 8 will deal with the role which various kinds of sexual and pornographic literature played in precipitating an interest and involvement in the swinging world.

Chapter 9 will deal with questions pertinent to just how happy, well-adjusted and content swingers are with their own lives and with their marriages. This chapter will also present material on how husbands manage to convince their wives to give sexual mate sharing a try. One of the most important findings uncovered by this research deals with the widely disparate consequences which different forms of adultery have for married couples; this too will be dealt with in Chapter 9.

Chapter 10 will discuss what actually goes on at the various kinds of swinging parties and get-togethers. Swingers govern themselves in accordance with a body of clearly defined normative expectations. The issue of jealousy and how it is handled will also be presented here.

Chapters 11 through 13 will deal with the children of swingers. Chapter 11 will focus on the sexual interests and social involvements of the swingers' older youngsters, while Chapter 13 will discuss techniques and philosophies of child-rearing prevalent among the swinging and the non-swinging couples. Chapter 12 will present a detailed coverage of the "method of frequent ejaculation," which is a birth control method I found to be extremely popular among the swingers' sexually active teenagers.

Through the eyes of society-at-large swinging is a highly deviant form of recreation. But within the ranks of the swinging population there are forms of socially shared erotic behavior which the majority of the swingers themselves consider to be highly nonconformist, deviant, and even bizarre, but which they tolerate among some of their fellows. Chapter 14 will focus on the bizarre end of the swinging continuum and the little that is known about it.

Chapter 15 will provide a summary discussion of what appear to be the major social antecedents of sexual mate sharing in America. Some material will also be presented here on the demographic origins of swingers. The chapter will conclude with a discussion of the psychological and marital consequences of swinging. The question of whether or not swinging poses any threat to the institution of marriage in the United States will also be considered here, along with the issue of whether or not swinging is likely to grow in popularity.

Why Study Swinging?

Over the past decade a number of books have been published which deal with sexual mate exchange among American middle-class suburbanites. Why, therefore, should another book be added to the already long list?

A major answer to this question is that we still know very little about what *causes* some people to pursue sexually deviant life styles while other people of very similar backgrounds do not. Up to now, all of the books published on sexual mate sharing have concentrated on swingers' feelings, sexual experiences and subjective motivation and have dealt very well with the philosophy and ideology behind swinging as well as with the kinds of activities that typically go on at swinging get-togethers. Such subjects are very interesting and will not be ignored in these pages. However, other books have not told us anything about the *kinds* of people from economically comfortable backgrounds who are prone toward becoming involved in and committed to sexual mate sharing on a prolonged basis.

This book can provide tentative answers to scores of questions about swingers that have long fascinated both layman and social scientist alike. It can do so because the findings it presents are based on data taken from two different groups of legally married, suburban middle-class people: (1) a group of 100 couples who regularly engage in sexual mate sharing activities, and (2) a group of 100 conventional, non-swinging couples who reside in the very same immediate neighborhoods as do the swinging couples. Through comparing and contrasting the responses of the swinging couples with those of the non-swinging couples a huge amount of meaningful and potentially very useful material was obtained about what it takes to become a swinger and why a very small minority of middle-class people choose to become involved in sexual mate exchange.

Inasmuch as swinging is very clearly a form of deviance, an additional matter to be focused upon is the extent to which the data collected on swingers jibes with the data of studies dealing with other, very different forms of deviance such as aggressive criminal behavior. Of particular interest will be the extent to which swingers, in contrast to other types of deviants, are socially and emotionally linked up with such conventional agencies of social control as relatives and kinfolk. If it can be shown that swingers have a number of points in common with some very different types of deviant and nonconformist people, such knowledge could prove very useful from the standpoint of advancing our understanding of deviance and of what produces and maintains it.

One of the liveliest areas of debate at the present time is that of whether or not such phenomena as sexual mate sharing, living together unmarried, urban communes, group marriage, the rapidly increasing divorce rate, the comparatively easy availability (for all but the shy) of premarital and conventional extramarital sex, etc., augur poorly for the safety and integrity of the family system as we know it. Many influential people regard the family institution today as being on extremely shaky ground. On the other hand, others perceive the various changes that seem to be occurring as posing no serious threat to the family system. Indeed, some contemporary theorists even view many of the changes (most of which are still very much in the process of occurring) as having a strong potential for strengthening rather than weakening the family system—over the long haul. The material presented in the chapters which follow sheds a good deal of light on the extent to which swinging and related forms of sexual nonconformity pose any kind of viable threat to the American family system.

One of the things that makes sexual behavior so fascinating to study is that it varies so greatly from one part of the world to another, from one society to another; and even within the same social class or community of a particular society it varies enormously from one group to another. Biologists and medical doctors have been telling us for a long time that there is actually very little difference in sexual makeup among human beings. Man represents a species of animal just as do dogs and cats and orangutans and monkeys. We know that dogs living in Ireland do not govern their sexual behavior any differently than dogs living in Iceland or in Polynesia or in the most conservative regions of southern Utah. While some dogs *are* more sexually active than others in all of these places, the percentage of unusually active dogs does not vary significantly from one part of the world to another. In stark contrast to this, among human beings the percentage who are highly active sexually does vary immensely from one geographic area to another.

The reason, of course, is that each geographic area represents a social setting complete with a learned system of norms and beliefs. Only man learns a system of normative beliefs and makes that system part of his reality. And man is the only animal who is profoundly affected in the way he thinks and behaves by the strength of his emotional attachments to those he loves and upon whom he depends for warmth and meaningful attention.

In sum, no one up to now has written about what swingers were like as people *before* they ever thought about becoming swingers. No one up to now has contrasted the childhoods of people who swing with the childhoods of those of similar socioeconomic backgrounds who do not swing. In addition, no one up to now has contrasted the past and present family lives of those who swing with the family lives of those who do not. No previous writer could do any of these things because no one up to now has obtained the kind of data that would permit handling such significant and important issues.

Let us turn now to sexual mate exchange in other societies and to its history within the context of our own American society.

Chapter 2

Mate Swapping in Cross-Cultural and Historical Perspective

Since the institution of the family is closer and more intimately tied to our personal lives than any other, the maintenance of objectivity in the course of studying its deviant patterns has always presented a serious problem. Fortunately, our efforts to arrive at objectivity in understanding sexual and family patterns in our own society which strike us as grossly deviant can be greatly facilitated by first directing our attention toward these very same social behavior patterns as they are engaged in by persons living in other societies.

There is evidence that "mate swapping" in one form or another has been going on for literally thousands of years. In his analysis of marriage, family and kinship customs in 250 societies, anthropologist George Murdock (1949) had this to say:

> Even after marriage it cannot be maintained that sex operates exclusively to reinforce the matrimonial relationship. To be sure, sexual intercourse between a married man and an unrelated woman married to another is forbidden in 126 of our sample societies, and it is freely or conditionally allowed in only 24. These figures, however, give an exaggerated impression of the prevalence of cul-

tural restraints against extramarital sexuality, for affairs are often permitted between particular relatives though forbidden with non-relatives. Thus in a majority of the societies in our sample for which information is available a married man may legitimately carry on an affair with one or more of his female relatives, including a sister-in-law in 41 instances. Such evidence demonstrates conclusively that sexual gratification is by no means always confined to the marital relationship, even in theory. It (sex) can reinforce other relationships as well, as it commonly does, it (sex) cannot be regarded as peculiarly conducive to marriage or as alone accountable for the stability of the most crucial relationship in the omnipresent family institution. (Murdock, 1949, p. 6.)

Anthropologists Ford and Beach (1951) have also reported that 39 percent of the 139 societies they investigated practiced mate exchange in some form. In particular, their work highlighted the prevalence of mate exchange among affinal relatives such as opposite sexed siblings-in-law and, in some cases, the spouse's opposite-sexed cousins.

Contemporary American swingers were by no means the first people to develop or discover comarital sexual practices, or to create norms for the orderly patterning of these activities. Indeed, some of the more sophisticated American swappers may well have adapted some of their particular swinging patterns from some of those about to be described!

Among the many African tribes practicing wife lending is the Banyoro of Uganda. Here swapping occurs among the spouses of any given clan. Briefly, the wife of a "brother" or clan fellow is regarded as "fair game" for sexual intercourse. Any sexual activity involving partners *outside* the clan, however, is defined as adultery and is punished. A wife may find herself on bad terms with her husband if she admits a man with whom her husband does not get along very well. But from the standpoint of the wider community her behavior would still be regarded as fully moral and acceptable. Numerous other tribes of East Central Africa could also be cited, all of which have long sustained quite similar customs.

Among the Masai of East Africa age grade groupings take the place of clans. Here premarital sexual license is permitted the adolescent warriors who live with their sweethearts in barracks. At the time of marriage all persons in the appropriate age category can demand coitus with the bride. The groom faces ostracism if he tries to prevent this; but interestingly, he apparently never does. Similarly, throughout marriage full sexual hospitality can be claimed and not refused by members of any given age group. Other African societies similar to the Masai in nature and form of wife-swapping customs include the Nandi, the Chagga, and the Wataweta.

Spouse-swapping activities are certainly not restricted to the African continent. In fact, such customs seem to be most prevalent in areas in and around the Pacific Ocean. Among the Southern Massim of New Guinea, membership in a specific age group places the individual in a special relationship to his fellows. This special relationship is called "eraiam." Each male of a particular fellowship has sexual rights over the wives of his fellow eraiam, and he typically uses and enjoys these rights frequently. Unlike certain other societies such as the Arunta and the Murngin, the husband's permission is not required for any given copulation, although respect and consideration for the feelings of the partner and for other relevant persons does seem to be the general rule here as in most societies where mate exchange is practiced.

Prior to the twentieth century the natives of such places as Tahiti, Tonga, and Hawaii had also exchanged marital partners on an overt and frequent basis. However, within all of these societies the swapping took place only within the boundaries of a given type of homogeneous group. Kinship or age grading or status and prestige or any one of a number of other factors could be the criterion upon

which members were initiated into a "swinging group."
(As will be shown later, age and social class serve as important criteria for contemporary American swingers.) A
crucial point is that all sexual activities took place only
within the context of the group. Sex beyond group boundaries was typically defined as unacceptable and "unfaithful," and would be punished consistent with the degree of
its perceived "immorality."

Norms confining mate-swapping activities to persons
within the group characterize most "interpersonal" type
mate-sharing cliques in contemporary United States almost as much as they do in such groups in preliterate
societies. Swapping behavior, as it is viewed in its correct
historical and anthropological perspective, was never
haphazard, disorganized or "promiscuous." The term
"promiscuity" denotes indiscriminate, highly casual and
haphazard sexual pairing without regard to any criteria of
partner selection. Small, homogeneous preliterate
societies ordinarily exert far greater control over their
members than a large, highly complex, pluralistic society
such as our own. A tight and well-structured system of
norms, rules and expectations can and indeed often does
occur as an integral part of a system of role relationships
that may strike Western man as being highly "permissive." Such a system of role relationships may have normative boundaries that are a great deal tighter and more
strongly and consistently enforced than most normative
boundaries that prevail here in American society. The difference is that these normative limits are drawn at *different* places with regard to such matters as sex, love, and
family interaction. The fact that the boundaries are established at points that are probably in greater harmony with
the primary needs and nature of human beings than our
normative boundaries are may constitute one explanation
as to why sex norm enforcement tends to be less of a problem in most preliterate societies than it is in our own society. It would appear that it is quite possible to have a
well-structured, well-ordered permissiveness.

According to numerous anthropologists, one of the key functions of wife exchange in terms of clan or age grade fraternity is that of demonstrating the solidarity of the group to the outside world. Most of the anthropologists who studied these societies agree that there is a communality of thought, feeling, and possession that is brought about by the lending of spouses. If this is so in primitive societies wherein swapping is the expected pattern, we should certainly expect to find such communality of thought, feeling and possession present to an even greater extent among swappers in the United States, inasmuch as such behavior is regarded as highly deviant here. When behavior binding a group together is regarded by out-groups as highly deviant, a strong and very intense in-group feeling of solidarity is normally needed in order for the component members to maintain their sense of direction, purpose and psychic integrity.

Many preliterate societies that practice swapping tend to do it in the context of groups that are fairly large, sometimes containing as many as 25 couples. On the other hand, many tribes such as the Siberian Chuckchee, Yukajhir, Tungus, and maritime Koryak confine their mate sharing to much smaller groups, usually involving just two or three couples. A sexual relationship must extend beyond the boundary of these groups in order to be defined by the society as "adultery." Periodic sexual exchange within the small group is regarded as normal, natural and desirable. The fact that these groups tend to remain stable over long periods of time has led some anthropologists to suggest that this particular form of mate exchange (quite common even among swingers in the United States) is merely a variation on monogamy.

Two other somewhat less commonly occurring forms in which spouse swapping is found are the "Mardi Gras" pattern, and the "sexual hospitality" pattern. Societies practicing the "Mardi Gras" form of mate swapping enforce strictly monogamous sexual patterns *most of the year*. However, on certain highly festive occasions which, depending on the society, may occur annually, semiannually, or once for each of the four seasons, a considerable amount of sexual freedom is permitted. This freedom quite commonly incorporates the exchange of spouses. In fact, in several societies the daily exchange of spouses for a period of about a fortnight is the primary manner in which the freedom is expressed. And it will usually occur within the context of feasting, partying, and sometimes even religious worshiping. The "Mardi Gras" pattern is found among certain of the aboriginal tribes of Australia. It can be suggested that socially sanctioned occasions of sexual license such as this may have the specific function of promoting the acceptance of rules and regulations of ordinary life. In doing what he or she is expected to do during each of the regular, mundane days of the year, each citizen of such societies can look forward to the special quarterly or semiannual or annual festival occasions when he or she can live out his or her sexual fantasies. Each festival occasion or "Mardi Gras" will sometimes last as long as two weeks; hence there is ample opportunity for much of the fantasy that has built up over several months to find socially sanctioned expression.

In still other societies, spouse sharing (or "lending," in this case) is regarded as the most ideal form of *social hospitality.* In the case of the maritime Koryak and the Eskimo groups, a man may bestow his wife or daughter upon a stranger as a gesture denoting (the expectation of) mutual acceptance and trust. Acceptance of this temporary sexual liaison allays the anxiety of uncertainty of the giver, and makes him feel that the stranger is not going to be dangerous. Sex is often believed by such people to possess a sort of benevolent magical quality that renders all participants congenial, friendly and compatible. Hence, refusal of the sexual favor by a stranger is often perceived as an insult or as a danger signal, and at least a few cases have been recorded in which fundamentalist missionaries have been executed for refusing. The 1960 motion picture *Savage Innocence,* starring Anthony Quinn as the mate-lending Eskimo, dealt with this theme quite beautifully.

Numerous anthropologists have documented similar emotional and vital economic significance for these sexual exchanges among the Eskimos. It has been found that these liaisons cement ties of friendship, provide for the inclusion of non-kin within the kinship circles, and provide assurance of continued cooperation and aid during difficult times. Eskimo wife exchanges also signify definite obligations among men similar to those existing among immediate family members. The spouse exchange customs further served to guarantee that no adult man or woman would ever be left for very long without a sexual partner. Of course, it should also be pointed out that female infanticide in large measure supported Eskimo wife lending. Most Eskimo groups traditionally suffered from a shortage of adult women.

Anthropologists Ford and Beach (1951) have also pointed out that "mate sharing" or "wife lending" often tend to be a part of a pattern of mutual hospitality, albeit hardly in the spirit of an easy exchange of gifts. Usually the permission of both spouses is necessary, and the sharing of women signifies the establishment of valued kinship bonds, such as "blood brotherhood."

A good example of "blood brotherhood" can be found among the Ruanda of East Africa, a society studied by anthropologist Pierre Gravel. Bartell (1971) quotes him at length as follows:

> When a man has to travel to a territory where he has no kinsmen, he establishes a blood brotherhood in the same manner in which he takes a bride. The same rituals are involved. The new blood brother is now entitled to the same kind of protection and shelter as a brother ... Marriage among the Ruanda is not a marriage of individuals, but of lineages. The woman's lineage united with the man's lineage is marriage. The wife becomes the wife of the lineage. It is through the family that a particular wife is assigned to a particular man. If

this man dies, his brother takes over the wife. In this case there is no ritual involved at all, since she is already the wife of the lineage. You don't just say to anyone, "Do you want to be my blood brother?" The rules that regulate relationships between individuals are now present. My blood brother owes me respect. Their society tells them that the woman I live with is the wife of the lineage. When I am not there, it is my brother who takes my place. Family-wise, he is me . . . They do not think in terms of having sexual access to their blood brother's wife. The first thing that comes to their mind will be protection from physical danger . . . The wife is not considered a possession and she is not given for such purposes. (Bartell, 1971, pp. 51–52.)

The reader should keep the above quotation in mind. It will become apparent in Chapter 5 that there is an almost uncanny similarity between the "blood brotherhood" form of wife exchange in the Ruanda society and the close, quasi-kinship ties that develop among many swinging couples here in contemporary United States. It is not at all uncommon for American swingers to have lists of fellow swingers who are living in different cities spread out all over the United States, Canada, and sometimes even Europe, Australia and New Zealand. Most of the people on these lists are not personally known by the typical swinging couple entrusted with such a list. However, when that couple has to travel (or vacation) in a distant state they can feel perfectly free about contacting one of the couples on the list in the city they are visiting. The host couple will provide room and board, psychologically meaningful companionship and sexual favors for the visiting couple and their children, and will expect the same consideration in their own travels. As will be shown later, most swingers never developed close or meaningful relations with their own kin. For many of them this nationwide swinging network of fellow swinging families provides an effective substitute: hence the label "quasi-kinfolk."

History of Mate Sharing in Western Societies

Most of the history of mate sharing must be considered nebulous at best. But in view of the fact that it has been considered a highly deviant practice since early Christian times, the lack of clear records cannot be viewed as surprising. That it is not a phenomenon new to the Western world, however, appears quite certain. A variety of literary sources extending as far back as the Middle Ages could be cited, all of which suggest that mate exchange was by no means unheard of among some civilized Europeans, particularly in England and on the northern part of the Continent. Indeed, during the Dark Ages in Europe sexual freedom among the elite may well have been far more the rule rather than the exception. Of course, the elite at that time represented a very tiny minority of the population; but it was this tiny minority (the literate leisure class) that produced virtually all of the literature of the period.

In one of the most fascinating discussions available, Lipton (1965) cites numerous historical and literary sources, all of which suggest that comarital sex orgies may have been especially widespread at times and in certain places during the pre-Christian era. In particular, the "Mardi Gras" pattern of sexual spouse sharing appears to have been very prevalent in societies located in what is now the Middle East, Turkey, Syria, and Israel. After approximately 200 B.C. these practices appear to have disappeared; but up until that time sexual orgies involving both single and married people were a very commonplace occurrence at seasonal festivals, feast periods, and also during religious holidays. It would appear that many of our ancestors of 2,000 to 4,000 years ago viewed frequent sexual orgasms publicly experienced (and with many different opposite-sexed persons in the context of orgies) as being a great facilitator of profoundly spiritual, deeply moving religious experiences. By 300 A.D. the norms had made a complete "about face," and sexual experience came to be viewed as antithetical to true spiritual and religious experience. In fact, even strictly monogamous sexual experience came to be viewed as antispiritual unless it occurred exclusively within the bonds of matrimony and only for purposes of procreation. Parenthetically, these new norms were not those of Christ, but rather of a band of extremely powerful ascetics whose philosophy became wrongly associated by the masses with Christian ideas.

Literature seldom if ever provides a mirror reflection of what social reality at any given point in historic time was like. But when a particular theme or content is found to be common to a number of works that had been written during a given period, it may be suggestive of what some (albeit the most literate) of the people during that period were intellectually preoccupied or behaviorally involved with.

Some of the case history letters collected by Wilson and Meyers (1965) strongly suggest that sexual mate sharing had been practiced in the United States as far back as the turn of the century. But by the same token, their material does not suggest that the practice became especially prevalent here until after World War II. Prior to that time swinging seems to have been confined primarily to small coteries of affluent iconoclasts, artists, and intellectuals living in or near major urban centers such as New York, Los Angeles, San Francisco, etc.

In his essay "The Secret Society," well-known social theorist Georg Simmel indicated that comarital sex orgies were occasionally held by some of Germany's intelligentsia during the first decade of the twentieth century. Then, as now, sexual mate sharing almost always took place within the context of "secret societies." Such "under the table" organizations serve many important purposes for their members:

> The first internal relation typical of the secret society is the reciprocal *confidence* among its members. It is required to a particularly great extent, because

the purpose of secrecy is, above all, *protection*. Of all the protective measures, the most radical is to make oneself invisible. In this respect, the secret society differs fundamentally from the individual who seeks the protection of secrecy. The individual can properly do so only in regard to particular undertakings or situations; as a whole, he can, to be sure, hide for certain periods of time, but his existence, except for very abstruse combinations, cannot itself be a secret. This is quite possible, however, for a societal unit. Its elements may live in the most frequent interactions; but the fact that they form a society—a conspiracy or a gang of swindlers, a religious conventicle or an association for engaging in sexual orgies—can essentially, as well as permanently, be a secret. In this type, then, it is not the individuals, but the group they form, which is concealed . . . the secret society is the suitable social form for contents which still (as it were) are in their infancy, subject to the vulnerability of early developmental stages. A new insight, a young religion, morality, or parts, is often still weak and needs protection, and for this reason conceals itself. Periods in which new contents of life develop against the resistance of existing powers are predestined, therefore, to witness the growth of secret societies . . . In general, the secret society emerges everywhere as the counterpart of despotism and police restriction, as the protection of both the defensive and the offensive in their struggle against the overwhelming pressure of central powers—by no means of political powers only, but also of the church, as well as of school classes and families. (Wolff, 1950, pp. 345–347.)

Thus, the secret society serves to fill many essential needs for people who desire continued participation in a behavioral form which tends to be viewed with intolerance and self-righteous scorn by a large proportion of the dominant society. Of course, any couple wanting to engage in comarital sexual behavior must, by necessity, find at least one other couple with desires and values similar to their own. This is obvious. But the less obvious functions served by the "secret society" are at least equally important. *Any* nonconformist person requires some degree of protection, emotional support, and social facilitation for "doing his thing" if he is to maintain a sense of personal stability. He is also quite likely to need a group for purposes of helping him to structure in his own mind a propitious direction of motives, drives, rationalizations and attitudes. In short, a coherent, well-structured ideology justifying and normalizing the behavior must become, to at least some extent, an integral, and indeed amalgamated, part of his own mind—the *emotional as well as* the intellectual part of it. For these reasons deviant subgroups tend to possess a number of traits in common. This is true regardless of what their specific goals or activities happen to be.

No discussion of the history of American mate exchange would be complete without a consideration of "Oneida," a community founded and developed by religious leader John Humphrey Noyes, first in Vermont and later in upstate New York. In this community every adult man in the group was regarded as being married to every adult woman in the group, although each man had a woman who was regarded as his "first" wife and with whom he normally lived and with whom he kept his private possessions. In his volume *Bible Communism*, Noyes advocated a high degree of sexual freedom, although he exalted at one and the same time the rigor and discipline of exacting emotional control as can be seen in his polemical discussions favoring coitus interruptus and karezza. The latter is a long, drawn-out, but quite pleasurable, method of sexual intercourse in which the erect penis is kept within the vagina for long periods of time.

The Oneida group was composed of hard-working, serious, pious men and women. The group nevertheless did enjoy a good many recreational and cultural pursuits, and could not be called ascetic by pioneer nineteenth-century standards. Central to the group's ideology was Noyes's notion that monogamous sexual (in contradistinction to *conjugal*) love was selfish and that it restricted man's erotic appetites unnaturally. He believed that any man or woman could love many times and many persons. "The more one loves, the more capable one becomes of loving his fellow human beings," he is known to have declared; this is a feeling which seems to be espoused again and again in interviews which I and others have had with contemporary mate-sharing swingers.

The children of the society seemed to have been well adjusted and well taken care of, and women were not required to accept attention from any man who did not appeal to them. Had it not been for the legal battle that the state of New York waged with Noyes and won in 1879 (after the Oneida community had successfully existed in the same place for thirty years), it is quite possible that the group might have been able to survive on a permanent basis. It is important to note that Oneida had not been suffering from any noteworthy internal strains or difficulties at the time of its forced dissolution.

The work of Kinsey contains a wealth of statistical data on the prevalence of extramarital sex. Fully 26 percent of the married women in Kinsey's sample had experienced at least one or more extramarital affairs. Nevertheless, throughout the total work only one brief and passing comment was made regarding "wife-swapping." Presumably it was not until after the data of Kinsey and his associates were already in that they realized that the phenomenon was widespread and worth closer investigation.

> There is a not inconsiderable group of cases in the sample in which the husbands had encouraged their wives to engage in extramarital activities. This represented a notable break with the centuries old cultural tradition. In some instances it represented a deliberate effort to extend the wife's opportunity to find satisfaction in sexual relations. In not a few instances the husband's attitude had

originated in his desire to find an excuse for his own extramarital activity. What is sometimes known as wife-swapping usually involves this situation. In another group of cases the husband had encouraged extramarital relations in order to secure the opportunity for the sort of group activity in which he desired to participate . . . It should be emphasized again that most of the husbands who accepted or encouraged their wives' extramarital activities had done so in an honest attempt to give them the opportunity for additional sexual satisfaction. (Kinsey, et. al., 1953, pp. 434–435.)

At no point in his brief discussion of "wife-swapping" did Kinsey present any statistics indicating its prevalence at the time of data collection. However, considering that the data were obtained during the late 1940s and early 1950s, and that about half of the sample resided in the state of Indiana, which is a substantially more sexually conservative state than those on the Northeast and West Coasts, the above quote certainly appears suggestive that comarital sex was fairly prevalent in the United States even as much as thirty years ago.

Along with the Kinsey reports of 1948 and 1953, the introduction of the birth control pill in 1960, and the public availability and widespread awareness of the Masters and Johnson findings in 1966, it is quite likely that the Roth decision of the United States Supreme Court in 1957 will be remembered as one of the major landmarks of the contemporary trend toward greater sexual freedom. It was with this decision that written material and artwork dealing with eroticism in a fully frank manner could, for the very first time since the Comstock laws of the 1870s, be publicly sold and distributed. It was with this very change of conditions that some evidence of "swinging" activity could surface. Prior to 1957, even the publishers of so-called "girlie" magazines tended to shy away from material which was "too descriptive," or which suggested that any people of "respectable" status actually approved of something like comarital sex or, worse yet, that anyone was actually able to experience this sort of thing without great suffering and punishment befalling them for their "misdeeds."

Along with enabling comarital sex to begin to surface to some extent, the Roth decision and other similar legal events of the late 1950s and early 1960s doubtless also had a significant hand in *creating* hundreds of mate-sharing swingers. This matter will be dealt with at length in Chapter 8. Suffice it to say here that the Thomas theorem—"When we are led to define things or ideas as real, those things or ideas tend to become real in their consequences"—is the mechanism through which this tended to occur. The Thomas theorem is popularly known as "the self-fulfilling prophecy" and it is in full harmony with the increasingly popular metaphysical idea that *we create our lives and our environments by the way we think.*

Since 1957, an avalanche of semipornographic material has been published and made available to the public. Much of this material has been sold only in large city "adult book stores," although quite a large amount of it, from as early as 1957, has been much more generally available. One of the more obscure of the numerous "girlie" magazines to commence publication during the 1950s was *Mr.* From its inception in 1956, it has been found on most large newsstands and it could be purchased by anyone who had the sixty cents to pay for it.

In 1957, *Mr.* began a monthly series of articles devoted to "wife-swapping." From its inception the series was alleged by its editor to be comprised entirely of "real-life case histories" sent in by letter by "just ordinary American citizens like you and I." By 1960, several other publications began to publish similar articles, but the *Mr.* effort remains the best known in swinging circles. And in 1965, the editors of *Mr.* published what was to become one of the most widely distributed paperback books on swinging: a book edited by Wilson and Meyers (1965) and comprised of what were alleged to be the best and most representative letters ever received by *Mr.* from actual swingers.

In the course of the two-year period during which I interviewed known swinging couples for this study, I learned from several reliable sources that for the first five years of *Mr.*'s publication of this special monthly column virtually all of its "case histories" had been fictionalized. But I similarly learned that with each successive month that this special column was published, the editor's office became progressively more swamped with letters. Many of these letters came from people who were dreaming about swinging and who wanted information as to how to go about entering what they had been led to believe was a highly glamorous life style. But many others came from people who actually did swing. As the editors of *Mr.* were primarily interested in highly enticing copy, they are alleged to have seldom published any actual letters. What they did publish was a highly glamorized, romantic picture of what it is like to be a contemporary American mate-sharing swinger.

With the publication and easy availability of materials such as these, virtually hundreds of people who had never even thought of the idea of swinging now began thinking of it as a viable and realistic alternative for their own lives. Without having come into contact with the concept of this particular type of answer to their craving for sexual variety, it is not entirely probable that they would have thought of it on their own. Conventional adultery they might well have thought of, but not the comarital sex pattern with its unique and highly unusual self-legitimating ideology. The very fact that virtually thousands of men picked up and purchased copies of publications such as *Mr.* suggests that unfilled erotic needs were quite widespread in our society back in the late 1950s, as they indeed continue to be today. Of course, for some people these erotic needs are rooted in learned, highly unrealistic expectations concerning the potentials of sex. There are many ways in which a person can attempt to come to terms with his learned needs and fantasies, and some of these inevitably entail "deviant" or "nonconformist" behavior.

Fictionalized but ostensibly authentic personal case histories such as those published in *Mr.* served to normalize in the minds of many readers (i.e., those who already had especially strong needs and predispositions) a particular, nonconformist mode of adjustment to everyday life problems and discontents. Through helping many men to normalize in their own minds the idea of comarital sex, the *Mr.* articles served to inspire many husband–wife discussions on the possibility of becoming swingers. Some of these discussions, and many of them were doubtless very heated, culminated in a resolution to explore further and to actually try out this nonconformist style of adultery.

Mr. and other similar publications were responding to a widespread, albeit unexpressed pattern of needs in American society. Yet, even though conditions were ripe at this time for a rapid proliferation of the comarital sex phenomenon, there was virtually no easy way in which prospective swingers could meet with other prospective (or experienced) swingers. Publications such as *Mr.* succeeded in planting the seed for the potentially fast spreading of the mate-sharing concept. But before this potential could even begin to be realized, water and an abundant supply of fertilizer would be needed.

By 1960, and again as a consequence of some landmark Supreme Court decisions, advertisements began to appear in a host of underground publications. A strong new demand for a new service had finally precipitated the emergence of numerous supply sources. First, highly sensationalistic weekly tabloids such as *National Informer* and *Midnight* began to publish advertisements from people desirous of meeting others of like mind. And by 1963, major young people's underground newspapers such as the *Los Angeles Free Press, Berkeley Barb*, and the *East Village Other*, began publishing similar ads. The typical format of such advertisements—a format still widely followed—can be illustrated by the following examples:

La-Laguna Area

Young, attractive, fun-loving, liberal-minded marrieds seek other young, attractive, fun-loving, liberal-minded marrieds to share young, attractive, fun-loving liberal-mindedness together. Photo with reply, please. [Address with post office number given.]

Groovy Couple

She: blond, blue-eyed, 25, 35-21-33, 5'2", 95 lbs., lovely, talented, affectionate, fun-loving uninhibited. He: brown hair and eyes, 33, 5'10", 150 lbs., talented, endowed, goodlooking, considerate, affectionate, uninhibited. Both: love nudism and French and Roman arts as well as plain ecstatic romps and good times between friends. Will travel. Only replies with photo from couples will be answered.

So. Calif. Marrieds Only

Small circle attractive young couples to age 30. Phone and photo with reply.

Advertisements such as these greatly facilitated the efforts of couples interested in meeting people of like mind. Such personal advertisements by 1963 had begun to appear not only in underground tabloids, but to an increasing extent in publications published specifically for swingers. Presently there are over one dozen magazines of nation-wide circulation which cater to the advertising needs of swingers. Such magazines, exemplified by *Swingers Life, Kindred Spirits, Select,* etc., are normally available in "adult book shops" for a price of about $3.00 per issue. Their availability and alleged superiority is also advertised in such tabloids as the *Los Angeles Free Press.* So indeed are swingers' publications catering to a regional readership such as *Just California, Pacific Northwest, New York and New England,* etc.

As merchants began to learn that swinging was not a figment of the imagination but a ready, viable market, other more facile ways began to emerge by which prospective swinging couples could meet and talk to each other. Important among these new ways were swinging bars and private swinging clubs.

Private, personal advertisements have always posed problems for swingers. Single men, for example, often misrepresent themselves as married. Similarly, many ads are placed by the merely curious, most of whom have no intention of ever becoming involved in swinging. One Encino couple told me of an advertisement to which they had responded which turned out to have been placed by a 12-year-old boy! The lad had been quite curious about the kinds of letters and photographs he would receive!

There have also been stories of harrassment by "moralistic" police and post-office officials. The incidence of complaints of this type dropped very sharply after a 1964 Supreme Court decision. But responding to swingers' ads has continued to entail an element of risk. Even today there are reports of prospective swingers inviting couples to their homes sight unseen—couples who later turn out to be exceedingly unattractive, uncouth, and in some cases, sadists. Since the 1950s, popular swinging literature has instructed prospective swinging couples to *first* arrange to meet each other over a couple of drinks at a convenient bar *before* making any kind of a commitment to exchange spouses. As a result of either ignorance or naïveté there are some couples desirous of entering the swinging world who continue to ignore this advice. Some of them get themselves into quite a bit of difficulty and embarrassment and become disenchanted with the idea of trying to become swingers as a result.

As the scores of magazine articles and books on swinging continued to create an increasingly greater need for swinging services, by the late 1960s major underground newspapers such as the *Los Angeles Free Press* began publishing a different kind of advertisement: they began advertising the swinging bars and private clubs referred to above. The following illustrate this pattern of ads:

Topley Too

NEVER CHARGES A COVER OR MINIMUM. NO DOOR OR MEMBERSHIP FEE. WE CATER TO THE SWING CROWD ONLY. 8875 Pico. LA.

"The In-Group"

We are an intimate group of young, attractive swinging couples with a different, more exciting approach to swinging. We may be just what you are looking for. Why not come to one of our parties and see for yourselves? We don't think you will be disappointed. Would an ad a mile long say any more? Call today and find out. [telephone number]

Searching Couples

You've seen "Bob & Carol & Ted & Alice." You've read "The Groupsex Tapes." You've discussed mateswapping. But you don't know why, where, or even *IF* you should get it started.

The place to find out nicely is The Swing in Studio City. The Swing has been written up in *PLAYBOY*, *LIFE & NEWSWEEK*, among others, as the first, largest, and most successful public Night Club catering to sexually freethinking people.

We provide a place for those like yourselves to meet casually and discuss the pros & cons of Swinging or whatever—or just come in and dance to our groovy bands and have some fun in a warm, friendly atmosphere.

[Telephone number] The Swing (Ventura at Coldwater) in Studio City. Open 8 p.m., closed Monday. Wed. is "Get Acquainted Nite."

"101"

Swinging 101 style is first class in every respect. We accept only couples in their 20s and 30s who are attractive and who are sure of their love for one another. Our private party mansion combines elegance with a feeling of belonging. The atmosphere of our weekend parties is erotic, yet comfortable and unpressured. Call anytime (except after 9:00 pm on Fri. & Sat.)

American Sexual Freedom Movement
Swingers—Nudists
*Personal Introductions
*Weekly Sexual Freedom Parties
*Over 4000 Members—since 1967
*Group Dynamics—discussions
*Ultra-Modern facilities including plush $100,000 estate
[Telephone number]
ASFM, 8235 Santa Monica Bl., LA 90046

Contempo
Where Aware Couples Meet
CONTEMPO is a club whose main interest is a people to people relationship with its couples. COUPLES swing parties every Friday and Saturday; non-members welcome. Party pad in Hollywood.
UPCOMING ACTIVITIES
Las Vegas trip 2/26-28
Cabin Party 3/17-19
Membership Information:
[Telephone number]

Couples & Singles
Let us take the problems out of meeting by mail and personal ads. Meet others with YOUR interests at our WEEKLY PARTIES or meet individually! More people join So. Calif. oldest (our 8th year) & largest (3,500 members) CLUB!

The In Crowd
Where FREE EXPRESSION is always your decision. In Orange County call Phil: [telephone number]; in LA call Jack: [telephone number].

Swinging Couples
Dial–A–Swinger
[telephone number]
Tell us your concept of a good swinging party. If it
rings true, we'll turn you on to where it's really
happening. Couples only. Call Jack & Joanne:
[telephone number]

Organizations such as those represented in the foregoing advertisements have made it far easier than ever before for people who think they might be interested in
swinging to explore it. Most of these organizations have
never required an immediate commitment from a couple.
A novice or prospective couple can go and "see for themselves" what the people are actually like. In so doing many
couples find that the majority of those they meet are not
really very different from themselves. One of the swinging
clubs I investigated even runs a special ten-week seminar
which couples who think they might be interested in
swinging can attend and learn about it and discuss its
various ramifications with those similar to themselves as
well as with the experienced swingers who run the classes.
They can do this without ever having to feel constrained
about making a definite decision to attend a swinging
party.

A further very important function served by such clubs
is that they screen all of the couples who indicate an interest in membership. Thus, inappropriate couples are
denied membership and social introductions are made
with care.

Advertisements such as those quoted above constitute in
and of themselves a socially meaningful kind of literature.
They reflect what a certain minority of our suburban
population is thinking, feeling, and needing at a particular
point in time. Indeed, by virtue of the steady proliferation
over the past few years of such advertisements and of the
clubs that place them, we can logically infer that the
swinging minority is probably growing larger. Like the

numerous articles about swinging that have appeared in semipornographic and even in some "straight" magazines, *these advertisements may well also be contributing to the growth of swinging.* This is so because their content has the potential for putting some direction into the often vague personal fantasies of men who have been led to believe that they have a strong need for sexual variety that cannot be adequately satisfied by their own wives.

Only time will tell whether these trends represent a kind of fad. However, comarital sex was clearly not a fad in the various preliterate societies discussed earlier. As it becomes increasingly "safe" and acceptable to practice comarital sex in the United States, it is possible that this now "deviant" phenomenon will develop a firm footing among a certain kind of couple.

Research on American Swingers

Despite the quite considerable fascination social scientists have had for spouse sharing on the contemporary American scene, comparatively little research has ever been conducted on the subject. Nevertheless, there are a few research efforts that are worth mentioning. They are important because they laid the groundwork for my own research, which will be dealt with in the chapters that follow. These early efforts also created an awareness that a very small minority of American couples might actually have found a new and different (for America) way of integrating sex with marriage and family life.

Up to now, anthropologist Gil Bartell (1971) has written the only truly scholarly, full-length book on comarital sex. His sample was comprised of 280 married couples, most of whom resided within the suburbs of greater Chicago. However, for variety he obtained about one-fifth of his swinging couples from suburban areas of Texas and Louisiana. Bartell's original curiosity about swingers was initially "turned on" during his graduate student days when he chanced upon a copy of *Mr.* The numerous "statistics" the magazine alleged regarding the purported "pervasiveness" of comarital sex in American suburbia seemed to Bartell to warrant corroboration by a qualified scholar.

Along with interviewing over 400 swinging couples over a three-year period, Bartell and his wife obtained a significant portion of their most fascinating data by actually attending swinging parties and observing interaction patterns. The Bartells had decided well in advance that they would never participate in the sexual side of the swinging festivities, and they found it was usually possible to remain at the larger parties for several hours without swinging and without even appearing conspicuous. Although it was necessary for both he and his wife to be nude at the various parties they attended, they found that by carrying around a drink all night and remaining together it was possible for them to observe quite a bit without ever feeling "out of place."

Apart from the nudity, Bartell found that many of the parties had an atmosphere not too different from that of a typical cocktail party. As most of the swinging usually occurred in the back rooms it was normally possible for the Bartells to remain in the neutral areas such as the living room and kitchen. On many occasions erotic and even coital activities would occur in these areas as well; but they found that most of the people held to a "do your own thing" attitude. A particularly interesting feature of the large swinging party was that on many occasions a large living room might have some couples engaging in erotic activities, some people standing around talking, some eating, some dancing, some drinking, and some actually playing cards—all at the same time! Yet, with all of these activities going on simultaneously, no one was ever made to feel under pressure to take part in any particular activity. In general, spontaneity was the rule at the parties the Bartells attended.

The Bartells found that 83 percent of the swingers they studied could be classified as middle-class and white; all were suburbanites, and they ranged in age from 18 to 70. The average ages for men and women participants were 32 and 28 respectively, and their average incomes were found to be well within a comfortable middle-class range.

Like other people who have studied swinging, Bartell found that the large majority of his respondents felt that their sexual nonconformity brought them closer to their spouses, and that it served to enhance sexual competence. On the other hand, Bartell uncovered a good many other findings which do not agree with those uncovered by other researchers. He found, for example, that one of the most outstanding characteristics of his group of swingers was that they tended to have remarkably few outside interests. He similarly found that the swingers tended to dislike "drugs, hippies, blacks, and liberals," and that they frequently sent their children to Sunday school even though they didn't consider themselves to be religious. Finally, 78 percent of his swinging wives were housewives who stayed at home full-time in order to look after their children. Most of these wives and their husbands viewed themselves as being bored with life.

James and Lynn Smith (1970; 1971) are another academic couple who conducted an extensive amount of research on comarital sexual behavior, particularly as it exists in the suburbs of the San Francisco–Oakland area of northern California. The bulk of the Smiths' work was based upon the questionnaire responses of 503 people who (1) were members of some sort of sexual freedom group, and (2) who at least occasionally attended sexually liberal activities or gatherings. In addition, they informally interviewed 200 sexual freedom participants, usually at parties.

The Smiths' married swingers were found to be a great deal more politically and socially liberal than those of Bartell's research. But, on the other hand, they were also found to be predominantly middle class. In fact, 72 percent of the male swingers were found to be in the professional occupations; 50 percent of all the Smiths' respondents could be classified as being within the top two (out of five) social classes. Only 2 percent were found to be in the lowest class.

In the process of managing their own private club for swingers, Matt and Kathleen Galant (1966a) managed to interview some 5,392 married couples, all of whom were involved to at least some extent in comarital sexual practices. These people resided all over the United States, although the South was the most heavily represented region. The Galants also found swinging to be an almost entirely middle-class phenomenon. Only 3 percent of the 5,392 couples from whom they obtained data could be described as blue-collar workers, and only 2.7 percent commanded annual family incomes of under $10,000 (early 1960s data).

A final research effort worth mentioning is that of Rubenstein and Margolis (1971), in *The Groupsex Tapes*. For this study the authors interviewed 628 married and single swingers (and some of their children) at various suburban and urban locations throughout the United States. They selected just 98 of these individuals for the intensive three-and-a-half-hour long interviews, and most of their book is comprised of quoted statements from these 98 individuals.

Rubenstein and Margolis claim that 93 percent of their respondents were upper middle-class—"the very group that sets national trends." Of the married couples they interviewed, 64 percent were in their thirties, 28 percent were in their forties, and 8 percent were aged 50 and over. Fully 85 percent of the married swingers were found to have children, and 55 percent of the children were in their prepubescent ages. Most of the couples had just two children.

Thirty-three percent of Rubenstein and Margolis's married couples had been involved with comarital sex for one to five years; 60 percent had been involved for five to twelve years; and 7 percent had been involved for more than twelve years. The authors concluded that the main reasons for married couples' involvement in sexual mate sharing appeared to be: (1) finding sexual variety with the consent of the spouse; (2) little likelihood of rejection; and (3) freedom to experience extramarital sex with little or no guilt. Concerning the last point, the group sex scene serves to produce an atmosphere of group approval and encouragement. Social psychologists refer to this as *social facilitation*. The fact that everyone else in one's immediate environment at a party is "doing it" makes it far easier for any given man or woman present to "do it" as well. Social facilitation is a powerful force behind many different kinds of deviance and nonconformity.

Like virtually all studies conducted up to now on swinging, Rubenstein and Margolis found that the large majority of their married swingers believed that their deviant recreational style was doing them and their marriages a great deal of good. Eighty-three percent of the married couples felt that the expanded sexual knowledge they had gained from swinging enabled them to develop a better understanding of themselves as men and women. Almost all of the couples believed that comarital sexual behavior served to produce a tolerance and freedom in them that inspired them into spontaneously sharing deeper levels of communication with their spouses than they had ever been able to experience before.

Of further interest is the fact that virtually all of the married couples in Rubenstein and Margolis's sample felt that they had been able to cultivate meaningful friendships through their swinging activities, and that these relationships carried over into a host of non-erotic activities such as cultural and sports endeavors and, in some cases, even shared family vacations.

The Importance of Ideology

Ideology is simply an organized and integrated system of ideas and opinions that governs the perceptions and reactions of a group or category of people. Ideology is socially programmed into the minds of people. And once a person makes the decision to accept an ideology (or if as a child he accepts it because it is the *only* set of viewpoints presented), his or her perceptions of the world from that point on will be different. More specifically, his or her perceptions will remain different for as long as he or she chooses to adhere to the new ideology which he or she decided to accept. The "reality" which you and I perceive from moment to moment is in very large measure *socially constructed*. In essence, reality is a byproduct of the shared meanings of the groups to which we belong and which are most important to us emotionally.

It is extremely difficult for most people to understand how some husbands and wives can take part in sexual mate-sharing behavior. Indeed, it is even harder to understand how middle-class Americans can do it than it is to understand how the residents of various preliterate societies can do it. Since we are not preliterates ourselves it is easy enough to attribute much of the preliterate's behavior to a lack of awareness or to the mere fact of being "primitive" and "uncultured." Yet the mechanism through which these "primitives" learned to view sexual mate exchange as "natural" and "good" is almost the same as that through which some nonconformist Americans have learned to regard it as "natural" and "good." The only difference is that in a preliterate society the people had been exposed to "swinging" as a "natural" and "good" part of life virtually from the moment they were born. They had never been exposed to any alternative ways of thinking or of perceiving the world. Their parents and other significant adults had always presented sexual mate exchange to them as being part of the natural order of the universe.

Because of the way they had been reared the preliterate peoples discussed earlier never had any reason for thinking of sexual mate exchange at a festival as being in any way competitive with or threatening to conjugal sex, marriage, or family life. Sex for these people represented one thing in some social contexts: namely recreation or fun or fulfillment of a responsibility. In the very different social context of the private hut or igloo it represented a moral obligation to their society to reproduce and to father and mother their offspring in an orderly and predictable way. Everyone knew that when the festival or party was over everyone was expected to return to his or her everyday responsibilities of family, kin, and society.

In American society many perfectly good marriages are needlessly destroyed everyday because of the wife's reaction at learning of her husband's adultery. In such cases the meaning that the extramarital sex has for the husband is very often entirely different than that which it has for his wife. To many husbands extramarital sex is viewed merely as an insignificant lark or as a means for assuaging loneliness when out of town, or as a means of satisfying erotic fantasies which he does not feel comfortable about dealing with or communicating about in the company of his wife. On the other hand, to many wives the mere suspicion of adultery strikes at the very heart of any feeling of security and of self-worth that they might have enjoyed. Sexual exclusiveness to many women is thus a "be-all and end-all" of marriage; as soon as there is evidence that the conjugal *sexual* relationship is not exclusive she immediately concludes that the situation is prima facie evidence by itself that the conjugal *psycho-emotional* relationship is not exclusive and that the marriage is not working or even that it has already disintegrated.

Women grow up in different peer groups and hence in different social contexts than men do. As such, the content of many of the belief systems that are programmed into them is very different than the content of that which is programmed into most men. To be sure, as the women's liberation movement becomes increasingly strong this situation will change. In fact, childhood peer groups today are nowhere nearly as sex segregated as they once were. But it is still true that from kindergarten through the twelfth grade most children still spend most of their time with their own sex and receive strong encouragement from their teachers and parents to do so. Most people think differently than and cannot completely "let their hair down" with the opposite sex because of this sex-segregated peer group situation which, hopefully, will eventually disappear.

Contemporary American swingers often talk about "faithful adultery" or "adultery without infidelity." To the uninitiated these terms seem quite absurd and often draw laughter. Yet it is precisely this conceptual distinction between "faithful adultery" and "unfaithful adultery" that allows preliterates to serenely take part in sexual partner exchange on occasions when the leaders of their communities tell them that it is permissible for them to do so.

The conceptual distinction between "faithful adultery" and "unfaithful adultery" is an integral and very central part of the contemporary American swinger's ideology. Most people in our own society cannot make such a conceptual distinction and most will doubtless never even want to try to learn to make it. Most people simply do not see themselves as needing the frequency and variety of sexual experiences that swingers see themselves (have sold themselves a bill of goods) as needing. In a society such as ours this is probably to the good. But for those of us who do not swing and who will probably never want to do so, it is useful to know how a person can arrive at a point where he or she can serenely mate swap without feeling any guilt or jealousy. Such knowledge can lead to a greater tolerance, compassion and understanding for people involved in this type of behavioral nonconformity. It can also help each one of us understand better how and why *we* got to be where we are in terms of attitudes, beliefs, values, and group identifications.

There are several other conceptual distinctions American swingers make that are also very similar to the conceptual distinctions people engaged in sexual mate exchange have been making down through the ages. One of the most important of these has to do with the concept of *monogamy*. Basically, what is monogamy? Is man intrinsically monogamous? Or is woman monogamous but man not so?

American swingers quite commonly talk about three different *kinds* of monogamy: (1) psychological or emotional monogamy; (2) residential monogamy; and (3) sexual monogamy. And this is the order of importance in which swingers place the three kinds of monogamy. Emotional and residential monogamy are both regarded as being of far greater importance than sexual monogamy as far as any "close" man–woman relationship is concerned. Preliterates and modern American swingers would answer the "Is man and/or woman monogamous?" question in the *affirmative* as far as the first two types of monogamy are concerned. But as far as *sexual* monogamy is concerned they would regard *neither* man *nor* woman as being instinctively monogamous.

This conceptual distinction also explains why American swingers tend to be highly anticommunist in their sympathies and belief systems. As we have already seen, most of them have "made it" in terms of success on the job market. Most of them have also been able to acquire quite a bit of personal and real property, and unlike the hippies of the 1960s they are not interested in sharing it with others through living in accordance with a communal life style. This is despite the fact that as hosts and hostesses of swinging parties they tend to be quite generous.

To the American swinger as to the resident of a preliterate society, sex is not seen as the "cement of marriage"; and neither is sex seen as a "be-all and end-all" of a marriage. To the American swinger psychological and emotional bonds tend to be viewed as the real cement of a marriage. After living together over a period of time two people tend to develop a kind of singular identity. They come to share intimate thoughts, aspirations, dreams, etc. Their lives intertwine into a shared unity of memory. The swinger has what for our society is the unusual ability to completely *compartmentalize* sex in the *recreational sector* of life, from sex in the intimate *psycho-emotional sector*. And as long as they are able to keep what goes on in one of these sectors from intruding on what goes on in the other sector they are able to function smoothly and serenely.

The men and women of preliterate societies operate in terms of similar compartments for the two different kinds of sexual experiences. But unlike American swingers *neither* the sexual bond *nor* the psycho-emotional feelings bond between a husband and wife is what holds a marriage securely together. In virtually all preliterate societies the *bonds of kinship* (which usually include many relatives on *both* the husband's side and the wife's side of the family) are what motivate the solidity of marriage. Divorce and separation tend to be quite rare in most preliterate societies. The kin family network tends to be far weaker and much less influential here in the United States than it is in preliterate societies. And among American swingers, as I shall clearly document in Chapter 4, the kin family network tends to be extremely weak indeed.

On the other hand, the need to lead a successful and respectable life seems to be as strongly internalized among swingers as it is among sexually monogamous middle-class couples. Hence, very few swingers take their marriage vows lightly. Whereas the swingers (psycho-emotionally and residentially monogamous as they are) do not regard sexual monogamy as a desirable or natural way of life for either sex, they *do believe* that it is absolutely necessary for non-monogamous sex to be patterned in accordance with a well-structured body of norms. Their purpose is to have their cake and eat it too. They both demand and want what they regard as the "good life" of beautiful suburbia and a normal family life with (psycho-emotionally) faithful spouse and children. And within the rubic of this "good life" they also want an abundantly rich, varied sex life with many different people as well as with their own lawful wedded spouse. In order to arrive at these seemingly incompatible goals they have internalized a normative ideology including a body of "rules of the game" which permit and encourage a rich, extramarital sex life.

Of course, people usually internalize new ideologies much faster at an intellectual level than at the "deep-down gut" psycho-emotional level. The fact that the intellectual part of man's brain can change at a much faster rate than the emotional part has created some problems for swingers. A person may "think" that swinging is a great idea only to find that he is really not a swinger at heart when put to the acid test—when he is actually faced with seeing his wife have sexual intercourse with another man. On the other hand, guilt feelings are usually much more easily dissipated. If a man or woman is intellectually motivated to become a swinger, guilt feelings tend to be rapidly extinguished with each new swinging encounter. After six or seven swinging experiences virtually all of a person's guilt and anxiety feelings will have disappeared. The term *extinction* is normally used by psychologists to refer to this process of gradually diminishing guilt with each new experience of the once forbidden act.

The importance of this process of "extinction" should not be taken lightly. Extinction has helped man to get rid of a lot of bad habits as well as countless unnecessary neurotic behaviors and anxieties. But it is also responsible for the Nazi Gestapo learning to exterminate Jews mercilessly. The morality of "extinction" quite clearly depends upon how and for what purposes it is used. Most people take advantage of the principle of extinction quite unconsciously. They continually repeat an act they want to be able to enjoy without feeling nervous or self-conscious or guilty. Their own perceived diminution of such uncomfortable feelings serves as a strong reinforcement for continuing to perform and to perfect the act. A key point is that from a purely intellectual standpoint a person could conceivably think of himself as a "real swinger" without ever having had anything whatever to do with actually participating in such behavior. But the full internalization of the swinging ideology at the deep emotional level requires that the person have actually freely participated in swinging activities at least a half-dozen or more times. Once a person has done that most of his or her deeply ingrained jealousy reactions, guilt, anxiety, awkwardness, etc., will have been extinguished.

The various elements of the swingers' ideology become further reinforced through frequent conversations with fellow swingers about the tenets of their belief system. In this regard listening to the spontaneous conversations of a group of swingers at one of their social get-togethers has much in common with listening to the informal conversations of a group of fundamentalist religious people. They spend a great deal of time discussing and rehashing the key points and premises which justify, support and regulate their nonconformist behavior. This frequent conversation about ideology and normative belief systems doubtless provides a continuing flow of needed reassurance. But it also reinforces in their own minds the swingers' beliefs in the face of what many of them perceive to be a widespread potential hostility toward swingers and comarital sex in the communities where they live.

There are some minor differences in the ideologies and normative belief systems of swingers as these relate to sex and marriage. But there is one difference which is of considerable importance and which needs to be clarified early in this book. Many swingers make a conceptual distinction between what they term *committed love* and *non-committed love*. The "interpersonal" swingers discussed in Chapter 1 are most likely to make this distinction, which still represents a minority opinion in the swinging world. To most swingers "love" can be permitted to apply only in the context of *conjugal sex* and would be regarded as potentially dangerous and threatening within the context of *recreational sex*, which is what swinging is. "Interpersonal" swingers, on the other hand, believe that it is impossible as well as undesirable to disassociate sex from love, and that the more one feels love for other people the more capable one becomes of loving one's self as well as one's family, legal spouse and others.

But such swingers emphasize that there are different kinds of love, and that what they term *non-committed love* need not interfere with the *committed love* which applies to marriage and family relationships. Most of these younger and usually better educated swingers insist that involvement in a small number of strong and very close non-committed love relationships enhances and improves their ability to be involved in a permanent, committed love relationship. Paradoxically, these "interpersonal" swingers seldom swing with as many different couples as most other swingers do. They tend to have just three or four "best friend" couples with whom they participate year after year. The large, impersonal party tends to be unpopular among this type of swinger, whereas the majority of swingers attend the large, impersonal type of swinging party on at least an occasional basis.

The concept of "non-committed love" perhaps can be clarified somewhat by comparing it to the emotions an unmarried courting couple who have been dating each other steadily for three or four months might feel toward one another. Such a couple feel themselves to be "in love." They may be having regular sexual intercourse together and they enjoy seeing a great deal of each other and sharing many different recreations together. However, at that stage they are *not* yet "committed" as far as any type of engagement for a future legal marriage is concerned. Thus, their love could be termed "real" albeit as yet "non-committed."

Of course, such "non-committed love" among unmarried lovers cannot be directly equated to the non-committed love felt by legally married people toward their best friends of the opposite sex. For the unmarried person legal marriage *could* and *may* eventuate as far as a particular love relationship is concerned. For married swingers it is known and realized by all participants that legal marriage cannot and will not eventuate. But, then, that is acceptable to the married swinger because legal marriage exists primarily for the legitimation of parenthood, *not* for the legitimation of coitus or living together. The couple in a non-committed love relationship can still see a great deal of each other and share many activities. Their sexual experiences together can still be *person-centered* as opposed to purely *body-centered*. Theirs is not a groggy-eyed romantic love that is heightened by prolonged physical separations and by an unwillingness to bring their felt emotions for each other to full fruition in sexual intercourse. To be sure, the easy availability of group-sanctioned sexual intercourse with the "loved one" has a wonderful way of removing the rose-colored smokescreen of blind idealization. Swingers never become *infatuated* with each other and they never romantically idealize each other in their private fantasies. They do not need to do so because the normative code of their group permits them to "live out" their love fantasies. The only real difference here between the "interpersonal" swingers and the majority (recreational and egotistical) of swingers is that the former are allowed by their groups to become more emotional with each other in lovemaking. They can have a "person-centered" as opposed to a purely "body-centered" relationship. They can enter into private conversations together and can feel free to say "I love you" whenever they wish. Most groups of recreational and egotistical swingers frown on saying things like "I love you" while involved in recreational (comarital) sex.

While conversations of a private nature are regarded as acceptable among many swingers, most comarital sex groups prefer to have their members confine such conversations to social contexts that do not involve sexual intercourse and other forms of erotic play. Of course, conversations about sex and about what is desired and enjoyed sexually are *not* regarded as private. To most swingers, when a couple is involved in sexual play at a party they should concentrate entirely on the experience of sexual enjoyment and *not* on private conversations or emotional feelings that the partners might (and probably should not) feel toward one another. For example, if a man is highly impressed by a woman with whom he is sexually involved at a party he should praise her heartily for her beautiful, seductive appearance and for her sexual competence. But he should *not* allow himself to get into the emotional type of "I love you's." His (or her) attitude should be, "I love the way you perform, look, and the way you sexually satisfy me," *NOT* "I love you as a person."

Finally, it is necessary to bear in mind that for swingers, sex and eroticism have developed into a veritable hobby and major recreational interest in the same sense as conventional husbands and wives often develop an interest in golf or tennis or bridge, which they pursue with a passion and often in the company of other married couples. To be sure, it is nowhere nearly as strongly approved in our society for a person to have a recreational interest in sex as it is for a person to have a recreational interest in such sports as tennis, golf, bowling, etc. In fact, even sports such as hunting and fishing which quite commonly serve to separate husbands from their wives and children for many weekends out of the year are not frowned upon to anywhere nearly the extent that sexual mate sharing is. This is so despite the fact that sexual mate sharing is a *common* interest a husband and wife *share together* and which they always practice *together* as a unit. (No husband is ever allowed into a swinging party unless he is accompanied by his wife; thus participation of a married couple as a couple is always assured.)

However, swingers do not perceive their recreational interest in sex as being in any way competitive with marriage and family life. Their ideology programs them into truly believing that it is not competitive, and one of the purposes of my research was to determine whether this aspect of the swingers' ideology is indeed true—whether participation in sexual mate sharing is indeed nonthreatening to the stability of marriage and family life here in American society. Usually what people believe to be so usually comes true for them; this is the "nutshell" essence of the self-fulfilling prophecy. But it is possible that the principle behind the self-fulfilling prophecy may not be valid in all cases.

Given the fact that an avocational interest in recreational sex is widely regarded in our society as being highly deviant, it cannot be considered surprising that so few people ever develop and sustain an interest in it. The question of why and how such an interest initially develops will be a major focus of Chapters 4 through 8 of this book. Suffice it to say here that for a variety of reasons sex has become a matter of far greater importance to swingers than it ever becomes for most Americans. By their behavior swingers have made it clear that they are willing to go far out of their way for sex and for the satisfaction of their fantasies of enjoying frequent sex with a variety of highly competent sexual partners. And since sex has become very much like a recreational sport to swingers, they place high value on sexual competence in both themselves and in their opposite-sexed partners. Just as it would not be satisfying to an expert tennis player to play his game with a beginner or with a moderately skilled opponent, so it is with swinging husbands and wives. They both look for and value a high degree of skill at the game of sex. And as will become clear in Chapter 11, this high value placed on sexual competence even affects the way they rear and relate to their offspring.

To be sure, sex is important to most Americans. There is evidence too that competence in the art of sex is becoming increasingly important: The sex therapy clinics of our major cities now have so much business that many of them cannot even handle it all. Our levels of aspiration for sexual enjoyment and our levels of expectation for sexually competent performances from our love mates are rising and may well be rising too high—unrealistically high—in many cases. But to swinging men and women sexual satisfaction and skill have become matters of *paramount importance* as total life goals. To the extent that the reader does not understand this point it will be very difficult for him to understand why swingers are willing to go to the trouble to which they very evidently go, and why they are willing to take what in some cases are quite considerable risks to both their personal and family lives.

As the author and researcher for this book it is not my purpose to either condemn or to approve the values and behaviors of the swingers. Some of the swingers' attitudes, particularly their willingness to take such risks and to go to such trouble for sexual variety, remain difficult for even me to understand. But swingers are very serious and sincere in the beliefs that they hold. As such I think they are truly fascinating people who are entitled to our sincerest efforts to understand them and to find out what they are about as people. To *understand* them does not imply approval or acceptance of any of their ideas.

Chapter 3

How the Couples
Were Selected

Swingers constitute a deviant population. Hence, the researcher is faced with the same kinds of problems in trying to obtain a representative sample of swingers as he is when he tries to obtain a representative sample of juvenile delinquents, car thieves, vandals, check forgers, burglars, tax evaders, homosexuals, or members of other deviant groups or categories. Most deviants are strongly desirous of keeping their activities and their deviant group memberships secret from residents of the larger community of which they are a part. In fact, among middle-class deviants this desire for secrecy might be expected to be especially strong.

There is no central registry that lists the names and addresses of all American swingers. Such a central registry does exist for social nudists who may legitimately attend American nudist resorts. But I am aware of no other sexually nonconformist group which maintains any such comprehensive list of its like-minded fellows. For security reasons, there was no way in which I as a researcher could have obtained either comprehensive club rosters or (from independent swingers) lists of all swinging couples known to a popular mate-sharing couple. Several of the couples I interviewed possessed lists of swinging couples living all over the United States, Canada and Europe. But these couples made it clear that such lists were considered highly confidential by the swinging community and could not be divulged even to university-sponsored researchers.

A further problem in obtaining a representative sample is that most sexually nonconformist groups are not homogeneous. To be sure, a person would not be considered a swinger as far as this research is concerned if he or she (1) did not have an image of himself or herself as a swinger, and (2) if he or she had not taken part in some comarital sexual activities over at least a six-month period of time. In addition, since this research was concerned with *married* swingers, all respondents necessarily had to be married. But within these limitations there are several potentially important differences among swinging couples. Whether a couple prefers to swing independently or as part of an organized club or group is one such difference which could have a marked bearing upon research findings. Whether a couple sees themselves as "interpersonal" swingers or as "recreational" or "egotistical" swingers is another such potentially significant difference. Just as there are no known data as to how many married swingers there are in the United States, we similarly have no way of knowing what proportion of swinging couples belong to organized swinging clubs, informal groups, or who practice their nonconformity on an independent basis. We similarly do not know what proportion of swingers prefer the "interpersonal" style over the "recreational" and "egotistical" style of swinging. Estimates abound, but there are no hard data; neither are there any feasible ways of ferreting out such hard data at this time.

The Swingers and Their Selection

I wanted to be fully confident that all swingers interviewed and tested were indeed (1) people who have engaged in comarital sexual behavior, (2) who actually did view themselves as swingers, and (3) who have been involved as a couple in the world of comarital sex for at least six months. I also viewed it as extremely important that all respondent couples be legally married and living with each other. The reason for this concern was simply that this study was intended to focus on the social antecedents and correlates of *comarital* sexual behavior, *not* just any form of sexual partner sharing. In short, since a major purpose of this research was to shed light on the dynamics by which legally married, suburban spouses move toward involvement in the activities of swinging groups, marital status had to be considered a matter of great importance in sample selection.

Secondly, since swinging had often been characterized in the popular literature as a deviant life style for the affluent, I also regarded it as appropriate to seek out middle-class swinging couples. Actually this was not difficult to accomplish, as virtually all swinging groups advertising in California during the period this research was conducted catered to a demonstrably middle-class clientele.

Thirdly, since I was very interested in the kind of life style the offspring of swinging couples commonly lead, I hoped to obtain a sample of swingers that would be composed primarily of people who actually were involved with parental roles. Along with being interested in the kind of life swingers' children lead, I was also interested in taking a systematic look at the kinds of child-rearing attitudes, values, and disciplinary approaches that prevail in swinging families.

Finally, because of the temporal and financial limitations under which this study had to be conducted, most of the swinging respondents had to be selected from among the ranks of organized swinging groups. It is recognized that questions could be raised regarding the issue of how representative of American swingers, or even of California swingers, the sample selected for this research actually is. There are several good reasons for believing the sample is adequately representative. These reasons will become apparent in the material that follows.

One hundred middle-class swinging couples were obtained for this study. All of the couples were legally married and all were living in suburban residential districts. All of the couples were obtained from suburban areas in and around Los Angeles and Orange Counties. Half of the couples were obtained from the San Fernando Valley suburbs of the city of Los Angeles.

Seventy percent of the swinging couples were obtained through the cooperation of organized sexual freedom groups, whereas the remaining thirty percent were obtained through the help of swinging couples who do not belong to any clubs. Some of the organized groups whose help was received cater exclusively to the needs of married mate-sharing couples whereas others do not. However, a major raison d'etre of both kinds of organizations was that of facilitating by means of parties, discussion groups, etc., the efforts of married swingers to meet compatible couples.

The age range among the swinging husbands and wives studied was fairly wide. The following table summarizes the ages of both the swinging and the non-swinging husbands and wives. The reader should remember that 100 swinging couples and 100 non-swinging couples were studied.

All of the couples enjoyed middle- or upper-middle-class incomes, and the husbands all held careers and owned attractive suburban homes that reflected that status. Almost two-thirds of the husbands and one-third of the wives (among both the swingers and the non-swingers) had graduated from college with at least a Bachelor's degree. However, even though the distribution of annual family incomes was essentially the same for both the swinging and the non-swinging couples, 62 percent of the swinging wives held regular jobs outside the home compared to only 33 percent of the non-swinging wives. This difference is a very significant one and will be enlarged upon in the chapters that follow.

TABLE 1
AGES OF HUSBANDS AND WIVES, SWINGERS AND NON-SWINGERS

	Husbands		Wives	
Age:	*Swingers*	*Non-Swingers*	*Swingers*	*Non-Swingers*
20–23	4	3	12	8
24–27	7	8	20	19
28–31	25	21	21	20
32–35	11	12	12	11
36–39	16	17	14	16
40–45	19	18	8	11
46 up	18	21	13	15

The number of children the various couples studied had is summarized as follows:

TABLE 2
NUMBER OF CHILDREN OF SWINGERS AND NON-SWINGERS

Number of Children:	*Swinging Couples*	*Non-Swinging Couples*
None	18	12
1	17	16
2	39	39
3	18	23
4 or more	8	10

Only half of the teenaged young people interviewed for this study were the offspring of the 100 swinging couples. Because I wanted a more complete picture of the personal and sexual lives of these youngsters it was necessary for me to search out an additional 24 swinging families with adolescent children. These additional swinging couples were very similar to the 100 upon whom this research focused. However, their family lives provided an abundant supply of additional fascinating material.

There was quite a bit of variability in the amount of time during which the 100 swinging couples studied had actually been actively involved with the comarital sex scene. All of the respondent couples reported themselves as having been involved to at least some extent in comarital sexual participation for a minimum of at least six months. The distribution for length of involvement in swinging among the couples studied was as follows:

TABLE 3
LENGTH OF INVOLVEMENT OF SWINGING COUPLES

Time period	Percentage
6 to 11 months	5
about 1 year	11
2 years	20
3 years	18
4 to 5 years	14
6 or 7 years	9
8 or 9 years	7
10 years	6
11 to 15 years	7
more than 15 years	3

There are several reasons why I decided not to interview any couples who had not been involved in swinging for at least six months. The point at which a married person becomes a swinger depends in very large measure on the *definition* of swinging that is being used. Virtually all of the material published up to now on swinging has agreed that the husband almost always has to convince his wife to try out the recreation of sexual mate sharing. The only noteworthy exception to this regularity is that of the considerable number of swinging marrieds who originally met each other as unmarried people attending swinging *singles* parties. In this study 38 of the 100 couples did originally meet each other as unmarried people in attendance at sexual freedom parties.

It is highly likely that a large but unknown percentage of wives (among those whose husbands broach this subject) cannot be effectively persuaded to try out this nonconformist life style. And some (again, an unknown percentage) of those who eventually do consent to "go along" do so very reluctantly. In essence, they resign themselves to "try out" swinging in order to please their husbands or even to save their marriages. And in all probability most of these "resigned" wives do not remain actively involved in the world of swinging for very long because their deeply internalized norms render them emotionally ill equipped to "take it."

Now from the standpoint of definitions, can these wives be considered true "swingers"? And more importantly, can the marital dyad (couple) of which they are a part be considered a "swinging dyad" or couple? I decided that the answers to these questions must logically be "no." These women do not have an image of themselves as swingers, and their marriages could not logically be considered swinging marriages. Hence, to include them in what is purported to be a sample of swinging married couples would very probably yield misleading data for the research as a whole. In fact, it is very possible that such wives may be far more similar in their background characteristics to suburban wives who do *not* swing than they are to wives who have been able to "adjust" to the world of comarital sex as reflected in their minimum of six months' involvement in same.

The Non-Swingers and Their Selection

The fact that this study employed a comparison group (control group) composed of regular married couples who do *not* swing renders it unlike any research heretofore conducted on swinging. One hundred legally married couples were obtained who were very similar to the swinging couples on such dimensions as age, neighborhood of residence, annual income, level of education, and presence or absence of children. Inasmuch as these factors have always been crucial determinants of life style, it was felt that the comparison group would provide a meaningful contrast with the group of 100 swinging couples.

Since every non-swinging couple was selected from within the same immediate neighborhood (usually within a block) as any given swinging couple, the control on the neighborhood of residence factor most closely approached a perfect match. The main reason for controlling on the neighborhood of residence factor was to have a control on such important dimensions as social context and life style.

The non-swinging couples were not advised of the fact that the study was to deal with sexual spouse-sharing among suburbanites. Even though each non-swinging couple was paid $10 for cooperating in the study, it was believed that such frankness might prove counterproductive with some people. In general, American suburbanites are oriented to privacy and tend to be somewhat distrustful and apprehensive with regard to the work of social scientists. Moreover, any stranger who goes around from door to door—as was necessary in this case—is often regarded with suspicion, regardless of the legitimizing university credentials he may carry. For these reasons, the non-swinging couples were told that the study was a university-sponsored, government-supported investigation of contemporary patterns of suburban family life. While this cover story was only partly true, none of it was false.

Nevertheless it was necessary to ascertain that each of the non-swinging couples was indeed a non-swinging couple and had never taken part in any form of sexual mate sharing. This was done during the course of the interviews.

An item designed to assess the tolerance limits of the non-swinging husbands and wives toward sexual mate sharing swingers was included in the non-swingers' questionnaire forms. The item asked six questions about a hypothetical swinging couple depicted as follows:

> "John and Mary are a happily married suburban couple, aged 33 and 31 respectively. They have two children. John has a Master's degree in electrical engineering and earns an annual income of $20,000. John and Mary enjoy many recreational interests and activities together. One of these is

that they engage about once every week in 'comarital sex' (mate sharing) with five or six other nearby married couples."

Let us consider the way in which the non-swingers responded to this hypothetical couple. Each non-swinger was asked whether or not he or she would object if John and Mary moved into his or her immediate neighborhood. The result was that fully 46 percent of the wives and 32 percent of the husbands *would* object. On the other hand, in the event that John and Mary were known by the non-swinging couples to be *already* living in the immediate neighborhood only 6 percent of the husbands and 4 percent of the wives would want to initiate direct action to make life difficult for them. Inasmuch as gossip tends to travel fast in many suburban neighborhoods the potential significance of these small percentage figures should not be underestimated. Just one hostile person has the potential of heaping a great deal of pressure and trouble on any nonconformist who is living in the same neighborhood.

Of perhaps much greater pertinence in assessing the tolerance limits of the majority non-swinging community toward swingers was the following item: "If I were an employer and John applied for a position in my firm (assuming he had appropriate career experience and education) I would have no objection to hiring him." The wives were again more likely than the husbands to register intolerance: 29 percent of them compared to 20 percent of their husbands indicated that they would *not* hire the man.

Each non-swinging husband and wife was asked quite directly whether or not he or she believed John and Mary's sexual behavior should be tolerated by the community or the law. Psychiatrist David Reuben (1970) in his highly popular book *Everything You Have Always Wanted to Know About Sex But Were Afraid to Ask,* made the statement that "ninety-eight percent of society doesn't really care about the sexual behavior of its members." The data I obtained for this research do not support Reuben. More than one quarter of the non-swinging couples I interviewed indicated that they did not believe that the community should tolerate comarital sexual behavior.

The non-swingers were also asked whether or not they would be willing to admit John and/or Mary into a social club of which they were a member: 58 percent of the wives and 48 percent of the husbands indicated that they *would object* were John and/or Mary to try to become a member.

Perhaps the most socially significant finding of all pertinent to the acceptance or rejection of our hypothetical couple is the one regarding whether or not the non-swinging husbands and wives would be willing to become friendly with John and Mary. Fully 50 percent of the non-swinging husbands and 30 percent of their wives indicated that they *would be willing* to become friendly with this hypothetical couple. It cannot be deduced from this that quite so many people would ever be likely to seriously consider becoming involved in sexual mate sharing themselves! But it should be noted that both the 50 percent figure and the 30 percent figure are *larger* than the 25 percent of the non-swinging couples who do not believe that comarital sexual behavior should even be tolerated by the community or the law.

On the basis of the foregoing, if swingers properly camouflage their activities (and most of them seem to do this rather well) they are likely to be quite safe. There does not seem to be any indication at all to the effect that people actually go out looking for swingers in order to purge them from the community. In fact, as a social researcher I have been constantly amazed at the number of middle-class people who do not even have an awareness of the fact that there is such a thing as comarital sexual behavior existing in many suburban communities.

Just under 40 percent of the non-swinging suburbanites who were asked to serve as respondents (and who qualified by being in the appropriate age group, living with spouse, etc.) proved willing to do so. A good deal of evidence has accumulated in recent years which strongly suggests that volunteers for virtually any kind of study tend to be more liberal, assertive, outgoing and socially aware than those who are reluctant to volunteer. The efforts of many highly respected researchers are especially revealing on this point. Yet, at the same time, these traits of assertiveness, flexibility, etc., are the very ones that have been found to accompany sexual nonconformity. Therefore, if the comparison group of non-swingers selected for this study differs at all as a group from their fellow non-swinging suburbanites, it would be expected that they would be at least slightly more similar than suburbanites in general to the mate-sharing swingers.

One of the implications of the foregoing for this research is that the non-swinging sample probably provides for *a more conservative test* of the several research hypotheses than a more representative group of suburban non-swinging couples would have done. In other words, if swinging couples are actually different from the majority of people in their areas of residence, then the "in-between" group differences revealed in the present study should eventually be shown by more elegantly designed research to be too small.

The non-swinging sample was compared and contrasted with the swinging sample on a variety of background characteristics, attitudes, beliefs, experiences, and so forth. I had hoped that through the data obtained from such comparisons something might be learned about possible antecedents (causes) of comarital sexual behavior in America, and about some of the non-sexual ways in which swingers differ from non-swingers of approximately the same age and social class.

If it could be shown that many of the background characteristics of swingers are similar to those of other kinds of deviant groups (i.e., groups viewed by the dominant majority in America as being deviant), I felt that something might also be learned about the antecedent social forces causing and precipitating the development of deviance in general.

Data Collection Procedures

Each husband and wife in both the swinging group and in the non-swinging group was asked to fill out a detailed questionnaire that dealt with a variety of topics pertinent to married life, children, child-rearing attitudes, political and social attitudes, sexual behavior both before and after marriage, courtship attitudes and experiences, current interactions with parents and kin, early family life during childhood, psychological adjustment, and other similar factors. Each respondent took between 60 and 90 minutes to answer all of the questions, and care was taken to insure that husband and wife filled out his or her form without collaborating in any way with his or her spouse. After the questionnaires were filled out each of the couples was interviewed at some length. The interviews with the non-swinging couples usually lasted about an hour while those with the swinging couples averaged approximately 3 hours. The interviews were tape recorded on cassettes and they were always carried out with couples rather than with individuals. However, in many cases the children of the couples (Chapters 11 through 13) were also interviewed separately.

I was responsible for obtaining all of the data to be reported in this book. I conducted the study originally in order to write a doctoral dissertation in family sociology at the University of Iowa.

While each of the one hundred swinging couples was paid $10 in return for the time and data they provided, it was clear that more than mere money motivated their willingness to cooperate. Ten dollars would have meant little to people of their comparative affluence. Moreover, the swingers seemed to enjoy talking about themselves and their life style. Perhaps the more a swinger discusses his sexual ideology with someone whom he feels is able both intellectually and emotionally to accept him as he is, the more thoroughly and firmly he internalizes that ideology and the more confident he personally comes to feel about it and about himself. However, this is not to suggest that these people are at all ambivalent about their ideology or behavior. Some data bearing on the psychological adjustment of the swingers involved in this study will be presented in Chapters 9 and 15 of this book.

My normal policy in obtaining the swinging sample was first to contact a club leader by telephone. Telephone numbers were obtained from advertisements published in the erotica section of the *Los Angeles Free Press*, which is southern California's major underground newspaper. If interest in cooperating was expressed, and it usually was, I would arrange for a private meeting with the leader and his wife during which I would go over the details of the study's methodology. I would usually ask for the addresses and telephone numbers of from 15 to 20 swinging couples, stressing that all participating couples had to be legally married and living in the nearby suburbs. I would also indicate a preference for couples with children, as many of the questions with which I was concerned dealt with offspring.

It is noteworthy that all of the club leaders approached cooperated fully on the matter of referring me only to those couples who met the various criteria for inclusion in the swinging sample. Every swinging couple in this study had indeed represented themselves to both myself and to their club leaders as being legally married and living in the suburbs. All of the couples selected viewed themselves as mate sharing swingers, and 82 percent of them had children.

None of the club leaders whose help I utilized had discussed the study with any of the members. They simply gave me the addresses and telephone numbers and let me contact each couple directly on my own. This I did, and 73 percent of the couples contacted in this way agreed to cooperate. Each couple was advised over the telephone that they would receive $10 for their help, and that the study was both university sponsored and government supported. (A grant from the National Science Foundation supported the study financially.)

Inasmuch as the refusal rate among the swinging couples contacted was comparatively low by contemporary research standards, it is not likely that there was any serious self-selection bias within the sample of the swinging married couples. Because the club leaders were ostensibly very busy people, it seems highly unlikely that they would have gone to the trouble of selecting only certain couples for me to contact. While it was not possible to obtain a fully representative sample of married swingers, the findings uncovered for this research can probably be considered tentatively suggestive for married, suburban swingers in the state of California. By the same token, the findings which are reported and discussed in the chapters that follow should be interpreted with some caution until such time as other studies become available which corroborate, refute, or qualify my findings.

Chapter 4

The Importance of Relatives and Kin

There is a very popular saying among social scientists that the most powerful forms of influence are those which arc least felt. When we are around people with whom we can let down our hair and our guard, our values and patterns of thinking tend to be effectively shaped in ways that are not even perceptible to us. To most people the family is the major place where they can relax and let down their guard. But the family is also the primary agent of social control and influence in any society. For this reason, any research into the etiology and social context of sexual mate sharing must carefully examine the nature and quality of swingers' relations with kin and particularly with parents.

The Formative Years

I asked the swingers many questions about their formative years in their parents' homes. The answers that they provided to these questions made it very clear that throughout their childhood and adolescent years they enjoyed significantly less cordial and less emotionally satisfying relationships with their parents than did the non-swingers. Only 28 percent of the swinging husbands remembered their childhoods as having been either "happy" or "very happy"; the figure for the non-swinging husbands was 65 percent. The analogous percentage fig-. ures for the wives were 35 percent (swingers) and 60 percent (non-swingers). On the other hand, 72 percent of the swinging husbands recalled their childhoods as having been "unhappy" or only "fairly happy"; only 35 percent of the non-swinging husbands said the same thing about their childhoods. The disparity between the two groups of wives was similar.

I also asked the respondents about how happy they recalled their family lives as having been during their teenaged years. Again the non-swingers were almost two-and-one-half times as likely as the swingers to remember their family lives during adolescence as having been "very happy" or "happy." The non-swingers were also a great deal more likely than the swingers to remember their adolescent years *as a whole* as having been "happy" or "very happy." The findings were almost the same as those obtained for happiness during the childhood years, although in all four groups there was a small drop in the percentage that remembered their teenaged periods as having been happy. This could be expected inasmuch as adolescence in American society is normally regarded as a period of stress and transition. Of course, most of this stress is not due to adolescence itself but rather to the pattern of expectations to which teenagers are subjected in America.

For most people the quality of family life is a powerful determinant of personal happiness. This is especially true in the formative years when the individual must reside with the family and depend on it for the satisfaction of many different strongly felt needs. All children need recognition, respect, and interaction with adults who are important to them. But when this interaction is sparse, unpleasant, or excessively strained, a child's sense of security is likely to remain undeveloped.

The swingers experienced considerably less gratifying relationships with their parents than the non-swingers did. Apparently the social distance in many of the swingers' families promoted a good deal more psychological differentiation from parents than is normal for children and teenagers. Only 32 percent of the swinging husbands and 36 percent of the swinging wives agreed with the statement: "My parents always respected me; I always felt free to discuss my problems with them." In contrast, 68 percent of the non-swinging husbands and 65 percent of the non-swinging wives agreed with the statement.

Data obtained on the frequency of informal communication in the family of orientation were found to corroborate these results. Only 17 percent of the swinging husbands and 24 percent of the swinging wives felt that they enjoyed informal conversations as children with their parents on a "frequent" basis. The analogous findings for the non-swingers were 36 percent for the husbands and 48 percent for the wives.

Both the interview and the questionnaire data clearly indicated that as teenagers the swinging husbands and wives had felt more tightly controlled by their parents than the non-swingers had felt. Only 39 percent of the swinging husbands and 33 percent of the swinging wives said that they were satisfied at the age of 17 with the amount of freedom and autonomy their parents permitted them. This compared to 69 percent of the non-swinging husbands and 66 percent of the non-swinging wives who were satisfied. On questionnaire items where the respondents were asked to estimate how authoritarian their parents were, some very similar findings emerged. However, here the swingers were a great deal more likely than the non-swingers to recall their parents as having been *either* highly authoritarian (much too strict) *or* too "couldn't care less" permissive.

And when the respondents were asked whether their parents had subjected them to more or fewer rules and regulations than their childhood friends of the same age and sex had been subjected to by their parents, there was again a marked tendency among the swinging husbands to have felt subjected to *fewer* rules than the non-swingers. Fully 43 percent of the swinging husbands felt that they had been subjected by their parents to fewer rules than their age mates; only 22 percent of the non-swinging husbands felt this way. On the other hand, 46 percent of the swinging husbands felt that they had been subjected to *more* rules and regulations than their age mates; only 29 percent of the non-swinging husbands felt this way. The data for the swinging wives were very similar, although they were even more likely than their husbands to feel that they had been subjected by their parents to *more* rules and regulations than their age mates.

On the surface these findings may appear to be inconsistent. How can excessive strictness and excessive permissiveness both be associated with low levels of happiness during childhood and adolescence? How can situations of too many family rules *and* too few family rules *both* be associated with a tendency to become interested in deviant forms of sexual behavior?

Even though authoritarian and "laissez-faire" permissiveness appear on the surface to be poles apart, a key point which both almost always have in common is a relative indifference and insensitivity on the part of parents to the feelings, interests, and unique individuality of children. Actually the authoritarian and the highly permissive parent have a great deal in common. Both tend to be adult-centered and quite disinterested in the needs and feelings of children. This leads to an inability to communicate with children on a relaxed, meaningful and informal basis. The authoritarian parent imposes his wishes arbitrarily and without considering the feelings of the child. The highly permissive parent is usually so uncomfortable about communicating with children that he just lets his children do whatever they want.

In assessing the quality of parent-child relations it seems likely that the issues that are of greatest importance are those of warmth, nurturance, and mutually enjoyable communication which occurs spontaneously and on a frequent basis. An atmosphere of mutual respect, warmth and interested responsiveness most consistently serves to facilitate and maintain a child's identification with his parents as role models. A cool or inadequately (emotionally) gratifying atmosphere in a home can almost always be expected to weaken children's identification with their parents. Moreover, a chronically cool environment will usually work to obviate a strong identification with the parents right from the start.

It is likely that a child can develop a strong emotional identification bond with his father or mother under a fairly wide range of different degrees of strictness and permissiveness. But if strictness or permissiveness tends to be accompanied by a cool, unfriendly environment in which little desire to communicate with the parents is inspired in the child, in which the child or teenager does not have the feeling that he is loved, trusted, accepted and respected as a person in his own right, and in which discipline is often inconsistent or erratic, then a very early sense of psychological autonomy and an inner need for rebellion may develop in that child or adolescent. A person who emerges into middle adolescence without a reasonably strong identification with either of his parents is very unlikely to have established any particular emotional commitment to the norms for which these parents stand. Correlatively, the less happiness a teenager's family life has given him, the *less* vested interest that teenager has in sustaining his parents' family norms and values. Also, the less happy a child's family life had been, the stronger that child's vested interest in later experimenting with a *different* set or sets of family values on his own.

Also of importance is the fact that people who as children had to frequently deal with authority *which they perceived* as arbitrary, capricious and unfair, usually grow up to be quite negative, suspicious and distrustful of all social rules and customs. Simply put, to the extent that a child views the authority to which he is regularly subjected as being uncompassionate and insensitive to his needs, feelings and opinions, to that extent is that child highly likely to grow up with a predisposition to be hostile and suspicious toward any authority or system of rules. Many people tend to regard these points as ivory tower theorizing. However, they are truly valid points with great practical significance and implications for the way we run our educational systems and family units. When these implications are acted upon we may confidently expect that all forms of deviance in America will become a very great deal less common than they are today.

There are three well-supported truisms in social science which will be referred to at appropriate points in this book because of their formidable importance in explaining how deviant inclinations develop:

> (1) A prerequisite for any kind of social influence is social interaction and meaningful communication.
>
> (2) The strongest, most effective forms of social control (influence) are those which are *least* strongly perceived or felt by those who are being influenced.
>
> (3) The more frequently two different people (or groups) interact with each other by mutual choice and desire, the more similar these two different people (or groups) become to one another in attitudes, values, hopes, desires, dreams, aspirations, behaviors, interests, etc. Also, the more frequently such mutually desired interaction takes place between two people, the more those two people come to love and/or like one another.

The first point is obvious common sense. Yet it is common sense that the parents of the swinging husbands and wives tended to chronically ignore. These parents clearly wanted their children to grow up as conforming, law-abiding citizens like everyone else. But despite such noble desires these parents typically either ignored their children much of the time or they depended upon the exercise of brute power to influence their children to do what they wanted them to do. For this reason the preswingers as children seldom *desired* communication with their parents for any warm, emotional gratification and satisfaction it might have provided them. In many cases, communication took place only when it was necessary, *not* for sheer pleasure and emotional gratification. The preswingers learned early in life to look outside their homes for warm, emotionally meaningful conversation. In essence, because meaningful communication seldom occurred, the parents of the swingers exerted comparatively little influence over them during their formative years.

> "Ahh, my home life is just a bad memory. Even now I don't like to think about it because it depresses me. Lots of times I wanted to open up to my parents, but the few times I did they just hit me over the head for something I said ... Sometimes they would just holler about how stupid I was or what kind of a sonofabitch I was. You know, they would give me a tongue lashing the few times I did open up with them about what went on at school." (35-year-old male swinger.)

Many of these parents unwittingly discouraged meaningful conversation with their offspring by constantly lecturing to them about the way they should have done or not done something.

> "Shit! As long as I can remember my mother and father never really talked to me. They lectured. Fuck! I know they meant well. But who can take having someone constantly telling you how you should be doing things. My parents were too fuckin' serious around us kids, especially me. I was the oldest and they were constantly getting into my hair about something. Even the few times I did try to talk friendly with them, after the first five minutes they were back to lecturing at me again." (28-year-old male swinger.)

This young man went on to point out how his three younger brothers and sisters gravitated toward quite conventional life styles as they grew older. Hence, an environment that is pathogenic for one or some of its members may not be pathogenic for all of its members. In the case of the above family the parents manifested a far less intense emotional preoccupation with the growth and development of their other offspring than they did with the elder son, who grew up to become a swinger. In short, the parents may have communicated in a satisfactorily meaningful fashion with the other children. With their pre-swinger son, on the other hand, they could only lecture. In the context of the intimacy of the home, constant lecturing, hollering, and correcting do not and cannot invite mutually meaningful communication.

The second point outlined above is usually far from obvious to the parent who wishes to influence his child. The parents of the swingers studied commonly resorted to force and coercion in order to get their children to behave properly. Many others simply ignored the undesirable behavior of their children. And still others behaved in a highly inconsistent way, beating and angrily swearing at their children on some occasions and totally ignoring the same disapproved behavior on other occasions.

Paradoxical as it may sound, people tend to be most strongly influenced in situations where they feel completely free to let down their hair, their guard, and their defenses. When people can freely discuss their mistakes and their wrongdoings without fear of recrimination and punishment they almost always remove their inner censors and open up their hearts. Groups composed of very close friends usually provide this kind of atmosphere. Mothers and fathers seldom provide it for their sons and daughters because they have too strong an emotional investment in the latters' propitious growth. But to the extent that parents do develop an ability *to listen* to their children and to serve as interested sounding boards with them, to that extent they inevitably come to wield a surprisingly huge amount of influence. Like adults, children resist when they feel that they are being strongly pressured. But when they are involved in mutually enjoyable social interaction they tend to be effectively influenced, with no pressure being felt. And because the child's defenses tend to be down he tends to absorb his parents' values without even being aware of doing so.

> "I didn't always agree with my parents and, in fact, I still don't. But our family always got along well together. I've always felt very fortunate that I had a very happy family life. And, believe me, that happiness has sustained me through some very turbulent times in my personal life. I always felt very close to my mother and father, and I would never want to do anything that would hurt or disappoint them. Even though I'm married now with a family of my own we still have many good times together ... I always enjoyed conversing with my parents. They never punished any of us kids for things we said. Somehow or other we usually arrived at decisions that were acceptable to our parents." (44-year-old non-swinging wife.)

Just as frequent interaction between people tends to make them become similar to each other, strained and unpleasant interaction among family members tends to make them become increasingly unlike each other. Such strained interaction similarly tends to promote early psychological differentiation and emotional independence from mothers and fathers.

> "I don't think I was much older than five when I first began to realize that I was never going to be able to really relax around my parents. They had their own friends and it seemed to me at the time that they were always with some adult. During these times I was always ignored. And when my parents were alone with me, like sometimes we would eat together, they insisted that I not interrupt them. There was only the three of us, yet I was never able to get a word in edgewise. I mean, I would always be hollered at for interrupting. Sometimes they would have the radio or the TV on

while we were eating. And it would be the same old story. I would be slapped or shouted down anytime I tried to say anything." (24-year-old swinging wife.)

It is quite common for young people growing up in such strained environments to become shy and to fail to develop the appropriate social and communication skills for effective interaction with age-mates. But like the woman whose statement is quoted above, most of the swingers had parents who were good sociability role models. The parents were remembered as almost always being with some other adult. And while this doubtless very often resulted in the children feeling neglected, it also (1) forced them to find their own resources for satisfying deep, social-emotional needs; and (2) led them to think of having a lot of chosen friends as being normal, natural, and *easy* to bring about.

Of course, it may also be that these young people (the swingers) had had the advantage of being born with highly resilient temperaments. It is quite possible that a home atmosphere that would have made an ordinary child become quite shy and inhibited with people resulted in the preswinging children becoming quite self-reliant, self-confident and independent minded. To be sure, the preswingers as children did not need to deal with much interpersonal anxiety. They were not afraid of people and quickly developed the social skills necessary for making friends. For reasons that are not clear from the data obtained, the parents' ignoring and frequent emotional neglect of these children never worked to undermine the children's feelings of confidence in their ability to make friends among age-mates and to have those age-mates respond in a friendly manner. Thus we can infer that the preswingers as children were somehow able to both develop and maintain levels of self-esteem which were high enough to permit an effective level of sociability in the peer group.

"I never remember being really shy. In fact, I used

to cut up a lot in class. I guess I did that a lot until I was almost in high school. But I had a good body then and I have a good body now. You know, I was respected by the other kids. Even though I never won any prizes for good behavior I was always invited to play football or basketball after school. I always had plenty of friends and I never could understand why so many kids my age liked to play by themselves. I couldn't stand to be alone, and I still can't. I always try to find someone to be with, and so far I haven't had any trouble at doing that." (38-year-old male swinger.)

But in a few cases the interviews suggested that the swingers may have been born with a stronger psychological constitution (temperament) than their siblings. Jack W., for example, had two older brothers, one of whom had died from an overdose of drugs five years prior to the interview, and one of whom was 42 years old but had never married.

"No, I don't think Artie is a homosexual. Like I told you, he lives in New York, and I don't get to see him very often. But last time I was back there he still had pictures of nude women hanging all over his apartment walls. He says he wants to marry but that he's too shy to get anywhere with anybody. Shit, I can't understand him. Nobody in our family ever could. When we were young, you know, he never seemed to have any friends, and he still doesn't have any. He's always off in a world of fantasy. He's managed to hold down a job steady enough; but that's about all I can say for him." (Jack W., 30-year-old swinger.)

The father had deserted this particular family when Jack was 2 and his oldest brother was 14 years of age. He recalled his mother as having been a strict disciplinarian with the older two boys. Jack had been spared much of this harsh treatment, but was paid little attention by his mother and other adult relatives. But he remembers being well liked by his age-mates at school and by the mothers of his best childhood friends. He escaped from his mother's home immediately after his high school graduation, at which time he came to Los Angeles.

Most of the swingers reported having had a difficult time with authority figures as children. Authority was something that was imposed rather arbitrarily and without any consideration for personal feelings and emotional needs. The swingers' identification with such authority figures as parents and teachers was thus seldom strong and complete. Compared to most people the swingers had been able to either make fun of authority or guiltlessly work out ways of evading it without getting themselves into trouble.

> "My parents would get mad at me really often. When I was in elementary school I used to be really frightened of them because they would both usually overreact a great deal to the things I did. But by the time I was 15 or so I would usually just bowl over in a fit of laughter whenever they would get really mad at me. I don't know why. I just couldn't control it. There they would be screaming at the top of their lungs about what kind of a sonofabitch I was and how they were going to kill me. And I'd be running from them in a fit of laughter that I just couldn't control. It got to the point where my mother especially would throw furniture and silverware and everything else at me, and I just couldn't stop laughing." (33-year-old male swinger.)

This type of situation at least suggests some degree of personal concern and ego involvement on the part of the parents for the child. Yet a large number of those with very similar stories mentioned how they were virtually ignored by their parents *most of the time*. Occasionally the parents would cease ignoring and suddenly be perceived by the child (now adult swinger) as overreacting to some real or imagined transgression. Several of the respondents who reported having been severely beaten by parents on a good many occasions similarly mentioned the fact that they were frequently ignored, and that the fact of being ignored resulted in their having a great deal more freedom then their peers of the same age and sex. Frequent physical punishment is often perceived in our culture as a sign of strictness and excessive control on the part of parents. The data collected for this study suggested that frequently beaten children may very often be under *less* control than seldom or never spanked children are. The frequent resorting to uncontrolled physical violence may more accurately be a mark of *inconsistency* in parents than of "strictness." And it may also mark a serious lack of interest on the part of the parents in the unexpressed feelings and needs of their children. The feelings and needs remain unexpressed because the child is never inspired to relate them to his parents; the child never comes to feel that he can *trust* his parents with confidential information about himself.

> "I remember my old lady used to go to card parties almost every day. She was never home when I came home from school. And I know she didn't work because I know she had a strong neurotic fear of being involved in the workplace. I had the whole house to myself almost every afternoon and I did a lot of crazy things. My dad had to double his fire insurance on the house because of some of the things I did . . . ha, ha, ha, . . . I remember one time I threw a bunch of plastic toys into the furnace and these heavy black particles started coming up through the radiators all over the house—even on the second floor. I was really scared shitless. I didn't know what to do to stop it . . . ha, ha, ha, . . . after about fifteen minutes it stopped. And when my parents came home they threw the funniest fit I ever saw in my life. [At this point respondent laughs hysterically for about three minutes.] All this black shit was on their valuable drapes and all over the ceilings! Oh shit, it was a blast!" (38-year-old male swinger.)

This pattern of parent behavior, bizarre as it may sound, was far from atypical among the backgrounds of the 200 swinging husbands and wives interviewed. In fact, 68 percent of them complained about having felt ignored by their parents; the husbands were even more likely to make this complaint than their wives were—82 percent of the swinging husbands had frequently felt ignored by parents and other family members. A 33-year-old swinging wife had this to say about the pattern:

> "My mom didn't work but she would frequently come home from wherever she was, even later than my father. My other sister Aggie and me had complete freedom to do whatever we wanted. Don't get me wrong. Both our parents would be constantly yelling at us almost every day that they would kill us if they found out we had done anything wrong when they weren't home. But we never had anyone to check up on us so we always did what we wanted ... Aggie would frequently bring boys in and by the time I was 14 I did the same thing. We had a lot of sex, and not all of it was of the old-fashioned kind either! We used to tease each other into doing all kinds of crazy things like take our dogs to bed with us. My parents never let us take our Irish setters into the bedroom areas when they were home. So when they weren't at home we went and did what we wanted. Believe me, by the time I was 17 I knew just about everything there was to know about sex. And neither me nor my sister ever got pregnant either!" (33-year-old swinging wife.)

Being ignored by the parents was very often combined with what (through the eyes of the preswingers as children) was the arbitrary and capricious exercising of authority. Nowhere was this more apparent than in the forcing of children to attend summer camps against their will. No fewer than 55 of the 200 swinging husbands and wives complained about having been *forced* to attend camp. Since 74 of the 200 had attended camp as children, it is clear that most of these people had attended against their will. Among the non-swinging husbands and wives, 46 (out of 200) had attended camp as children, and only 3 out of that number complained of having been forced to go. And all three of these men and women indicated that now as adults they were happy that they had had the summer camp experience. *None* of the 55 swingers who had been forced to attend camp as children were at all happy about having had the experience. Indeed, most of them continued to feel quite bitter about it.

> "The least happy times of my life were those I spent at summer camps. Don't get me wrong; I wasn't homesick. I might have been a bit homesick the first two or three weeks of my very first summer at camp. My parents forced me to go for five straight summers. Anyway, my feelings were those of anger and bitterness, not of homesickness. I never missed my parents when I was away. But I did miss my freedom very much. And I missed the girls. Even when I was ten I felt totally out of place in an environment without any girls. None of the other kids could understand how I felt; but shit! Camp is a bloody monastic environment. I couldn't have been more uptight if I had been placed in reform schools every summer. Because camp is a prison in a way. Even when you're in some very expensive camps, and my parents sent me to some very expensive ones, you're still in a prison because you can't do what you want and go where you want to go. All of your time is organized for you and you have no control at all over your own life . . . Camp is just a refuse dump a lot of parents resort to every year in order to escape from their kids for eight weeks. And that's true of even the most expensive camps." (34-year-old swinging husband.)

Hence, the parents of most of the swingers interviewed tended to have been very insensitive to, unaware of, and non-caring about the deep psychological feelings and needs of their children. Many of these parents may have been basically selfish; summer camp may have provided them with a respectable means of "getting rid of" their children for the summer without being suspected (or suspecting themselves) of neglecting their children's psychological and emotional well-being. In America summer camps tend to be blindly viewed by most adults as being a very rewarding, "fun-type" experience for children. Thus, many of the parents of these swingers may well have been regarded by other adults in the neighborhood as being ideal and very generous parents. The swingers made numerous comments suggesting that such had been the case.

Evidently not all of the swingers had passively adapted to their annual confinement at summer camps. One of the husbands bragged enthusiastically about how he had gotten himself "kicked out" of one "very expensive" camp when he was 14.

> "I finally decided I wasn't going to take it anymore! So you know what I did? I put a shit into my counselor's bed! Yeah! I shit into a towel, wrapped it up and put the fuckin' thing into my counselor's bed! Holy shit—it was a blast! Several of the kids saw me do it, and the next day I was discharged as being psychiatrically unfit for camp! Isn't that a blast! Ha ha ha ha! My old man beat the shit out of me when I got home and my old lady started me out on fuckin' psychotherapy at about that time. But at least I fuckin' well got what I wanted! I got out of that fuckin' prison and I got my fuckin' freedom back!" (36-year-old swinging husband.)

Happiness of Parents' Marriages

Other forms of instability were also much more common among the families of the preswinging husbands and wives than among the families of the non-swingers. For example, the swingers were more than three times as likely as the non-swingers to have come from homes broken by divorce. And many of them recalled very vividly the arguments that had gone on among their parents up to and even after the divorce. Of course, 56 percent of the swingers' parents had never been divorced. But even among this group the level of marital satisfaction must have been unusually low. The swingers were significantly more likely than the non-swingers to rate their parents' *intact* marriages as having been less than happy. In other words, *even among those respondents whose parents had never been divorced*, the swingers rated *their* parents' marriages as being significantly lower in overall quality than did the non-swingers.

These findings are of particular importance. Social scientists have long known that the marriage of parents often serves as a role model for the next generation. This is one reason why bad marriages often run in families and tend to persist generation after generation within the same family. Residing in a home in which the parents are frequently fighting can also cause the growth in the children's minds of distorted viewpoints about the opposite sex.

How happily married a mother and father are can have a marked bearing upon the development of nonconformist tendencies in children. In many ways the marriage of a child's mother and father serves as a kind of model of what marriage in general is like. This image will, of course, be modified as a child grows older, and as he has a chance to observe many other marriages, and as he becomes more aware of the institution of marriage through reading, study, and the fictionalized depictions of motion pictures and television. Nevertheless, despite these later modifying influences, the saliency and immediacy of the parents' experience with marriage is likely to retain a pronounced effect upon the attitudes and feelings about marriage that offspring have, even as adults.

Finally, since the marriages of the swingers' parents tended to have been a great deal less happy and satisfying than the marriages of the non-swingers' parents, this too could be expected to have rendered the minds of the swingers much more open to the exploration of different types and styles of marriage and family alternatives. The model represented by the parents' marriages very often served as a poor advertisement for the benefits of pursuing a conventional marital style. Moreover, since the traditional family system with all of its conventional answers evidently did not do a satisfactory job at dealing with the preswingers' emotional needs when they were children, this too could be expected to have helped to promote an unusually low level of loyalty and trust for traditional answers.

Psychiatric pathology may also have been more prevalent among the homes of the preswingers. Only one respondent admitted that her father had spent the majority of his adult life in a mental hospital. However, lesser forms of pathology may have played some role in shaping the preswingers' views about family life and about the potential of a conventional home life for promoting happiness and contentment.

> "My mother was always drunk. Every day when I came home from school she would be totally bombed. I was ashamed to bring any of my friends home. But I also felt sorry for her and tried to get her to stop drinking. She would keep cussing at me and after a while I would just leave and go to a friend's house. My mom died during my junior year of high school, and I felt guilty about it for a long time. I couldn't bring myself to forgive myself for ignoring her so much and for not being nice to her. My dad was no help either, as he would constantly blame me because I was home with her a lot more often than he was. It took five years of in-depth psychotherapy after my mother died before I finally began to feel some sense of relief and freedom." (27-year-old swinging wife.)

Alcoholism and/or excessive use of alcohol by a parent was mentioned by 32 percent of the swinging wives and by 27 percent of the swinging husbands. None of the nonswinging husbands and wives mentioned this problem. And while there may well have been some incidence of alcohol abuse among the non-swingers' families, it is significant that none of them volunteered any indication that it had been a problem in their homes.

To be sure, not all of the swinging husbands and wives were dissatisfied with their mothers and fathers and with the home that they had provided. About 15 percent of the swinging respondents enjoyed what would have to be considered very high quality relationships with their mothers and fathers, and most of these people referred to their childhood and adolescent years as having been "very happy." The important point to remember, however, is that more than four times as many non-swingers as swingers praised the virtues of their parents and often referred to the many happy times that they had enjoyed during their formative years in their parents' homes. All of these findings collectively suggest that an emotionally unsatisfying home life combined with a history of divorce and parental friction serve to greatly increase the chances that a person will gravitate toward deviant interests and particularly toward swinging. However, these factors are not enough to cause an interest in swinging. Nor is their absence enough to prevent the development of such an interest.

Some of the most fascinating data the social sciences have been able to offer the public come out of the analysis of statistically *deviant cases*. Statistically deviant cases as far as this study is concerned would include all of those swinging husbands and wives who *did* enjoy the advantages of growing up in happy, emotionally satisfying homes. Six of the husbands and seven of the wives in this group thought their own parents might possibly have been swingers, and three of the respondents (two wives and one husband) "knew" that their own mothers and fathers had also been swingers.

> "My mom and dad started swinging when I was 16. They were unbelievably open about it and often discussed the subject with us kids because, you know, they would often have these discussion

> groups in their living room. And me and my brother were usually around when these people came over. I can't recall my mom and dad ever arguing about swinging. But they often reminded my brother and me that it was something that outsiders might not understand and that we shouldn't discuss it at school or with any of our friends. My parents were always 'avant-garde' in a lot of ways and I was always very proud of them for their daring." (29-year-old swinging wife.)

This young wife went on to describe how she and her brother were often invited to important adult discussions, including those pertinent to swinging. Thus, it may well be that one reason why she had been able to adjust happily to her home life and to her parents was that she had never been ignored and had always believed that she was an important and well-respected, loved member of her family. Parenthetically, her younger brother (two years her junior) had also embarked upon a successful, well-adjusted adulthood.

> "I don't know, but I have a sneaking suspicion that my mom and dad did some swinging of their own. They never said anything to me about it but they often spent weekends away from home and a lot of the things they used to say to each other when they didn't think I was around makes me think they were swingers . . . They were very protective, but they were also very good to me. I really can't complain, man. I was always a very lucky guy." (26-year-old swinging husband.)

All of the swinging respondents who enjoyed good parent–child relationships during their formative years were continuing to enjoy them presently as adults. It is interesting too that none of these people had been very geographically mobile. All were still living within an hour's driving distance of their parents. Similarly, all had appeared to have contracted especially happy marriages as far as all appearances were concerned.

Chapter 11 of this book will present data pertinent to how most of the swinging husbands and wives of this study were programming their own children into thinking and behaving like future swingers. These data offer additional insights as to why becoming a swinger does not necessarily entail coming from an unhappy family background. Most of the swingers' children who were interviewed for this book had had very happy childhoods.

Current Relationships with Parents and Kin

Considering that a very large proportion of the swingers had experienced strained, unsatisfying relationships with their parents during childhood and adolescence, it might well be expected that the swingers and the non-swingers would differ a great deal regarding their current relations with parents and kin. It might also be expected that as adults they would interact with relatives significantly less often than would the non-swingers.

In point of fact, swingers of both sexes reported significantly less interaction with relatives than did the non-swingers, and the disparity between the two groups was greater for the wives than for the husbands. Among the non-swinging couples, only 25 percent of the wives and 35 percent of the husbands interacted with their relatives *less often than once in three months.* The comparable figures for the swingers were 62 percent for the wives and 54 percent for the husbands. While significant for both sexes, these findings were particularly strong for the wives. Fully 46 percent of the non-swinging wives saw their relatives at least a few times per month, compared to only 15 percent of the swinging wives.

Even when we confine our attention to couples whose relatives reside within the same immediate metropolitan area, the swingers still interacted with their kin substantially less often than the non-swingers. Among the wives living near their kin, 42 percent of the non-swingers saw their relatives once or more per week compared to only 17 percent of the swingers. Only 14 percent of the non-swinging wives living geographically close to their kin saw them less often than once per month. In contrast, almost half of the swinging wives saw their kin this infrequently. The analogous findings for the husbands were quite similar, although not quite as many swinging husbands as swinging wives were alienated from their parents and kin.

As was pointed out in the first section of this chapter, the preswinging husbands during childhood and adolescence had been *more likely* than the preswinging wives to have gotten along poorly with their mothers and fathers. Now, as adults, the wives were on worse terms with their parents than their husbands were with theirs. This is true even though three-fifths of the swinging wives had initially become involved in sexual mate sharing in the first place as a result of the unrelenting pressure of their husbands. Be that as it may, they had changed over time more than their husbands had. In essence, involvement in sexual mate sharing had made them even more alienated from parents and siblings than it had made their husbands.

While sexual mate sharing in general is viewed as highly deviant by most Americans and particularly by the older, parental generation, it is highly likely that it is viewed as even *more* deviant for women than it is for men. American society has long had a double standard as far as sexual behavior, both before and after marriage, is concerned. And even though this tradition is weakening, for a married woman with children to occasionally involve herself in sexual mate sharing is viewed with abhorrence by most Americans. Most Americans would clearly disapprove of such behavior in married men with children as well, but the degree and extent of the moral revulsion would probably be weaker. Therefore, it would appear quite logical that involvement in swinging would affect kin relationships among women to a greater extent than among men. Also, women in almost all societies are more closely tied to the family (by virtue of their roles and the way in which they are socially programmed) than men are. Hence, since swinging is more deviant for women than it is for men, the amount of intellectual and emotional autonomy from parents and kin needed in order to *persist* in this behavior over a long period of time would doubtless have to be substantially greater for wives than for husbands.

A great deal of data were obtained from the swinging husbands and wives suggesting that as a group they were indeed a great deal more psychologically autonomous from parents and kin than the non-swingers. For example, as adults the swingers were found to agree far less with their parents than the non-swingers did with theirs. In fact, the swingers saw themselves as disagreeing with their parents on virtually every issue of personal importance. Commonly, even people who as adolescents had comparatively poor relations with their parents change considerably as they become parents themselves. Some 82 percent of the swingers studied were parents, but there is no indication that this had brought them closer emotionally to their own parents. As a case in point, 42 percent of the non-swinging husbands and wives felt that they presently agreed "a very great deal" with their parents about ideas, values, and opinions which they deem important in life. The comparable percentages for the mate-sharing husbands and wives were 7 and 5 percent respectively. On the other hand, 52 percent of the swinging husbands and 55 percent of the swinging wives reported "very little if any agreement" with their parents about major issues; only 12 percent of the non-swinging husbands and 14 percent of the non-swinging wives felt the same way. Similarly strong differences between the swingers and the non-swingers were found concerning emotional closeness to their mothers. These differences were particuarly noteworthy for wives: 42 percent of the non-swinging wives, compared to only 9 percent of the swinging wives, presently feel emotionally close to their mothers.

Finally, the respondents were asked to describe the importance to them of their relatives (including parents and siblings) in their overall scheme of things. As expected, wives were less likely than husbands to view relatives as "unimportant." But swingers of both sexes were significantly more likely than the non-swingers to view their relatives as being "unimportant." Only 28 percent of the non-swinging husbands and 12 percent of the non-swinging wives viewed relatives as "unimportant." For the swingers the analogous findings were 51 percent for the husbands and 37 percent for the wives. On the other hand, only 11 percent of the swinging husbands and 15 percent of the swinging wives viewed their relatives as being "very important" in their overall scheme of things. The analogous figures for the non-swingers were 36 percent for the husbands and 48 percent for the wives.

Generally speaking, the swingers did not have the strong feelings of animosity toward their brothers and sisters that they felt toward their parents. However, many of them indicated a desire to avoid frequent contact with siblings on the ground that they aroused unpleasant memories. Many of the swinging respondents indicated that they invariably came away from social contact with brothers and sisters feeling depressed, and that this tended to be so regardless of whether or not the parents or other relatives had also been on hand at the family gathering. Still other respondents expressed the feeling that their married siblings were deliberately avoiding them; the swinging wives were particularly prone to express this sentiment, although a minority of the husbands expressed it as well.

> "Seeing any of my relatives is the worst possible downer to me. I really haven't got anything against my sisters at all; but even seeing them is a downer. We have nothing in common and I just don't like to be reminded of all the shit that went on in the past." (37-year-old swinging wife.)

On the other hand, 7 percent of the swinging wives indicated that they often wished they were closer to their brothers and sisters. The husbands of these women seemed to have a difficult time understanding how their wives felt in regard to this issue. To them the less contact they have with both their own and their wife's family, the better. Yet, some of these women felt hurt by the shunning of some of their relatives.

> "When I was growing up I was always extremely close to my younger sister Edie. Even when we were in high school we were almost inseparable. But my bitch of a mother always had it in for me. And after I went away to college my sister began to drift away from me. Right now we don't even live far apart. She and her husband live in Torrance [about 25 miles away], but Mac and I haven't seen her in well over three years now. My mother has filled her mind with all this bullshit about what a sinful life I'm leading. She's also stricken me from her inheritance. So I guess she's got Edie kissing her ass lest she get disinherited too. Really, my mother isn't worth shit. I know it sounds awful for me to say this, but I wish she'd go jump in the ocean and drown herself!" (32-year-old swinging wife.)

Such pungently hostile feeling toward parents were not at all uncommon among the swinging respondents. Interestingly, the wives tended to be a good deal more overtly hostile in their attitudes toward parents than the husbands were. But some of the husbands emphasized their feelings of hurt and anger too.

> "Oh shit! Don't even mention parents to me! My fuckin' parents are just a bad memory. My old lady could never get it through her thick skull that I can't just turn around and live my life the way she wants. My dad disinherited me and I felt bad about it for two or three months after I heard about it. But shit! I'm my own man! What the fuck am I supposed to do? I've made it this far on my own—I'll be able to make it all the way on my own. I don't need my old man's fuckin' money. My old lady keeps

> feeding me all this shit about love when she calls
> me. My father won't even lift up the receiver.
> Neither one of them know the first fuckin' thing
> about what love is." (38-year-old swinging hus-
> band.)

The idea of being able to "let your hair down" with the
people you see socially came up again and again during
the interviews, especially when visitation with parents
and married siblings was brought up. Only about one-
seventh of the swingers felt that they could really "let
their hair down" with their close relatives. And in the final
analysis this is doubtless the most basic reason for the cool
and very infrequent interaction of the swingers with their
parents and siblings.

> "Say, I work pretty hard at my job. And when I
> come home and get ready to go out socially with
> my wife I want to know that I'm going to be seeing
> people I can shoot the breeze with—you know what
> I mean? That's even more true when we invite
> people to come here. Life's too short and I get far
> too little time off for me and my wife to be wasting
> our time with people who we can't feel at ease with.
> And that includes my own mother and father. I
> know it sounds sort of amoral on my part. A lot of
> people tell me I ought to try to get on closer terms
> with my parents. But we never were close and I feel
> it's too late now to do anything about it. My wife
> and I—we have a lot of friends we *do* feel close to.
> We both decided a long time ago—those are the
> people we are going to see." (41-year-old swinging
> husband.)

On the basis of these findings, it seems that the emotional dependency which normally prevails between children and their parents never became firmly established in
the families of orientation of most swinging husbands and
wives. This is critical because it is the strong emotional
bond between individuals and their families that makes
the family system an extremely powerful conservative so-

cial force for most of society. Since that bond and the strong controls did not develop effectively for most swingers, they acquired quite early in life a sense of personal freedom that permitted the exploration of deviant alternatives for self-expression and coping with life's stresses. Most people, because of their deeply internalized norms, are profoundly affected by the attitudes and perspectives of their parents in ways of which they are scarcely even aware. A close emotional bond (and this can never be forced to come about) greatly facilitates the degree and thoroughness with which norms can be internalized. It is in this manner that the range of behavioral alternatives for most people becomes effectively narrowed.

Of course, even people on excellent terms with their parents will differ with them on at least some issues. But they are likely to differ with them on far fewer issues (and to a lesser degree) than those who are not on such good terms with their parents. And most importantly, they are *highly unlikely* to assume viewpoints disparate from those of their parents on highly significant life issues, such as marriage and family life styles. Disagreements, when they occur, will tend to be confined primarily to the less important issues of life.

Yet at the risk of belaboring the obvious, the swingers' rebellion against their parents was nevertheless *limited* in scope. They did not rebel against such middle-class notions as "hard work and study bring happiness and the good life." They did not rebel against the high value their parents placed upon money, upon owning an attractive suburban home, and upon the desirability of holding a good, stable job. Finally, like their parents the swingers valued the idea of achieving popularity with peers. They did not rebel against their parents' council to be competitive with their peers. Particularly as regards the development of social skills the swingers tended to be highly competitive.

Chapter 5

Relationships With Friends, Neighbors, and Organizations

Alienation from relatives and kin is a background factor which deviants and nonconformists of almost all kinds have been found to have in common. Moreover, the more highly nonconformist a deviant interest is, the more alienated the practitioners of that type of deviance are likely to be from their relatives and kin. Time is also an important variable. A long-term involvement in a highly deviant life style is more likely to be associated with alienation from relatives and kin than a short-term involvement in the same type of deviance. These generalizations have all been shown by this research to be true for mate sharing swingers. But how about social involvements with *chosen friends*? Do these tend to suffer too as a consequence of being involved in deviant activities?

Relationships With Friends

A great deal of research has been published in recent years showing that deviants and nonconformists of all kinds tend to be less popular than people who fit into the mainstream. In fact, even juvenile delinquent gang members have been found by numerous scholars to have fewer close friends, less friendly relationships with people, and poorer social skills, than boys of the same age and social class who are law abiding. Several years ago sociologist Morris Weinberg (1966) similarly found that social nudists tended to have significantly fewer close friends than non-nudists of the same age, sex, and social class. Adolescents and young adults heavily involved with drugs and/or alcohol have also been found to suffer from unpopularity and from low self-esteem. Indeed, it has often been suggested by psychiatrists that isolation from meaningful social contacts is itself commonly a potent factor in precipitating an initial involvement in certain forms of deviance; this is especially true for drug abuse and undisciplined use of alcohol.

In light of the foregoing I naturally expected to find that the mate sharing swingers would have significantly fewer friends than the non-swingers and that they would see those friends a good deal less frequently. However, in stark contrast to what was initially expected, I found that the current adult lives of the mate sharing swingers were not at all socially isolated. In fact, I found that the swingers interacted *with people in general* a good deal more often than the non-swinging husbands and wives did. This was true despite the fact that the non-swingers interacted with their relatives significantly more often than the swingers did with theirs.

More specifically, 49 percent of the swinging husbands and 45 percent of the swinging wives were found to visit with their friends *"more often than* once per week," compared to only 13 percent of the non-swinging husbands and 21 percent of the non-swinging wives. At the other extreme, only 2 percent of the swinging husbands and 7 percent of their wives said that they visit with friends only once per month or less often. The analogous findings for the non-swinging couples were 40 percent for the husbands and 26 percent for the wives.

Further analysis revealed that number of years in swinging had no effect on frequency of social involvement with chosen friends. The question arises, however, as to whether the friends with whom the swingers interacted were exclusively fellow swingers. This definitely does not appear to be the case, given the swingers' affinity for belonging to community organizations. The interview data clearly indicated that most of the mate sharing respondents developed an early dependency on the peer group of chosen friends for a variety of satisfactions, most of which they could not get from their parents. Moreover, the average swinging couple only gets together with fellow swingers for sexual mate sharing about once every twelve days; but over 80 percent of the swingers couples were found to visit with their friends *once or more per week*. Only about one-third of the non-swinging couples visited their friends that often.

Fully 67 percent of the swinging wives viewed their friends as being of greater personal importance than relatives and kin; only 26 percent of the non-swinging wives felt the same way. Among the husbands the differences were equally great: 85 percent of the swingers but only 42 percent of the non-swingers felt that friends were of greater importance than relatives.

According to Goode (1963), some 79 percent of the housewives interviewed in a Detroit area study indicated that relatives were of greater importance to them than friends, while only 17 percent thought that the importance of friends surpassed that of relatives. Yet, whereas 74 percent of the suburban California non-swinging wives of this study similarly thought relatives were more important to them than friends, only 35 percent of the swinging wives thought so as well.

Clubs and Organizations

Involvement with clubs and social organizations is commonly used by social scientists as an indicator of the strength of a person's bonds with his community. The degree and extent of a person's social participation is known to have an especially strong effect upon his level of personal happiness. For these reasons I asked the respondents how many social organizations in their community they belonged to in the past year, and how many meetings of such clubs and organizations they normally attended each month. Informal swinging and other sexual freedom groups that meet within the community were ruled out for both of these questions.

Only 29 percent of the swinging husbands and 27 percent of the swinging wives were found to belong to *no* clubs or formal social organizations. Quite surprisingly, this compared to 55 percent of the non-swinging husbands and 36 percent of the non-swinging wives. Indeed, 19 percent of the swinging husbands and 14 percent of the swinging wives belonged to *three or more* clubs or formal social organizations at the time of the interviews, compared to only 10 percent of the non-swinging husbands and 13 percent of the non-swinging wives.

Regarding the perhaps more important issue of *how many meetings* of clubs or organizations the respondents attended each month, the differences between the swinging and the non-swinging couples were somewhat smaller. But the swingers still revealed a more frequent and more active participation in clubs and community organizations than the non-swingers did. For example, 19 percent of the swinging husbands and 20 percent of the swinging wives attended an average of four or more club meetings per month. In contrast, only 8 percent of the non-swinging husbands and 16 percent of the non-swinging wives attended that many meetings in the average month. At the other extreme, only 43 percent of the swinging husbands and 37 percent of their wives attended *no* club meetings in the average month. Among the non-swingers, 59 percent of the husbands and 49 percent of the wives attended *no* meetings of clubs or community organizations in the average month.

The swingers belonged to very much the same organizations as did the non-swingers. For example, the husbands belonged to the Kiwanis, the Rotary, the Lions, the Elks, etc., while the wives belonged to various women's club groups. Many of the couples were affiliated with their local chambers of commerce, and even with the Parent-Teachers Association. On the other hand, the swinging husbands were substantially more likely than the non-swinging husbands to play an active role in the affairs of the national and/or international organizations associated with their businesses or professions. As a case in point, the non-swinging husbands were less likely than the swinging husbands to have attended an out-of-state business or professional meeting during the past twelve months.

The swingers cited a range of reasons for belonging to their respective clubs and community organizations. Many of them simply stated that they wanted to live a rich and varied life, and that this necessitated associating with important and influential people resident within the local area. On the other hand, twelve of the swinging couples revealed that membership and involvement in respected community organizations was a good way of maintaining camouflage as sexual mate-sharing swingers, and that it was a way of determining whether or not any rumors or hints of rumors might be floating around town about them.

While twelve out of one hundred couples certainly isn't many, there is strong evidence in the remarks made during the interviews that "maintaining a proper image" was a major reason behind membership in and attendance at PTA meetings. The swingers were about as likely as the non-swingers to belong to the PTA despite the fact that slightly fewer of them had children: 82 percent of them were parents compared to 88 percent of the non-swinging couples. Among the husbands 15 percent of the swingers and 8 percent of the non-swinging were members of their local PTA. Among the wives 25 percent of the swingers and 29 percent of the non-swingers were members. The swingers were more likely than the non-swingers to attend meetings with their spouses. Many of the swingers were genuinely interested in the activities and discussions that went on at their local PTA meetings. But many of the swingers, including many of those who enjoyed and actively participated in the PTA meetings, were concerned about "keeping tabs" on what parents of their children's friends might be saying about them.

As for the various civic and women's club organizations, most of the swingers who were active members expressed considerable enthusiasm for their own participation. They enjoyed what they were doing and had every intention of continuing their "double life," so to speak. These people were able to compartmentalize and segregate their highly nonconformist sexual lives in such a way that the people in the "public sector" of their lives would not become aware of their nonconformity.

In sum, the swingers had more "good friends" (among the ranks of non-swingers) than the non-swinging couples had, and they interacted with them significantly more frequently than did the non-swinging couples. In addition, the swingers were also somewhat more actively involved in community organizations and clubs than the non-swingers. And when it is recalled that the swinging wives were almost twice as likely as the non-swinging wives to be employed outside the home, it becomes clear that the swinging wives studied for this research led highly active lives. These facts, if they should later be borne out by other researchers, are of considerable theoretical importance. For they suggest that sexual mate sharing does not need to be associated with withdrawal from community involvement.

Neighbors

Besides relatives and chosen friends, neighbors constitute another group which has traditionally been very important as a source of informal social conviviality. However, unlike friends, neighbors are not deliberately chosen; people end up with a collection of neighbors as a direct result of where they happen to live. It might be expected that swingers would perceive neighbors as posing a kind of threat. A substantial fraction of the swinging couples did say that they often worried about the possibility of relatives dropping in unannounced at the wrong time. Friendly relationships with neighbors might substantially increase the likelihood of being inopportunely surprised by visitors.

I checked the extent of the respondents' informal relationships with their neighbors. And, not surprisingly, 61 percent of the swinging husbands and 62 percent of the swinging wives characteristically get together socially with neighbors less than four times per year. This low frequency of interaction with neighbors was true for only 43 percent of the non-swinging husbands and for 36 percent of the non-swinging wives. The fact that almost twice as many swinging wives as non-swinging wives were employed outside the home could account for some of this difference. The less often a woman is home, the less often she is likely to see her neighbors. Nevertheless, the marked difference between the two groups of husbands, all of whom were employed, suggests that swingers tend to be highly selective in terms of their patterns of friendship and peer relations.

Friends as a Kin Network Substitute

Since most of the swingers as children never enjoyed warm, emotionally satisfying relationships with their mothers and fathers, they learned to depend from a very early age upon their peer groups of chosen friends for their social and emotional satisfactions. Since none of the swingers ever suffered from a fearful inborn temperament or from a low interpersonal anxiety threshold (shyness), and since their parents in spite of their shortcomings in other areas had served as effective sociability models, the swingers had always enjoyed social skills and a strong sense of personal freedom in choosing and enjoying friends. And despite certain psychological problems common among them during their early adulthood years (which will be dealt with in Chapters 9 and 15), none of them had ever felt lonely or socially isolated. All had always had friends, and over 80 percent of them had always enjoyed the "special" companionship of "close friends."

Despite the fact that as adults almost all of the swingers enjoyed an extensive network of friends that extended far beyond the bounds of comarital sex, most of their "closest" or "best friends" were (at the time of the interviews) fellow swingers. This was especially true for the interpersonal swingers, but it was also true for most of the recreational swingers as well. In fact, for at least 60 percent of the swinging couples I interviewed, their fellow swingers had become a kind of *quasi-kin group*—a functional equivalent of what for most Americans would be a group of very close relatives.

Seventy-two percent of the swinging couples indicated that they frequently got together socially with fellow swingers for plain, ordinary, non-sexual sociability. Fifty-seven percent of the couples, in fact, got together with their swinging friends for non-sexual sociability an average of at least once per week. Quite commonly during these occasions the children would be brought along. And among those swinging families with teenaged children it was not at all uncommon for the mothers and fathers on such occasions to be quite sexually inactive while the children would be in another part of the house actively engaged in their own overt erotic activity (see Chapter 11).

Such groups of close swinging friends have become for many sexual mate sharers a quasi-kin group providing much of the in-group intimacy that conventional people usually find through close and frequent interaction with relatives. A minority of swingers (15 percent in this study) prefer *not* to develop any close friendship ties at all with the people with whom they swing, and some of these people strongly prefer the impersonal anonymity that large group sex encounters with total strangers afford. But if the swingers of this study are at all typical of their kind, it can be stated with confidence that most swingers feel a bond, and in some cases a very strong bond (particularly among long-time swingers), with fellow mate-sharing swingers everywhere.

A particularly remarkable feature of this strong group bond is the tendency among many swinging couples to carry and maintain lists of fellow swinging couples (whom they have never met) who reside all over the United States and, in some cases, all over the world. Couples entrusted with such lists feel quite free about contacting the recommended couples when they travel through the various cities where the listed couples reside. Some 26 percent of the swinging couples I interviewed possessed such lists, and all made extensive use of them. Entire swinging families will occasionally go off together on weekend vacation trips. While the eroticism of the adults in such cases seldom takes place around the children, the closeness of the friendship bond found among some of these couples tends to be strikingly similar to that which commonly prevails among blood relatives in the more conventional world.

One couple enthusiastically told me of how they had to make a business trip to Atlanta. Even though this couple had their three children along, they still proceeded to contact a listed mate-sharing couple whom they had never met before. This couple also had children; they put the visiting couple up at their home for four nights during which time, among other things, they engaged in a variety of family type recreations together.

Seven of the couples interviewed had done an extensive amount of summertime travel, often with their children. All of this group of respondents were particularly enthusiastic about their use of the lists.

> "Well, two years ago we took the kids on a ten-week tour across the country. Up to that time we had never actually used the lists which we had been given. But our name and address had been on one of those lists for some time, and over a three-month period we had been visited by some lovely people from all over the country. Usually they would just

stay for one night. The idea is to stay with families
who are like yourselves instead of at some expensive motel. You see what I mean? . . . Anyway, when
we set out we were a bit nervous at first. You know,
you don't like to impose on people, especially those
you've never even met. Well, we were literally
amazed! Out of 70 nights on the road we only had
to use hotel or motel facilities for 24. We had the
most fantastic time. And let there be no doubt
about it. It was the people who made it fantastic—
the people—not any of the things we saw or did."
(47-year-old swinging husband.)

One of the most interesting uses to which such lists were
sometimes put was that of providing a "home away from
home" for husbands whose occupations required them to
make frequent out-of-town trips. Six of the couples I interviewed held reciprocal understandings with swinging
couples living in distant cities. Most such relationships
did not entail any kind of financial charge because the
husband of the family visited would just as often be required by *his* job to visit Los Angeles. One of the couples
had such relationships with fellow swinging families in
seven different cities: New York, Chicago, St. Louis, Min-
neapolis, Denver, Houston, and Dallas. Another couple
had such understandings with families in five cities, and
tentative understandings with families in three others. All
of the remaining four families had reciprocal understandings with fellow swinging families in at least three American cities to which the husband most frequently had to
travel. The cities listed above were the most commonly
represented along with Seattle, Portland, Vancouver, B.C.,
Phoenix, Washington, D.C., Atlanta and Miami.

"Before I became involved in this thing I used to
dread making these trips. I hate to even admit that
because I really love my work. In fact, I always
enjoyed my job. But I'm the type of guy who needs
to be around people. And I used to get so goddam
lonely once I pulled into my hotel for the night and

the day's business was finished. Like I've read in several places that that's the time when most husbands are likely to be unfaithful to their wives in the first place—because they're lonely. You know what I'm talking about? I used to screw around at such times. I'll be the first to admit that. And it wasn't because I didn't love my wife. It was because I was just so goddam lonely. And the lonelier I got the more horny I became, it seemed. Well, with this new set-up we've got now I don't have to be lonely. Fortunately Chicago and Denver are really the only out-of-town places I'm ever asked to go now. And our swinging friends in both places are so close to us I'm sure we couldn't feel any closer if we had grown up in the same family. Jack lives in Chicago, and he has to come to Los Angeles at least once every five weeks. And he knows this place is literally his whenever he comes here. And I feel the same way when I go there. Now, Frank in Denver we haven't known as long. But it's getting to be the same way." (49-year-old swinging husband.)

This particular husband had been very close friends with Jack for over 15 years. Jack and his wife had lived in Los Angeles for many years before he and his family were required by his company to move to Chicago. However, most such relationships with swinging families in distant cities get started by referral or through use of the nationwide lists. To be sure, many swinging families are not interested in serving as "hotel substitutes" for "total strangers" living in distant cities. On the other hand, fully half of those swinging husbands who were required by their businesses to travel frequently were interested and very often quite enthusiastic about the idea of sharing their home with swinging husbands visiting Los Angeles on business trips from distant cities. It appears likely that personality factors (i.e., high sociability) along with personal needs and desires for such a reciprocal service both help to determine what a swinging couple's attitude on the matter might be.

Lest the reader think the wives feel put upon by being expected to occasionally share their homes with traveling businessmen, the following comment can be seen as typical for swinging wives whose husbands must frequently travel:

"It makes life much more interesting for me because all of these guys have a lot of interesting things to say. You know, you get to hear some perspective in things that's different from your husband's for a change. I don't know; it really keeps me on my toes. I love it. I think it's a sort of hidden dividend of being a swinger." (42-year-old swinging wife.)

Two of the swinging families had another interesting use for the nationwide lists: namely that of a summertime child exchange.

"Our fifteen-year-old son Jimmy had been bugging us for a long time about travel to different parts of the country. Both of our kids love to travel, so one summer we decided to let them do it. We have these friends back in Coral Gables, Florida, and we decided to switch kids with them for four weeks. Our kids were delighted with the idea and so were theirs. Our kids were anxious to see what life was like in Florida, and theirs were anxious to come to California. So we put our kids on a Greyhound bus with a generous supply of money so that they could have some fun along the way. Fiona and Vince are more protective of their kids than we are. They put them on a plane and flew them out here. The result was that we had their kids about a week longer than they had ours. But they all had a wonderful time. And at the end of the summer I got the feeling that they all appreciated their own homes a lot more than they had before the summer began. (46-year-old swinging wife.)

In the case of the second family, the children were sent away for at least a weekend every six or seven weeks to the home of some geographically distant swinging couple. The children were always eager to go because of friendship ties and romantic love relationships that they had developed with age-mates in these distant families. In the summertime this family and their children traveled around the western states a great deal, stopping at the homes of fellow swinging families along the way, and occasionally trading off children for weekend outings.

The sharing of family outings with fellow swinging families living within the immediate Los Angeles area was much more common. Fully 56 percent of the swinging families I interviewed got together occasionally with fellow swinging families for camp-outs, trips to the beach, backyard barbecues, and short vacations. This practice was more common among interpersonal swingers than it was among recreational or egotistical swingers. The latter drew fewer of their closest friends from among the ranks of fellow swingers and, for the most part, were less children-oriented. In other words, they were more inclined than the interpersonal swingers to keep their children out of their social recreation.

During the summer months 28 percent of the swinging families averaged one such family get-together per weekend, and 8 percent of those interviewed synchronized their vacation schedules with those of their closest friends so that they and their children could go away together. It is interesting to note that none of these families had more than semi-annual contact with their parents and/or other blood relatives. Again, it appears that the clinging together commonly found among many groups of swinging families serves as an effective substitute for the kind of kin group interaction which most American families share with blood relatives.

A further interesting earmark of the swingers' recreational style which will be commented upon at greater length in Chapter 9, is that the swinging couples tended to engage in most of their social and recreational activity *together* on a husband–wife unit basis. The non-swinging couples, on the other hand, engaged in much more of their activities outside the home on a sex-segregated basis. Social scientists commonly apply the label "joint" to the former recreational style and "segregated" to the latter. Husbands and wives whose recreation is *joint* tend to get along much better together than those who prefer the *segregated* style. We often hear the cliché: "The family that prays together stays together." Recent social science research has made it clear that the family that does *anything* together on a frequent basis is more likely to stay together than families whose members go their separate ways for recreation.

The quasi-kin group status of the swingers' friendship networks was further reflected in the support, among 6 of the 100 swinging families, of teenaged "love groups." The "love groups" will be dealt with at length in Chapter 11. Suffice it to say here that they are parent-sponsored sexual freedom groups for the swingers' own teenaged children. This research focused upon 18 teenaged "love group" members; they came from 14 swinging households. Six of these 14 families were among the 100 swinging families upon whom the major part of this research focused. The remaining 8 came from 24 additional swinging families with adolescent offspring.

The swinging parents who sponsored the "love groups" tended to be very close. They spent a great deal of time together and engaged in a wide variety of social activities. Through the eyes of the vast majority of adults in their respective communities they surely would have been viewed with great scorn and probably would have been arrested had their activities been divulged. Sharing a faith and a strong and sincere confidence in the judiciousness of what they were doing served to bring them together into a very close, harmonious coalition. Oddly enough, the teenagers involved could very easily have taken care of their own sexual needs without the aid of their parents. But because they deliberately planned sexual activities for their children the swinging fathers and mothers involved with the "love groups" tended to feel "different" (i.e., deviant) even among the ranks of many of their fellow swingers.

A further illustration of the quasi-kin group nature of swingers' friendship networks can be seen in the frequent use of tiny bumper sticker symbols on their automobiles. Thirty-seven percent of the swinging couples I interviewed used such symbols on the rear bumpers of their cars. The stickers are about one square inch in size, and they enable swingers to recognize each other anyplace they might be driving throughout the United States and Canada. Just how prevalent the use of such stickers might be in other parts of the country is not known. Many of the husbands and wives with whom I talked were dead set against their use. The interpersonal swingers were especially likely to be opposed to use of the stickers. The three main objections to their use were: (1) they might endanger family privacy; (2) they might suggest an "open invitation" to swingers with whom a sexual relationship might not be a good idea; and (3) their use might lead some members of the "square" community to suspect them of improper behavior.

An aditional way in which some swingers endeavor to help one another is through the so-called "shitlists." "Shitlists" or "blacklists" are maintained and passed around to a sizable minority of the most active swingers. "Shitlists" are comprised of couples who have violated major swinging norms such as those against chronic intoxication, the overt manifestation of jealousy, violence, grossness, uncleanliness, rudeness, etc. They also include the names and addresses of couples trying to gain entrance into the swinging world, but who for various reasons are deemed grossly inappropriate candidates. Along with the above factors, obesity, excess age, gross unattractiveness, low education, and low socioeconomic status are major factors determining whether a couple might be placed on such a list. To be sure, many of the couples I interviewed had never heard of, had never been offered, and/or did not want a copy of the "shitlist." Interpersonal swingers who swing for long periods of time with the same group of very close friends tend to be comparatively uninterested in "shitlists." On the other hand, recreational and egotistical swingers are very often interested in such lists, and often take an active part in helping to keep them up to date.

Like people with a large number of relatives and kin, swingers very often try to keep as much as possible of their personal and job-related business within their quasi-kin group. Again, this tends to be more true of recreational and egotistical swingers than of interpersonal swingers, primarily because the former tend to meet many more fellow swingers; hence, they have many more contacts. At most of the larger swinging parties (those with seven or more couples in attendance) many business calling cards are exchanged. Swingers often go out of their way in order to trade with fellow swingers, and in some cases will even accept a lower profit margin (i.e., will sell at a bigger discount) in order to do business with a fellow swinger. Some of the contacts made at the larger swinging parties may never be renewed again, or may not be renewed for a period of many months or even years. Yet despite the fact that a particular client may not be seen again socially at a swinging party, doing business with a fellow swinger is viewed by many swingers as an appealing thing to do.

To be sure, not all of this is due to "intra-clan" altruism. Some of the salesmen swingers bragged about having contracted some of their best and most profitable deals at swinging parties. Some of these deals ran well into the tens of thousands of dollars and many of them brought about a great deal of valued repeat business. The idea of keeping one's business within the large "swinging family" smacks of "blood brotherhood." It suggests that a bond is operating among many of these sexual nonconformists which is taken quite seriously and which holds considerable psychic and financial rewards for those involved.

Chapter 6

Religious and Political Views and Involvements

The institutions of religion and politics have a profound effect upon people in American society. And the family institution in turn has a very strong impact upon religious and political institutions through the ways in which it programs the loyalties and belief systems of its younger members. In this chapter we shall explore the past and present attitudes of the sexual mate-sharing swingers toward religion and politics. The data I obtained from the swingers pertinent to religion and politics turned up many interesting surprises and offer us further valuable insights into the highly idiosyncratic personality structures of sexually nonconformist husbands and wives. These data provide some further insights into the antecedent causes of involvement in sexual mate sharing.

Religion and the Swingers

On the basis of our knowledge that swingers practice sexual mate exchange for sheer fun and recreation, it seems all too easy to predict in advance how they might differ from non-swingers on matters pertinent to religion. However, the relationship between swinging and religion is far from being quite as simple and straightforward as some might imagine.

Sociologists often define religion as being an organized set of ideas which imbues both life and death with a sense of meaning, destiny, and purpose, and which attempts to explain the unexplainable. Life in all societies and at all social class levels is fraught with uncertainty and with seeming injustice. Death, in particular, has always been a major problem of man; and it has always been a matter about which he has continually sought some viable explanation which could provide some semblance of serenity of mind.

Perhaps this is why virtually all societies the world over have historically had some form of religion. Not all people in all societies have practiced religion or have seemed, on the surface, to have had a need for it. But anthropologists over the years have assembled an impressive amount of data suggesting that all societies have had some form of religious ideology.

In the United States, as in most Western nations, people tend to confuse the *spiritual* functions of religion with the *social control* functions. In the large majority of societies around the world religious institutions serve spiritual purposes *only*. In most regions religious representatives do not try to tell people how they must behave, and they do not instill people with a feeling of fear lest they might behave in ways that are different from those prescribed. All societies do have institutions of social control. But the social control functions of most societies tend to be taken care of by the kin group and family. Informal social control among members of local communities also tends to be strong in most places. Religion, in contrast, tends to concern itself with serving man's spiritual needs rather than with telling him how he must or must not run his life.

In contrast to most other parts of the world, the religious institutions supporting the Judeo-Christian tradition have been as much concerned with fulfilling social control functions as with serving man's spiritual needs. And in many cases, particularly in the case of Roman Catholicism and the fundamentalistic Protestant denominations, the preoccupation with social control has been far more visible than any preoccupation with serving spiritual needs.

Religious institutions have long had a powerful influence upon life in America. Indeed, many of the most basic elements of American civilization were shaped, in part, by religious ideology. As powerful an institution of social control as religion is, however, *its influence is mediated largely through the family rather than through the efforts of religious functionaries.* It is the parents who introduce children to church and to Sunday school in the first place, and who later exercise coercion to ensure their attendance at these religious events. Similarly, it is the parents who interpret and impart religiously based values and knowledge in the intimacy of the home day after day, year after year. The two or three hours spent per week in the charge of religious functionaries ordinarily cannot begin to exert as much of an impact upon the child's developing social reality as can the far greater amount of time spent with parents.

As parents in very large measure serve as the main mediators of religious values, it might normally be expected that given a relatively conventional social setting, people who develop a degree of emotional estrangement from parents and kin are similarly likely to do so with respect to the religious institutions their parents represented over the years. The more close, intimate, and emotionally rewarding the interaction between children and their parents, the closer the similarity of the child's values to the parents' values is likely to be. We have already seen that parent-child relations had been considerably less mutually rewarding for the swingers than had been the case for the non-swingers; during their formative years the swingers did not perceive their relationships with their mothers and fathers as being anywhere nearly as emotionally satisfying and happy as did the non-swinging respondents. And we have also seen that the swingers and the non-swingers differ greatly from one another in terms of present-day interaction with relatives, parents and kin. It is in light of these earlier findings on parent-child and present-day kin relationships that much of the swingers' attitudes toward conventional political and religious institutions can be accurately understood in a meaningful way.

Each of the swingers and non-swingers was asked to indicate his or her usual frequency of church attendance, both as a 15-year old as well as presently as an adult. These data are summarized in Tables 4 and 5.

TABLE 4
"ABOUT HOW OFTEN DID YOU ATTEND ORGANIZED RELIGIOUS SERVICES AS A 15-YEAR OLD?"
(in percentages)

	Husbands		Wives	
		Non-		*Non-*
Response Categories	*Swingers*	*Swingers*	*Swingers*	*Swingers*
Weekly or more	49	49	55	52
One to three times per month	18	23	23	17
Two to six times per year	12	9	12	19
Once per year or less	21	19	10	12
Never attended	13	10	7	8

TABLE 5
"ABOUT HOW OFTEN DO YOU NOW ATTEND ORGANIZED RELIGIOUS SERVICES?"
(in percentages)

	Husbands		Wives	
		Non-		*Non-*
Response Categories	*Swingers*	*Swingers*	*Swingers*	*Swingers*
Ten or more times per month	7	25	3	29
Once every one to three months	7	16	13	19
Once or twice per year	18	32	32	27
Never attend	68	27	52	25

The reader should find it very interesting to compare and contrast these two tables. It is particularly noteworthy that the swingers recalled having attended organized church services equally as often as the non-swingers recalled having attended organized church services when they were about 15 years old. Fully 49 percent of the swinging husbands and 55 percent of the swinging wives recalled having attended church services once or more per week when they were 15 years of age. The figures for the non-swingers were not noticeably different. Evidently, the demands and expectations of the parents of the swingers-to-be had not been significantly different than those of the parents of the non-swinging husbands and wives. But perhaps the manner and spirit in which they imposed these demands on their children was markedly different and less friendly and loving than had been the case for the parents of the non-swinging husbands and wives.

In any case, while there were no meaningful differences in frequency of remembered church attendance as 15-year olds, we observe in Table 5 that today as adults the swinging husbands and wives have broken away from organized religion to a far greater extent than have the non-swingers. Fully 68 percent of the swinging husbands and 52 percent of the swinging wives reported that they never attend religious services anymore. Among the non-swingers only 27 percent of the husbands and 25 percent of the wives never attend anymore.

To be sure, the frequency of organized church participation has gone down for the non-swingers just as it has for the adult population in American society generally. But we are primarily concerned here with the fact that the swingers in the course of their late adolescence and early adulthood became alienated from organized religion to a far greater extent than did the non-swinging husbands and wives.

Among the non-swinging husbands 10 percent never attended religious services as 15-year olds; today among this same group 27 percent never attend. For the non-swinging wives 8 percent never attended as 15-year olds; today 25 percent never attend. In contrast, among the swinging husbands only 13 percent never attended as 15-year olds; at the present time fully 68 percent never attend. And for the swinging wives, 7 percent never attended as 15-year olds; today fully 52 percent never attend.

I also looked at the specific organized religion or denomination in which the respondents were born and raised. And again, with the sole exception of the "no organized religion or agnostic" category, there were no meaningful differences between the swinging and the non-swinging groups. Thirteen percent of the swinging husbands and 8 percent of the swinging wives grew up as agnostics or with no religion; the analogous figures for the non-swingers were 1 percent for the husbands and zero percent for the wives.

While only 13 percent of the swinging husbands grew up as agnostics or with no organized religion, 68 percent of them see themselves as being without organized religion today. The comparable figure for the swinging wives is 58 percent, up from 8 percent when they were teenagers. Among the non-swinging husbands 23 percent see themselves as being without organized religion today compared to 22 percent of the wives. Again, virtually none of the non-swinging husbands and wives remembered themselves as having been without organized religion when they were teenagers.

In sum, the swingers became "dropouts" from conventional, organized religion to a far greater extent than did the non swingers, even though *both* groups tend to be significantly less involved now than they had been as children and as teenagers.

Further indication of the comparative alienation of the swingers from organized, conventional religious institutions can be seen in their pattern of responses to several attitude items that were included on the questionnaires. One such item read: *"Organized* religion is one of the greatest sources of hate, intolerance, and oppression the world has ever known." It is interesting to note that fully 65 percent of the swinging husbands and 61 percent of the swinging wives registered agreement with the statement compared to only 25 percent of the non-swinging husbands and 26 percent of the non-swinging wives. On the other hand, 56 percent of the non-swinging husbands and 57 percent of the non-swinging wives disagreed with the statement; but only 18 percent of the swinging husbands and wives disagreed.

Of interest too is the fact that 86 percent of the swinging husbands and 76 percent of the swinging wives did not feel that children should be required to attend Sunday school classes in religion. Among the non-swingers only 31 percent of the husbands and 26 percent of the wives felt the same way.

Bearing these findings in mind, it cannot be considered surprising that the swinging couples were far less likely than the non-swinging couples to have married in church. Fully 83 percent of the non-swinging couples had had a church wedding, compared to just 49 percent of the swinging couples. Forty-seven percent of the swinging couples had had a civil ceremony only, compared to 12 percent of the non-swinging couples. The remaining couples had experienced both a civil and a church ceremony.

At first glance the foregoing findings would appear to suggest that swingers tend to be very strongly "this world oriented" and basically disinterested in spiritual matters. But as suggested earlier, the *spiritual* functions of religion are very often confused by both scholars and laymen alike with the *social control* functions. As a group the swingers certainly evidenced a much greater rejection of *conventional* religion than did the non-swingers. Researchers such as Bartell (1971), the Smiths (1970), Walshok (1971), and Rubenstein and Margolis (1971), have similarly presented evidence suggesting that swingers tend to be quite nonreligious in comparison with the general middle-class American population. But none of this material suggests that swingers are any more likely than most American suburbanites to reject the notion that man has a spiritual nature. Nor does any of this material suggest that swingers have less of a *need* for spiritual sustenance than most people do.

Psi Phenomena and the Swingers

For the past fifteen years psychic phenomena has been one of my strongest professional interests. I have been particularly interested in those aspects of this field which pertain to such phenomena as astral projection ("out-of-body experiences"), apparitions, communications with discarnate entities, "life after life," and reincarnation. Popular literature as well as professional research in this area has proliferated immensely over the past two decades—the very period during which popular involvement with organized religion here in American society has undergone a very marked decline.

My interest in this field led me to include several items pertinent to paranormal phenomena on the questionnaires and in the interview schedules which were used for this research. One of these items simply asked the respondents whether or not they accepted the reality of extrasensory perception as an established fact. Another item went further: it asked the respondents whether or not they could accept as authentic and valid some of the many reported cases of alleged communications with and visitations from the discarnate spirits of deceased persons. Additional questions dealt with such psychic occurrences as "out-of-body" experiences, reincarnation, and "life after life" experiences.

The data obtained in response to these questions do not provide any support at all for the widely prevalent view that mate-sharing swingers are so completely enmeshed in their sensate pleasures that any form of spiritualism for them is a totally superfluous consideration. In fact, for the husbands, fully 74 percent of the swingers but only 43 percent of the non-swingers were able to accept the notion of extrasensory perception being an established fact. These differences were found to be highly significant, even though the analogous differences between the two groups of wives were much smaller: 78 percent of the swinging wives and 67 percent of the non-swinging wives were able to accept the existence of extrasensory perception.

Of course, the phenomena of extrasensory perception only borders on the spiritual. But a belief in the possibility of communication with and visitations from discarnate entities, on the other hand, would appear to lie at the very heart of matters spiritual. Among *both* the husbands and the wives the mate-sharing swingers were found to be significantly more accepting of the possibility of communication with and visitations from discarnate entities than the non-swingers were. For example, 40 percent of the swinging husbands and 53 percent of the swinging wives accepted such communications and visitations as being possible, compared to only 16 percent of the non-swinging husbands and 34 percent of the non-swinging wives.

Out-of-body experiences are doubtless the most significant of all psychic and occult experiences because of the obvious implications that they hold in regard to survival of bodily death. In recent years, many outstanding books have been published on this subject, particularly by such people as Robert Crookall, Raymond Moody, Elizabeth Kübler-Ross, Brad Steiger, Herbert Greenhouse, David Wheeler, Harold Sherman, and Archie Matson. (Readers who might be interested in exploring this subject further will find the bibliography at the end of this book helpful, as it includes books by the above authors and others.)

Fully 43 percent of the swinging husbands and 54 percent of the swinging wives believed in the reality and authenticity of out-of-body experiences. They believed, in essence, that human personality can exist independently of the physical body. In contrast, only 16 percent of the non-swinging husbands and 35 percent of the non-swinging wives believed in the possibility of out-of-body experiences. None of the non-swinging respondents admitted to having had any out-of-body experiences themselves. Interestingly, 7 percent of the swinging husbands and 15 percent of the swinging wives claimed that they themselves had experienced an astral projection at least once in their lives.

The non-swingers were also much more hostile than the swingers were to the idea of reincarnation. Many of them denounced the very idea of reincarnation as being "anti-Christian." Less than one-tenth of the non-swinging respondents thought that reincarnation was possible. On the other hand, more than one-third of all the swingers interviewed believed in at least the possibility of reincarnation. In fact, almost a quarter of them indicated feeling convinced of the reality of reincarnation. (See the bibliography at the end of this volume for works by Ian Stevenson, Helen Wambach, Brad Steiger, and Morey Bernstein, if you are interested in exploring the subject of reincarnation.)

The major ostensible purpose of religious structures is that of satisfying man's needs for spiritual sustenance—at least this is the message most religious functionaries in America endeavor to convey. We have seen, however, that contemporary organized religion is actually an institution primarily concerned with *social control*. With this in mind, two points seem to emerge with considerable salience: (1) from early childhood onward, swingers seem to have been unusually refractory to most kinds of control. They did not want to permit themselves to be controlled or to have their minds programmed and conditioned by authority figures. And (2) conventional religion is *not* the only structure which can fulfill spiritual functions. In fact, it *may* be that the better publications on metaphysics as well as such paranormal topics as out-of-body experiences, communication with discarnates, and reincarnation, fulfill the spiritual needs of many people far more effectively and thoroughly than do the conventional religious structures with which most Americans are familiar. And it could be that one reason why material on metaphysics and psychic phenomena does this for many people is that it does not demand attitudinal and behavioral allegiance to any preconceived constellation of normative proscriptions and prescriptions.

When I first came into contact with books on out-of-body experiences and communication with discarnates I found myself overcome with a vastly greater feeling of serenity regarding the matter of life after bodily death than I had ever experienced through years of exposure to many different kinds of conventional religious indoctrination, including Roman Catholicism, Latter-Day-Saintism, and moderate as well as fundamentalistic Protestantism. In fact, the course in medical sociology which I regularly teach has presented me with the opportunity to explore the practical applicability of books on the paranormal for "death therapy." I have observed numerous cases in which the families of terminally ill patients have thanked me profusely for introducing them to such books and materials. I have seen even devoutly religious people claim far greater spiritual benefit from these materials than from the host of conventional religious teachings to which they had long been exposed. But perhaps most impressive of all have been the very positive unsolicited reactions I have received from initially "non-spiritual" students, some of whom had originally been somewhat hostile to the idea of being required to read some of this material for a sociology course.

Therefore, it may very well be that materials on the paranormal are far more effective at satisfying the spiritual needs of well-educated, contemporary Americans than conventional religious institutions are. Whether or not spiritual needs are intrinsic to the basic, underlying nature of man is still a matter of some debate. Some scholars feel that these needs are learned and are not endemic to man's nature. On the other hand, virtually all of 650 or more societies covered by the *Human Relations Area Files* do provide some means by which their members can satisfy spiritual needs. This by itself constitutes a fairly convincing argument that man everywhere, regardless of the social context in which he is reared, does have a lasting preoccupation regarding what happens to his sense of self after the death experience. If the structures designed to deal with this preoccupation turn out to be inadequate to the task, new structures are bound to gradually emerge. The contemporary large-scale increase of interest in spiritualism and metaphysics (concomitant with a diminution in organized religious participation) would seem to illustrate this point.

To the traditionalist a mate-sharing swinger is anything but a "spiritual" person, inasmuch as he is "preoccupied" with the sensate pleasures of his "animal nature." But to many swingers, particularly the younger, well-educated ones, man's animal nature is an integral part of his spiritual nature, and that until biological death (i.e., death of the outer shell which is contained by the soul) the two cannot be separated. A good many swinging couples view the "square" population as being highly materialistic and fundamentally *non*-spiritual in orientation; the weekly church attendance is viewed as being fraught with sham and pretense and as being motivated by the programmed desire to conform to middle-class community expectations rather than by genuine inner spiritual strivings and convictions.

Most of the sensory awareness programs in which some of the swinging couples have taken part place a very strong emphasis upon man's underlying spiritual nature as well as upon the desirability of "getting back to nature." Yoga and other health approaches which have been borrowed from the gurus of oriental religions similarly place a strong emphasis upon the notion that man has a spiritual nature, and that he cannot find true happiness until he endeavors to recognize, understand, and accept his own spiritual nature as well as that of his fellows. Moreover, the group sex behavior of many preliterate societies commonly took place within the context of religious worship. (See especially the volumes by Henriques, 1959, and Lipton, 1965.)

Of course, there are other factors which might partially

explain the greater tendency for swingers than for most
people to become interested in psychic phenomena and
the occult. To be a swinger is to be a "deviant" or "nonconformist." And, until very recently, for a person to be
interested in the psychic was itself considered "deviant."
Indeed, people who devote a great deal of time to psychic
matters are still considered "deviant" by large numbers of
middle-class Americans.

Since swingers are already "deviant," it might well be
considerably easier for them to develop interests in other
"deviant" areas than it would be for non-deviants. In fact,
the weak family relations which made it so easy for many
of the swingers to become interested in sexual mate sharing might possibly have been the very same factor which
enabled them to easily become interested in psychic and
occult matters. This combined with a lack of intellectual
and emotional allegiance to any conventional organized
religion, might have also made it easier for the swingers
than for the non-swingers to become interested in and to
explore psychic phenomena.

But there is also the possibility that swingers are more
likely than most people to have had meaningful occult
experiences. One man, a 34-year-old who had been swinging for four years, recounted to me what for him had been
an extremely moving event. This man, whom I shall call
Mario, had always viewed himself as a strictly down-to-
earth, practical type of person for whom spiritual matters
held little interest or relevance. Yet one evening, when he
was about 24 and a graduate student at a Los Angeles
university, he chanced to notice his father standing on the
outside balcony of his apartment as he was driving his car
into his apartment parking lot. And most importantly,
Mario had a friend sitting next to him in the car who also
saw the man standing on the balcony. The friend had
never met Mario's father.

Mario quickly parked his car and ran upstairs to his
apartment to see what his father wanted and to find out
how he had managed to get in. His father lived 480 miles

away in the San Francisco suburbs, and he knew that his father did not have a key to the apartment. When he opened the locked door Mario was even more flabbergasted to find his apartment in total darkness and his father not there. The door leading to the balcony was similarly locked and the area was in total darkness.

Dumbfounded, Mario sat down to catch his breath. Inside of about five minutes the telephone rang. It was his mother calling long distance from San Francisco to advise Mario that his father had suddenly dropped dead that afternoon on the golf course. Even more amazingly, it turned out that the very clothes in which the father had died were the ones that Mario and his friend had seen being worn by the father's apparition.

After this experience Mario was not motivated to return to any active involvement in formal, organized religion. But, as he claims, his attitude toward death and the survival of human personality underwent a vast change. He found himself spending many hours in the library reading hundreds of books and articles on the paranormal. And he claims that this reading and study served to make him happier and more serene about life and death and their purpose than he had ever thought he could be.

In another case recounted to me by one of the swinging wives, an out-of-body experience had been involved. In this case the woman (Marta) had come down with a severe case of acute appendicitis. One Sunday afternoon she was overcome with severe pains. An ambulance was quickly summoned by her husband. However, before help even arrived she found herself suddenly on the ceiling looking down upon her body and observing the distressed conversations of those standing around her. She had never had anything akin to this experience before, but she found herself feeling strangely calm and peaceful.

She continued watching her limp body for several minutes. And then she found herself riding in the car of her doctor who was enroute to her home to help her. The doctor had two assistants in the car whom Marta had never met.

She listened closely to their conversations and was particularly amused at how her doctor swore profusely as he arrived at a certain signal light just as it turned red.

Immediately upon arriving at her home the doctor gave Marta an injection. Within seconds she was back in her body and wriggling around in the throes of the worst pain she had ever known.

About a day later, after her operation had been successfully completed, Marta discussed the experience at considerable length with her flabbergasted doctor. The doctor was particularly astounded at her recounting of the minute particulars of the conversation he had had with his assistants en route to Marta's house. And he was especially astounded at her mentioning of his swearing fit at the exact street corner at which it had occurred.

Almost a fifth of the swinging respondents spontaneously detailed either major or minor psychic experiences which they at one time personally had had. Further discussion here of the specific nature of these psychic experiences is beyond the scope of this book. Suffice it to say that these experiences were very real for those who had savored them. In most cases such experiences tended to motivate the person into wanting to read about and study the psychic. And in virtually all cases the person's philosophical outlook on life was changed at least in part.

But the increased belief in and interest in matters spiritual toward which personal psychic experiences tended to lead did not tend to inspire the development of any ascetic or "moralistic" orientation. Throughout the interviews the swinging couples tended to stress what they saw as being the importance of individual responsibility for personal behavior. The idea that *anything* is "moral" except that which impinges on the happiness and well-being of fellow human beings is the theme which pervaded most of the interviews. And I think it can be concluded that it is a keynote of the swingers' ideology and belief system. To the swinger, spiritual or what some might call "religious experiences" (such as those recounted earlier), tend to support the theme of individual responsibility. In short, for those swingers who do accept some spiritual or religious system, God wants man to behave responsibly and to not inflict pain, suffering and unhappiness upon his fellows. To them what is "moral" is that which leads to happiness and fulfillment. Happy people find it easy to be compassionate, loving and good to others; unhappy people usually find it difficult to be compassionate and loving. However, swingers recognize that what leads to happiness for one person or couple will not necessarily do so for another.

Metaphysics as an Alternative to Religion

During the course of the interviews I found 35 percent of the swinging respondents to be ideologically committed to a metaphysical perspective and outlook on life. I further found that the widespread acceptance of and belief in psychic and occult powers was in some measure a reflection of the swingers' serious involvement in metaphysical study. Twenty-two percent of the swinging families, for example, attended metaphysical meetings and study groups an average of once or more each month. And most of them usually engaged in this activity as a total family unit. Only two percent of the non-swinging families indicated any interest at all in metaphysics; most of them had no awareness at all of metaphysics or of what it is.

Metaphysics can be defined as "the branch of philosophy that systematically investigates the nature of ultimate reality." Let there be no mistake about it: metaphysics *is* a religion to many of those who practice it. In fact, in California, metaphysical organizations are accorded the legal status of "churches" with all of a conventional church's attendant privileges.

Even more significant is the fact that many of metaphysics' most central tenets are rooted in the Bible, and more specifically in the teachings of Christ. The most important of these are represented by the following Biblical quotes:

(1) "The kingdom of God is within you."

(2) "I and the father are one."

(3) "All of you are equal unto me."

(4) "According to your faith, so be it unto you."

(5) "As a man thinks, so is he."

(6) "All things are possible to him that believes."

(7) "Call no man your master, not even I. But one is your master and He is the God within you."

(8) "Why call ye me good? There is none good save one. And He is the father (within each and every human) who has sent me."

(9) "Seek first the kingdom of God (within you) and all these things will be added unto you."

(10) "It is not what a person eats that defileth a man, but rather what issueth forth from his lips."

(11) "Greater things than these shall ye do."

(12) "In all your ways acknowledge Him, and He will direct your paths."

(13) "It is not I but the father (within) who doeth these good works."

(14) "If therefore thine eye be single, they body shall be filled with light."

(15) "Enter into thy closet, shut the door behind thee and pray to thy father which seeth in secret."

A careful study of these fifteen quotations will teach the reader a very great deal about how a significant minority of the swinging population is able to effectively integrate their sexual nonconformity into a coherent moral and religious philosophy of life. Many swingers repeatedly use these quotes in their informal conversations as they strongly emphasize the importance of positive thinking and of a positive self-image. They also emphasize the point that *for them* the *correct translation* of the extramarital sex commandment is "Thou shalt not commit *infidelity*," *NOT* "Thou shalt not commit adultery."

Many swingers also champion the importance of twice-daily meditation (quotes 14 and 15). They believe that God exists within the mind of each and every human being, but that most people never learn how to contact their own God-mind.

Metaphysics accepts the pantheistic doctrine that God is in everything throughout all of nature. Metaphysicians believe that God is infinite energy and that man is just one manifestation of this infinite energy. They further believe that man's physical body is merely a temporary vehicle which is also composed entirely of energy which possesses a very low level of vibration. The personal soul of a person is, according to this perspective, the essence of the God-within. It includes the personal consciousness and the immortal part of man including his unique purpose. It is energy functioning at a very high level of vibration and it serves to coordinate the physical and mental energy including heartbeat, breathing, flow of blood, digestion, etc.

If it is indeed true that "All of you are equal unto me," that "I and my father are one," and that "The kingdom of God is within you," then it logically follows that each and every human being on earth contains within him or her the *universal God-mind*. Those who learn to contact the higher mind inside of themselves through one of the techniques of meditation soon find that their problems begin to get solved. And this includes practical and money problems as well as medical and psychological problems.

Because God does exist within, the metaphysical philosophy directs man to find his own unique, individual purpose *and his own truth* by and through a disciplined program of meditation. The disciple of metaphysics is instructed to determine the morality, appropriateness and goodness of his planned behavior by this program of going into his own higher mind. Indeed, he is instructed *to plan* his behavior *before* engaging in it by first meditating; and this applies whether his plans pertain to career, love, morality, recreation, or anything else. Twenty-two percent of the swingers interviewed indicated that this very medi-

tation convinced them of the morality of sexual mate sharing *for themselves*. These respondents stressed that their
conclusions can apply only to themselves and the intimate
relationships of which they are a part. This in a nutshell is
how the metaphysical religion allows a person to legitimate in his or her own mind the recreation of sexual mate
sharing. Of course, to many people the swingers are delud-
ing themselves for their own "immoral" self-gratification.
The swingers, however, do not think they are doing this.
And for them that is all that really matters.

Metaphysics rejects the traditional ideas of heaven and
hell. The swingers involved in metaphysical groups tend
to strongly believe that the kingdom of heaven is here and
now and lies *within*. They reject the concept of "sin" in its
conventional sense. Still, they frequently cite two quite
specific definitions for the word "sin": (1) sin is merely a
lack of awareness, and (2) sin is any action that represents
less than perfect love for another human being. To
metaphysician swingers, justice for "wrongdoing" or "un-
awareness" is brought about through the operation of
karma. They believe, in essence, that life is a school comprised of a wide range of positive, neutral, and negative
experiences, and that all people pass through an unlimited
number of incarnations and discarnations on their way
toward full and complete perfection. The cruel or unaware
person will simply experience a larger ratio of negative
over positive experiences during his next few incarnations
and discarnations. In this regard they believe that *all*
people are "saved" no matter how "wicked" they might
have been. All souls have a purpose, and those with
"wicked acts" entrenched in their karma will simply have
to assign themselves some "corrective learning experiences" at some later date. Human personality is an
energy, and energy can never be destroyed or in any way
annihilated.

Prayer, including "family togetherness" prayer, is very
important to metaphysician swingers, and most of them
partake in it a very great deal. *However*, prayer to them is

an *affirmation;* it is *not* begging or beseeching as is customary in conventional prayer. To beg, according to the metaphysical philosophy, is to say that we do not *already* have the answer we need within ourselves. To the metaphysician we *do* have the answer; it exists in the universal God-mind within us, and we get at it through going inside of our higher minds in meditation. This, in essence, is the meaning behind quote numbers 14 and 15 cited above.

While the metaphysician swingers believe that each person is indeed equal to God Himself, they stress that this knowledge must never allow a person to go off on an "ego trip." They stress that it is the *personal ego* that prevents a person from effectively meditating, "losing himself," and finding his God-mind. Everyone *must* love himself in order to effectively love others and to be successful and happy. *But* this "self-love" must be love for the God-within, *not* for the personal ego which is a blinding smokescreen.

A central ingredient of metaphysical prayer is intense *visualization* accompanied by a sense of belief, faith and *expectancy.* This point will be commented upon further in Chapter 12, when the problem of birth control will be considered. Suffice it to say here that metaphysical visualization is being widely used today by practitioners of holistic medicine. All manner of diseases and disorders have been successfully treated by means of this method, including some cases of terminal cancer (see especially Simonton, 1976).

A final major tenet of metaphysics is the principle that *thought creates form.* "As a man thinks, so is he"—quote number 5—aptly sums it up. In essence, thought is a powerful energy form; thoughts are things (which in turn are energy) and can affect and create matter.

Hence, swingers are strong protagonists of positive thinking and of visualization. In fact, I found this to be true even among swingers who were not at all interested in metaphysics or in any other spiritual topics. Their positive thinking and metaphysical affirmations were credited by many of them as having contributed substantially to the success of their marriages and to their sexual and social competence. The "self-fulfilling prophecy" may well be in overt operation here: "when we define certain things or ideas as real, those things or ideas tend to become real in their consequences." The swingers *expect* to be sexually competent and to have strong marriages; thought creates form, and so they do remain sexually competent and sustain strong marriages.

In sum, metaphysics has been able to do for many swinging couples what conventional organized religion has (sometimes) been able to do for ordinary, conventional married couples. *It has* imbued their lives with a sense of meaning, destiny and purpose, and *it has* given them a firm faith and conviction about the existence of life after this earthly life. In fact, for a group very often accused of being highly "anti-spiritual" and "exclusively body-centered" (as opposed to "person-centered"), the swingers interviewed for this study enjoyed a far stronger conviction about the spiritual nature of people and things and about the certainty of an afterlife, than most ordinary Americans enjoy. Few of the ordinary churchgoers I interviewed shared this kind of strong faith; unlike the majority of the swingers, most of them confessed to anxieties about death and the annihilation it might bring. Similarly, among those respondents who did pray, the non-swingers were far more likely than the swingers to feel that prayers are not answered. To the metaphysician swinger it is inconceivable for a positive affirmation (prayer) not to be answered.

The Conventionally Religious Swingers

About 20 percent of the swinging couples preferred to maintain at least some degree of participation in organized religion, even if it was not very frequent. Several of these people labeled themselves "liberal Christians," and some of them conveyed the impression of being quite well-read on religious topics. One such swinging wife asserted that people like Billy Graham are doing far more to alienate people from the ranks of organized religion than are people who are actively hostile to religious practice. She suggested that Graham and his followers almost constantly intimate that only they (i.e., strict, fundamentalist Christians) have an exclusive franchise upon the love and devotion of Jesus Christ, and that all others are really not Christians at all even though they may call themselves such. This attitude which prevails on religious radio broadcasts tends to present the public with a very rigid, uncompassionate image of Christianity and of Christian teachings. Above all, it tends to suggest that there is only one correct interpretation of and approach to Christian teachings, and that those who reject this approach will not be "saved."

The "liberal" approach, as this woman suggested, tends to stress the fact that the people for whom the Bible was written are not the intellectual equivalent of today's Americans. The people of twenty centuries ago were almost all very poorly educated by today's standards, and they tended to react to almost everything on a purely emotional rather than on an intellectual or thoughtful, intuitive basis. Poorly educated people, like very young children, tend to be basically incapable of thinking in the abstract. They tend to think purely in concrete terms. (Very young children in our own society are typically taught elementary arithmetic with concrete objects such as apples or beads. This helps them to conceptualize in their young minds the idea that 3 plus 2 equals 5. Without the help of concrete objects it would be very difficult for them to understand simple arithmetic.)

The very same difficulty in regard to thinking in the abstract can be illustrated by certain experiences social change workers have had in working with people in underdeveloped parts of the world. In a South Sea island community, for example, a social change worker wanted to convince the people of the importance of using toothpaste in brushing their teeth. Pictorial advertisements were displayed all over the island showing a fisherman in the process of catching a large fish. Upon the fish hook displayed in the photograph was a large tube of toothpaste. And anxiously trying to bite into the "bait" was a large fish.

The social change worker in this case succeeded in selling a great deal of toothpaste. But the toothpaste was not used for its intended purpose. It was instead used by the people as fish bait!

In another case a social change worker in an isolated Peruvian community was concerned with teaching the people the importance of sanitation, and particularly about how flies can spread germs when they are permitted to alight upon feces and other forms of garbage. The residents of this community loved to attend movies; they particularly loved Walt Disney-type cartoons. With this in mind, the worker presented them with a beautifully made cartoon about a half-hour in length in which flies and their disease-spreading capabilities were carefully depicted. Upon the motion picture screen the flies and the germs were naturally shown as being far larger than they are in real life, in order to get the concepts across in an interesting and entertaining fashion.

The people very much enjoyed the film and even asked to see it again. However, the social change worker was flabbergasted and exasperated when several of the leaders of this Indian community approached him and said, "Gee, boss, we may have flies down here, but none of them are anywhere nearly as huge as your flies! We're glad we don't have to worry about your kind of flies spreading germs here in our community!"

Christ evidently recognized very well the importance of getting across certain ideas to people who, for want of education, had never developed any capacity for thinking and assessing ideas in the abstract. People who can only think in the concrete cannot for example, be expected to digest the implications of statements such as, "The kingdom of God is within you," and "Call no man your master; not even I. But one is your master and He is the God-mind within you." Similarly, they cannot be told, "Thou shalt not commit adultery except for certain situations or circumstances." The exceptions would have confused them to the point at which the ultimate message of this and other commandments would have been totally lost. Hence, in order to effectively deal with this problem God is depicted in the Bible as having specified all of His commandments in a concrete, non-confusing manner with no exceptions or elaborations given. This approach was necessary in order to bring stability and order into the disorganized, non-intellectual world of 4,000 years ago.

One of the few church-attending swingers in the sample asserted that the mind is the greatest gift God has bestowed upon man, and that man has a moral responsibility to use it. The fundamentalistic approach, he pointed out, saves man from the responsibility and privilege of having to use his mind; it makes all of life's decisions for him. In this approach, all man ever needs to do in his search for truth is to check with the Scriptures. The fundamentalistic approach assumes that man can only think in the concrete, and that if an answer was valid for an illiterate society of 2,000 to 4,000 years ago, it is equally true for the modern, highly complex society of today. In line with this, the fundamentalist assumes that all moral laws are rooted in the ancient Scriptures rather than in the basic question of what in any given social context might most effectively lead to man's happiness and creative fulfillment. Indeed, to the fundamentalist true happiness can only be achieved through the steadfast following of the ancient moral laws. And they try to impose this concept by doing everything possible to make their followers feel guilty about any violations of these ancient moral laws—even though such violations may not have inflicted any harm upon anyone.

In line with this, "thou shalt not commit infidelity" (rather than "thou shalt not have extramarital sex") could quite possibly be the *correct translation* of the "thou shalt not commit adultery" commandment, just as many swingers believe. It is important to remember that the

Bible handed down to us was *translated* from the original by a group of highly ascetic fourth century monks. It is thus inconceivable that the highly ascetic views of these monks did not have a significant bearing upon their translation and interpretation of the scriptures which, parenthetically, were never written by Christ or by God in the first place. The beliefs of the political and religious leaders during the Spanish Inquisition several centuries later served to render our Bible even more anti-sexual and anti-spiritual in its general tone. This is one reason why the metaphysics oriented swingers came to view truth as being rooted in the "universal God-mind" which can only be gotten at through a disciplined program of meditation.

In sum, the mate-sharing swingers researched for this study provide strong evidence of being quite alienated from the *conventional* social structures of organized religion. In a *conventional* sense they *are* nonreligious. As a group they seemed to have become estranged from organized religion during the years of late adolescence and early adulthood. As a group the swingers were found to manifest no evidence that as children they were any less involved than the non-swingers were in the practice of organized religion. Of course, the possibility exists that many of the swingers up until the age of 15 found themselves *in* the church each Sunday morning, but not *of* it. It is likely that the relatively estranged relations which a significant portion of the swingers had as children vis-vis their parents served to facilitate the development of feelings of estrangement toward the parents' religion and their style of practicing same.

On the other hand, while the swingers were found to be strongly rejecting of organized religion, they turned out to be a good deal *less* rejecting than the non-swingers of unconventional spiritual beliefs. For example, they were found to be significantly more likely than the non-swingers to be actively involved in metaphysical study groups, and to accept the possibility of visitations from and communications with discarnate entities. There was also a very marked tendency for the swingers to be strong believers in extrasensory perception. In essence, the swingers did not provide any indication at all that as a group they were "anti-spiritual."

Politics and the Swinger

Data were obtained on the political affiliations of the respondents. The most striking difference between the swingers and the non-swingers was that far fewer of the former were affiliated with *any* political party. Each respondent was asked to identify himself or herself with *one* of the following four options: (1) Republican; (2) Democrat; (3) Independent; and (4) Uncommitted and not interested in politics. Among the swingers 33 percent of the husbands and 34 percent of the wives classified themselves as "independents," compared to only 9 percent of the non-swinging husbands and 11 percent of the non-swinging wives. In addition, 28 percent of the swinging husbands and 22 percent of the swinging wives checked that they were "uncommitted and not interested in politics," compared to only 3 percent of the non-swinging husbands and 5 percent of the non-swinging wives. Moreover, just 9 percent of the non-swinging respondents claimed that they did not vote in the last presidential election; 31 percent of the swinging respondents claimed that they did not bother to vote.

These differences regarding political party affiliation suggest a sense of detachment and even a feeling of exasperation on the part of many swingers with conventional party politics. This becomes even more apparent in light of numerous findings by political science researchers indicating that people who identify themselves as "independents" tend to be significantly less likely than those who identify themselves as Republicans or Democrats to be interested or involved as voters in politics.

However, while the swingers indicated a significantly greater amount of detachment and estrangement from conventional party politics than did the non-swingers, they were also, as expected, less likely than the non-swingers to identify with the Republican party. Just 17 percent of the swinging husbands and 21 percent of the swinging wives identified themselves as Republicans. In contrast, fully 52 percent of the non-swinging husbands and 43 percent of the non-swinging wives considered themselves Republicans. As for the Democratic party, 22 percent of the swinging husbands and 23 percent of the swinging wives were members; this compared to 36 percent of the non-swinging husbands and 41 percent of the non-swinging wives. Again, the fact that more of the non-swingers than swingers were members of *both* the Republican and the Democratic parties is explained by the much stronger tendency among the swingers to have identified themselves as either "independent" or as "uncommitted and not interested in politics."

Of course, it must not be concluded from the foregoing that swingers lack political attitudes, values and opinions. They do indeed have such attitudes, values and opinions, and they hold many of them with deep emotional intensity and conviction, as we shall soon see. But swingers do not seem to want or to have time for direct personal involvement in the conventional political institutions. Indeed, they appear to be almost as estranged and disenchanted with the conventional political institutions as they are with the family, kinship and conventional religious institutions.

Seventy-four percent of the swinging husbands and wives labeled themselves as "liberal" in their political views as opposed to "middle-of-the-road" or "conservative." Only 30 percent of the non-swinging husbands and wives similarly labeled themselves as "liberal." However, it remains for us to survey the swingers' political attitudes on *specific* issues in order for us to fully appreciate the very great differences in the thought-styles and philosophies of life between the two groups. For the swingers were found to be *far more liberal* than the non-swingers on virtually *every* political and social opinion issue questioned. And it is one of the paradoxes of this study that despite their relative lack of involvement in politics the swingers exhibited considerably greater vehemence than the non-swingers in discussing their opinions. The swinging husbands, in particular, seemed to want to talk a great deal more than the non-swinging husbands did about political and social issues. They seemed to be far less content than the non-swinging husbands with the way things are; but they also seemed to feel more powerless and exasperated about doing anything about it. As an interviewer I very often had to remind the swingers that political and social attitudes were not the major subject of the research. But by the same token, the swingers' attitudes reflected a far greater amount of compassion and tolerance than did those of the non-swingers; they very often held very strong opinions about issues that did not even affect them in any personal way.

Fully 78 percent of the non-swinging husbands and 76 percent of the non-swinging wives considered themselves to be part of the "silent majority." This was true for only 26 percent of the swinging husbands and 42 percent of the swinging wives. Similarly, only 22 percent of the swinging husbands and 25 percent of their wives concurred with the viewpoint that "old-fashioned respect for law and order is what this country really needs." Among the non-swingers 75 percent of the husbands and 68 percent of their wives agreed.

The swingers tended to be a great deal more concerned about individual rights than the non-swingers were. And this concern was strongly reflected in their responses to several questionnaire items. For example, among the swingers 71 percent of the husbands and 84 percent of the wives believed that "It is the constitutional right of any high-school student to wear long hair to school if he so wishes." Among the non-swingers only 43 percent of the husbands and 52 percent of the wives agreed. Forty-seven percent of the swinging husbands and 50 percent of the swinging wives indicated a positive attitude toward the hippies and flower children. Among the non-swingers only 15 percent of the husbands and 14 percent of the wives shared this view. Particularly revealing was the distribution of responses to the statement: "Duties are more important than rights." Fully 51 percent of the non-swinging husbands and 56 percent of the non-swinging wives agreed, compared to only 15 percent of the swinging husbands and 21 percent of the swinging wives.

I also asked the respondents about the effect they felt that recent Supreme Court decisions about censorship and pornography had had. Sixty percent of the swingers felt that these decisions had been "too restrictive," compared to only 12 percent of the non-swinging husbands and wives. On the other hand, fully 45 percent of the non-swingers felt that the decisions had "seriously threatened moral standards." Only 4 percent of the swinging husbands and wives felt that way. The remaining couples felt that the decisions had "established reasonable guidelines."

The swingers' concern for human rights and individual freedoms was also reflected in their pattern of responses to the statement: "Religious groups should not be permitted to use legal and political means for purposes of trying to impose their standards of behavior on others." Fully 94 percent of the swinging husbands and wives agreed with the statement, compared to only 42 percent of the non-swinging respondents. The swingers were also more than twice as likely as the non-swingers to endorse the statement: "Curfew laws which restrict all persons below a certain age rather than just those who are disruptive, disorderly and inconsiderate, constitute a violation of teenagers' constitutional rights as free citizens."

I also asked the respondents about their attitudes toward marijuana. Marijuana is banned at all swinging parties. But some of the swingers did confess to occasionally using it when they are relaxing at home alone with their families. Among the swingers only 13 percent of the husbands and 15 percent of the wives thought that marijuana use should continue to be against the law. In contrast, 52 percent of the non-swinging husbands and 67 percent of the non-swinging wives felt that marijuana use should continue to be illegal.

On the issue of patriotism the differences between the swingers and the non-swingers were especially great. Emotions tended to run high on this issue, particularly among the swingers. Fully 58 percent of the swinging husbands, compared to only 20 percent of the non-swinging husbands, strongly agreed with the statement: "We should be patriotic toward the human race and *not* toward any particular nation."

Several questions were asked about the military draft, all of which yielded very strong and noteworthy differences between the swingers and the non-swingers. I asked the respondents to react to the statement: "Young men who have *personal* moral scruples against physical aggression and violence should be exempt from the draft." Among the swingers 65 percent of the husbands and 78 percent of the wives agreed; among the non-swingers only 27 percent of the husbands and 41 percent of the wives agreed. Even when I asked the respondents whether they thought men with personal moral scruples against violence and aggression should be exempt from *combat* but *not* from the draft, almost twice as many of the non-swingers as of the swingers felt that they should not be exempt.

I requested reactions to another statement which read: "Three to five years in prison is entirely too severe a sentence for draft resisters." And here 78 percent of the swinging husbands and 75 percent of their wives agreed. But among the non-swingers only 33 percent of the husbands and 42 percent of their wives agreed.

Questions pertinent to the military draft, the war in Vietnam, protest demonstrations, and Watergate, tended to arouse the strongest feelings. Many of the respondents had been affected either directly or indirectly by the war in Vietnam, and about two-thirds of the swinging couples (including virtually *all* of the interpersonal-style swinging couples) assumed what many people might regard as a radically liberal stance toward it and the military establishment. The extremely strong feelings of powerlessness, estrangement, anger, rage, disillusionment and exasperation with the federal government tie in well with the swingers' feelings of detachment toward the family and religion, and may partially account for their overall detachment from active political involvement.

> "I don't believe that any nation has the right to make cannon fodder out of human life. That's exactly what happened in this Vietnam thing. Human beings are not dispensable pawns in the service of some perverted sense of national honor. I believe that honor and pride and patriotism are all potentially lethal values and that they proved themselves to be such during the Vietnam conflict as well as in Nazi Germany. I believe that human life is infinitely more important than any political cause. It is certainly more important than preserving national honor." (28-year-old swinging wife.)

> "I'm so goddam sick and tired of hearing about these fuckin' POWs! Shit! They're all a bunch of John Bircher reactionaries who don't give a shit about those who aren't interested in partaking in their stupid war games! ... I know they went through some horrible times, but all the same I find it very difficult to feel any sympathy for them. I find it hard to feel any sympathy for any fuckin' reactionary. I firmly believe that every American soldier who died in Vietnam died in vain—all 55,000 of them. I feel that everyone who suffered any injury in Vietnam suffered entirely in vain. And I believe that the sooner every citizen of this country faces the fact that they all suffered and died totally in vain the better off we will all be and the safer we will be from any possibility of future wars. The United States was every bit as guilty as North Vietnam for what went on. And that's no shit!" (28-year-old swinging husband.)

"Well, I'll tell you, I'd rather be a live communist any day than a dead American! You know what I mean? I never had any sympathy for the communist philosophy and I certainly wouldn't want to live under it. But if I had to choose between that and death I still say I'd rather be a communist. As long as you're alive there's always hope. You know what I mean? I mean you can always do something. When you're dead you can't do anything." (31-year-old swinging husband.)

"This may surprise you, but I can easily forgive Nixon for Watergate. Like I say, that may surprise you coming from the mouth of a guy who has become increasingly radical over the past few years. But I believe that Watergate is nothing more than a smokescreen which was deliberately designed to divert our attention away from the infinitely greater evil of the selective slavery system and the Vietnam War. I can forgive Watergate because I think there is at least a slight amount of shysterism in all of us. I can forgive shysterism because I can understand it. I don't like it, but at least it is a human foible. But I cannot forgive, and I know that until the day I die I will never forgive this business of taking young men and forcing them against their wills to risk their lives and to suffer and die for a totally useless cause. That's the same to me as treating human life as though it were a bunch of slabs of meat. Watergate is of absolutely infinitesimal moral significance compared to Vietnam or to the appointing of four ultra-rightist uncompassionate pigs to the Supreme Court. . . . I wouldn't have impeached Nixon for Watergate. But I would have strung Nixon and Lyndon Johnson both up by their balls for the indescribably cruel torture and immorality they heaped upon hundreds of thousands of our young men. Believe me, everytime I so much as hear the word 'Vietnam' even in casual conversation, I want to puke. That's how strongly I still feel about it!" (42-year-old swinging husband.)

"Well, we encouraged our two sons not to register

for the draft and they never did. One of them is 25 now and the other is 23, and neither of them has ever been caught for not registering. I don't think they ever will be. And we have several friends who got their sons to take the psychiatric 'out.' There are lots of psychiatrists in this city who will write any letters that might be necessary to exempt a young man from the draft. A '4-F' is better than conscientious objector status because with a '4-F' you don't have to waste any of your life working as a slave for the government. It's bad enough they make you pay taxes all of your life. Why the hell should a man be required to donate some of the best years of his life to a disinterested, insensitive government! The government has gone too far in its control over people. A man has to look out for his own neck first. That's what I always tell my sons." (52-year-old swinging husband.)

"Listen, I don't even believe World War II was necessary! Back in 1939 or 1940 we should have put all of our resources into the production of an atomic bomb and we should have continued that effort even after Pearl Harbor without becoming involved in the war. In fact, in those days it would even have been possible to keep the war-mongering public ignorant of Pearl Harbor. Anyway, if we had put all our resources into the production of the bomb, we could have paid a bunch of volunteer militia $100,000 per man to fly over to Germany and Japan and just drop it. That could have been done in 1942 at the latest, and literally millions of lives would have been saved. I believe that all wars are totally unnecessary and that there is no conceivable evil greater than war. War is the greatest of all evils!" (34-year-old swinging husband.)

"The fact that personal moral scruples against fighting mean nothing to the government is in my way of thinking a very dangerous sign. When I was growing up I had always felt very proud about being an American. But maintaining the draft in order to keep this lousy war going made it very clear to me that I could no longer be proud of my country. In fact, I am frankly very ashamed of the United States for what it has done and for the total lack of regard it has for human life, and especially for the lives of our young men. It treats human life as though it were mere chattel—like it was nothing more than mindless pawns without feelings—in the service of some vague and misguided goal of national honor. I feel that our country is sick! . . . Did you read about how many adults back in Ohio approved of the Kent State shootings? If that's what being an American means to some people they can just take it and shit on it! I'm sorry for sounding vulgar, but I just can't help how I feel." (26-year-old swinging wife.)

"Draft resisters pose no risk to the community. I believe that only dangerous people belong in prison. No matter how you cut it, draft resisters simply ain't dangerous people." (35-year-old swinging husband.)

"I think a lot of the draft resisters are cowards. But there's been a lot of evidence recently that a certain percentage of people are born shy and cowardly—you know, they have low pain and anxiety thresholds. And a lot of these people are either too poor or too ignorant to take the right steps to protect themselves against the government. A lot of them are poorly educated and come from families where there is no awareness of viable legal options. To punish someone for being a coward is just as immoral as discriminating against someone because he's Black or a Jew or a Chicano. You can't crucify people because of their inborn characteristics. No one chooses to be born a coward any more than they might choose to be born a member of any other minority group. And even when they do manage to get a coward into combat his presence there is more likely to screw things up for the others. I don't see how a coward can really help out in a

combat situation." (39-year-old swinging husband.)

In conformance with the foregoing, the swingers were
significantly more sympathetic than non-swingers toward
the idea of young people participating in protest demonstrations. Among the swingers 76 percent of the husbands
and 74 percent of the wives approved of student demonstrations. Among the non-swingers only 57 percent of the
husbands and 49 percent of the wives approved.

The swingers were far less likely than the non-swingers
to cling to the old sentiment that children should be seen
and not heard. Most of the swingers felt that young people
have the right to speak out and that they deserve to be
heard. Fully 71 percent of the non-swinging husbands and
72 percent of the non-swinging wives believed that "Youth
has gone too far and should have more respect for authority." Only 29 percent of the swinging husbands and 31
percent of the swinging wives were able to register agreement with this sympathy.

As a final example of the strong psycho-political differences between the two groups I asked the husbands to
react to the following very strong question: "Assume for a
moment that you are a soldier in the Army. Suppose that
the colonel in charge of your group orders you to line up
and shoot some 60 to 70 women and children of the
enemy. Would you do so?" Fully 36 percent of the non-
swinging husbands answered in the affirmative. Only 19
percent of the swinging husbands said "yes."

Social Views

While only a few of the swingers had ever been actively
involved in the women's liberation movement, they were
significantly more likely than the non-swingers to be sympathetic toward the goals of "women's lib." For example,
among the swingers only 33 percent of the husbands and
35 percent of the wives endorsed the statement: "Basically
a woman's place is still in the home." In stark contrast,

fully 62 percent of the non-swinging husbands and 71 percent of the non-swinging wives endorsed it.

The greater independent-mindedness of the swingers can also be seen in their strongly positive attitudes toward wives working outside the home. I asked each respondent to react to the statement: "It is desirable for married women to work before they become mothers even if they don't need the money." Fully 72 percent of the swinging husbands and 68 percent of the swinging wives agreed that it *is* desirable. And many of them gave lists of reasons as to why they thought so even though no reasons were called for by the item. On the other hand, among the non-swingers only 38 percent of the husbands and 46 percent of the wives agreed that it *is* desirable for wives to work prior to parenthood regardless of whether or not they need the money.

Of course, women who do not work outside the home are likely to remain far more "sheltered" and "narrow" in terms of their range of ideas than those who do. It has already been pointed out that at the time of the interviews the swinging wives were almost twice as likely as the non-swinging wives to be gainfully employed outside of the home. It is very possible that the greater exposure that these women had had over a long period of time to the world of men and of non-family related ideas served as one of the key factors of influence enabling them to eventually move more easily toward a swinging life style.

One of the particularly important differences between the swingers and the non-swingers was the far stronger tendency among the former to view sex and love as two entirely different and distinct human needs. The differences between the two groups of wives were particularly noteworthy in regard to this matter. Only 32 percent of the non-swinging wives could agree that sex and love are two different and entirely distinct human needs. In contrast, fully 68 percent of the swinging wives agreed that they were two different and distinct needs; and most of the others checked "uncertain." Among the husbands 82 percent of the swingers saw sex and love as being two different and distinct human needs; this compared to only 46 percent of the non-swinging husbands.

Not surprisingly the swingers were also a good deal more liberal than the non-swingers in regard to the abortion issue; 85 percent of the swinging husbands and 87 percent of their wives agreed with the statement: "Abortion is usually the most sensible solution for the problem of unwed teenage pregnancy." Among the non-swingers only 51 percent of the husbands and 42 percent of the wives agreed with the statement.

A similar question was posed: "A 19-year old college girl becomes pregnant out-of-wedlock. Everything else being equal, would you recommend an abortion for her, or would you recommend that she see the pregnancy through to term?" Here fully 90 percent of the swinging husbands and 94 percent of the swinging wives indicated that they would recommend the abortion. Among the non-swingers only 62 percent of the husbands and 54 percent of the wives would recommend abortion over "seeing the pregnancy through."

A small number of respondents intimated that an unwanted childbirth was a just and proper punishment for anyone who would become pregnant prior to the age of college graduation. This is reflected in the slightly more permissive pattern of responses to the following question: "Do you believe that women should be free to obtain medically safe abortions whenever they desire to do so?" *None* of the swinging husbands and wives responded with a "no" to this question; among the non-swingers 21 percent of the husbands and 25 percent of the wives responded with a "no."

Parenthetically, I found that some of the permissiveness of the swinging couples on matters concerning abortion had been influenced by their involvement in metaphysics. Most metaphysicians believe that the soul does not enter the fetus until quite close to the time of birth, and that until that time the growing embryo and fetus is within the force field of the mother. Recently quite a bit of data eminating from research on hypnotic age-regression has confirmed the view that the soul or sense of self enters the fetus shortly before birth. (See especially the work of Helen Wambach (1977) cited in the bibliography at the end of this book.)

The swingers' attitudes toward divorce also tended to be much more in line with the values of "women's lib" than was the case for the non-swingers. As a case in point the respondents were asked to react to the following statement:

> "Divorce becomes a matter of social significance only when there are children involved; divorce among young, childless couples in no way threatens or undermines either the family or the social structure."

Family sociologists have long argued that the family does not even exist prior to the time that children come into the world, and that any divorce that occurs before that time logically cannot affect the family. In fact, many social scientists argue that marriage exists primarily to legitimate parenthood, not sexual intercourse and not living together. However, the non-swingers were less likely than the swingers to share this view. Only 42 percent of the non-swinging husbands and 50 percent of the non-swinging wives agreed with the foregoing statement. In contrast, among the swingers 80 percent of the husbands and 62 percent of the wives agreed with it.

An additional statement concerning childless divorces to which the respondents were asked to react was: "In divorce cases involving childless couples under 35, no legal provision should be made for alimony." Among the swingers 85 percent of the husbands and 63 percent of the wives indicated agreement. Among the non-swingers only 53 percent of the wives and 63 percent of the husbands indicated agreement.

While staunch traditionalists concerning marriage were

in the minority in both the swinging and the non-swinging samples, they were clearly a good deal more common among the latter. This was reflected in the pattern of responses to the statement: "People should try to continue their marriage when one or both of them becomes dissatisfied, even if there are no children involved." Among the swingers only 13 percent of the husbands and 17 percent of the wives agreed. On the other hand, among the non-swingers 37 percent of the husbands and 32 percent of the wives agreed.

I also asked the respondents whether they deemed it proper for a married man to take another woman to lunch. While some of the respondents insisted that it would depend on the circumstances, among the swingers fully 93 percent of the husbands and 92 percent of the wives gave an outright "yes." Among the non-swingers only 74 percent of the husbands and 69 percent of the wives indicated "yes." Of course, considering the non-swingers' conservatism on most of the other questions, their relative liberality on the issue of a husband taking another woman to lunch might be considered somewhat surprising and unexpected.

Equally interesting were the differences in attitude between the swingers and the non-swingers on matters pertinent to changing the dating and courtship norms. Generally speaking, the non-swingers (wives particularly) were much more likely than the swinging respondents to feel that the male should be expected to retain the exclusive burden of assuming the assertive role in asking women for first dates. Only 49 percent of the non-swinging wives felt that women should have as much right as a man to propose a date. In contrast, 81 percent of the swinging wives felt that women should have as much right as a man to propose a date. The differences among the husbands on this issue were less: 83 percent of the non-swingers compared to 95 percent of the swingers favored the idea of women asking men for dates.

During the past few years there has been an increasing

amount of research evidence pointing out that the large majority of *both* sexes feel uncomfortable about assuming the assertive role, and that most men and women would prefer to foist the responsibilities of the assertive role upon the shoulders of the other sex or upon somebody other than themselves. Such evidence suggests that shyness and low interpersonal anxiety thresholds are a good deal more common among people in American society than had formerly been thought. The pattern of reactions to the following statement provided further corroboration for the view that most women do not want anything at all to do with assuming the assertive role vise-à-vis the male sex:

> "The norms should be changed to make it equally as socially acceptable and expected for females to ask males for first dates as it is now and would continue to be for males to ask females."

Among the wives only 46 percent of the non-swingers and 69 percent of the swingers agreed with this statement. The husbands, evidently wanting to relinquish some of the burden of always having to assume the assertive role, were more enthusiastic: 94 percent of the swingers approved compared to 69 percent of the non-swingers.

Of the many questions I asked, there was *only one subject* with respect to which the swingers favored *greater* restrictions than the non-swingers: this was the issue of population control. In essence, with regard to potential population-control programs the swingers seemed to be a great deal more willing than the non-swingers to have some of their freedoms taken away. Of course, the "Zero Population Growth" people have been arguing for the past several years that actual freedom in any society goes down as population size and density go up. Somehow, sexual mate-sharing populations are more responsive to such arguments than most middle-class suburbanites tend to be; while the latter tend to be more responsive than swingers to arguments in favor of nationalism and patriotism and to the renunciation of individual safety, freedom, and emotional well-being, for the benefit of these values. Thus it appears false to suggest that swingers and other types of nonconformists tend to be *entirely* in favor of freedom in all of its many ramifications, and that conventional middle-class suburbanites tend to be in favor of a plethora of restrictive controls in all areas of life lest their society become overrun by anarchy. Different groups tend to favor a different set of freedoms and restrictions.

To exemplify the differences in attitudes among the respondents on matters pertinent to population control the following statement was posed:

> "In light of the current situation of uncontrolled population growth and the many severe problems that it creates, no couple anywhere should be legally permitted to procreate more than two children."

Fully 57 percent of the swinging husbands agreed with the statement compared to only 26 percent of the non-swinging husbands. Among the wives 48 percent of the swingers agreed, compared to only 24 percent of the non-swingers. On the other hand, among the swingers 32 percent of the husbands and wives *disagreed* with the statement, compared to 55 percent of the non-swinging husbands and 50 percent of the non-swinging wives.

And to a much stronger statement I asked each respondent for his or her reaction: "Husbands whose wives conceive for a fourth time should be required by law to undergo a vasectomy." Only 3 percent of the non-swinging husbands and wives registered an affirmative reaction. In contrast, 29 percent of the swinging husbands and wives approved of the idea.

Even though the public has become more aware of the American population problem over the past several years, it is likely that a key reason behind the non-swingers' greater resistance toward the idea of doing something about it is the fact that, compared to the swingers and the "avant-garde" college set, the non-swingers had long been influenced by a strong mental-emotional link between the idea of sex and the idea of babies. The connection between sex and babies that is programmed into the minds of most Americans throughout the course of growing up seems to be very much in the process of weakening at the present time, particularly among youthful populations. The parental generation probably fears this change because of the de-inhibiting, freeing consequences to which it may give rise as far as sexual behavior among young people is concerned. The rapid spreading of contraceptive knowledge and ideology tends to be especially feared by many conventional middle-class suburbanites for this reason. The daily newspaper, the television newscast, magazine articles, etc., have all contributed to a situation in which the more intelligent and literate of second and third grade elementary school children frequently have an awareness of contraception that surpasses that which their own parents had had at the age of 20 or even older.

Nudity and Social Nudism

I asked each of the couples whether or not their family ever went nude around the house. Forty-eight percent of the non-swinging couples indicated that their families *never* went nude around the house. Not surprisingly, only 8 percent of the swinging couples similarly indicated that social nudity was *never* practiced in their homes. On the other hand, fully 67 percent of the swinging couples indicated that social nudity was *frequently* practiced in their homes. Only 11 percent of the non-swinging couples indicated that they frequently practiced social nudity at home.

Thirty percent of the swinging couples occasionally attended nudist resorts, although only 9 percent of the couples were actively involved in outdoor nudist club activities at the time of the study. Not surprisingly, none of the non-swinging couples had ever been to a nudist resort, and many of them seemed somewhat shocked and surprised that I would even ask them if they had ever been to such a place.

Six of the nine swinging couples who were currently members of outdoor social nudist clubs were members of the Elysium Fields Nudist Resort in Topanga Canyon near Los Angeles. This is significant inasmuch as Elysium Fields is one of the very few sexually permissive nudist resorts in the United States. They permit touching and fondling and virtually any other kind of bodily contact in the public areas of their resort except sexual intercourse and oral-genital play. In contrast, most social nudist clubs have a reputation for a puritanical asceticism toward sex. Members are frequently not even permitted to look at fellow nudists for more than a second or two. While social nudists by definition go nude, at most typical American nudist resorts members, even on cloudy days, feel constrained to wear sunglasses. These permit members to relax and not worry about being suspected by anyone of "looking" too long at someone.

The swingers were almost unanimous in condemning traditional social nudism as downright "antisexual" and "hypocritical." For this reason in addition to two others: (1) the sedentary type of activities commonly engaged in, and (2) the "narrow range of personal interests" they viewed nudists as having, the swingers tended to stay away from regular nudist resorts.

Among the couples who continued to regularly attend nudist resorts, three claimed that they were doing so primarily for their children. And among the couples who *occasionally* attended such resorts, eighteen told me that their children constituted a major reason for their doing so. They viewed nudism as instrumental in helping people to develop a healthy attitude toward their bodies and toward their sexuality. In addition, children's activities at nudist camps are far from sedentary. Evidently, many of the adults in attendance derive a good deal of satisfaction out of watching the children and young people at various kinds of play activities such as swimming, volley ball (both in and out of water), and tennis. All of these play activities are usually coeducational. Even prepubescent children seldom play for very long in single-sexed peer groups.

In contrast, nudity within the swingers' private homes seems to be an integral part of their life style. And 58 percent of them have built special fences in their backyards that permit the private—at home—practice of outdoor social nudism among their children, other family members and fellow swingers. However, most of these swinging families are nude indoors far more than they are outdoors. Many of them eat a good many of their meals nude and pursue a good many of their ordinary indoor activities nude.

Only 11 percent of the swinging husbands and 9 percent of the swinging wives claimed to have gone nude around the house much when they were children in their parents' homes. It is interesting that among the *non*-swinging wives 12 percent indicated that they had gone nude quite a bit around their houses as chiildren. The non-swinging husbands, on the other hand, were the least likely group to have gone nude when they were children: only 3 percent had done so.

Chapter 7

The Premarital Dating and Courtship Years

We have seen how swingers are significantly more likely than non-swingers to be emotionally and intellectually detached from such major social institutions as the kin family network, politics and conventional religion. While such detachment can go a long way toward prompting and enabling a person to consider and explore nonconformist solutions to the problems of everyday life, it does not provide any clear clues as to why a person might hit upon the *specific* form of nonconformist deviance of sexual mate sharing. The comparative dating and sex histories of the respective samples of this study provide such a clue.

The respondents were asked to indicate the grade in school when they first felt a strong romantic interest in an age-mate of the opposite sex. According to the work of family life researcher Carlfred Broderick (1966, 1972), the large majority of American children have strong romantic interests and emotional attachments as early as the third grade. Yet the differences between the swingers and the non-swingers on this issue were strong and convincing. Thirty-one percent of the swinging husbands and 37 percent of the swinging wives had felt strong romantic interests as early as kindergarten through the third grade. In contrast, this had also been the case for only 11 percent of the non-swinging husbands and for 9 percent of the non-swinging wives. Only 16 percent of the swinging husbands and 24 percent of the swinging wives had been at the eighth grade level or older when they first felt a strong romantic interest. The analogous figure for the non-swingers was 44 percent for both the husbands and the wives.

Of particular relevance to the foregoing are two of Broderick's (1972) findings. First, the earlier children became romantically interested and emotionally attached to age-mates of the other sex, the more socially skilled and competent they were, and the more *same-sex friends* they were likely to have. Secondly, Broderick found that 43 percent of the children who developed early romantic interests did *not* enjoy cordial, rewarding relationships with their parents. In comparison, only 15 percent of those who did *not* develop such early romantic interests had troubled relationships with their parents. The reader will recall the earlier finding that swingers tend to interact with chosen friends significantly more frequently than non-swingers do, and also that they were quite well skilled socially. The reader should further recall the closer attachment and involvement of the non-swingers with their mothers and fathers. From these data and from those of Broderick, *it would appear that early learning of the emotional gratifications from heterosexual-social interaction is one of the key preconditions for selecting erotic forms of deviance over other forms of deviance.*

There is a very important conceptual distinction which must be drawn at this point between romantic love needs and purely sexual needs. From the time of Freud both scientists and laymen have had a tendency to confuse sexual and romantic love needs with each other, particularly as far as such needs affect preadolescent boys and girls. To be sure, purely sexual-erotic needs do not seem to exist in human beings prior to the onset of adolescence. There are some human societies in which preteens do engage in sexual intercourse. But such behavior appears to arise largely out of a desire to imitate older brothers and sisters. Of course, once such preteens find that they can experience orgasms through erotic play they have received a powerful reinforcement (reward) for their behavior and have developed a *learned* (as opposed to inborn biological) need for further erotic behavior with the opposite sex.

Romantic love needs pertain to the desire for close, frequent, friendly interaction between a particular boy and a particular girl. Romantically involved people of *any* age want to share many different activities and experiences together. They want to be in each other's presence as much and as frequently as possible.

Up to now most social scientists have taken the position that romantic love needs are learned and are not inborn. However, in recent years a considerable amount of data have become available suggesting that there might be a strong inborn component to romantic love needs, and that in some people such needs may be so strong that even a close, emotionally satisfying family life with parents and siblings cannot markedly attenuate it. The following comment made by one of the swinging husbands clearly suggests that something far more than the need for sex may be operating:

> "I can remember like when I was in the second grade. I enjoyed playing baseball and wrestling and doing a lot of other things with kids of my own sex. But there was something about playing with girls that I liked better than playing with boys. And I remember that for a while my preference for playing with girls got me into a lot of trouble with everybody. The teachers at school were hollering at me because they wanted me to play with the boys. I was getting it from my parents at home. They wanted me to be a real boy and play with the boys. Some of the mothers of the girls I was playing with didn't like me and they would chase me away screaming that I should play with boys. And the worst thing of all was that my friends of my own sex were beginning to tease me and make fun of me

for always wanting to play with girls. Even when I was playing baseball with kids of my own sex it seemed that I was the only one who always wanted to have girls on my team." (34-year-old swinging husband).

This man went on to talk about how he continued to play with two girls in particular throughout his elementary school years in spite of a considerable amount of negative reinforcement (criticism and even some punishment) from age-mates, his own parents, teachers, and some of the other parents in his immediate neighborhood. I want to stress that this case is by no means atypical for the swinging husbands and wives of this study, and it raises the question as to whether "conformity to peer group norms" is really anywhere nearly as important as some people have suggested in explaining the strong romantic attraction which some children feel for opposite-sexed age-mates quite early in their elementary school years.

> "You may think I am kidding you when I tell you this. But I kid you not. When I was only five years old and in kindergarten I was so extremely infatuated with this girl who was in my class that I used to walk all over town after school in a daze just dreaming about her. I was too shy at that time to say anything to her. In fact, it took me until I was in the second grade to actually reach the point where I managed to make close friends with a particular girl. But once I did I saw more of her than I did of any of my same-sex friends." (27-year-old swinging husband.)

Most of the swinging husbands had been quite successful throughout their childhoods as far as getting along well with same-sexed peers was concerned. In American society success with the same-sexed peer group is usually a precondition for success with age-mates of the opposite sex. This generalization tends to be especially true for boys. Yet at least one of the swinging husbands I interviewed had remained socially unsuccessful with his own sex until he was into his high school years.

> "Before I entered kindergarten I didn't have any boys to play with. No kidding, I was scared shitless for a long time whenever I was around kids of my own sex. But I can't say I was ever lonely either because there were three girls on my block who were in my class throughout elementary school. And we used to do our homework together, we played together after school, and on Saturday afternoons we often went to the movies together. I never thought anything of it. They were my friends and I enjoyed being with them. And as you can see, I ended up marrying one of them! ... I guess the thing that saved me with the kids of my own sex was my musical ability. As you know, I can play the piano real well. I can play the trumpet and I can even play the guitar a little bit. I was in the school orchestra from the time I was in the second grade and when I got to high school I joined the school band. Musically I was the most talented kid in my school and I earned a lot of recognition for that. I was always all thumbs at playing any kind of contact sport. But I was able to get away with it because of my music. Today for the first time I can honestly say I have a lot of good male friends. But until I became involved in this swinging thing my best friends were all girls." (21-year-old swinging husband.)

The swinging wives were much more likely than the non-swinging wives to remember having been tomboys. This, rather than specifically romantic interests, may have accounted for some of their early predilections for heterosexual-social interaction. But when I asked them about this most of them could recall instances of demonstrable romantic feelings that accompanied their tomboyish proclivities.

> "Yeah. Until I was 13 or 14 years old I think I was pretty much of a tomboy. But I was very fond of my

boyfriends too, though. I can remember a lot of
times at school when I even got in trouble with the
teachers in order to save one of my boyfriends from
catching it. I cared about them. In fact, I cared
about them more than I ever cared about any
people of my own sex." (22-year-old swinging wife.)

"Ha! Was I a tomboy! Christ! You'd better believe
it! Let me tell you I caught more snakes and lizards
and frogs than any boy I know. And I could beat
most of the boys at baseball and even football. In
fact,—ha!—I think I still can! My ass was always
red from being kicked and spanked by either my
dad or my mom. I was Peck's bad boy—with a
clitoris and a cunt! Ha, ha, ha!" (25-year-old swinging wife.)

Still, some of the swinging wives who claimed to have
had very early romantic interests were evidently not tomboys. The following quote illustrates this pattern:

"Oh, I always hated anything that would cause me
to get dirty or hurt. I never liked any of the games
the boys liked to play. Even today I still can't understand them. But there was this boy who lived
down the block from me. He always hated boys'
games too, and we played together quite regular
from the time we were only three or four years old.
I really loved him and I remember he told me he
loved me a lot of times! I was really heartsick when
his family moved away. I was in the fifth grade
then, and we corresponded for over two years. But I
never saw him again, and we sort of stopped writing because we couldn't think of anything to say."
(26-year-old swinging wife.)

Freud suggested that all human beings go through a
so-called "latency stage" which lasts roughly from age 5
through age 12, and during which children tend to be indifferent to and sometimes hostile toward age-mates of
the opposite sex. Since Freud's time dozens of anthropologists have shown that whenever and wherever

there is widespread indifference and/or hostility toward age-mates of the opposite sex among 5- to 12-year-olds, that indifference or hostility is a byproduct of family and community prescriptions and expectations for children of that age group. In most of the world's societies and to an increasing extent in our own contemporary American society heterosexual-social interaction is the rule among preadolescent children, *not* the exception. Still, while most of the non-swingers had become romantically interested in opposite-sexed age-mates prior to the eighth grade, very early romantic interests were more common in the backgrounds of the swinging husbands and wives. As a case in point, only 4 percent of the non-swinging husbands and 5 percent of the non-swinging wives could recall having had a strong romantic interest in an opposite-sexed age-mate as early as kindergarten or the first grade. But among the swingers fully 20 percent of the husbands and 16 percent of the wives could recall having had such a very early interest.

First Dates

The speed with which the various stages of heterosexual-social involvement were passed through was also significantly greater for the swingers than it was for the non-swinging husbands and wives. For example, among the husbands 68 percent of the swingers had had their first date by the age of 14, compared to only 48 percent of the non-swinging husbands. Among the wives 61 percent of the swingers had commenced dating by the age of 14, compared to only 44 percent of the non-swinging wives. Eighteen percent of the non-swinging husbands and wives had waited until at least the age of 17 before they started dating. Among the swingers only 9 percent of the husbands and 8 percent of the wives had waited that long.

"I never even thought about dating, man. When I was a kid I didn't even know what a date was. I just

started doing it. There was never a time when I
didn't have a lot of girl friends that I liked. My
sisters always brought girl friends home too. So
there were always girls around my house. I used to
play ball with them, play cards with them. When
my family went on outings there was always some
girl there who wasn't my sister. Saturday and Sunday afternoons I used to go to the movies with my
friends and there was almost always a girl or two
with us. It's crazy, but I never thought of that as a
date. One day when I was about 11 some friend of
my girl friend's mother saw us at the movie theatre
and she said something like 'your mothers allow
you to date at such a young age?' At the time we
didn't even know what she was talking about. It
was just natural for us to do things with our
friends, and she was one of my best friends." (36-
year-old swinging husband.)

A few of the swingers had experienced some shyness
during the early teenaged years. But this shyness tended
to have been short-lived thanks to the efforts of the same-
sexed peer groups of which they had been a well-accepted
part.

"Actually I didn't start dating until I was fifteen,
although I wanted to start a lot sooner than that. In
my day most of the kids bitched because of the restrictions their parents put on them. But I really
think the worst restrictions are those which people
impose on themselves. I'm glad that I wised up to
that fact early enough to be able to enjoy my teen
years . . . My best friend had a girl friend and he
used to invite her up to his room after school and
they'd play music together, and I was envious as all
hell. One day I was at this party and he and his girl
friend introduced me to this girl. Well, I guess she
must have liked me because she went out with me a
lot of times after that. And by the time I was sixteen
I wasn't afraid to start conversations with girls. I
think spending so much time with that one girl

gave me the confidence I needed to strike up friendships with a lot of other girls. And the more friendships I struck up, the more confident I became."
(30-year-old swinging husband.)

Frequency of Dating

The respondents were also asked about how many dates
they had averaged during a typical month of their junior
year of high school. This type of question has an equal
bearing upon the matter of social skills and upon the relative absence of social-heterosexual interaction anxiety
(shyness) as it has upon romantic or sexual needs, interests or desires. With this in mind, 36 percent of the
swinging husbands and 48 percent of the swinging wives
averaged *at least* five dates during a typical month when
they were high school juniors. The analogous figures for
the non-swingers were 18 percent for the husbands and 27
percent for the wives. It is interesting to note, however,
that 18 percent of the swinging husbands and wives averaged *no* dates per month at this time; but among the non-
swingers 26 percent of the husbands and 30 percent of the
wives were not dating.

An important point which these data make clear is that
a large minority (almost half) of the *non*-swinging husbands and wives had begun dating early in life (by age 14)
and had had active dating careers throughout their high
school years. Hence, while the swingers were indeed significantly more active than the non-swingers, it is quite
clear that early and frequent dating is *not by itself* a cause
or a precipitating agent of sexual mate-sharing behavior.

Love and Going Steady

Although the swingers had "gone steady" with only a
slightly greater number of persons before marriage than
had the non-swingers, they began "going steady" at significantly earlier ages. Thirty-five percent of the swinging
husbands and 51 percent of the swinging wives had "gone
steady" by the age of 15; among the non-swingers only 20

percent of the husbands and 38 percent of the wives had started this early. Forty percent of the swingers said they had been "in love" *four or more times* prior to their first marriage, compared to only 7 percent of the non-swingers.

Forty-two percent of the swinging husbands had "gone steady" with *four or more* women prior to their first marriage. This was true for just 34 percent of the non-swinging husbands. However, among the wives the differences between the two groups were considerably smaller. For example, 35 percent of the swinging wives had "gone steady" with *four or more* men prior to their first marriage; but this had also been the case for 30 percent of the non-swinging wives.

Not surprisingly, the swingers were also considerably more likely than the non-swingers to recall social activities with the opposite sex as having been more important to them than social activities with their own sex. While significant for both sexes, these findings tended to be particularly striking for the husbands.

A revealing questionnaire item called for a response to the statement: "At the age of 20 or so I could have done without the opposite sex for three or more months at a time if circumstances had forced me, and still have remained basically happy and secure." Fully 46 percent of the swinging husbands and 50 percent of the swinging wives registered *disagreement* with this statement, compared to only 20 percent of the non-swinging husbands and 29 percent of the non-swinging wives. These findings are both striking and highly meaningful, particularly for the husbands. They are somewhat weaker for the wives, primarily because 55 percent of the swinging wives were already married by the time they were 20 years of age. Only 36 percent of the non-swinging wives had married that early.

In fact, one of the strongest findings of this study was that swingers tended to marry significantly earlier than the non-swingers. Among the husbands, 39 percent of the swingers had married by the time they were twenty compared to only 12 percent of the non-swingers. Forty-one percent of the non-swinging husbands were 25 years of age or older when they married, compared to just 23 percent of the swinging husbands. Among the wives only 4 percent of the swingers married at 25 years of age or older; this compared to 20 percent of the non-swinging wives.

On the surface, marrying early may not appear to be suggestive of a particularly libertarian approach to life. But it should be remembered that reasonably systematic, well thought-out philosophies of sex, marriage, life, etc., very seldom develop before the age of 21, 22, or even later. Many of the swingers seemed to have had a strong need during their adolescent and early adulthood years to assert their autonomy and independence from family and other institutions of social control. Getting married early is one of the key ways in which autonomy and independence can, as far as an individual's subjective feelings are concerned, be asserted.

From the standpoint of the present, most of the swingers expressed rather negative views toward early marriage, including their own. Such negative views, on the other hand, did not extend to early unmarried cohabitation, a point which will be explored in later chapters. As will be shown, many more swingers than non-swingers eventually divorced their first spouses, finding that they themselves had been too inexperienced and immature to realize that their first spouses' needs, values and beliefs had been far too different from their own to make for a serene and emotionally satisfying existence. Many of the swingers did not know themselves very well during their adolescent and early adulthood years.

Two other findings help us to understand the courtship background of the swingers even better. The first of these concerns the age of first sexual intercourse. Among the husbands 71 percent of the swingers compared to only 41 percent of the non-swingers had had sexual intercourse by the age of 17 or younger. Among the wives 48 percent of the swingers and 22 percent of the non-swingers had started experiencing coitus at 17 years of age or earlier. In fact, 40 percent of the swinging husbands and 23 percent of the swinging wives were fifteen years old or younger when they started having sexual intercourse. This compared to only 17 percent of the non-swinging husbands and 4 percent of the non-swinging wives. For a middle-class American group these figures are clearly quite high. Moreover, only 4 percent of the swinging husbands and 1 percent of the swinging wives were 22 years of age or older when they first commenced having coitus; the analogous figures for the non-swingers were 26 percent for the husbands and 31 percent for the wives.

The second finding concerns the number of people with whom coitus had been experienced prior to first marriage. Here again very striking differences were noted between the two groups. *The distinction between the swingers and the non-swingers was not whether they had experienced premarital coitus, but rather the number of partners with whom they had experienced it.* For example, a large percentage of the swinging husbands didn't even know how many women they had had sexual intercourse with prior to marriage. Fully 47 percent of the swinging husbands estimated that they had copulated with at least twenty or more women prior to marriage; none of the non-swinging husbands had had premarital coitus with more than five women, and indeed only 16 percent of them had had it with more than two women. In contrast, 88 percent of the swinging husbands, in spite of their early marriages, claimed to have had premarital coitus with more than two women.

I was also interested in determining the number of "monogamous" or comparatively long-term or "steady" premarital sexual relationships the swinging and non-swinging respondents had had. I decided that sexual intercourse *fifteen or more times* with the *same* partner might be reasonably regarded as a fairly accurate barometer of comparative stability in sex-love relationships prior to marriage.

I found that 38 percent of the swinging wives had had

premarital coitus fifteen or more times with each of two or more partners, compared to only 13 percent of the non-swinging wives. Among the husbands 41 percent of the swingers had had premarital coitus fifteen or more times with *three or more* partners, compared to only 19 percent of the non-swingers. At the other extreme, just 5 percent of the swinging husbands were virgins at marriage compared to 22 percent of the non-swinging husbands. Among the wives 14 percent of the swingers were virgins at marriage, compared to 40 percent of the non-swingers.

The swingers' unusually large amount of premarital sexual experience can be seen as reflecting their strong erotic and heterosexual-social interaction needs. But it can also be seen as having contributed significantly to their developing of a strong, *autonomous* interest in sex. Simply put, an "autonomous" interest in sex refers to the ability and proclivity to be able to view sex as a hobby, as a kind of recreational pastime which swinging is by definition. Almost all women and most men in American society are in many ways programmed from an early age onward to link up the idea of sex with the idea of love and of long-term emotional commitment. It is for this reason that most people do not have and cannot have an autonomous interest in sex. Sex for most people cannot be thought of independently of love or romance or potential marriage. For the married swinger (when he or she is engaged in sexual mate sharing as opposed to conjugal erotic activity) sex is normally defined, viewed *and enjoyed* as sex and sex alone, fully independent and autonomous of all other emotional feelings, considerations and socially recognized statuses. It should be recognized that premarital sex cannot *by itself* ever give rise to the development of an autonomous interest in sex. However, for young men and women who happily engage in premarital sexual relations over a long period of time and with many different partners with whom no emotionally meaningful, stable love relationship has been built up, an autonomous *lifelong* interest in sex and eroticism as a desirable end in its own right is highly probable and indeed almost certain. Simply put, *a non-monogamous style of premarital sex probably foreshadows a non-monogamous style of marital sex.*

I asked the respondents about the premarital sexual standards that they had held at about the age of 21. Generally speaking, attitudes and values are more difficult for people to remember than actual experiences. Nevertheless, the differences that emerged between the swingers and the non-swingers were still quite substantial. The most permissive statement I posed regarding premarital sexual standards read as follows: "I believe that full sexual relations are acceptable for the female before marriage even when she does not feel particularly affectionate toward her partner." Only 4 percent of the non-swinging wives registered agreement with the statement, compared to 37 percent of the swinging wives. Among the husbands 69 percent of the swingers saw fit to agree, compared to only 18 percent of the non-swingers. When this "permissive" statement was turned around to refer to male behavior, similar differences emerged between the swingers and the non-swingers.

But in spite of this strong permissiveness, the swingers strangely enough did not seem to be any less romantic in terms of their *current* attitudes toward love and marriage than the non-swingers were. For example, I asked all of the respondents whether or not they agreed with the statement: "Love is more important than practical considerations." Among the wives 48 percent of the swingers *agreed* compared to 43 percent of the non-swingers. Among the husbands 36 percent of the swingers and 37 percent of the non-swingers agreed. These differences are obviously very small and are in no way suggestive of a diminished romantic orientation among the swinging couples.

I also asked the respondents whether or not they felt that romantic love was an important ingredient in a successful marriage. Among the wives 79 percent of the swingers and 73 percent of the non-swingers felt that it was.

Among the husbands 68 percent of the swingers and 81 percent of the non-swingers felt that it was. Similar very small differences between the two groups emerged when I asked the respondents whether or not they agreed with the statement: "Being in love gives life meaning and direction." Roughly 85 percent of all four groups indicated in the affirmative.

SUMMARY

In sum, the swingers of this study became romantically interested and involved with the opposite sex significantly earlier in life than the nonswingers did. They had also started dating earlier and passed through the stages of increasingly intense courtship and sexual involvement both earlier in life and at a faster rate than the non-swingers. The swingers learned early that boy-girl social relationships provide some of the greatest rewards that life has to offer. They developed (and to some extent may have had at the outset of life) a significantly stronger need for social-heterosexual interaction than did the non-swingers. This strong need (in combination with their history of gratifying involvement with the other sex, and their detached, emotionally cool relations with parents and kin) served to assure that, if they were to move toward deviant or non-conformist roles, these roles would revolve around social-erotic endeavors rather than around some other activity or interest.

Chapter 8

Pornographic Literature

Until the late 1960s very few middle-class people had ever even heard of sexual mate sharing. Still fewer realized that this sort of social-recreational behavior—rare though it was—existed and occurred primarily in middle-class circles. The question therefore arises as to how the phenomenon spread so widely over the past few years. Surely there have always been people in America who possessed the background characteristics of (1) emotional detachment from parents and kin, and (2) an early and strong heterosexual interest and involvement. But these two background characteristics, important though they seem to be, are clearly not sufficient by themselves to cause a person to become involved in sexual mate sharing. Before a person can become interested (much less involved) in sexual mate sharing there must first be something to introduce him to the subject in an appealing and alluring manner. Few people are likely to have invented comarital sex on their own.

People who *subjectively* feel and believe that they have a strong need for sexual variety have always been rampant throughout the American population. But most people tend to be fearful of being in the vanguard of anything new, and sexual mate sharing is no exception to this. In order for the swinging population to have undergone any proliferation over the years some kind of stimuli would have had to have been available on the social scene (1) to create an illusion of prevalence, and (2) to provide a credible, easy-to-follow "cook book" formula for entrance and for active involvement in the swinging world. Even though the kind of personality likely to be attracted to swinging might well be less afraid than most of being in on the "avant-garde," swinging is so nonconformist a recreational activity that a considerable amount of serious reflection is likely to be engaged in prior to involvement in it, particularly among middle-class suburbanites with careers and reputations to worry about. And the data of this study tend to support this expectation.

Very few people anywhere are likely to have the courage to turn their fantasies of highly unconventional behavior into reality. It requires far too much work, willingness to take risks, perseverance, and dedication to a particular nonconformist ideal. There had long been a precedent for conventional adultery, for seeing prostitutes, call girls, pickups, as well as for carrying on affairs with secretaries and mistresses. Given the widespread availability of "illegitimate" sex through these conventional means, why would anyone want to gamble on something that was not tried and true—particularly when one's wife's awareness *and* her willingness to involve herself too would necessarily have to be solicited? At the very least it seems highly probable that some very strong learned needs were involved, and that pornography and a low tolerance for being alone both helped to contribute to the generation of these needs.

It will never be possible for us to know how many people independently thought up something equivalent to co-marital sexual behavior. But by the 1950s there must have been a fairly widespread need for some kind of patterned, well-organized extramarital sexuality, and it remained for some social force such as pornography to give direction as well as a morally acceptable rationale and meaning to the satisfaction of these needs. Without the stimulus of pornography and its accompanying advertisements for "swingers" these strivings would have had to have either gone unsatisfied, or they would have had to have been satisfied by way of the more conventional extramarital sexual outlets.

With the passing of the Roth decision of the United States Supreme Court in 1957, it finally became possible for very frankly written books, articles, advertisements and other non-pictorial erotica on a wide variety of sexual subjects to become generally available. Magazines with highly glamorized and often fictionalized case histories of alleged sexual mate sharing activities among American suburbanites became socially significant earmarks of this new emancipation of the press. To the sophisticated reader many of these "case histories" must have seemed highly improbable at best. But there were also many people reading these magazines who had deep needs to accept as true that which they were reading. More importantly, the blueprint for involvement in swinging which these articles presented could be followed by at least some people; it could inject some structure and order into the chaos of undifferentiated fantasizing about subjectively felt needs for extramarital sexual pleasure.

The dynamics of the "self-fulfilling prophecy" may well have been operating here in full force. People respond not only to the objective features of a situation, but also and at times *primarily* to the *subjective* meaning that the situation holds for them. Once people have assigned some meaning to a situation, their consequent behavior and some of the consequences of that behavior become determined by that ascribed meaning. These highly glamorized magazine articles incorporated much of the ideology and some of the techniques behind successful involvement in swinging which are still recommended even today by leading couples of the swinging world.

> "Before Wes showed me all these books and advertisements about swinging I had had two brief af-

fairs. I didn't really love either of these men, but I did have a hankering for—I guess you would call it adventure. I raised hell at first. A wife is supposed to raise hell when her husband suggests something like having sex with other people. But deep down I felt relieved. Both Wes and I knew that swinging was the answer for us. And the material we read gave us the knowledge and the confidence that we needed to take the appropriate steps. And it might surprise you, but neither of us has had any desire at all to be unfaithful since we started swinging." (32-year-old swinging wife.)

It can be argued that there are far more men and women around with fantasies about sexual freedom than there are men or women who would commence taking serious steps to actualize these fantasies. No matter how widespread and openly available a certain kind of literature becomes, if the actions recommended by a particular literature are considered highly deviant by most people in a society, *only some* of the readers will seriously consider involvement in these activities. I would suggest that this is so no matter how attractive the particular deviance may appear at the moment, and no matter how much readers might envy those who are alleged to be actively involved in it. A key task of the social scientist is that of pinpointing some of the ways in which couples who do take the time and trouble to involve themselves differ from the many who confine their deviant desires to fantasy and/or to occasional *conventional* adultery without the knowledge of the spouse. Some of these factors have already been identified.

In effect, people with rich premarital sexual histories are probably especially prone to be attracted to this literature and to tabloids in which advertisements for swinging organizations are commonly carried. Those readers with estranged kin relations can probably be expected to take what they read more seriously than those who do enjoy emotionally close relationships with their blood relatives. And those with the most frequent exposure to this pornographic literature are the ones who are most likely to pattern their own future sexual behavior after that which is depicted in the material they read. Being required by one's job or career to spend a great deal of time out of town likewise increases the likelihood and frequency of exposure to all types of pornographic literature, including that which depicts a sexual mate-sharing scenario.

Hence, not surprisingly, 56 percent of the swinging husbands at the time of the interviews were required by their occupations to do some out-of-town travel. This compared to only 34 percent of the non-swinging husbands. Perhaps even more revealing is the fact that 72 percent of the swinging husbands had been required to do some travel in the service of their careers at the time they first began to seek active involvement in the world of comarital sex. Indeed, not only were the swinging husbands more likely to travel than the non-swinging husbands, but they were also likely to do so more frequently. At the time of the interviews 42 percent of the swinging husbands had to make at least six business trips per year; only 12 percent of the non-swinging husbands had to make that many trips per year. And again, the frequency of travel for the swinging husbands had been even greater when they first commenced comarital sexual behavior.

> "I represent a large drug firm that is headquartered back in New Jersey. My work requires me to do a lot of traveling. Most of it is right here within the state of California. But regardless, I am away about as many nights as I am home here with my family ... When I first got involved in this about six years ago I used to become quite lonely after I'd finished dinner and went back to my hotel room. Lots of nights I would just walk the streets until I got tired. Sometimes I went to movies or nightclubs and sometimes I would have a few drinks in the hotel bar. But one of the things I did to kill the time was to go into some of those adult book stores and browse around. I learned a lot that way, and

> I'm sure that if I had not done all this traveling I never would have spent much time with this adult literature. I don't know whether I would have ever read enough of it to have learned about wife-swapping." (48-year-old swinging husband.)

Some of the men first became acquainted with the sexual mate sharing ideology while in the military. Even though military life is quite temporary for most men, few if any jobs necessitate as much geographic instability as do those connected with military endeavors.

> "Well I was stationed at this base in Texas and, well, I thought I knew everything at the time. Christ! I didn't know how really innocent I was. This buddy of mine showed me this magazine with articles about swinging. I remember when I first read that shit it blew my mind. I couldn't believe what I was reading hardly. Anyway, me and my buddy went into town and he showed me these sexy magazine stands. I never saw anything like it. I come from a small town in Oklahoma, and I think I had been just too goddam sheltered. Anyway, the next time I was away on leave I told my wife about it. Let me tell you, it really blew her mind when I told her." (33-year-old swinging husband.)

Not all of the swinging husbands had been lonely or isolated from significant women in their lives when they first became exposed to sexual freedom-oriented literature.

> "No, I'm always far too busy to be lonely. But Christ! If you have to spend any time at all in the downtown sector of any of the major cities of this country you're bound to come into contact with this material sooner or later. I think you'd have to be either totally blind or totally lacking in curiosity not to. You know, I'm not being facetious, but I heard where they even have pornography in braille now! No shit! I've never met any blind swingers, but that'll be the next thing in this sexy world of ours!" (39-year-old swinging husband.)

> "You wanna know how we first heard about swing-
> ing here in southern California? You're gonna
> laugh at this, but I first learned about it when my
> daughter, who was only 12 at the time, brought
> home a copy of the *Los Angeles Free Press*. Neither of
> us had ever read the *Free Press*. But I was curious
> and I sat down and read it. And I couldn't believe
> some of those ads. It was the ads that really blew
> my mind!" (40-year-old swinging husband.)

The interviews revealed that for 75 percent of the swinging husbands the availability of a literature about sexual
mate sharing was a major factor in precipitating the desire to experiment with and explore this activity. This included many of the husbands who had commenced their
involvement in sexual freedom festivities while still
single. The remaining 25 percent, for whom a literature
about sexual mate sharing had not been important, had
all gravitated toward comarital sex by way of swinging
singlehood; in other words, they had met their current
wives at sexual freedom parties for single people. None of
the wives in this study had ever taken the lead in terms of
introducing the idea of swinging to their husbands. Thus it
seems to have been the husband's introduction to and
awareness of the swinging literature that made the crucial
difference.

Most of the swinging husbands I interviewed talked
about how they often killed lonely hours browsing
through the inventory of "adult book stores" during
periods while they were away from home on business
trips. These men all recalled encountering the glamorized
case histories of alleged swinging couples. For some of
these men the case histories seemed to provide the sense of
direction that they had been seeking. The literature provided a formula that could be tried, followed, and experimented with. The formula was imperfect and often
misleading. But it did present a picture of middle-class
husbands and wives with a strong interest in rich, purely
erotic experiences. And these people were depicted as
satisfying their interests and needs within the context of

an ideology which did not threaten the quality or solidarity of marriage and family life. Basically, these materials provided an exciting, well-structured solution to the felt need for sexual variety.

For most people, and for women especially, the need for sex and erotic gratification is socially conditioned from early childhood on into being closely associated with at least some of the following: love, romance, close emotional attachment to one partner, marriage and family life. Preswinging men quite characteristically see themselves as having strong needs for these experiences too. But for them the need for sex is very often conceptually and emotionally distinct from the need for these other things. Sex for them is very often a strong, autonomous need and interest in and of itself.

The marriage relationship of preswingers, no matter how gratifying, had not satisfied erotic needs in a comprehensive manner. Most of the preswinging husbands had dealt with this psychological unrest by engaging in occasional *conventional* (as opposed to consensual) extramarital sex. They would seek the companionship of "call girls" or other women desirous of sexual intercourse. And this was done primarily when the men were far away from home. Many of these husbands had enjoyed close psychological relationships with their wives and so felt guilty and uneasy about these affairs.

> "Well, for about two years I fucked around with other women. Don't get me wrong. I felt damned guilty about it. My wife and kids have always been important to me, and even with all the fucking around I always felt that my wife was the best damned lay in town. But somehow I just wanted more—not necessarily more sex, but I just had this burning curiosity to see what other women were like. I don't know if I can explain it. Christ, I don't think I can understand it myself. Anyway, when I read about all these swingers my eyes practically popped out of my head. I knew right away that

swinging was the answer to all my problems and
that I'd have to find a way to convince my wife of
that fact." (31-year-old swinging husband.)

This particular man had married when he was only 19
years of age. It is possible that this might have partially
contributed to his strong curiosity about what other
women are like sexually. On the other hand, even at 19 he
had already experienced an unusually rich premarital
sexual life with more than a dozen women, including his
wife.

It seems likely that a key reason why many of the swinging husbands had not been satisfied with their conjugal
sex life at the time they first took up swinging was simply
that they had grown to expect too much out of sex. Many
of them harbored highly unrealistic expectations for sexual gratification that no one woman could possibly
gratify. Many of the husbands I interviewed actually admitted this. They pointed out that they loved their wives
and wanted to preserve their marriages, but that they had
to find a way to make their marriages adapt to their strong
needs and fantasies relative to sexual variety.

Very few men or women in this or any other society
ever develop the grandiose fantasies and expectations relative to sexual variety and enjoyment that were common
to the swinging husbands of this research. The premarital
sex histories of these men contain an important clue as to
how and why such unrealistic expectations developed. It
was *not* the premarital sex itself but the gradual learning
to skillfully seek sexual gratification (with many different
women) as an end in its own right, quite independent of
emotionally meaningful relationships, that may well have
made these men come to expect too much from the
monogamous type of sexual relationship that customarily
prevails within marriage. As suggested earlier, it would
appear that a non-monogamous style of *premarital* sex
foreshadows a non-monogamous style of *marital* sex.

SUMMARY

A wide array of swinging literature, including glamorized case histories and advertisements for swinging clubs and services, could never have been sufficient *by itself* to promote an interest and involvement in swinging. Before such a literature can proliferate, there must be a sizable group of people who are relatively estranged from parents and conventional social control agencies, and who find heterosexual interaction to be immensely gratifying. People with rich premarital sexual histories (such as those of most of the swingers in the sample upon which this study is based) are especially attracted to this literature and/or to libertarian-humanistic publications such as the *Los Angeles Free Press* where advertisements for swinging organizations are commonly carried. In short, before a person is likely to move toward swinging there must first be an autonomous state of mind (freedom from the usual controls); a strong, autonomous heterosexual interest; and literature which shows the way. Without the swinging literature (and, later, contact with experienced swingers), potential swingers would very likely never even become aware of comarital sexual behavior. They would have to find some other way of adapting to their situations.

Finally, it is worth repeating that it was *non-pictorial* literature that introduced the swingers to the world of comarital sex. Color photographs of nude men and women engaging in a wide variety of sexual acts together are arousing a great deal of controversy today. But neither pornographic picture magazines nor erotic films can plant the seed of desire for comarital sex participation into peoples' minds. Nor can they point the way toward actual swinging involvement or lead middle-class married men and women into believing that becoming swingers is a truly feasible alternative for them. Photographs can arouse sexual desire, but only *the written word* can effectively point the way toward involvement in the world of comarital sex.

Chapter 9

Marital and Psychological Adjustment

Of all the questions people ask about swingers, those pertinent to happiness and adjustment are the most common. Both the layman and the scientist tend to be very curious about this issue. Many people have read brief reports written by psychiatrists in newspapers and magazines. These reports, by and large, have been far from flattering to swingers. Most psychiatrists have depicted swingers as being severely maladjusted, unhappy and immature. But by the same token, most psychiatrists have based their judgments upon their knowledge of those swingers whom they have seen as clients as part of their regular practice. None of these doctors has ever tried to obtain a reasonably representative sample of swingers outside of the psychotherapeutic situation. And, prior to the current study, no one had ever compared and contrasted a group of swingers with a group of non-swinging married couples of the same age, neighborhoods of residence, and socioeconomic status.

It is not my purpose in writing this book to defend swingers or swinging. But at the same time it is obvious that an accurate picture of sexual mate-sharing husbands and wives cannot be obtained from a study that restricts its attention *exclusively* to those who are receiving some form of psychotherapy. Swingers in therapy cannot be viewed as representative of the population of all American swingers.

As I pointed out earlier, it will probably never be possible to obtain a fully and completely representative sample of swinging husbands and wives. But this research investigation at least did focus on swingers who were selected from outside of clinical settings. With the data obtained from these sexual mate-sharing husbands and wives and from the non-swinging husbands and wives, it should be possible to make some valid generalizations about marital and psychological adjustment of swingers. The findings I am about to present do not represent the final or definitive word on the subject. But I do believe that they are much more likely to be closer to the truth than anything else that has previously been published on the subject.

Marital Adjustment

There is probably no better index of marital adjustment than marital happiness. If a person says that he or she is happily married, the chances are good that at least at that particular point in time he or she *is indeed* happily married. All of the 400 respondents of this study were separately asked about the happiness of their respective marriages. This question was contained on the written questionnaire, and there was no interaction between a husband and his wife during the period when they were filling these out. Specifically, the question asked: "As marriages go in American society, about how happy would you say your marriage is?" And the respondents could select one of five alternative answers: "very happy," "happy," "fairly happy," "unhappy," and "very unhappy." It has been shown in many studies that very few people ever check "unhappy" or "very unhappy," and even among people getting a divorce, "fairly happy" tends to be the option most commonly checked. The point I want to stress here is that people who check the last three options (i.e., "fairly happy," "unhappy," and "very unhappy") tend to have a great deal in common. On the other hand, those who check "very happy" normally tend to be more excited about the high quality and satisfying nature of their life situations than do those who check "happy." With this in mind, let us examine the findings which are summarized quite clearly in Table 6.

TABLE 6
EXTENT OF SUBJECTIVE MARITAL HAPPINESS
AMONG SWINGERS AND NON-SWINGERS
(in percentages)

Response Categories	Husbands		Wives	
	Swingers	Non-Swingers	Swingers	Non-Swingers
Very happy	56	43	58	49
Happy	29	33	23	31
Fairly happy	13	20	15	18
Unhappy	2	4	4	2

First of all it is apparent that more swingers than non-swingers indicated that their marriages were "very happy." In fact, 56 percent of the swinging husbands and 58 percent of the swinging wives checked this option, compared to only 43 percent of the non-swinging husbands and 49 percent of the non-swinging wives. On the other hand, the swinging and non-swinging wives did not differ from one another in terms of the prevalence of marital dissatisfaction—as measured by indicating "fairly happy" or "unhappy." But among husbands fully 24 percent of the non-swingers were less than "happy" compared to only 15 percent of the swingers.

Even though I am committed to keeping this book sufficiently non-technical so that it can be easily understood, I do want to point out that when appropriate statistical tests were applied to these data (Table 6), the differences between the swingers and the non-swingers were *not* found to be statistically significant. In other words, even though these data suggest that swingers may be somewhat more likely than non-swingers to have very satisfying marriages, conventional statistical tests say that the differences could have been obtained by chance. Of course, if future studies uncover similar differences between swinging and non-swinging couples, we might be somewhat more confident in suggesting that swinging is slightly related to (but is not in and of itself a "cause" of) marital happiness and satisfaction.

The Differential Consequences of Adultery for Marital Happiness

Even though none of the non-swingers had ever taken part in any sexual mate-sharing activities, 34 percent of their marriages *had involved* conventional (non-consensual) adultery at some time in the past. More specifically, 31 percent of the *non*-swinging husbands and 5 percent of the *non*-swinging wives had been sexually "unfaithful" to their spouses. In only two of the 100 non-swinging families studied had *both* members of the same couple been sexually "unfaithful" at some time in the past. And there were only three cases among the non-swingers where *only* the wife but *not* the husband had had extramarital sexual experience.

Thirty-four percent is comparatively small, but it still represents over one-third of the non-swinging sample as having had extramarital sexual experience. I was therefore quite curious as to how happy those non-swinging marriages that had involved adultery were, compared to the non-swinging marriages that had never involved adultery. In addition, I wanted to determine whether or not the impact of adultery upon marital happiness was essentially the same in *both* the swinging and the non-swinging samples. This is an important matter to explore as it has long been argued that adultery is itself prima facie evidence that a marriage is deteriorating and may be headed for the "rocks." Indeed, it is also widely believed that adultery is a prime cause or symptom of marital deterioration. Table 7 summarizes the data obtained for this study on the relationship between adultery and marital happiness *for the non-swinging sample only.*

TABLE 7
"AS MARRIAGES GO IN AMERICAN SOCIETY, ABOUT HOW HAPPY WOULD YOU SAY YOUR MARRIAGE IS?"

	(in percentages)			
	Non-Swinging Husbands		Non-Swinging Wives	
Response Categories	Adulterous Unions	Non-Adulterous Unions	Adulterous Unions	Non-Adulterous Unions
Very happy	27	52	41	53
Happy	41	29	41	26
Fairly happy or unhappy	32	19	18	21
N =	(34)	(66)	(34)	(66)

As is plainly apparent, adultery *does* have a strong bearing upon marital happiness for *non*-swingers, and *especially* for non-swinging husbands. Usually it is the wife who is thought of as being the "victim" when it comes to extramarital sexual relationships. Yet the *non*adulterous *non*-swinging husbands were almost twice as likely as the adulterous non-swinging husbands to indicate that their marriages were "very happy." Indeed, almost one-third of the adulterous non-swinging husbands viewed their marriages as *less than happy;* as a group they were far more likely than any other category of persons studied to view their marriages as being less than happy. The wives (the alleged "victims") in the adulterous non-swinging marriages were comparatively unlikely to express discontent with their marriages; only 18 percent were "less than happy" with their marriages.

At the risk of hazarding an overly hasty judgment, it could be that many of these wives had driven their husbands to adultery and that they were continuing at the time of this study to be insensitive to their own role in precipitating their husbands' marital discontent. In any case, these data strongly suggest that for most marriages adultery tends to be associated with a more negative set of consequences for the adulterer (i.e., the husband) than for the "victim" of adultery (usually the wife).

However, the most important finding of all to emerge from these data can be seen in a comparison of Table 6 with Table 7. Table 7 indicates that for *non*-swinging husbands and wives regular *non*-consensual adultery *does* tend to be associated with marital unhappiness, while Table 6 tells us that sexual mate-sharing swingers are happier and more content with their marriages than married couples who do not swing. The *happiest* of the non-swingers were the wives who were in *non*-adulterous unions: 53 percent of them considered their marriages "very happy." Their non-adulterous husbands followed closely behind, with 52 percent saying that they regarded their marriages as being "very happy." *However*, fully 58 percent of the *swinging* wives and 56 percent of the *swinging* husbands indicated that they regarded their marriages as being "very happy." In other words, the swinging husbands and wives were *more likely* than the non-swinging husbands and wives *who had never had anything to do with adultery* to label their marriages as being "very happy."

Even more impressive are the figures on marital happiness for "interpersonal" (as opposed to "recreational" and "egotistical") style swingers. Forty percent of the swingers studied were strongly "interpersonal" in their style of swinging (see Chapter 1 for an explanation of these categories). And among these "interpersonal" swingers fully 62 percent of the husbands and 65 percent of the wives labeled their marriages as being "very happy." But of even greater importance is the fact that *none* of the "interpersonal" swingers labeled their marriages as being *less than happy.*

It would be very wrong to assert that comarital sexual behavior *causes* marital happiness. However, these data do suggest that *it may be associated* with marital happiness for those who practice it. It is important that the reader recognize, however, that to say that *A* is associated with *B* is very different from saying that *A* causes *B*.

The major upshot of these findings is that there are different forms or types of extramarital sex just as there are different forms or types of *pre*marital sex. It has long been known that the different forms or conditions of premarital sexual intercourse give rise to vastly different consequences for the participants. In essence, different forms or conditions of extramarital sexual intercourse similarly seem to be associated with widely varying consequences for the participants and their marriages. Adultery, like premarital sex, is a "mixed bag"; it is not a simple, homogeneous category of human behavior.

But neither can it be assumed to be as potentially "safe" as premarital sexual relationships. In point of fact, for the vast majority of Americans *any* form of adultery has a far greater potential for harm than does premarital sex confined within mutually loving relationships. Only very few married couples can practice "safe" adultery, simply because very few married couples can come (or even *want* to come) to an agreement with each other that extramarital sex is morally right and proper for themselves under a highly specific, well defined, and mutually understood set of circumstances. The data of this study strongly indicate that before *any* couple can practice "safe" adultery, they *must* come to such an agreement with each other.

The Importance of Shared Meanings

In order for a couple to become successful swingers, the meaning which the concept of adultery holds for them both as a couple and as individuals must undergo a thorough transformation away from the conventional meanings of the term. They must come to fully accept the idea of "faithful adultery" or "adultery without infidelity."

As an illustration, three particularly pertinent questions were asked of each respondent in this study. First, they were asked to react to the following statement: "It is possible to engage in a great deal of extramarital sexual intercourse without being at all unfaithful or genuinely untrue to your marriage partner." Among the swingers 87 percent of the husbands and 89 percent of the wives registered agreement. Among the non-swingers the analogous figures were only 15 percent for the husbands and 7 percent for the wives. The differences between the swingers and non-swingers may have been even greater except that some of the former did not equate comarital sex with "extramarital sexual intercourse." Some of them commented after filling out the questionnaires that swinging to them was not *extra*marital sexual intercourse because it was an experience shared as a couple. However, most swingers do view swinging as a *type* of extramarital sex. They characteristically insist upon the conceptual distinction between "faithful adultery" and "unfaithful adultery." To them swinging is seen as belonging to the former category.

A second item asked for reactions to the statement: "When adultery occurs, it is usually symptomatic of the fact that the marriage is not going well." Again, less than 20 percent of the swinging husbands and wives indicated agreement with this statement, compared to almost 80 percent of the non-swinging spouses.

In the case of a third item I separately asked each husband and wife the following:

> "Suppose your husband (wife) admitted to occasionally experiencing some sexual intercourse 'on the side,' and indicated to you that it was purely by reason of a need for sexual variety and that he (she) loved you no less than he (she) ever did even though he (she) definitely planned to continue occasionally enjoying such extramarital sex. Assume that the marriage had been happy and satisfying up to this point. Would you consider a divorce? Would you consider a separation?"

Over 80 percent of the non-swinging husbands and wives indicated that they would indeed "consider a divorce" if they ever found themselves in a situation such as that depicted. Moreover, 93 percent of the non-swingers would "consider a separation." In contrast, only 4 percent of the swinging husbands and wives indicated that they would consider *either* a divorce *or* a separation.

The very great differences between the swingers and the non-swingers in regard to the way in which they responded to the foregoing three items illustrate very clearly the fact that adultery means something very different to the swinging husbands and wives than it does to the non-swinging husbands and wives. This, in a "nutshell," may partly explain why the swingers rated their marriages as being happier than the non-adulterous non-swingers rated theirs, and why the non-swingers who had been involved in adulterous marriages were the *least happy* (in terms of *marital* happiness) of all the groups. As social scientists often explain it, the two groups *define the situation* in radically different ways. The "self-fulfilling prophecy" enters in again here. When people come to define a certain event in a certain way (i.e., "adultery is proof of lack of love and commitment and therefore warrants a divorce or separation"), that event's mental definitions and expectations tend to become *real* in their consequences. In other words, if the offended spouse learns of the adultery, divorce or separation *is indeed* highly likely to occur. It is highly likely to occur because it is part of the participants' pattern of culturally programmed expectations. They had been socially conditioned to view sexual monogamy as a kind of "be-all and end-all" of marriage.

The fact that the adulterous swingers and the adulterous *non*-swingers represent the two extremes of marital happiness (with the non-adulterous non-swingers "in the middle") becomes even more interesting when it is realized that the *amount and frequency* of extramarital sexual experience among the non-swinging couples was only a *very tiny fraction* of the amount and frequency of extramarital sexual experience among the swinging husbands and wives. The swinging couples studied for this research attended one swinging party approximately every twelve days. And at each swinging party most husbands and wives have sexual intercourse with two or three persons of the opposite sex, not counting their legal spouses. Those non-swinging husbands and wives who had had adultery, on the other hand, had had it only very few times and with very few partners—in most cases only one. In addition, their affairs tended to have been very brief and sporadic as well as guilt ridden. Thus it is apparent that even the frequency of extramarital sex has nothing to do with the consequences that such behavior may have for a marriage.

And as a final consideration the non-swingers tended to view their extramarital sexual experiences in terms of being "affairs." Swingers virtually never even use the word "affair," because in their view they are not having "affairs" with the partners with whom they "swing." In essence, to the swinger an erotic fling at a party is not definable nor labeled as an "affair," in spite of the fact that some of the swingers have known their sexual companions at parties for many, many years. But again, these long-term friendships are not defined by any of the swingers involved as being in any way competitive with their respective marriages.

Value Relevance and Relative Consequences

Up to now no social scientist has contributed more to an understanding of the consequences of different kinds of sexual behavior than Harold Christensen (1969; 1970). His work has clearly demonstrated that few if any of the various consequences to which nonconforming sexual behavior has been alleged to give rise are actually caused by the sexual behavior itself. In essence, the real cause of negative (and quite often positive) consequences is that of the pattern of internalized norms and expectations of the participants involved in the behavior. In simple terms, Christensen's "principle of value relevance" is that the values people hold are relevant to their behavior and to the outcomes and effects of that behavior. What people believe or perceive or desire or expect determines how they are likely to act and react in reference to the situations that they face. In fact, what people believe and expect to happen is very often of far greater importance than any other factor in determining what is likely to happen as a consequence of a particular behavior.

As an illustration of Christensen's "theory of relative consequences," it is now known that among young people engaging in premarital coitus those who are not quite able to fully accept their behavior as morally right for themselves run a considerably higher risk of unwanted pregnancy than those who do accept their behavior as morally right for themselves. Young people who are less accepting of their own sexual behavior are less likely than others to discuss it with their partners before commencing a lovemaking session. They are also a good deal less likely to discuss or to employ contraception, because to do so would render their behavior all the more deliberate and premeditated.

Of course, in order for negative consequences to be least likely to occur, an individual's acceptance of his behavior must occur on both an emotional level *as well as* on an intellectual level. The emotional part of man's mind is always a great deal stronger and more influential than the intellectual or reasoning part. And most importantly, man's values are rooted in emotion, *not* in the intellect. An individual's loyalty, emotional dependency, and love for people significant in his life paves the way for his relatively uncritical internalization and strong-willed maintenance of those norms and values which are held and promulgated by those "significant others" such as family members.

Because it is not rooted in strong feelings and in emotional dependencies upon others, the intellectual part of man's mind can change far faster than the emotional part. In fact, the intellectual part tends to be comparatively autonomous while the emotional part tends to be quite strongly dependent upon the ideas of other people who are significant in a person's life. When someone does not fully accept his behavior on *both* an emotional as well as on an intellectual level, negative consequences are far more likely than when he does accept his behavior on both of these levels.

Internalized, emotion-rooted values and norms are not static, however, and people's reference groups and significant others do change somewhat over time. Guilt feelings and the person's very emotionalized values that support them can be extinguished through a repetitive experiencing of the particular behavior that at first precipitated guilt feelings, and through the taking on of new significant others who provide new values and a supportive ideology for the behavior. Behavior therapy, otherwise known as reinforcement or social learning therapy, is based upon this assumption; and it has enjoyed a great deal of success among people suffering from phobias, compulsions, anxiety states, etc. Very often, as a person's guilt feelings become extinguished, he gradually begins to realize (1) that his previous reality was not a necessary or indispensable reality, (2) that in many ways a person creates his own reality by the perceptions he chooses to recognize, and (3) that he can still accept, love, and respect people in his background without uncritically accepting everything that they happen to believe.

Christensen's theory of relative consequences is also important from the standpoint of shedding additional light on the causes of comarital sexual behavior. In America a considerable amount of autonomy from the kinship system and other agencies of conventional social control is necessary for enabling people to explore such deviant alternatives as comarital sex. However, Christensen's work has sensitized us to the point that such autonomy is probably related to the exploration of deviant sexual alternatives *only in social settings where full and complete sexual monogamy is espoused.* In societies where the kinship and religious institutions do not program

young people to believe that all forms of extramarital sexuality among married persons are wrong, we would not
expect to find sexual mate sharing associated with emotional autonomy or estrangement from the kinship system
or from the conventional religious structures. In short, in
order for involvement in any particular behavior to be
associated with estrangement from parents, relatives or
kin, that particular behavior must first be defined by the
dominant norms of a society as deviant and undesirable.

In a highly pluralistic society such as our own, it might
further be expected that comarital sexual involvement
would not be associated with estrangement from parents
in those cases where the parents were remembered as having espoused liberal, sexually permissive (albeit unconventional) norms vis-à-vis their young. Only three of the
200 swinging husbands and wives studied indicated that
their parents had ever discussed swinging with them. And
an additional six swinging husbands and seven swinging
wives thought that their parents might possibly have been
swingers. It is significant that all of these individuals were
on friendly, cordial terms with their parents at the time of
the study, and most of them visited with their parents
quite frequently.

In sum, for some couples comarital sexual behavior
would doubtless be "poison," while for others (a very
small minority of American society) it may constitute a
great boon to their relationships. However, the good or
bad consequences will not be directly caused by the
swinging behavior itself, but rather by (1) what its
participants think of their behavior, and (2) by the degree
of homogeneity or congruence in the internalized norms of
a particular husband and wife on matters pertinent to the
morality of comarital sex.

Convincing Initially Unwilling Wives to Swing

Except in cases where swinging husbands and wives
meet each other as single people prior to marriage, the
socialization process for swingers almost always involves

an effort by the husband to involve his wife in swinging. Such was the case for 62 percent of the swinging couples studied for this research. This 62 percent represents *all* of the husbands and wives who had not been already involved in some aspect of organized sexual freedom prior to marriage.

Most wives are at first very reluctant to try swinging, and only after some successful and highly enjoyable encounters do some of them gradually come to define swinging as worthwhile. Interestingly, various studies on sexual mate sharing have suggested that once the female begins to enjoy swinging she very often becomes even more enthusiastic about it than the male. This may be partly due to the multiorgasmic potential which most and quite possibly all women enjoy.

I asked the 62 wives who had been initially reluctant to swing whether or not they had experienced any internal turmoil as a result of their husbands' strong encouragement for becoming involved in the world of sexual mate sharing. Thirty-eight of the 62 wives indicated that they had suffered "a very great deal of turmoil." On the other hand, 13 of the 62 wives indicated that they had suffered only "a moderate amount" of turmoil, and the remaining 11 wives said that they had suffered "only a small amount of turmoil." Hence, we can see that for almost two-thirds of the wives who had not been swingers at the time of marriage, the initial movement toward this form of sexual nonconformity had been far from easy.

Quite commonly when a husband wishes to interest his wife in swinging he will leave some swinging literature and perhaps some related pornography where she is likely to find it. The wife characteristically (in line with her socially learned role) reacts with strong negative emotional feelings. This can be called *stage one*, or the *revulsion* stage. Depending upon the depth and strength of her revulsion, she is likely to glance over the material out of curiosity. This revulsion stage can be relatively short-lived, or it can be permanent, depending upon (1) the strength of the woman's internalized norms, (2) her ties to her own kin family network, (3) how strong her marriage and her emotional attachment to her husband are, and (4) the quality and success of the first one, two, or three swinging encounters. In any case, this stage is likely to be fraught with a considerable amount of open weeping in her husband's presence (an example of role-playing rooted in internalized normative expectations) and loud emotional argumentation.

Assuming that the woman's background is not too conservative and that the husband manages to offer primarily intellectual and ideological arguments about why they should at least try swinging (e.g., honesty, openness, sharing sexual variety together as recreation, etc.), she is likely to move slowly toward *stage two*, or *resistance*. During this stage she begins to learn that some very respectable people like herself swing. The husband may even invite a couple that swings, in for a chat. He will perhaps keep his wife in the dark about the sexual behavior of the couple for the first couple of hours. Since the wife usually will have established some rapport with the couple by the time the conversation turns to swinging, she typically finds it impossible to react in a strong negative or insulting manner. In essence, the apparently normal and appealing nature of the visiting couple has in part neutralized and normalized their deviance for the wife.

The argumentation between husband and wife during this second stage tends to lack the emotional fervor which prevailed during the revulsion stage. The wife reacts primarily with her own intellectual arguments as to why she should not swing. The husband counters these with the appropriate points from the swinging ideology.

The resistance stage can last for several months. If the husband is successful, the wife is likely to move to *stage three*, or the *resignation* stage. During this stage the wife resigns herself to trying out a swinging party. At this stage the most crucial factor is whether or not the first experience with swinging is pleasant. Those couples adequately familiar with the swinging ideology and alerted to the possible pitfalls will usually avoid serious problems. On the other hand, naive couples may make serious blunders during their first one or two swinging encounters. They may arrange to meet a couple sight unseen at a motel; or they may invite a couple to their home without having previously investigated them. A few of the people interviewed for this study had had extremely unpleasant experiences because they had violated the principle that one must never commit oneself and one's spouse to a swinging encounter without having first interacted with the other couple at a bar or restaurant or in the company of mutual friends. It seems likely that for many couples such unpleasant experiences could send the wife back from the resignation stage to the revulsion stage, and at the same time reduce the husband's desire to press the issue further.

After resignation the *fourth stage* for many women is *acceptance.* This stage usually arrives after a few favorable swinging experiences. Some swinging wives remain at the acceptance stage while others, after additional swinging experiences, move on to *stage five—enthusiasm.* At this stage they find that they no longer feel guilty and they begin to relish swinging to an even greater extent than their husbands.

Yet with a large number of couples, almost all of whom are comparatively new to the swinging scene, the wives tend to remain very much back at the resignation stage, and many of them fluctuate between resignation and resistance. In essence, these wives simply occasionally "go along" in order to please their husbands or to "save" their marriages. It is my contention that such couples cannot be called true swingers, as they have not yet undergone all of the necessary attitudinal changes.

Furthermore, one of the major conclusions of this research is that those wives who do get beyond the resignation stage to either the acceptance or the enthusiasm stage tend to have backgrounds very similar to those of their husbands in terms of (1) emotionally unsatisfying formative years in the parental home, (2) emotional detachment and comparative alienation as adults from parents and the family network, and (3) a history of early interest and involvement in social-heterosexual activities and of romantic attachments from an early age onward. On the other hand, those wives who do not get beyond the resignation stage (even though they may go through the motions of "swinging" from time to time in order to please their husbands) tend to have backgrounds that are comparatively similar to the backgrounds of the non-swinging wives.

A swinging relationship in which the husband is enthusiastic but the wife cannot get past the resignation stage is not likely to become a stable, active swinging dyad. Just as a few experiments with homosexual behavior do not necessarily make a person a homosexual, a few swinging experiences are not a sufficient condition to render a couple a true swinging couple. *In the world of swinging, couples function as units;* and in order to be an effective unit the component parts must complement each other. The value systems of the two parts of the dyad (couple) must be reasonably congruent and complementary.

The concept of *value congruence between spouses* is commonly referred to in family research. The greater the number of characteristics a husband and wife have in common, the greater the likelihood that the couple will achieve satisfaction. Behaviors such as sexual mate sharing or premarital sex cannot in and of themselves create conflict and disharmony among people; these behaviors alone cannot cause a relationship to deteriorate.

What can and does matter greatly is what a person thinks and feels about his or her personal behavior, and the degree of congruence between the internalized norms of the spouses. Harmony between mates as to what their values and expectations are for their relationship is of crucial importance. If both mates have (or develop) similar expectations as to what they want sexually from their relationship, they have a high likelihood of success. Husbands and wives who are not especially happy with each other, or whose normative perceptions of social reality (especially as they relate to sexual mate sharing) tend to be markedly disparate, ought to avoid this form of nonconformist recreation. It could precipitate a deterioration of such a marriage.

Other Elements of Marital Adjustment

There are many factors which contribute to or detract from marital happiness. We have already seen that the marriages of the swingers studied for this research compare very favorably with the marriages of the non-swinging couples as far as general marital happiness is concerned. Let us now examine how the swingers and the non-swingers compare with each other in regard to some of the major correlates of marital satisfaction and contentment.

It is safe to say that anyone who feels ignored or slighted by his or her spouse is not likely to remain happily married for long. Many marital relationships tend to go through stages. During some of these the husband and wife share almost all of their activities together and they spend a great deal of time with each other. No one likes to feel that he or she is being forced to "take a back seat" in terms of the interests and priorities of his or her spouse. In American society people are programmed to depend very heavily upon their husbands and wives for the satisfaction of many of their most important emotional needs. Thus, to what extent can swingers and non-swingers of this study confidently depend upon their spouses for emotional support and sincere personal interest?

Each of the respondents answered the question: "Do you feel that your spouse spends enough time with you and shows enough interest in you?" And while the differences between the swinging and non-swinging couples did not turn out to be statistically significant, the swinging couples were clearly more satisfied with the amount of sincere attention and interest they were receiving than the non-swinging spouses were.

For example, 19 percent of the non-swinging husbands answered "no" to the above question, compared to only 8 percent of the swinging husbands. Similarly, among the wives 15 percent of the non-swingers answered "no," compared to only 10 percent of the swingers. On the other hand, 47 percent of the swinging husbands and 49 percent of the swinging wives indicated *very strong satisfaction* with the amount of time and interested involvement they commonly receive from their spouses. Among the non-swingers only 36 percent of the husbands and 39 percent of the wives were this well satisfied.

In a related question I asked: "Are you reasonably well satisfied with the amount of (non-sexual) affection your spouse spontaneously displays toward you around the house?" Inasmuch as the swinging husbands and wives were receiving a copious amount of *sexual* affection from many different people, it might be expected that the swingers would be prone toward lower levels of satisfaction here than the non-swingers. But again, the swingers were *more* satisfied than the non-swingers, and this time significantly so. Fully 29 percent of the non-swinging husbands were *not* satisfied with the amount of spontaneous displays of affection they had been receiving from their wives. This compared to only 12 percent of the swinging husbands. Among the wives, however, the differences were smaller: 18 percent of the non-swingers and 15 percent of the swingers indicated that they were not satisfied.

On the other hand, among the swingers 42 percent of the husbands and 51 percent of the wives were *highly satisfied* with the amount of spontaneous affection displayed toward them around the house. Among the non-swingers only 26 percent of the husbands and 39 percent of the wives were this well satisfied.

Many men and some women in our society tend to be quite shy about saying "I love you" to their spouses *even when they want to do so.* The expression of such warm, loving and romantic feelings very often does not come easily. But those husbands and wives who are able to easily express such feelings almost always find their marriages on safer, more secure ground than those who cannot.

With this in mind I asked each husband and wife: "Does your husband (wife) seem to have an easy capacity for occasionally saying 'I love you' to you?" And again I found the swinging husbands and wives to be more readily able than the non-swingers to say things like "I love you" to their spouses. Twenty percent of the swinging wives answered "no" to the question, compared to 29 percent of the non-swinging wives. Among the husbands only 8 percent of the swingers answered "no," compared to 37 percent of the non-swingers.

For many decades anthropologists have viewed commensalism (eating together) as a key indicator of social acceptance, mutual admiration and liking, and of social equality. Hence, I asked each couple to indicate about how many nights per week they generally eat dinner together as a family. Only 7 percent of the swinging couples and 9 percent of the non-swinging couples indicated that they usually eat dinner together less than three nights per week. However, 62 percent of the swinging families eat dinner together virtually every night of the week most weeks; this compared to just 54 percent of the non-swinging families. Inasmuch as these differences are not statistically significant, it can conservatively be said that the swingers eat dinner with their spouses and children about as frequently as do the non-swingers.

Each respondent was also asked to estimate the number of minutes he or she normally converses informally each day with his or her spouse. This may or may not have been an easy question for the respondents to answer, and many gave what could be considered improbably large estimates. However, even though it is not possible to give strong credence to these data, it is interesting that the swingers did see themselves as communicating informally more often with their marriage partners than did the non-swingers.

Of course, the most intense and potentially emotional of all forms of communication is that which is involved in sexual intercourse. Since swingers are free to experience a great deal more sexual intercourse *outside* of marriage than the non-swingers are, it might reasonably be expected that their overall sexual frequency *with their own legal spouses* would be *less* than that prevalent among the non-swingers.

I asked each couple to indicate the number of times they usually have sexual intercourse *with each other* (within the confines of marriage) during a typical week's time. And the differences between the swinging and the non-swinging couples were great and in some respects amazing. The responses (in percentage) ran as follows:

	Swinging Couples	Non-Swinging Couples
6 or more times weekly	23	2
4 or 5 times weekly	32	14
2 or 3 times weekly	34	36
zero or once weekly	11	48

These findings perhaps testify as strongly to the swingers' very strong interest in sex as they do to their commitment to share many different kinds of experiences together. Many of the comments made by the various respondents strongly suggested that even *inside* of marriage the swingers tended to make fairly frequent sexual experience a *priority item of business*. Some of them were concerned about rehearsing various sexual maneuvers and skills for their oncoming swinging parties and other social festivities!

As a case in point, the non-swinging couples very seldom had sexual intercourse at any time other than the time of retiring. And none of them ever copulated outside of the privacy of a bedroom. Usually they had the lights out and would do it under the covers with at least some garments on. In contrast, the swinging couples tended to systematically set time aside during the day for their sexual play together. They wanted to be wide awake and alert during their sexual fun together. Comments made by the various couples also strongly suggested that the swingers were far less self-conscious than the non-swinging couples about engaging in sexual play while the children were around. Few of the swingers ever copulated in front of their children; but by the same token they had no inhibitions about telling their children that they wanted to be alone so that they could "make love" with each other "in peace" and undisturbed. The non-swingers, on the other hand, viewed it as desirable to keep their sex life a secret from their children. Indeed, even long after their children had gone to sleep there tended to be a constant worry among many of the non-swinging couples that their children might awaken and "hear something."

A further very striking difference between the swinging and the non-swinging couples was that the latter tended to disagree with each other a great deal more on the question of how often they should have sex. Fifty-eight percent of the non-swinging couples indicated that they often disagreed with each other on this issue. In the case of 52 of these couples the husband wanted more sex than his wife; in only 6 cases did the wife have a bigger sexual appetite than the husband. Among the swinging couples, on the other hand, only 8 couples frequently differed with each other in terms of how often they wanted to copulate with each other. And in 6 of these 8 cases the wife was the partner who wanted more conjugal sex than the husband!

Swingers quite commonly assert, and those interviewed for this study were no exception, that non-conjugal sexual intercourse at parties serves to heighten their erotic interests and arousability. Many of the swingers asserted that sexual mate sharing is a powerful aphrodisiac for all people who truly accept and enjoy it. It would appear that most commonly the swinging experiences work to effectively fuel the participants' fantasy life. In fact, merely watching others engaged in erotic play also serves as an effective fantasy arouser and sexual aphrodisiac. Swinging husbands and wives take these fantasies home and their own conjugal sexual lives thus tend to be strongly affected.

I asked each swinger whether or not he or she felt that his or her sexual relations *within* marriage had improved at all since he or she had first begun engaging in sexual mate sharing. Fifty-three percent of the husbands and 46 percent of the wives felt that their sexual relations *within* marriage had improved "a very great deal" since first becoming involved in swinging. Thirty-three percent of the husbands and 39 percent of the wives thought that their conjugal sex had improved "somewhat" or "slightly," and only 13 percent of the husbands and 14 percent of the wives felt that there had been no improvement. Only one swinging husband and one swinging wife felt that their conjugal sex had become worse since commencing co-marital sexual behavior.

As a check on the aphrodisiacal impact of sexual mate exchange upon conjugal (husband-wife) sex, I asked each swinging respondent whether or not he or she ever discusses details of his or her individual sex trades with his or her own spouse. Over 60 percent of the swinging husbands and wives indicated that they frequently discuss the details of their individual sex trades with each other, and most of these people further indicated that such discussions "turned them on" sexually to their spouse a very great deal. Only 5 percent of the swingers said that they never discuss sex trades with their own husband or wife. The remaining 33 percent indicated that they "sometimes" discuss sex trades with their own husbands or wives.

It is possible that the significantly greater sexual activity rates of the swinging couples even within their own legal marriages reflect a higher inborn sexual drive. The data presented in Chapter 7 lend strong support to this possibility. Of course, many social scientists impugn the notion of an inborn sexual drive differential among people; but none of them have ever presented any evidence supporting the position that there is not such an inborn drive. People's sexual lives are influenced by the norms and expectations of the groups of which they are a part. But norms and expectations do *not* appear to fully control or entirely determine human sexual behavior. I think the unusually high rate of sexual activity prevalent among middle-class swingers resident in conservative American suburbia testifies quite strongly to that effect.

Of course, many swingers became involved in comarital sex expecting it to contribute to a better and more frequent conjugal sex life; and for them it has. However, almost one-third of the swinging husbands asserted their belief that a high rate of sexual frequency will almost always assure a high degree of sexual competence and skill. These men insisted that sexual skill was little different than athletic prowess, and that just as strong muscles require constant daily exercise in order to remain in top shape, remaining sexually competent and highly skilled similarly requires a dedicated effort and daily exercise. The swinging wives were much less likely than their husbands to stress the "sexual muscle development" and "practice makes perfect" philosophy. But many of them did point out that they had never known they were "multi-orgasmic" until they had taken up swinging. Many of them also credited swinging with making their orgasms more intense, and with making their husbands more cognizant of how to please a woman sexually. Both the husbands and the wives stressed that swinging had made it a good deal easier for them to communicate with each other freely about their sexual likes, preferences, and fantasies. This last point may be of especial importance inasmuch as few of the non-swinging couples seemed to be able to communicate "heart-to-heart" on matters pertaining to sexual desires.

Common among the expectations of popular psychiatrists is that people who engage in comarital sex deprive themselves of a rich emotional satisfaction and intimate social relatedness that coitus ideally ought to provide every time it is experienced. The intimation, of course, is that impersonal sex is mutually exclusive with warm, emotional, loving sex, and that the latter kind of sex can only be engaged in on a totally monogamous basis if it is to be genuine and real. According to this conception, non-monogamous sex could seldom if ever contain for its participants any of the elements of warmth, emotional intimacy, and love.

Given the popularity of this view I considered it quite appropriate to ask the respondents whether or not they feel that they derive enough emotional satisfaction and relatedness out of their sexual expression. If swingers' approach to coitus and eroticism tends to be purely pleasure oriented and "body centered," then presumably they should register less satisfaction than the non-swingers with the amount of emotional sharing and intimate personal relatedness they derive from their conjugal copulations.

The foregoing popular expectations were not borne out by the data I obtained. In fact, among the wives I found the swingers to be significantly *more* satisfied than the non-swingers with the amount of emotional satisfaction and relatedness they normally derive from coition. And among the husbands the findings also favored the swingers, although the differences were not as substantial as were those for the wives.

More specifically, among the wives only 9 percent of the swingers and 20 percent of the non-swingers indicated that they did not feel that they were deriving enough emotional satisfaction from sex. Among the husbands just 17 percent of the swingers and 27 percent of the non-swingers were similarly dissatisfied. On the other hand, *very high* degrees of satisfaction were registered by 25 percent of the swinging husbands and 46 percent of the swinging wives; and among the non-swingers, by 23 percent of the husbands and by 38 percent of the wives.

Of course, a moralist could counter these data with the

assertion that a swinger does not really know the first thing about what "real" emotional satisfaction and person-to-person relatedness in coitus is because he has never actually experienced it. The data presented here do not rule out the possibility of very different mental yardsticks being applied by the two groups for such things as amount of person-to-person relatedness and emotional satisfaction. However, on the basis of the data presented there certainly does not appear to be any suggestion that swingers are any more likely than non-swingers to *feel* deprived or impoverished in regard to conjugal emotional relatedness usually experienced. It is almost always an individual's *subjective feeling* of deprivation which can and often does cause negative effects such as divorce, recriminations, etc. If an Eskimo who has never experienced anything different says that he is quite comfortable sleeping on hard ice we had best believe him even though we ourselves may not be able to understand how this could possibly be.

In another somewhat related question I asked:

"Which of the following describes your experience with sexual intercourse?

Very enjoyable	Neither pleasant nor unpleasant
Mostly pleasant	Mostly unpleasant
Occasionally pleasant	Very unpleasant."

The responses of the 200 swinging husbands and wives were *exclusively* confined to the first two alternatives: "very enjoyable" and "mostly pleasant." In contrast, only 82 percent of the non-swinging husbands and 71 percent of the non-swinging wives confined their answers to the first two alternatives. In other words, even among those who contended that they usually do derive enough emotional satisfaction and relatedness out of their sexual expression, some of the non-swingers found their comparatively infrequent sexual intercourse to be only occasionally (or less often) pleasant.

Some of these differences may be explained by the much richer knowledge that the swinging couples had regarding human sexuality. The swingers tended to make sex a priority item in their daily round of activities, and becoming highly competent at sex and its enjoyment had become a veritable hobby and recreational pastime to most of them. Thus it cannot be considered suprising that 75 percent of the swinging wives and 84 percent of their husbands indicated that they found sexual intercourse "very enjoyable," and all of the others checked "mostly pleasant."

One of the most obvious reasons why more of the swinging wives greatly enjoyed their marital sexuality was that almost all of them could confidently look forward to an orgasm virtually any time they had sex, whether with their own husband or with some other man. To a far greater extent than the non-swinging wives they *knew* what pleased them sexually and they had a sufficient sense of personal freedom to permit them to spontaneously tell their husbands what they wanted in terms of erotic play. They expected far more from sex than the non-swingers.

This is *not* to imply that the swinging wives always experienced an orgasm in every *copulation* with their husbands. The point is that almost all of them were able to experience at least one orgasm every time they had sex. Sometimes that orgasm was experienced in regular penile-vaginal copulation and sometimes it was experienced in oral-genital sex or in one of the many techniques of erotic foreplay. The non-swinging wives, on the other hand, tended either to "put down" the importance and desirability of orgasms, or they did not want to talk with the interviewer about the issue of orgasms. Of the non-swinging wives who did talk, only about 25 percent were able to experience regular orgasms while in the course of foreplay or intercourse with their husbands.

As a final index of marital adjustment I was interested in determining how *equalitarian* the marital relationships of the swingers and non-swingers were. It has been known for a long time now that the more democratic the power relationship is between a husband and his wife the happier and more satisfying their marriage is likely to be. However, the differences between the swinging and non-swinging couples in regard to this issue were almost nil. I found that approximately 75 percent of *both* the swinging and the non-swinging couples had equalitarian marital relationships and that all of the remaining 25 percent were husband dominated. All of the couples indicated that they usually tried to discuss their differences with each other. Nevertheless, in the case of deadlocks the husband was the partner most likely to win out in 80 percent of all the swinging and non-swinging marriages.

Selling the Self on Marital Adjustment

At the risk of belaboring the point somewhat, I think it is definitely in order to present some additional data on how the swingers are able to convince themselves of the "non-toxic" influence of their sport upon their marriages. One of the main messages of this book is that what a person truly believes about something directly affects the consequences of participating in that something. If a person can honestly and truly convince himself or herself of some idea, no matter how outlandish that idea may appear to others, then that idea will work for that person. Consider, for example, how hypnotized subjects are able to painlessly walk barefoot on hot irons. The swingers have convinced themselves of many ideas, a large portion of which would be summarily dismissed as highly outlandish and unthinkable by the majority of the population. These ideas are collectively contained in what has been referred to up to now as the swingers' *ideology*.

Many people contend that swingers have "absolutely no values at all." It is my contention that swingers could not successfully do what they do for very long and still remain without a governing value system. Swingers do have a well-structured value system, but it is a *different* value system than that which most of us share. As I shall point out later in this chapter, many swingers went through a period of life (usually late teens and early twenties) when they really did lack a (for them) viable value system. But sooner or later most of them *substituted* a new ideology or value system for the old one with which they had grown up. In essence, a deviant value system regarding sex and marriage (but *not* regarding the desirability of financial success, hard work, popularity, social skills, etc.) *replaced* the conventional one. And this happened comparatively easily for most swingers because of reasons outlined in Chapter 4.

To be sure, I am *not* emphasizing these points with the desire of encouraging readers to consider the idea of swinging for themselves. I, personally, am *not* a swinger and, in point of fact, I could never become one. My desire is merely to understand swingers. And through understanding swingers I believe that a number of truths can be (and indeed have been) derived which have helpful implications for everyone, no matter how liberal or conservative or conventional they might be in their sexual and marital beliefs and values. People need to be much more careful than they usually are regarding the beliefs they accept about themselves, other people, and the consequences of certain actions they or others might have taken. "According to your faith (belief), so be it unto you" (Matthew 9:29 of the Bible).

Let us now look at the extent of belief among the swingers in their own swinging value system. I asked the swingers to agree or disagree with the statement: "Swinging poses absolutely no threat to my marriage or to my love relationship with my wife (husband)." Eighty-four percent of the swinging wives and 86 percent of their husbands agreed; only 1 percent of the swinging husbands and 7 percent of the wives disagreed; the remainder checked "uncertain."

I further asked (separately) each swinging husband and wife whether the general overall quality of their marriage had improved at all since they had begun engaging in sexual mate-sharing behavior. Fifty-three percent of the swinging husbands and 51 percent of their wives said that they felt that their marriages had improved "a very great deal" since they had started swinging. Only 4 percent of the husbands and 15 percent of the wives felt that swinging had had no effect upon their marriages. No one felt that swinging had made their marriage worse. The remainder of the respondents felt that swinging had improved their marriages either "somewhat" or "slightly."

Thirdly, I asked each swinging respondent to indicate whether or not he felt that the general quality of his life had improved to any extent since he had first become involved in the world of comarital sex. Of the husbands 67 percent indicated that their lives had improved "a very great deal"; 60 percent of the wives felt the same way. On the other hand, only 4 percent of the husbands and 11 percent of the wives felt that there had been no improvement in their lives. Several of these people told me that their lives had already been quite pleasant long before they had ever become involved in swinging. No one felt that their lives had become worse as a result of swinging.

Jealousy

To most Americans it is inconceivable that a person could allow his or her own spouse to engage in casual sexual intercourse with another partner in his or her own home. To the swinger, on the other hand, to do so is most often seen as an aphrodisiac to the regular husband-wife sexual relationship. Why do some people experience strong feelings of jealousy over extramarital sex while other people seem to seldom or never experience such feelings? The answer lies in the ways in which people respond to the traditional programming received from parents, kin, and religious officials. Since the swingers reacted negatively to much more of this programming than the non-swingers they were faced with the problem of finding and developing a new and different value system. In other words, the swingers had to find their own truth and they had to find a way of programming their own minds with it.

When the swingers initially decided to involve themselves in the activities of the swinging world they necessarily had to face up to the swinging belief system. Like any other type of group, swingers are reluctant to accept among their membership any individuals whose beliefs might pose a threat. Because jealousy is a potentially dangerous emotion, virtually all swinging groups maintain strong norms relative to its expression, and some groups even go so far as to deny the legitimacy and acceptability of jealousy feelings among swingers altogether. No person wishing to become involved in sexual mate sharing has to accept the normative ideology of any particular swinging group, club or organization. *But all* persons wishing to become swingers must convince the members of *at least one* swinging group that they share and are willing to abide by that group's rules and policies. People whose feelings of jealousy cause them to become involved in fights (physical or verbal) are almost always ejected from the swinging scene. Quite commonly such people become blackballed throughout much of the swinging population within a given geographic area.

Swingers do not offer us any suggestive answers to the age-old question of whether sexual jealousy is inborn or learned. However, if the potential for sexual jealousy is inborn (and there is some indication that it may be), long-term involvement in swinging serves to effectively neutralize it. Swingers who involve themselves with groups that view jealousy in a disparaging way and which insist that jealousy is entirely a learned emotion usually do not experience any jealousy feelings at all when they swing. On the other hand, some swinging groups view sexual jealousy as an acceptable emotion so long as (1) it does not disrupt swinging activities or lead to recriminations of any kind, and so long as (2) it serves the aphrodisiac function for husband-wife sexual intercourse away from the party scene. As I have already pointed out, many swingers *expect* swinging to have this aphrodisiac function for conjugal coitus, and so it does.

Along with the system of normative ideas which all swingers are expected to accept and abide by, swingers also avoid jealousy feelings by structuring the *context* of extramarital sex in such a way as to minimize the possibility of any threat to their primary marital relationship. They pursue sex as a *shared* leisure-time activity with others and ordinarily will not allow their same-sexed fellows to see their spouses outside of a prearranged party situation or when they themselves are not around.

Most swinging couples also express concern that the couples with whom they swing enjoy reasonably happy marriages which they want to maintain. Similarly, most swinging groups will not permit single men to participate, nor will they allow married men to attend parties without their lawful wedded wives. Attendance at a swinging get-together with a paid call girl or even a mistress, for example, is rarely permitted because the man in question is not taking the same risks nor making the same contribution as everyone else. Single men might want to find someone with whom to fall in love, or they may be after "sexual conquests." And people in less than satisfying marriages may be looking for a way out of them. In either case, such people are regarded as having "less to lose" than married people whose relationships are solid. Yet strangely enough many swinging groups *do* welcome single women. This is a common inconsistency that is very widespread in the swinging world.

Almost all swinging groups have strong norms prohibiting their members from falling in love with one another. Some groups do permit the spontaneous expression of tender feelings, but expressions such as "I love you" are quite commonly feared and disapproved of within the context of swinging festivities. Interpersonal swingers tend to be more permissive than recreational or egotistical swingers in regard to this point. But interpersonal swingers typically enjoy long-term relationships with the couples with whom they swing.

Again, the idea is to protect and defend the marital unions of everyone involved, yet still enable everyone to enjoy playful, recreational sex. To be sure, most swingers value the emotion of friendship with the couples with whom they share their recreational pursuit. The expression of warm friendship and sincere human concern within the context of sexual mate exchange is seldom ruled out. But there is a very marked difference between the warmth of friendship and the emotional desire for sexual and social-emotional exclusivity that comes with the initial stages of the romantic falling-in-love experience. Swingers believe that couples with good, strong marriages are highly unlikely to "fall in love" with someone to whom they are not married. They further believe that the freedom to live out sexual fantasies with almost anyone of their choosing within the party context serves to greatly reduce the probability of ever "falling in love" (or of ever developing a desire to do so) with someone other than the legal spouse. In short, they believe that the only people who "fall in love" are people with a void in their emotional and/or sexual lives.

As pointed out earlier in this book, interpersonal swingers often make a conceptual distinction between "committed love" and "noncommitted love." These people do not see deep, long-lasting friendships with their swinging partners as competitive with the *committed* type of love characteristic of a sound marriage. Friends who see each other very often are regarded as "loving" one another, but in a *noncommitted* way. They do not live together, pay each other's expenses, or have children by each other. Again, the swingers believe that human beings (both male and female) are intrinsically monogamous from a psycho-emotional and residential standpoint, but polygamous from a *sexual* standpoint.

Adopting new beliefs about the meaning of adultery is

only the first step in the process of reducing jealousy feelings so as to allow multiple extramarital relations. These new beliefs must be internalized on an emotional level. It requires much longer for a set of nonconformist norms to become internalized on this deeper emotional level than for them to become internalized on an intellectual level. When strong feelings of jealousy do emerge at swinging parties it is not usually because the norms against falling in love were violated.

Most often the problem is this: one of the party participants was a novice at sexual mate sharing and had accepted the swinging norms on an imperfect, intellectual level and not on a deep, emotional level. Not everyone at a large swinging party is likely to be a long-time swinger. Sometimes upon hearing about sexual mate exchange a man will become extremely excited and will enthusiastically bring the matter to the attention of his wife. Such a man will quite often perceive himself as being very much in need of sexual variety, and he will fantasize about all of the real or imagined rewards he might derive from becoming a swinger.

The problem, of course, is that such a man will very often direct so much of his psychological energy toward reforming his wife that he completely forgets about himself and the real implications of what he thinks he wants to do. He does not confront the fact that he is going to see his wife undressed and engaging in sexual activity with other men. If, as often happens, she enjoys the experience, his expectations are upended and he loses his balance and his "cool." Jealousy attacks him in his guts with the force of a strong blow.

Experienced swingers also report occasional feelings of jealousy. These feelings are usually much milder than those of the novices—and far less likely to issue in rage. The veteran swingers usually keep their feelings to themselves until they arrive home. Then, as we have seen, jealousy becomes a sexual "turn-on"—even though most couples are likely to be quite physically tired after having spent several hours in an orgiastic social setting.

When so many of their swinging friends talk enthusiastically about how they arrive home from a party even more erotically charged toward their spouse than when they left, the expectation of similar feelings in themselves arises even in those who are relatively new to swinging. Sociologists have long argued that even very intimate feelings tend in large measure to be a predictable by-product of the normative ideology of the most meaningful reference groups of which a person is a member.

Divorce History

Divorce statistics might be another reflection of the relative happiness and adjustment of swinging versus nonswinging couples. It is widely assumed that sexual mate sharing leads to marital discord, family disorganization and divorce. And in fact, 49 percent of the swinging husbands and 34 percent of the swinging wives had at some time been divorced, in comparison with only 15 percent of the non-swinging husbands and 14 percent of the non-swinging wives. Yet it cannot be concluded that swinging and divorce go hand in hand. In this study, *none of the divorces occurred after a man or woman had become active in comarital sexual behavior.* Factors other than swinging seem more useful in explaining the higher divorce rate for swingers. For example, as I documented in Chapter 7, the swinging men contracted their first marriages at unusually early ages. They tended to have entered first marriages with women to whom they had felt strongly attracted on a physical level, and they first married after very short courtships. In essence, they entered into marriage before any kind of adequately comprehensive knowledge and appreciation of the values and personal attributes of the girl could be realized at a rational, intellectual level.

Much of the research on courtship behavior has shown that "love" during the early months of a relationship tends to serve as a smokescreen blinding the "lovers" to many of the most essential personal attributes of each other. This element, combined with the weak social control of the family and the strong psychological autonomy of pre-swinging men, undoubtedly functioned as a powerful social force pressing toward early marriage. In American society, being married is often seen by teenagers—because of the way they are socialized—as constituting a key indicator of adult status. And the status of independent, fully autonomous adult is one which the pre-swinging men tended to crave unusually early in their youth, too early even to have given serious consideration to the nonconformist option of "living together" unmarried for a while. In any case, it is likely that only being legally married could have effectively reinforced the feeling of complete adulthood which was so important to many of these people. (Many of these people did practice "living together" prior to their second marriage, when they were in their mid-twenties.)

A quite common outcome of these first marriages was that the men gradually began to find their partners "too conventional" for them. In fact, during the interviews several of the swinging wives made similar points in regard to their first husbands. Usually within from one to three years of the marriage a clash of values between the pre-swingers and their first spouses gave rise to a great conflict, alienation, and unhealable cleavages.

Upon being divorced, and often before, the pre-swinger began hanging around politically liberal and/or socially unconventional groups of young people. "Swinging singles" groups and sexual freedom organizations in particular tended to be frequented on a fairly regular basis. Indeed, 38 percent of the swinging couples of this study claimed that they actually met their present spouse at "swinging singles" parties. In short, for many of the couples, swinging actually preceded the current marriage. This point is of considerable significance, for it provides us with a viable explanation as to why the swinging couples were as happy, and in some respects even happier with each other, than the non-swingers were, even though as a group they were far more likely to have experienced at least one divorce in their lifetime.

It would appear that when the swingers chose their second spouse they tended to be quite careful about selecting someone whose major life values, outlooks on life, recreational interests, and personal understandings, were reasonably similar to their own. Virtually all family sociologists are agreed on the point that a reasonable homogeneity of major life values and interests between a husband and a wife is a major precondition of marital success and happiness. Among the many swingers who had experienced a divorce, the first marriage had not entailed such a homogeneity, whereas the second one did. Of course, only a study that followed up *the same couples* for many years could ascertain the extent to which the swinging couples of today remain legally married to each other throughout their lifetimes.

Personal Psychological Adjustment

It is doubtful whether there is any more valid or reliable method of assessing psychological or emotional adjustment than through looking at a person's happiness. A person who is subjectively happy most of the time is almost always a well-adjusted person. Over the past several decades psychologists have constructed so-called "personality tests" averaging anywhere from 300 to 600 questions in length. But it has recently been shown that not even these lengthy and elaborate instruments are as consistently valid as is this *one* simple question: "Generally speaking, about how happy would you say you are these days?"

The results revealed no statistically meaningful differences between the swingers and the non-swingers, either for the husbands or the wives. Seventy-seven percent of the swinging husbands and 73 percent of the non-swinging husbands indicated that they were either "very happy" or "happy." Among the wives, 80 percent of the swingers and 79 percent of the non-swingers said that they were either "very happy" or "happy." The wives, however, were evidently happier than the husbands in *both* the swinging and the non-swinging groups, as over 40 percent of them indicated that they were *"very* happy." Only 30 percent of the husbands were *"very* happy"—the same figure for both the swingers and the non-swingers.

At the other end of the spectrum, 3 percent of the swinging *and* the non-swinging wives were "unhappy." Among the husbands, 3 percent of the swingers and 4 percent of the non-swingers were also "unhappy." The remaining respondents indicated that they were only "fairly happy."

In a related question I asked the respondents: "At this point in your life do you have a pretty comfortable sense of personal fulfillment?" And again, no meaningful differences emerged between the swinging and the non-swinging couples. But *again,* the wives in both groups indicated stronger feelings of personal fulfillment than their husbands did. (Twenty-eight percent of them felt *exceedingly well fulfilled* compared to only 16 percent of their husbands.)

Among the swingers only 17 percent of the husbands and 8 percent of the wives said that at the present time they did not have a comfortable sense of personal fulfillment. This compared to 15 percent of the non-swinging husbands and 10 percent of the non-swinging wives. But 75 percent of the swinging husbands and 79 percent of their wives did feel fulfilled in life. This compared to 68 percent of the non-swinging husbands and 87 percent of the non-swinging wives.

One of the strongest criteria of personal adjustment in this or any other society is that of satisfaction with one's job or career. I asked two questions regarding this matter, the first of which was: "If you were twenty years old and had the chance to start all over again, would you select an occupation at least roughly similar to the one which you are now in?" And 78 percent of the swingers and 79 percent of the non-swingers indicated "yes," they would.

In the second question I simply asked the respondents to indicate the degree or extent of personal satisfaction they normally derived from their occupation. (It should be recalled that only 33 percent of the non-swinging wives were employed outside the home compared to 62 percent of the swinging wives.) Only 5 percent of the swingers and 2 percent of the non-swingers were "dissatisfied" with the amount of satisfaction they were deriving from their occupations. On the other hand, 29 percent of the swingers and 31 percent of the non-swingers indicated that they were deriving "a very great deal" of satisfaction out of their careers; 32 percent of the swingers and 42 percent of the non-swingers were deriving "a considerable amount" of satisfaction from their work. In essence, the differences in career satisfaction between the swingers and the non-swingers were very small and not statistically significant.

Boredom

The question of personal boredom with life often comes up with reference to those who practice sexual mate sharing. Of course, all human beings everywhere seem to require some entertainment and recreational activities. Research from hundreds of cultures throughout the world is very clear and consistent on this point. Psychiatrists too will usually agree that the various defense mechanisms and escapes are fundamentally healthy. They become pathological only when the individual develops an undisciplined dependency upon them and his or her efficiency, growth and adjustment become impaired.

In the United States there are literally hundreds of recreational pursuits which people depend on to a greater or lesser extent for fun and relaxation. However, it is important to observe that a very high proportion of our most popular forms of recreation appeal to just one sex and are usually practiced on a sex-segregated basis. In fact, some of the sports that are most popular among married men, such as hunting, golf, fishing, etc., are of this sort.

Moreover, such sports as baseball, basketball, and football, which are widely practiced by younger men, are almost never played coeducationally. Nor do wives usually sit in front of a television set watching such games along with their husbands.

Husbands who enthusiastically practice such activities with other men weekend after weekend are almost never accused of "copping out," or of being excessively bored with their lives, or of pathological escapism in order to avoid facing up to psychological or relationship problems which may often include wives and children. But in reality they may actually be "escaping" a good deal more than swingers. Unlike comarital sex, their recreations cannot be practiced by a married couple together. In order to practice them it is usually necessary for a person to remove himself physically and mentally from home, marriage and family for a greater amount of time and with a higher degree of frequency than is commonly necessary for sexual mate sharing. There is a very great deal of research data showing that husbands and wives who play together (and who share most of their recreational interests together) usually stay together. And there are no data anywhere suggesting that it is more difficult for a man or woman to develop a dependency or "addiction" to baseball, golf, or football (or upon watching a television set as a spectator for these), or bridge parties, than it is to develop an "addiction" to sexual mate sharing. In point of fact, it would appear that a person can become addicted to anything.

Sex segregated though they usually are, golf, bridge, hunting, fishing, and football are all socially approved activities in our society. Swinging, on the other hand, is not. Indeed, one of the most common reasons given for involving teenagers in the various sports and athletic activities is that they will distract youth from their burgeoning sexuality. Americans are socially conditioned and programmed to feel uncomfortable about things sexual, but not about things athletic or sex segregated.

Even extreme and potentially destructive forms of escapism are likely to go relatively ignored in a complex, impersonal kind of society such as ours unless these forms violate norms that are deeply imbedded in what to many people are unquestioned traditions. Swinging, no matter how infrequently a couple may partake in it, violates just such norms. Many people cannot help responding with fear and anxiety to the idea of swinging, as its very existence places the veracity of the very core of their social reality in doubt—a reality comprised of much-repeated norms as to what a "decent" person's relationship to marriage and family life can be expected to be. While our society has developed a heterogeneity of moralities in connection with sex, marriage and family, many people maintain a trained incapacity to feel tolerant or serene about the existence of normative pluralism.

Three questions with specific relevance to the boredom issue were asked of each of the respondents. Firstly, they were asked: "In general, would you say that your life is busy enough?" And there were no significant or meaningful differences between the swingers and the non-swingers for either the husbands or the wives. In fact the very slight differences which did obtain tended to favor the *swingers* as being less likely to be bored.

Secondly, the respondents were asked: "Do you often find yourself with too few interesting or meaningful things to do?" Among the husbands 85 percent of the swingers indicated that they did not often find themselves with too few interesting or meaningful things to do, compared to only 71 percent of the non-swingers. Among the wives the analogous percents were 84 for the swingers and 82 for the non-swingers. In essence, for this question the swinging husbands (but not the wives) were significantly *less likely* to be bored than the non-swingers.

Thirdly, each respondent was asked: "Do you sometimes feel that people like yourself have too much leisure time?" Only 28 percent of the non-swinging husbands answered "emphatically no," compared to 46 percent of the swinging husbands. On the other hand, among the swingers only 7 percent of the husbands and 10 percent of the wives answered "yes" to the question; this compared to 9 percent of the non-swinging husbands and 12 percent of the non-swinging wives. So again, there is some suggestion in these data that swinging has no effect at all upon the tendency of wives to occasionally feel bored. On the other hand, the data also suggest that being a swinger may serve to slightly reduce the tendency to boredom among husbands.

Of perhaps some relevance to the boredom issue is the question of how many hours a person typicaly spends per week watching television. A high frequency of television viewing may or may not be indicative of boredom in individual cases just as it may or may not be indicative of loneliness or of inability to communicate effectively with one's spouse and children or with lethargy or with a narrow range of personal interests. But inasmuch as people who spend many hours in front of a television set are often accused of these things it may be meaningful and worthwhile to consider where the swingers and non-swingers of this study stand in regard to this matter.

Among the husbands 25 percent of the swingers and 8 percent of the non-swingers estimated that they watched an average of "one or less" hours of television per week. Among the wives this was true for 17 percent of the swingers and for 8 percent of the non-swingers. On the other hand, among the swingers 18 percent of the husbands and 27 percent of the wives averaged eleven or more hours of television per week. For the non-swingers 31 percent of the husbands and 44 percent of the wives watched this much television. The upshot of these data is that swingers do watch significantly less television than the non-swingers. However, there did not appear to be any "television addicts" among either the swingers or the non-swingers.

As a final check on the "boredom" question I asked each husband and wife to give me an estimate of the number of books he or she had read within the past year. People who read a great deal are often presumed to have more active minds, to be more verbally articulate, and to be less likely to suffer feelings of boredom than those who do not read very much. Unfortunately, it turned out that both the swingers and the non-swingers gave me improbably large estimates, and I had to decide not to take the data seriously. Suffice it to say that the differences between the swingers and the non-swingers on this issue were almost nil.

Alcohol and the Swinger

Many of the swinging couples I interviewed made a point of stressing that an undisciplined use of alcohol is unknown in swinging circles. Virtually all of the books and articles published on sexual mate sharing up to now have similarly pointed out that swingers tend to be very moderate in their use of alcoholic beverages, and that a few of them don't even drink at all. The ideology propounded by almost all veteran swingers similarly stipulates that any use of alcoholic beverages in excess of two drinks on any given occasion will have a deleterious effect upon sexual drive and sexual performance, and that it may also cause halitosis. The shared belief systems prevalent in swinging circles also tend to view an excess consumption of alcohol as indicative of a "cover-up" for shyness and social inhibition.

People who have difficulty controlling their intake of alcohol swiftly become blackballed in the swinging community. Since very little alcohol is typically provided at swinging parties, most swingers find it easy enough to limit themselves to just one or two drinks. The swinging club owner-managers with whom I talked also made it very clear that the undisciplined consumption of alcohol is very much against swingers' etiquette even though "social drinking" is normally involved at swinging festivities. However, there are some swingers who will not drink at all prior to an erotic event. Indeed, like alcohol, food is also believed by many swingers to have a dampening effect upon sexual competence and performance. Swinging men tend to be particularly concerned about performing creditably at the parties they attend. Their wives, on the other hand, convey the impression that they are considerably less "up tight" about the "performance" issue.

I asked each swinging husband and wife to indicate the number of alcoholic drinks he or she generally consumes at a typical swinging get-together. In interviewing the non-swinging couples I substituted the word "social" get-together for "sexual" get-together. And while these two words are certainly not equivalent, many of the swinging husbands and wives assured me that their own drinking behavior as well as that of other swingers they know is no different at non-sexual, social get-togethers than it is at specifically sexual or "swinging" get-togethers. They also pointed out (see Chapter 10) that the first two or three hours at most swinging parties are almost never given over to sexual activities, and that this is when most of the drinking and eating occurs.

Among the husbands 37 percent of the swingers indicated that they usually average either "one or none" alcoholic drinks at social (swinging) get-togethers. Among the non-swinging husbands only 19 percent said that they usually averaged "one or no" drinks. Among the wives, 48 percent of the swingers said that they averaged "one or no" drinks, compared to only 31 percent of the non-swingers.

On the other hand, when we focus upon the percentage of people who drink *three or more* alcoholic drinks per party, we similarly find the non-swingers to be significantly more active drinkers than the swingers. Only 39 percent of the swinging husbands indicated that they usually average three or more drinks per party; this compared to 65 percent of the non-swinging husbands. Among the wives 32 percent of the swingers averaged three or more drinks per party; the analogous percent for the non-swingers was 42.

Hence, we see that among the husbands the swingers

seem to drink significantly less alcohol than do the non-swingers even though some of them (39 percent) *do* transcend the swinging norm of a "two drink maximum" per party. And while the swinging wives also drink less than the non-swinging wives, the differences between the two groups of women did not turn out to be statistically significant.

I also asked the respondents whether or not intoxication ever arises at their social or swinging get-togethers. Among the husbands 62 percent of the swingers and 48 percent of the non-swingers said that it "very seldom or never" happens. Among the wives 55 percent of the swingers and 51 percent of the non-swingers indicated that it "very seldom or never" occurs.

Yet despite their normative ideology, intoxication does appear to happen with some regularity among a minority of swingers. This is so, even though frequent intoxication is suggested by the data I obtained to be between two and three times more commonplace among the non-swingers than among the swingers. For example, 13 percent of the swinging husbands and 8 percent of their wives said that intoxication arises "sometimes or frequently" at their get-togethers. But among the non-swingers the analogous percents were 25 for the husbands and 23 for the wives.

I also asked the respondents to react to the statement: "I never or very rarely become intoxicated from too much drinking." Here the differences appeared to be somewhat greater between husbands and wives than between swingers and non-swingers. For example 21 percent of the swinging husbands and 29 percent of the non-swinging husbands admitted that the statement was *untrue* for themselves. Among the wives, only 15 percent of both the swingers and the non-swingers said that it was untrue for themselves.

On the other hand, these data suggest that 79 percent of the swinging husbands and 85 percent of their wives seldom or never experience intoxication. And while it can be argued that these respondents may have "faked good" in order to create a favorable impression of themselves and of swinging, much the same can also be said for the responses of the non-swingers. The analogous percents for them were 71 for the husbands and 85 for the wives.

As a final check on the respondents' use of alcohol the following item was included on the questionnaires: "When it comes to alcoholic beverages, I never have any difficulty refusing further drinks once I feel that I have had enough." And among the swingers only 4 percent of the husbands and 3 percent of their wives answered "untrue"; among the non-swingers 9 percent of the husbands and 6 percent of the wives indicated "untrue." Again, even though this kind of question may be likely to invite some distortion of the truth, the data obtained strongly suggest that swingers have at least as much self-control in regard to alcohol as do the non-swingers.

Anomie

Simply put, *anomie* is a feeling of not being a part of anything. It is a depressing feeling of detachment from one's community and from one's society. "Anomie" can also mean normlessness, hopelessness, alienation, and confusion as to the meaning of life and as to one's place in life. McClosky and Schaar (1965) found in what is probably the most penetrating study to date on the subject, that highly anomic people tend to be socially isolated and tend to have experienced a high degree of upward or downward social mobility. They also found anomic people to be characterized by high guilt, low self-confidence, a high contempt for weakness and an intolerance of human frailty, low social compassion, low overall satisfaction with life, pessimism, negative thinking, strong feelings of political futility, and low sense of social responsibility.

In effect, "anomie" is a kind of umbrella term that is widely used among social scientists to refer to a number of conditions, some of which have already been dealt with, particularly in Chapter 6. But questions about anomie have very often come up in the course of the many public lectures I have given on swinging. Because some deviant groups have been found to be quite high on anomie the tendency has been for most people to suspect swingers of similarly being quite high on it. It was for this reason that I decided to determine where the swingers of this study stood on a scale of anomie.

I used the highly respected and fully validated nine-item scale that had been developed by McClosky and Schaar (1965) to measure personal anomie. And, in general, the findings tended to suggest comparatively low levels of anomie for both the swinging and the non-swinging husbands and wives. In other words, compared to Americans in general, the couples of this study would have to be considered comparatively well-off regarding anomie. In fact, only the *non-swinging wives* had as many as one-fifth of their members in the "high" anomie ranges. Everything else being equal, low anomie would be expected for well-educated, middle to upper middle-class suburbanites. But beyond this it should be noted that the non-swinging respondents did score significantly *higher* on anomie than the swinging respondents did. In other words, even though most of the scores were low, the scores of the swingers still came out significantly lower than did those of the non-swingers. These findings provide support and corroboration for the material discussed in Chapter 6, where it was pointed out that swingers do tend to be significantly more tolerant, compassionate, and politically liberal than the non-swingers. And while the swingers were indeed found to be detached from their relatives, kin and neighbors, they were found to be significantly less detached from chosen friends.

Personality and Self-Image

Swingers are *extroverts*. The most immediately conspicuous and demonstrable difference between the non-swingers and the swingers is that the latter tend to be highly outgoing, articulate, and immediately friendly. With very few exceptions I found the swingers to be amazingly effective in their ability to "warm up" to strangers very rapidly. To be sure, more of the husbands than the wives seemed to possess these highly outgoing, very articulate qualities. But they were nevertheless apparent in most of the wives and in nearly all of the swingers' children as well.

For more than a decade now psychologists have been interested in the relationship between sexual "permissiveness" and personality. In 1964 I conducted an elaborate study on this subject in Salt Lake City and among a large sample of students on the campus of the University of Utah. Using a major personality test I found that sexually liberal men and women differed significantly from the conservatives on several dimensions of personality. The liberals scored substantially higher than the conservatives on level of self-esteem, sociability, social presence, social spontaneity, flexibility, empathy, assertiveness, leadership capacity, and tolerance. On the other hand, the sexual conservatives scored better than the liberals on such scales as responsibility, conformity, and self-control.

The Utah study also uncovered a very strong and convincing relationship between happiness and heterosexual interaction. The more satisfied a person was with his or her extent of heterosexual interaction the happier he or she was likely to be. For the male respondents no other single factor correlated more strongly with happiness than satisfaction with heterosexual interaction. Shy (but heterosexual) men were by far the least happy people in the study. For the female respondents the relationship between happiness and being involved socially with the other sex was less strong than it was for the men; but it was still a noteworthy statistical relationship. Thus it appears evident that women can do without men a very great deal easier than men can do without women.

In the current study I similarly found the swingers to be significantly higher than the non-swingers on self-image and on sociability. Some thirty separate questions relating to "self-image" and "self-esteem" were included on the written questionnaires. And most of these items yielded small differences favoring the swingers over the non-swingers. For example, in responding to the statement: "I am generally considered a warm and affectionate person," 86 percent of the swinging wives responded affirmatively, compared to just 72 percent of the non-swinging wives. Among the husbands 71 percent of the swingers responded affirmatively, compared to 60 percent of the non-swingers.

However, a few of these "personality" questions revealed differences suggesting that swingers may have somewhat more volatile, labile personalities than most people. For example, in response to the question: "Do you have ups and downs in mood without obvious reason?" 47 percent of the swinging wives responded in the affirmative compared to only 32 percent of the non-swinging wives. There were no differences between the two groups of husbands on this question; 30 percent of both groups responded in the affirmative.

Psychotherapy

Of the various barometers of psychological adjustment employed by this study, only one revealed data suggestive of greater problems among the swingers than among the non-swingers. A common albeit crude index of adjustment is that of whether or not a person has ever experienced any kind of psychotherapeutic help for personal problems. And among the husbands the data revealed that virtually twice as many swingers as non-swingers had experienced at least some psychotherapy in their lifetimes (36 percent versus 18 percent). Among the wives it was 35 percent for the swingers compared to 24 percent of the non-swingers. Of course, despite these differences, it should be noted that almost two-thirds of the swinging husbands and wives had never in their lives experienced any psychotherapy.

These findings would have to be considered somewhat surprising in light of the fact that the swingers came out at least as well and in most cases somewhat better than the non-swingers on such indices of adjustment as personal anomie, subjective personal happiness, self-image, satisfaction with employment, marital happiness and satisfaction, absence of boredom feelings, social involvement with friends, moderation in the use of alcoholic beverages, etc. Indeed, if the swingers had had a greater tendency than the non-swingers to "fake good" on these various adjustment questions, one might well wonder why they failed to follow through on the questions pertinent to the experiencing of psychotherapy! Parenthetically, psychologists James and Lynn Smith (1970) similarly found that 40 percent of their swinging respondents had experienced some form of psychotherapeutic help at some time in their lives.

Despite the comparatively high incidence of psychotherapy among the swingers, none of them admitted to having seen any psychiatrists or clinical psychologists within a twelve month period of the time they were interviewed. Hence, it may be that the psychotherapeutic history of many of the swingers had been due to youthful adjustment problems rather than to current difficulties. It may have been a by-product of the greater effort they had to expend during later adolescence and early adulthood to "find themselves"—to establish a firm personal identity and an acceptable (to them) morality. As the data indicate, the swingers appear to be as happy and in many cases even happier *now* than the non-swingers. But as I *also* documented in Chapter 4, the data also show that the childhood and teenaged years of these same swingers had been a good deal less happy and serene than those of the non-swingers. Thus it would appear that the more serious adjustment problems of most of these people were primarily a thing of the past.

On the basis of the data of this study it seems probable that swingers do tend to be significantly less stable and serene than most people during the first 25 or so years of their lives, but that after they have lived through this long period and grappled successfully with its problems they emerge with a degree of personal happiness and adjustment to life which at the very least seems to be no different than that which ordinary people at the same social class level enjoy.

A further point of relevance to these findings is the possibility that the swingers may have required considerably less of an impetus than the non-swingers for the seeking out of psychotherapeutic help in the first place. The seeking out of psychotherapeutic help is in and of itself a non-conformist and *deviant* thing to do. Sociologist Derek Phillips (1963) published some strong evidence documenting the point that people with a variety of psychiatric problems are more likely to be rejected by others if they are known to have sought out psychiatric help than if they had endeavored to grapple with their psychological problems entirely on their own without professional help. Phillips found that the residents of a southern Connecticut community whom he interviewed were especially likely to be rejecting toward a *man* who had sought out psychiatric help—much *more* rejecting, indeed, than they were toward a woman with the *same* psychiatric problem who sought help.

Presumably in part because of the pioneer tradition of rugged individualism there has long been a firm norm in American society that people should "pull themselves up by their own bootstraps," "grab the bull by the horns," and solve their own problems. This normative expectation has always been especially strong as far as the *male sex* is concerned.

Now, since swingers are deviants as far as the traditional norms are concerned, and since judging by the quality of their relationships with their parents they had been deviant in numerous particulars for quite some time, it is very likely that considerably less of an impetus may have been needed in the first place to move them toward a therapist than may have been needed in the case of the non-swingers. The severity of a psychological problem necessary to motivate the seeking out of psychological help may well have been much greater for the non-swinging men than for the swinging men. The swinging men, inasmuch as they already viewed themselves as "different," may well have felt perfectly free about seeking professional help under a considerably lesser degree of provocation than might have been necessary for the non-swingers. In their laboratory study of deviance, psychologists Freedman and Doob (1968) found that people who had been made to feel deviant tended to pursue a nonconformist course of action on the various laboratory exercises to which they had been assigned. In short, people who consider themselves deviant in one way typically find it easier to deviate in other ways than most people do.

Physical Health

Finally, I asked the respondents to rate the condition of their physical health. And while almost no one rated his or her health as "poor," the swingers were substantially more likely than the non-swingers to use the term "excellent" in rating their health rather than "good." To the extent that the personalities of the swingers tended to be more exhibitionistic and outgoing than those of the non-swingers such a response tendency might possibly be expected, at least to a mild extent. Of course, it should be remembered that the swingers and the non-swingers were of approximately the same ages.

In any case, among the husbands 79 percent of the swingers compared to only 53 percent of the non-swingers rated their physical health as "excellent." Similarly, among the wives 77 percent of the swingers and 46 percent of the non-swingers rated their health as "excellent." Most of the remaining respondents used the term "good" to rate their health; only about 6 percent of the swingers and non-swingers used the terms "fair" or "poor."

Almost all people who are regularly involved in any form of sexual mate sharing receive a very great deal of strong albeit subtle encouragement to keep their bodies as physically fit and attractive as possible. Like nudists, swingers see each other nude a very great deal. And especially at the large, impersonal swinging parties which many of the "recreational" and "egotistical" swingers very much enjoy, the competition among participants (both men and women) for sexual favors can be very great indeed. To be sure, the swingers enjoy this competition. But they enjoy it because they are able and willing to take the necessary steps to keep their bodies healthy and sexually appealing.

Some writers have claimed that swingers are no more "good looking" as far as *facial* appearance is concerned than the majority of the population of their own age. However, everyone who has studied swinging—both journalist and scholar alike—agrees that swingers maintain their bodies in a maximally attractive condition for their respective chronological ages. My own impressions are in harmony with this assessment. I personally found the swinging wives to be more facially attractive than the non-swinging wives whom I interviewed. In effect, most people would probably consider them to be at least somewhat "prettier"; and I don't think any judge would consider any of them to be either ugly or obese.

On the other hand, the swinging husbands looked little different than the non-swinging husbands. Just as many of them were balding, and just as many of them could easily be placed in the "non-handsome" category. Nevertheless, fewer of the swinging husbands had developed "pot bellies," and even those who did appear somewhat unattractive nevertheless displayed warm and friendly personalities which undoubtedly helped them a great deal. Many of these husbands had wives who were considerably more attractive than they themselves were. Among the non-swingers I almost never got the impression that a wife was more attractive than her husband; far more typically the non-swinging husband appeared to be considerably more attractive than his wife!

Swingers who do not pay adequate attention to their physical appearance tend not to be invited to very many of the more desirable parties. Few of the swingers seem to need any normative pressure or encouragement to keep fit. Most of them speak enthusiastically about exercises they enjoy doing and health diets they enjoy keeping. Such interests in health and physical fitness and appearance may simply be a reflection of basic personality traits, some of which may include some of the same traits that facilitated their involvement in the swinging world. In any case, it seems highly probable that the swingers' concern about physical fitness and attractiveness together with their positive thinking and confidence about their competence in these matters probably helped to facilitate the realization of these very qualities for them. In other words, a concern for physical fitness usually works to promote better health, everything else being equal.

When people belong to groups that meet frequently and regularly and which maintain an enthusiasm for a set of values that includes health and physical fitness, these people are likely to feel highly motivated to live up to those values. To be sure, groups with strong physical fitness and health values do *not* have to be swinging groups or nudist groups! Indeed, they can revolve around *any* shared set of interests. But the group members must truly like one another; they must enjoy being around one another and sharing experiences with one another. A person who is a member of a group whose interests and values are only mildly important to him or her is not likely to be significantly influenced by that group's interests and values, or by how the members might react to his or her deviation from major group values.

Finally, the swingers unusually frequent rate of sexual arousal and of sexual intercourse may itself constitute at least a minor but important factor in promoting physical fitness, good health, and trimness of figure or physique. It is now known that each time a person has sexual intercourse the body burns up a *minimum* of 150 calories.

Under conditions of the prolonged sexual arousal and foreplay common among most swingers, between 250 and 400 calories are burned up for each sexual arousal leading to orgasm. In point of fact, sexual activity is itself an outstanding form of exercise. And when it is regularly supplemented with other forms of physical exercise it doubtless serves as an effective boon to good health and appearance.

Chapter 10

At the Swinging Parties

It should be clear on the basis of what has been said so far in this book that swingers go through a great deal of trouble in order to practice their brand of fun and recreation. Why is it all worthwhile for them? What actually goes on at their parties and erotic get-togethers that makes swingers want to keep coming back for more? This chapter is intended to shed some light on what goes on at sexual mate-sharing events. It will also focus on some of the normative pressures and expectations to which swingers enthusiastically subject themselves while in a party environment.

Types of Swinging Parties

There are basically four different types of swinging parties: (1) unstructured, non-intimate; (2) structured, non-intimate; (3) intimate, unstructured; and (4) intimate, structured. All of the parties and get-togethers discussed by the swingers interviewed for this study could be easily classified under one of these four categories. Most swingers have a preference for one or another of these forms. But only about 15 percent of the swingers I interviewed have restricted themselves entirely to just one type of party.

Most swingers have experimented with different types of parties, and most of them plan to continue to occasionally attend parties that are outside of their usual preference category. As a group the swingers investigated for this study averaged one swinging party per twelve days.

An *unstructured, non-intimate* party is large and usually involves between seven and forty couples, with approximately fifteen to twenty couples being the most common. Such parties tend to have a "cocktail party" type atmosphere, and they assume a fairly high degree of social skills in the participants. Both women and men are expected to take the assertive role in terms of introducing themselves to each other. Such parties tend to be held in large, private homes, hotels and motels, and in special mansions that are either owned or rented by private swinging clubs and organizations.

The unstructured, non-intimate type of party situation tends to be favored by many "recreational" swingers and by virtually all "egotistical" swingers. "Interpersonal" swingers very seldom attend such parties. But if and when they do they usually attend with one or two other swinging couples with whom they are very well acquainted. Couples in attendance at these parties are likely to vary a good deal from one another in terms of age, and they are likely to come from all over a particular metropolitan area. Thus, the swingers at such parties tend to be only mildly acquainted with each other, and some of the couples in attendance may not know anybody.

One of the paradoxes of this form of party is that novice couples are likely to be present. Unless such couples are quite attractive and quite socially skilled, and/or unless there are at least two or three other couples present with whom they are fairly well acquainted, such a party situation is likely to prove quite anxiety provoking for novice couples.

These parties are "unstructured" in the sense that no particular activities are prearranged or scheduled to take place. In effect, what happens at these parties happens on an unplanned, spontaneous basis. Participants in this type of party scene are expected to "make it happen" for themselves. And even novice couples are usually accorded only a minimal amount of help from people present who might be sponsoring them.

Structured, non-intimate parties are similar in most respects to the unstructured, non-intimate variety. The major difference is that party activities are *planned*. The host and hostess of such parties will have worked out an elaborate schedule of organized activities that are to take place at various times during the course of an evening.

These parties also tend to be large, although not quite so large as the unstructured, non-intimate type of party. These parties are usually held in private homes, and the number of couples commonly invited seldom surpasses sixteen. The most typical number of couples likely to be present is between eight and twelve. And occasionally a smaller number of couples will be invited. One or two couples who are newcomers to swinging are also likely to be present at such parties. The demands made upon such couples are fewer than at the unstructured, non-intimate party because structured games and activities are provided which ensure everyone's participation and which obviate the necessity of anyone aside from the host and hostess having to assume the socially assertive role.

Interestingly, the structured, non-intimate type of party is *less* commonplace than the unstructured, non-intimate type. However, it too tends to be favored by "recreational" swingers to a far greater extent than by "interpersonal" swingers. In addition, the couples present are likely to be in their later thirties, forties, and fifties. Despite the "easier" set of demands it makes upon newcomers to swinging, the structured, non-intimate type of party is seldom attended by swingers in their twenties and early thirties.

Better than 90 percent of all parties that could be considered as "intimate" fall into the third category of *intimate, unstructured*. Such parties or "get-togethers" (as they are usually called) seldom involve more than four couples and very often involve only two or three couples, all of whom are likely to be "very good friends" who have known each other for a long time and who share numerous non-sexual activities with each other as well. Newcomers to swinging are seldom found at such "get-togethers." However, newcomers occasionally meet other newcomers at the large, impersonal parties, and they form groups among themselves that become "clubs" that will eventually hold their own "intimate, unstructured" get-togethers. In effect, couples preferring this type of party tend to be quite "cliquish."

As might be expected, the intimate, unstructured get-together is most popular among interpersonal swingers. However, recreational swingers occasionally hold their own small parties in their own private homes. When they do they will invite couples whom they met and enjoyed at a large, impersonal party. But unlike the interpersonal swingers, recreational swingers seldom try to sustain long-term associations with fellow swingers.

The least common form of swinging party is the *intimate, structured* variety. Limited almost entirely to couples in their forties and older, this type of party usually involves between three and five couples at a private home where all or most of the activities have been pre-planned by the host and hostess. The couples in attendance are likely to be very good friends and they are likely to have known each other for a considerable number of years. Each participant at such a party will be expected to engage in erotic acts with every opposite-sexed guest in attendance. And he or she will do this in accordance with a prearranged schedule of sex games and sexual mate exchange.

This prearranged schedule of activities tends to be quite similar to that which obtains at the much larger "structured, non-intimate" type of party. For example, a host or hostess may schedule two 45-minute swing periods and four 45-minute erotic games periods for a particular evening. During any particular "swing period" each party guest goes off with an opposite-sexed partner to whom he or she has been assigned through games of "spin the bottle," drawing straws, key games, games involving being blindfolded, etc. In other words, the individual guests do not have the responsibility of making their own contacts; but everyone present at such a party is automatically assured of having as much of an opportunity for full participation in sexual mate sharing and erotic games as everyone else. The highly skilled person enjoys no more opportunity at such a party scene than the less socially skilled person. Highly outgoing people, however, are seldom found at such parties. Younger couples are also seldom present.

At this point another conceptual distinction is in order: *"closed"* swinging versus *"open"* swinging. "Closed" simply means that the sexual behavior of any couple is expected to take place in privacy behind closed doors. "Open" swinging, on the other hand, means that a couple may engage in sexual intercourse, oral-genital sex, or any other type of erotic activity (involving one couple or a group of couples or two women and a man, etc.) either privately or out in the open. In the "open" style doors do not need to be kept closed and, indeed, most of the sexual activity takes place in open areas such as on the living room rug or in the hallways or den of a particular home. In California preferences for "closed" swinging are becoming increasingly uncommon. Almost all of the people I interviewed for this study swing "open" or "semi-open" (i.e., in private bedrooms but with the doors left open). Couples preferring the "closed" style tend to be in the "over 40" category and of more conservative social and political persuasion.

Organization of Time at Swinging Parties

Most swinging parties last between six and eight hours. They generally commence around 8:00 P.M. and end some time between 2:00 A.M. and 4:00 A.M. Very often couples will "sleep over" until the following morning. But unless a party is earmarked beforehand as being "for an entire weekend," there are not likely to be any sexual activities the following morning. Full weekend parties are not common; only about one party in twelve is for more than one evening. And not all couples remain on the scene for the full length of a party. In the case of "intimate" structured or unstructured parties all of the guests are likely to depart within a half-hour of each other. But in the case of the "non-intimate" parties people are seen coming and going the entire evening. The larger the party, the greater the tendency for participants to remain for only a portion of an evening. In fact, it is not at all uncommon for two couples to depart together from a "non-intimate" party and return to one of their homes for their own unplanned "intimate" get-together. Many people who dislike "non-intimate" party settings attend them on occasion anyway in order to meet like-minded fellows with whom they might establish "intimate" long-term swinging fellowships.

One point which surprises many people is that swinging parties *of any kind* very rarely involve sexual play for an entire evening. At most of the large "unstructured, non-intimate" parties sexual activity is very much available all evening to those who might want it. But even at "unstructured, non-intimate" gatherings it is uncommon to find anyone involved in sexual activity prior to 10:30 or 11 o'clock. This tends to be true even when the hostess responds to each doorbell ring stark naked, as occasionally happens.

In effect, parties are designated as starting at 8:00 P.M., although sometimes the host and hostess (or the swinging club manager) will designate a looser hour of commencement such as "between 8 and 9 P.M." In the case of "intimate" parties held at private homes the guests will usually begin arriving at about 8:20, and by 9 o'clock all who had been invited are likely to be in attendance. But in the case of the larger, "non-intimate, unstructured" parties the guests are not likely to be completely in attendance until 10 or even 10:30 P.M. Generally speaking, they will flow in at a very slow trickle from about 8:15 until 10:15 or thereabouts. In the case of the large "non-intimate, structured" party the guests will usually be in attendance by 9:30 as the structured, organized erotic festivities usually begin at approximately 10:00 P.M.

The first two or three hours at most swinging parties are commonly given over to non-erotic activities. During this period everyone remains fully clothed; the wives are likely to be attired seductively and quite sexily, while the husbands are likely to be attired in attractive, informal slacks and sport shirts. But again, this avoidance of sexual activity during the first part of an evening is only very rarely a normative expectation. In short, even highly experienced swingers seem to need a "warming up" period, even when they are with people whom they have known for many years.

Pleasant, spontaneous informal conversation tends to be the main activity during the first part of a swinging evening. At most parties the majority of the guests are seated during most of this period. However, at the "unstructured, non-intimate" parties the guests are more likely to be standing and circulating around the room in much the same way that they might at a typical cocktail party, except that here husbands and wives often circulate together.

At the smaller, more "intimate" parties conversational interaction tends to be quite "coeducational" throughout the entire evening. This is interesting because at most social gatherings involving husbands and wives in the "straight" world the guests tend to involve themselves in conversation with members of their own sex for much of the evening. Swingers tend to feel uncomfortable about prolonged same-sex interaction. And when, for example, a group of husbands is seen standing around in the kitchen or in the corner of some room talking with each other for more than ten minutes or so, one of the other guests (either male or female) is likely to yell out a teasing remark which is designed to bring the men back to a "coeducational" conversational setting. The same thing applies when a group of wives is seen conversing among themselves without any husbands present, although wives are generally less often seen engaged in same-sex conversational interaction at parties than husbands are. However, as I shall point out later in this chapter, same-sex *erotic* interaction (i.e., "lesbian" sex play) is very common at swinging parties whereas swinging *husbands never* engage in homosexual eroticism.

Most (but not all) swinging wives take great pride in their ability to prepare and serve very tasty but low-caloried snacks. There is quite a bit of friendly competition among swinging wives in this regard. Hence, various snacks and hors d'oeuvres, and occasionally eating from smorgasbord or buffet tables, provide swingers with a considerable amount of pleasure during the first part of their party evenings. Wine, beer, coffee and tea, are the most common beverages provided with this food. With the exception of Hawaiian drinks which are sometimes served, hard liquor and mixed cocktails are seldom provided at swinging parties. The swinging ideology discourages heavy eating as well as heavy drinking as both are believed to undermine sexual competence and erotic "staying power." But on the other hand, a wife can save her inadequately "performing" sexual partner some degree of embarrassment by humorously attributing his erection problems to his having enjoyed her "outstandingly well-prepared hors d'oeuvres" too much. In such an instance she would doubtless encourage him to stimulate her via various techniques of manual massage and oral-genital play.

At the larger parties light drinking, eating, and conversing with fellow swingers are the only activities likely to take place prior to the start of sexual festivities. But at the smaller, more intimate parties other kinds of activities occasionally occur. For example, small swinging cliques may even play bridge for the first two or three hours of an evening. Billiards and table tennis are very popular pastimes among swingers and are often practiced at the parties. Some of the younger swingers told me that tennis or handball or swims in the home swimming pool very often precede erotic festivities. Swingers almost invariably keep their swimming pools fenced in sufficiently to prevent anyone outside from looking in. Thus, swimming, when it is incorporated into party activities, tends to take place with all participants fully nude. By the way, the home swimming pool is an excellent "ice breaker" for swingers inasmuch as it provides an easy justification for the swift removal of clothing in a mixed social setting. Usually the host will suggest a swim; and those of his colleagues who are anxious to get the sexual activities started will quickly commence removing their clothes. Observing this action makes it comparatively easy for all but novice swingers to similarly undress.

A minority of swinging groups practice social nudism throughout an entire party evening. In effect, they remove their clothes as soon as they walk in the door. Even among these swingers sexual activity is not likely to begin prior to 10 o'clock of a particular evening. One of the large swinging organizations I contacted and which threw large, "unstructured, non-intimate" parties at the rate of eight or ten per month, provided for quite a bit of optional party nudity. At this organization's parties some of the guests would typically remain nude throughout an entire evening. But they had to agree to remain outside of the central foyer and pool table area for as long as they had no clothes on. In other words, they and their associates with the same preference could remain nude for as long as they wished so long as certain predesignated "neutral areas" were kept free of nudity (and eroticism).

The term "ice breaking" is commonly used by swingers to refer to what goes on between the non-sexual activities of a party and the time when most or all of the guests are involved in sexual mate-sharing festivities. It is taken for granted among swingers that being able to enjoy an orgy is a key reason for taking the time and trouble to attend a particular party in the first place. Hence, in the rare cases when 10:30 has arrived and no erotic activity has as yet begun some of the guests begin to feel fidgety and uncomfortable. One of the greatly valued skills in swinging hosts and hostesses is that of knowing how to cleverly but subtly initiate the sexual fun of the evening. For swingers throwing "structured" parties this tends to be less of a problem inasmuch as their often pre-published programs specify that swinging will commence at 10:15 or 10:30 with a "daisy chain" or with a game of blindfolded "hide and seek" or "spin the bottle," etc. But for the majority of swingers who prefer more spontaneous, less structured activity, the transition period offers a special challenge to the host and hostess which veteran swingers very much enjoy.

Some of the more popular techniques for "breaking the ice" include dimming the lights, putting red or orange light bulbs in the lamps, playing romantic music on the stereo, or playing a recording of the sounds of a woman having an orgasm. A minority of swingers show erotic movies. Occasionally a host or hostess will introduce some new sex device he or she has recently found or which he or she considers to be particularly humorous. Sometimes Polaroid snapshots are brought in. Incense burners may be lit, and especially appealing perfumes may be introduced by the hostess.

However, even among some intimate swinging groups it is not particularly uncommon to find a member who is highly adept at "getting the ball rolling." Some swinging groups contain members whom some people might regard as crude in their approach or unduly loud. Yet such members often provide a highly appreciated service for their fellows at swinging get-togethers. One woman who enjoys the nickname "Penis Envy" among her swinging friends told me that after a certain amount of time she "just can't help unzipping some man's fly if things appear to be dragging too much." She doesn't care what time it is or whether the man she selects is in the midst of enjoying a tasty snack. If she feels the urge, she has the type of personality (and reputation among her friends) that permits her to give in to it. Outside of swinging circles this type of person would be considered highly deviant. But in the swinging community and social (party) context, her behavior is tolerated, accepted, and by some people it is even appreciated.

The Sexual Mate-Sharing Festivities

Much more than merely sexual intercourse and related foreplay goes on at most swinging parties. Only a small minority of the most highly structured parties restrict the range of sexual activities in which their participants may participate. And even among this small group of parties it is not unusual for the participants to engage in non-coital sexual activities, especially if "closed" as opposed to "open" swinging is featured. Behind closed doors only the people directly involved in a sexual activity know what is going on with themselves and their partner or partners.

The female swingers of this study averaged 4.5 orgasms per party, 2.3 of which were experienced through regular sexual intercourse and its attendant foreplay and afterplay activities. The husbands averaged only 1.8 coital orgasms per swinging get-together; their total number of orgasms per party averaged just 2.8. The orgasmic capacity of men being far more limited than that of women accounts for the orgasmic differential, and it also accounts for why wives often become more enthusiastic than their husbands about involvement in swinging parties. Unless the deeply internalized value system of a woman impedes her from moving to the "enthusiasm" stage (see Chapter 9), she will typically experience more party orgasms than her husband. And since she is ordinarily the marriage partner who assumes the larger part of the responsibility for preparing and serving the attractive snacks (and for deciding who is to be invited) she can also look forward to being the main recipient of praise for the successful way in which her party was managed and run.

Generally speaking, the husbands who come to enjoy swinging parties the most over long periods of time are those who (1) tremendously enjoy, and (2) are highly competent at arousing women sexually. Oral-genital ("French") sex-play and a wide variety of manual massaging and stimulating techniques consume the large majority of that quantity of party time which is given over to sexual activities. And while most of the sexual activities involve people functioning as couples, many group sexual activities almost always occur at swinging parties. Almost all swinging groups, small or large, "structured" or "unstructured," sooner or later encourage all of their members to take part in these group sexual activities. Individuals or couples who act reserved about this are often perceived as having "too many hangups"; they are usually among the less popular swingers.

Even within swinging circles women have a considerably slower initial arousal time than men do. Since swingers pride themselves on their sexual competence and knowledge, very few of them would even dream of commencing their party erotic activity with coital behavior. Almost all of the swinging husbands like to brag about how long they can postpone their own initial party orgasm and ejaculation. In fact, this is one of the many items about which there is considerable competition among swinging husbands. Usually the goal is to give their first sex partner at a party *at least one* orgasm before they themselves engage in any coital activity. Frequently they will even decline fellatio during this period, although very brief periods of fellatio may be experienced during the initial stages of sex play with a female partner. Some of the husbands, particularly those in their later thirties and older, try to give their initial partner two orgasms before they begin to move toward orgasm themselves. Again, this is done mainly through a variety of techniques of cunnilingus (mouth-genital caresses on the woman) and manual massage. Shortly after the women has had her initial party orgasm (or during the time she is having her second) he will usually commence penile entry.

When a man has not yet had his first orgasm with a female partner who has already completed her second orgasm (with him), he may be "petered out." In effect, she may be his second or third partner of the evening. This problem is usually handled by the woman then turning her full attention to pleasuring the man. She will usually do this by fellating him over a prolonged period of time and also through various techniques of manual massage. Occasionally an electric massaging device may be brought in, although massaging devices, vibrators, and other sex gadgets are normally reserved for the end of an evening, if and when they are used at all.

To be sure, swinging husbands would have to be considered unusually sexually active for their ages. This is particularly so for those who are forty and over. But a good deal of medical research has indicated that the frequent use of *any* organ or human capacity *strengthens* that organ or human capacity. In essence, it is very probable that most forty-year-old Americans could easily equal the swinging man's frequency if they had some reason for wanting to do so. They would not be able to accomplish this overnight, however. It might require several months, just as several months' effort in a gymnasium might be required to strengthen a particular arm muscle or to lose a certain number of pounds. But by gradually making an effort to increase sexual frequency and competence virtually any man or woman can probably experience sex a good deal more often than they are experiencing it at the moment.

Under the relatively uncommon (in California) conditions of "closed" swinging, each party liaison is usually given between forty-five minutes and an hour. Most swingers usually allow their own spontaneous feelings and desires to determine how much time they stay with a particular partner. In any case, once sex with a particular person has been concluded the couple will head for the living room or to what I labeled the "neutral" area. Usually one of the partners will say something like "let's go see what Mack and Elsie are doing," or "hey, it sounds like they are really having fun in the next room; let's go see what they are doing." At this point the liaison may break up or they may go on together to join some type of group sexual activity that may involve several couples.

Group sexual activities usually involve a great deal of massaging. Of course, all participants are nude, so there is a great deal of visual stimulation. In the United States men tend to be a great deal more "visual" than women. But among swingers there tends to be considerably less difference between the sexes in this regard. Swinging women, either because of their different inborn sexual constitution and/or because of their learning experiences, demonstrate as much of an ability to become "turned on" by visual stimuli as men do.

Group sexual activity is not an invariable component of all swinging parties. But according to my own research data it *is* a typical component. Group sex may involve anywhere from three to twenty or more people, all climbing all over each other and massaging each other in a wide variety of ways. Group sexual activity also involves cunnilingus and fellatio, and occasionally one or two of the participants in such group sex orgies will become involved in penile-vaginal sex; although this is not usual, there are rarely any norms against it. In cases where only three people are involved in a group sex encounter, at least two of those people will invariably be women. Group sexual activities involving a plurality of men are almost unknown in swinging circles.

Swinging groups very seldom have any formal norms against male homosexual behavior. But regardless of that fact *male* homosexual activity virtually never occurs among swingers. This is interesting because at least half of all swingers operate under the premise that human beings are basically "bisexual." And most swinging wives do participate in a substantial amount of lesbian behavior at their swinging parties. Fully 68 percent of the swinging wives interviewed for this study indicated that they participate in lesbian activity at least occasionally, and 92 percent indicated that lesbian activity does occur at their parties, and with some regularity.

As a rule lesbian sexual behavior does not normally commence until the later part of a swinging evening—usually around 1:00 A.M. or thereabout. It occurs after most of the husbands appear to have "petered out" and lost their enthusiasm for further sexual activity. Lesbian activity is greatly enjoyed by most of the wives who engage in it, and it does tend to occur in "open" or public areas of the house. It almost invariably draws an audience of husbands who flock to watch it. Observing group sex among a group of women is a strong sexual stimulus for almost all men, and even those who had already enjoyed two or three party orgasms and ejaculations will invariably gain back some of their erotic desire as a result of witnessing lesbian activity for a half-hour or more.

Most of the swinging wives admitted that "turning their husbands back on" is indeed a conscious motive for becoming involved in lesbian group sex activity. But as far as *most* wives are concerned it is very definitely a *minor* motive. Several of the wives accused me of being a "male chauvinist pig" for even so much as suggesting that they make love to each other primarily in order to provide a sexual stimulus for their husbands! Thus, it seems quite clear that the major motive for lesbian activity at swinging parties is *enjoyment*. Swinging women very much enjoy this activity for what it provides them, although few of the women seem to have arrived at the point at which a swinging evening would be incomplete for them without lesbian activity. But a few of them (i.e., 6 percent) did indicate that "only a woman can really understand another woman and what pleases her sexually." This small group did not enjoy the free and easy husband-wife communication that the large majority of the swingers enjoyed. And their husbands, by their own admission, were less competent than the majority of swinging husbands at the art of pleasing women sexually.

Of those who do engage in lesbian activity at parties, 15 percent indicated that they enjoy such activity at least somewhat better than they enjoy sexual activity with a man. And an additional 20 percent said that they enjoy it equally as much as they enjoy sexual activity with men. Only 2 percent of the women who engage in lesbian activity at parties do so despite the fact that they do not enjoy it. The majority of the women interviewed who engage in party lesbian activity (i.e., 63 percent) indicated that they definitely enjoy lesbian sex play, but not as much as sexual activity with a man.

Most of the lesbian sex play that occurs at parties occurs in groups of three or four or more women. Only very rarely do women at parties break up into couples for sexual activity. Mouth-genital caressing as well as various kinds of manual massaging are the main activities engaged in. Women also use vibrators and battery operated dildos with each other a very great deal. The usual practice is for each woman in a group to have her turn at being pleasured by all the other women in the group simultaneously. Occasionally a person will pleasure someone else at the same time that she is being pleasured. But this practice is less common because most women find it difficult to savor the sexual pleasure while they are trying to concentrate on "giving it" to someone else. The same applies, by the way, to male-female sexual contacts, whether they occur in groups of three or more people or in couples. In essence, the usual procedure is for one person at a time to "do the work" on another person. Each person takes his or her turn and tries to deliver as much as he or she can, or at least as much as he or she has received from the other person or persons involved.

In recent years an increasing amount of scientific data have become available on lesbian activity. One of the key points to come out of this research is that involvement in homosexual activity (whether it is male or female) does *not* constitute an indication of homosexuality, although men who voluntarily engage in homosexual activity outside of a sex-segregated prison environment are much more likely to be true homosexuals than women who freely engage in lesbian sex play outside of prison are likely to be true lesbians. Generally speaking, in order for a person to be a true homosexual or lesbian *two* factors must be present: (1) the person must *prefer* sexual activity with a person of his or her own sex to sexual activity with a person of the opposite sex; and (2) the person's self-definition (self-image) must be that of a homosexual (lesbian). In effect, if a person does not agree that he or she is a homosexual (lesbian), then he or she cannot correctly be considered as such. None of the respondents interviewed for this study could be considered a male or female homosexual.

One of the most fascinating facts about lesbian activity (as opposed to lesbianism) to become available in recent years is that the more *heterosexual* coitus a girl experiences and enjoys, the more likely she is to become involved in *at least some* lesbian sexual activity. Women who experience many premarital orgasms either through masturbation and/or through boy-girl sexual intercourse are far more likely to experience some lesbian activity during their adulthood than women who enter marriage sexually inexperienced or who do not enjoy any form of sexual stimulation very much. It appears that for women (but not men) the more a person both experiences and enjoys sex the more she is prone to experiment with many different forms of sexual stimulation and the more likely she is to try out lesbian sex play. Yet we see in the current study of swingers that frequent enjoyment of lesbian activity does not serve to discourage women from frequent sexual intercourse with their husbands and other men or from wanting to continue living with their husbands and caring for their children.

After a group of wives has completed a lesbian sex play session it is not at all unusual for some of the husbands to commence sexual advances again. In fact, during the time that the women are playing with each other sexually it is not at all uncommon for a husband to try to join in and begin petting a woman whose body appeals to him. Thus, lesbian sessions very often become heterosexual group orgies after a certain amount of time has passed—usually thirty-five or forty minutes or more. The wives never try to stop the husbands from joining in, even though most of them stalwartly insist that they become involved in lesbian activity because they enjoy engaging in sexual activity with the other wives and not in order to sexually reinterest and rearouse their "petered out" husbands. (However, some of the wives believe that their husbands often learn how to be more effective lovers through watching women engaged in lesbian sex play.)

Some of the most fascinating scenes at swinging get-togethers take place in the living rooms of "unstructured, non-intimate" parties. After the sexual festivities have gotten underway it is not at all unusual to find people in the same large room engaging in a wide variety of markedly disparate activities. Some people may still be nibbling on food and chatting with each other, some may be playing cards, different couples will be engaging in sexual intercourse or oral-genital sex in various corners of the room or behind furniture, some might be dancing to music, and some might be engaged in exercises of group massage. Some of the people will be nude, others might be in various stages of undress, and some might still be fully clothed. Few of the participants during the early stages of an evening's sexual activity are likely to assume a passive, voyeuristic role, although one or two people may be doing this. Men are more likely than women to be cast in the voyeur role; in order to appear inconspicuous they are likely to hold a drink in their hands and stand watching and talking with or alongside of someone else in a similar situation. At the large "unstructured, non-intimate" type of party men are expected to assume the assertive role with women. And as in any large group of people not all on hand are likely to be equally competitive or equally adept at doing this. Novice women and their husbands at the larger parties are similarly likely to require a greater amount of time than most guests in terms of becoming involved in sexual activity. Such couples are not required to take any action; if they wish they are perfectly free to remain sexually uninvolved all evening long, although there is bound to be a certain amount of psychological discomfort in remaining passively uninvolved over long periods of time.

Even so, some journalists as well as some social science scholars have studied the swinging party scene (usually the large "unstructured, non-intimate" type of party) by attending, through invitation, several such parties. They have attended with their wives and have presented themselves as novice swingers or as people very interested in the possibility of becoming swingers.

Not all swingers feel comfortable about engaging in sex out in the open in front of everyone. Still others feel quite free about joining or being joined by another couple or couples for a group sex experience, but they do not wish to be observed by anyone else on the scene or by anyone with whom they are not already very good friends. Not all such people confine themselves to the "intimate" type of party. Many relatively "private" (for swingers) people actually prefer attending the "non-intimate" sort of party; but they want to be able to do their thing "behind closed doors" and away from any possibility of being observed by others. Yet many such people feel uncomfortable in the small, "intimate" type of party setting that invariably takes place among close friends in a private home or apartment. Thus, even though they are swingers themselves, they do not want to have any swingers amid their circle of "best" or "closest friends."

It was partly in order to deal with the demands of such people that commercial clubs for swingers began to emerge during the early 1970s. Two such private commercial clubs operating in the San Fernando Valley suburbs of Los Angeles hold their twice-weekly parties in large mansions which they either rent or own for that purpose. As might be imagined, the membership dues for some of these organizations tend to be quite substantial. One such club charges $500 per year per couple and another charges $300 plus $20 per party per couple. But such organizations provide a means through which novice swingers can meet others of like mind and socioeconomic background. (Novice couples are permitted to attend two or three times without being required to pay the membership fee.) In addition, they provide a means by which swingers preferring a "non-intimate" type of party atmosphere can have it and still swing in total privacy without having to worry about being observed in sexual activity by anyone.

One such club spent many thousands of dollars in order to divide their party mansion into a large number of rooms of widely varying sizes and shapes. They call these rooms "caverns," and some of them are so small as to only be accessible by crawling on hands and knees through narrow hallways. Shoes must be removed.

Some of the "caverns" are large enough to accommodate twenty or more people while others can accommodate only two people; and even then their bodies are likely to touch the floor and the ceiling at the same time. Each "cavern," whether large or small, is carpeted with lush, very soft, spongy carpets. The objective was to make the "feel" of the carpets as soft and sensuous as possible. In some of the cavern rooms mattresses are provided; in others, there are soft sleeping bags; and in some cavern rooms tiger or leopard skins are provided. Some of the rooms contain nothing but the soft, lush carpeting.

A few of the smaller cavern rooms had mirrors on the ceiling and walls. However, the rooms with mirrors were in most cases large enough to accommodate two or three couples. But these rooms could be and often were used by two people alone. Each couple in attendance at the mansion had to find their own cavern room; no one was ever assigned to any person or room. Several of the largest rooms of the mansion also had mirrors attached to the ceilings and walls. And various colored lights and incense burners were also available in most of the cavern rooms. But lights throughout the mansion were adjusted so as to remain relatively dim at all times.

In addition, a large public area was provided. Here participants were expected to be fully clothed at all times—an expectation rarely found at swinging parties held in private homes. The public area contained the only entrance. In addition, it also contained billiard tables, bridge tables, a swimming pool, buffet tables with food and drink, lush furniture, etc. According to the manager of this club the police had arrived on a number of occasions to investigate the large number of cars parked in the environs. They had always behaved quite courteously and in every case left without incident and without making anything of their suspicions as to what might have been going on in the huge non-public sector of the mansion.

Norms and Expectations

Swinging groups vary somewhat in terms of the normative expectations they maintain. But most groups insist that everyone has a right to turn down any particular sexual invitation. In effect, a woman can say "thanks but no thanks" to any man, and she does not need to offer any reason.

At some of the larger swinging parties couples are permitted to remain sexually inactive all evening long if they wish. Novice couples may decide not to become sexually involved at a particular party. Similarly, menstruating wives may prefer not to swing on a particular occasion; but because they tremendously enjoy the atmosphere and the company they attend the party. And, of course, their husbands are perfectly free to engage in all the sex they might desire with the other wives who are there.

By the same token, it is *not* usually contranormative for menstruating wives to fully involve themselves in all sexual activities, and many of them do just that. Rubber pads are often used in cases where it is deemed appropriate. In addition, a menstruating woman may elect to achieve her party orgasms exclusively through non-coital means. She may, for example, depend exclusively upon hand-genital or mouth-genital stimulation. No man may force her into having sexual intercourse if she does not wish to do so. On the other hand, many men find it quite satisfying to stimulate a woman to a non-coital orgasm, particularly if they themselves have already had at least one orgasm with another woman.

At the smaller, more intimate parties, on the other hand, the set of expectations is somewhat different. First of all, with the exception of any novice couple who might have been invited, everyone on hand will be a good friend of everyone else. It is thus taken for granted that acceptance of an invitation to attend a small, intimate party among close friends presupposes a willingness and a desire to "swing," although true "swinging" can occasionally entail only oral-genital and hand-genital eroticism. In a two, three, or four couple situation, for example, it would be ludicrous for someone to be in attendance with the specific intention of declining all sexual invitations for any and all kinds of erotic play. In an "intimate" setting such a person would not be likely to remain a good friend for very long.

But there are other less "intimate" kinds of invitations the acceptance of which also presupposes a willingness to participate and to "play the game" according to direction. The "*structured*, non-intimate" type of party is an important case in point. At such parties a range of sexual and erotic play activities is usually scheduled according to a fairly rigid set of rules. Everyone is expected to have arrived by a certain hour and to assume the specific roles that are assigned to him or her at specific time intervals. For example, at 10:00 P.M. some hand-genital erotic play may be scheduled, and if woman *A* is told to join husband *J* for this activity she must be willing to do so. From 11:00 until 11:45 a copulation session may be scheduled, and woman *C* must be willing to go off with whatever husband draws her straw or "spins the bottle" in her direction. This high degree of structure helps many people, draws them out of their shell and ensures that everyone will participate equally. But most swinging personalities are not at all comfortable with this structured system and they will avoid invitations to swinging parties that are earmarked to operate in this highly organized, structured fashion.

By the same token, the host and hostess in charge of operating a structured party will almost always exercise considerable care in terms of whom they invite. The "intimate, structured" party is always highly predictable because it involves pretty much the same group of guests every time. Such people are likely to have been close friends over a long period. But in the case of the "non-intimate, structured" party which may contain ten or more couples, each prospective guest wants to feel assured that only his or her kind of *attractive* people will be invited. Couples who take chances and invite a couple without being confident beforehand that they will "fit in" usually lose their popularity fairly quickly as swinging hosts of structured parties.

To be sure, those operating "unstructured, non-intimate" parties also exercise considerable care as to who enters their doors. But less care is necessary in the large, "unstructured" setting. This is because membership fees are often charged and couples will ordinarily not be accorded membership unless they appear to have good, solid marriages. In this regard, only 27 percent of the couples interviewed told me that they *might* under certain circumstances be willing to swing with a couple that was not happily married. Everyone else indicated that their sexual partners must have happy marriages.

Another widespread rule in swinging circles specifies that swingers must confine their extramarital sexual behavior to sexual mate-sharing get-togethers. In other words, they must never see fellow swingers for sexual reasons outside the context of a party situation. And they must not have extramarital sexual intercourse with someone who is not himself or herself a swinger. A major purpose of this second rule is simply to protect swingers against the possibility of contracting and spreading venereal diseases. This norm seems to be obeyed by swingers in that none of the husbands and wives interviewed for this study had ever contracted any form of venereal disease.

Obedience to the first norm—i.e., confining extramarital sex to swinging get-togethers—was far from complete. Fully 47 percent of the swinging husbands and 43 percent of their wives had had sexual intercourse *with fellow swingers outside* the context of the swinging party situation. However, almost two-thirds of these people had "open marriage" understandings with their spouses. In other words, the husbands and wives had agreed with each other beforehand that each would be free to have sex with whatever fellow swinger each wanted to have it with and whenever they might want to have it. Inasmuch as such understandings violate the norms of most swinging clubs and groups, these couples kept their "open marriage" agreements to themselves; they did not talk about them within the context of any of the swinging get-togethers they attended.

The large majority of the couples with such understandings were "recreational" swingers. Only four of the "interpersonal" swinging spouses admitted to ever having had any extramarital sex outside of the sexual mate sharing context since they had first become swingers. These four people represented two couples, both of which had arrived at "open marriage" understandings.

Up to now much of the popular literature on swinging has suggested that a major advantage of sexual mate sharing is that it insures against that brand of extramarital sex which *is* indicative of "infidelity." However, at least 17 percent of the swinging couples I interviewed had been involved in what would have to be considered "unfaithful" adultery after they had become swingers. Such involvement did not appear to have harmed their marriages in any noticeable way. But the fact that *at least* 17 percent of the swingers had been involved in it does make clear that becoming a swinger does *not* assuredly negate the future possibility of conventional adultery ("infidelity").

As might be expected, all swingers are sworn to confidentiality in regard to such matters as whom they might have met at swinging parties, sexual preferences, personal idiosyncrasies of their fellows, the sexual behavior of swingers' teenaged children, etc. This norm is evidently very seldom violated, as none of the people whom I interviewed knew of any violations of the confidentiality norm.

Most swinging groups and organizations also have norms against teasing or making fun of people with erection failures, unattractive bodies, etc. People with persistent problems of a type that disrupt or interfere with the activities at swinging parties are simply not invited back again. Erection problems tend to be defined by swingers as "'temporary" and as invariably surmountable. Hand-genital and mouth-genital techniques are prescribed by and for group members any time erection failures occur, and such ancillary techniques appear to be very much a part of the swingers' ideology. Therefore, people who tease tend to be viewed by most sexual mate sharers as "gross," "discourteous," and "uncultured in the ways of swinging." People who engage in such behavior tend to swiftly develop bad reputations.

On the other hand, it is not considered a violation of good decorum to politely advise party participants that they need a breath deodorant or some similar item. The bylaws of two of the groups I studied specifically pointed out that members should never feel hurt as a result of being asked to spray their mouths, because failures of mouth deodorants or of body deodorants are to be expected at swinging parties and that "such failures are human and perfectly natural."

By the same token, swingers are expected to keep their bodies clean and sweet smelling both before and during all sexual mate sharing festivities. The bathroom is the busiest room of the house at virtually all swinging parties, and both women and men are quite likely to go there after or even during each sexual liaison. Many swingers have built sinks, bidets, and showers in their basements in order to accommodate many people and in order to compete with similar amenities offered by their fellow swingers. Many swinging party liaisons shower together as part of their erotic fun.

In addition to keeping their bodies immaculate, swingers are also expected to keep their homes as clean as possible. Carpets and rugs, in particular, must be kept immaculate because many sexual activities occur on the floors. In addition, clean sheets must be placed on all the beds, and any large sofas must be kept as clean and sweet smelling as possible.

One of the things which many people find particularly exciting about their involvement in swinging is the fact that they never know who they are going to meet at some of the larger, "unstructured, non-intimate" parties. Several of the men and women interviewed told me of having met major state and local political officials at some of the parties. Twelve of the couples spoke about having swung with recognizable television and motion picture stars. None of the couples indicated that meeting well-known people was a regular thing at swinging parties. But at least a small handful of Los Angeles area swinging couples seem to meet well-known people at approximately every tenth or eleventh *large* swinging party they attend.

Many swinging groups also encourage their members to confine as much as possible of their business to fellow swingers. Before "abortion on request" became legally available in 1973, swingers had little if any difficulty in getting their abortion needs taken care of through enlisting the services of their sexual mate-sharing doctor friends. Attorneys, real estate brokers and salespeople similarly find much of their business confined to fellow swingers, as do dentists, stock brokers, and a wide variety of other business functionaries.

Another norm which swingers take quite seriously has to do with noise. In the case of small parties this is not an issue. But in the case of the larger get-togethers it is a cause for some concern. Even the largest swinging parties tend to be surprisingly quiet. There is no shouting, swearing, or disorderly conduct. When it appears that some person or group is making too much noise, either the host or someone else will come over and express concern about it. Most of the time when the noise level does become excessive it is because someone has the stereo on too loudly. The main concern here is that someone on the outside who harbors intolerant attitudes toward sex orgies might come to investigate the noise and learn what is really going on inside the house. Interestingly, the large bulk of party noise occurs *before* the sexual festivities begin to get under way. But the transition time (between non-sexual and sexual activities) can also entail some noise, and during this period the concern of the host couple and of other dedicated couples present tends to be heightened.

None of the couples interviewed had ever had their party activities interrupted because of noise. But the possibility that noise could attract the wrong people was a source of some concern to many of the couples who frequently attend the larger swinging parties.

Of much greater concern than noise per se is the parking situation at some of the parties. A large number of cars parked in a suburban, residential neighborhood tends to attract the police. It also tends to entail a type of noise that is often disturbing to other residents in the neighborhood. When people start the engines of their automobiles between 2:00 and 4:00 A.M., and when this happens with some degree of frequency and regularity, some people become suspicious and curious as to what may be going on. One large San Fernando Valley club had to move their party facilities out of a mansion located in a plush residential neighborhood because they were convicted of violating "zoning laws." The noise of people going home at the end of a party (and the parties had been held by this club about eight times per month) caused several neighborhood residents to investigate and to complain. Upon learning that the mansion was owned by a commercial sexual mate-sharing organization their dedication to finding some legal means to expunge them from the neighborhood was strengthened. After over one year of legal maneuvering, having been unable to convict them of violating anything else, the club was finally forced out of the neighborhood on the grounds of a "zoning law" violation.

Since that time most of the larger swinging clubs and organizations have worked out ways of avoiding (1) the problem of having many cars parked in a residential neighborhood, and (2) the noise and disturbance of many people turning their engines and headlights on between two and four in the morning in order to go home. Specifically, arrangements are now made to have people park their cars in one or two (and sometimes as many as three) nearby shopping center parking lots. Upon parking they are instructed to wait until an assigned time when the host or hostess will drop by to pick them up. Between 8:00 and 10:00 P.M. many hosts of larger parties now make several such trips to pick up their swinging guests. This procedure has imposed quite a bit of inconvenience on swinging couples, but no one who follows this procedure has ever had his doorbell rung during a party by a police officer. Similarly, no one following this procedure has ever been accused of violating "zoning laws" or any other kind of law. (Parenthetically, couples holding swinging parties in *their own* private dwellings could not be legally convicted in California of violating "zoning laws." However, if their parties are held in a house or mansion rented by a commercial organization specifically for the purpose of sexual mate exchange they can be legally convicted of violating zoning laws.)

The inconvenience tends to be somewhat greater when people are ready to go home. Usually the host will shuttle the first group back to the parking areas at about 2:30. But the last couples may not be ready to leave before 4:00 or 4:30 A.M. To an increasing extent now the services of a professional chauffeur are being used so that the host and hostess or club managers do not need to devote their time to the shuttling of their guests. In any case, the shuttling procedure commonly entails a number of steps designed to keep noise to a minimum: (1) the car is started while the garage door is still closed; (2) headlights remain off until the car has been driven out of the neighborhood; (3) no car radios are used; and (4) conversation is restricted to inside the house and inside the car. In addition, car windows are kept closed until the car is outside of the neighborhood.

Again, it should be stressed that this procedure is needed and used only when a large party involving more than eight couples is held. And even then it tends to be used only by those couples and club managers who hold such large parties in the same residential location with considerable frequency and regularity.

Eighteen percent of the couples interviewed had quiet alarm systems in their homes or swinging locations. These could be deployed in the event that a police officer or some other stranger came to the door at a time when sexual festivities were in progress. All of these couples were partial to the large, "non-intimate" type of party setting; none of the couples who usually hold small parties owned such systems. The most commonly used quiet alarm system caused the lights to blink on and off about five times. In another case the alarm caused the lights to go out for ten seconds, and then go back on again. All such alarm systems could be easily triggered by pressing an inconspicuous switch located near the front door.

Cameras and tape recorders are almost never permitted at swinging parties. Swingers believe in savoring the "eternal now" for all that it is worth. Cameras and recording devices are viewed as interfering with this. In addition, there are obvious security reasons why such items are not used at parties; these need not be recounted here.

Pictorial pornography similarly sees very little use in swinging circles. At the larger parties 8 mm. or 16 mm. erotic films are sometimes used by some of the guests as ice breakers. But at any type of swinging party their use is far from regular. Hard-core pictorial pornographic magazines are almost never used by swingers. These facts may seem somewhat strange to some readers inasmuch as pornography pertinent to sexual mate exchange had been a major factor in precipitating their initial interest and involvement in this activity (see Chapter 8). But the literature that had aroused their initial interest and awareness of swinging had been primarily *non*-pictorial in nature. As a group, swingers purchase very little pornography. They have the inner resources to be able to live out their sexual fantasies directly rather than vicariously.

Normative expectations pertinent to birth control and contraception assume a prominent place in swinging circles. However, most swingers tend to trust those among their fellows whom they know well. Swingers very seldom subject each other to any kind of cross-examination about the contraceptive precautions they have taken.

In general, husbands over 40 and husbands whose wives had already given birth to two or three children are likely to have had vasectomies. Vasectomy is a very common topic of conversation in swinging circles. Virtually everyone has a strong opinion about it, although not all of these opinions are positive. Worry about possible interference with the sex drive or with sexual competence tends to be a more widespread concern among swinging men than worry about the possibility of eventually wanting to have additional children after a vasectomy has been performed. Of the husbands of this study who had had a vasectomy none had any complaints about sex drive or performance. But some of them knew of men either inside or outside of swinging circles who had subjectively perceived themselves as having been harmed as a result of vasectomy.

Several of the younger couples I interviewed practiced the "method of frequent ejaculation" (see Chapter 12) and used vaginal foams as a supplement. In addition, many of the women were on the pill, and some of them had an intrauterine device. The diaphragm and jelly also turned out to be more popular than I had expected, and even ordinary condoms were occasionally used by some of the husbands—although only two of them depended on condoms for regular use.

Bearing in mind that many of the couples depended upon various forms of birth control and contraception, the following list will give the reader some idea as to the methods each couple depended upon the majority of the time:

Vasectomy .... 34 percent
The Pill ....23 percent
Diaphragm and Jelly .... 13 percent
Method of Frequent Ejaculation
   & Foam .... 12 percent
Intrauterine Device .... 7 percent
Vaginal Foams .... 5 percent
Hysterectomy .... 4 percent
Condoms .... 2 percent

While contraceptive counseling and help is readily available to all swingers who want it, each swinging couple is deemed fully responsible for contraception. Because the swingers fully accept their sexual behavior as morally right for themselves, they feel no apprehension about talking about contraceptives and birth control with their legal spouses as well as with fellow swingers. Indeed, they discuss contraception as readily, easily and serenely as they discuss with their various sexual partners what pleases them sexually.

But despite their contraceptive care, 13 percent of the swinging wives had had at least one abortion since the time they first began swinging, and 21 percent had had at least one abortion in their lives. Among the *non*-swinging wives 12 percent had had at least one abortion in their lives. Only one non-swinging wife had had two abortions, but 10 percent of the swinging wives had had two or more abortions in their lives. Almost all of the swingers viewed abortion as an excellent backstop to contraceptive failure, and none of those who had had an abortion indicated feeling any guilt as a result of the experience. Indeed, most of the wives who had had an abortion blamed unnecessary social programming for any guilt which some women might suffer as a result of having an abortion. Several of them also cited their metaphysical religious beliefs (see Chapter 6) as further helping to prevent the possibility of any guilt reactions developing.

Norms against excessive use of alcohol and against the use of physical and verbal violence have already been commented upon at some length. All swinging groups have such norms, and all couples active in swinging tend to be quite mindful of them. Popular couples will very often take it upon themselves to courteously warn any of their fellows who seem to have imbibed too much wine or other alcohol, or who seem to be too loud or agitated or likely to move toward verbal or physical aggression. Among close friends (or when close friends are present at a large party) these friendly warnings always seem to be sufficient to bring a person into line. At larger gatherings they do not always work. When they fail to bring about the desired effect the person and his spouse is usually taken out by the host and driven home or placed in a nearby motel room. Serious or persistent violators of the norms of good taste and decorum are simply not invited to future parties. But violations tend to be few in number and the large majority of them are disposed of easily and with a minimum of embarrassment to everyone concerned.

Finally, the swingers have a good many informal normative understandings among each other as to what kind of person would or would not be a suitable guest at a swinging gathering. Major norms such as those against inviting singles, call girls, etc., have already been covered. But beyond this swingers, like most people in our society, want to have a good time and let down their hair with people who are like themselves in most ways. They want to swing with people who are equally as well educated, aware and culturally sophisticated as they are, and who own homes that are at least on an equal par with the homes of other couples in their group. In essence, they want to be with people who are "just like us" in as many respects pertinent to socioeconomic status, life style, social skills and personality as possible.

Of course, swingers are much more tolerant and liberal than most middle-class suburban Americans. And fully 82 percent of them told me that they would have no objections to swinging with a black couple. But it is interesting as well as significant that none of those interviewed had ever actually swung with a black person or with a member of any other racial minority group. Perhaps at some time in the future they will have the opportunity to have their "liberality" tested in regard to this matter.

Competence and Performance

Swingers love swinging and most of them will go to a considerable amount of trouble in order to practice it with a good deal of regularity. But as any sexually experienced person knows, sex is not all fun. It is also *work*. It requires dedicated effort and commitment to bring a woman to one or more orgasms, and to truly satisfy her. Similarly, it requires dedication and effort on the part of a woman for her to be able to consistently throw truly successful and enjoyable parties, and for her to be able to remain attractive to men as well as capable of sexually pleasing them.

However, on the basis of the hundreds of hours I devoted to interviewing the swinging couples I was left with the impression that swinging parties are almost always more demanding of husbands than they are of wives. And as a group the husbands to a greater extent than the wives would be happy with a slightly reduced frequency of attendance at swinging parties. As I pointed out in Chapter

9, it is not easy to convince most women to become involved in swinging; but most of those who can be successfully convinced end up being more enthusiastic about it than their husbands. Perhaps this should not be considered surprising: they (1) usually experience significantly more orgasms and other sexual pleasure per party than their husbands, and (2) they do not need to work anywhere nearly as hard as the men do in order to achieve orgasms. And (3) at "unstructured, non-intimate" parties they are not expected to assume the socially assertive role in striking up liaisons with the other sex to anywhere nearly the extent that the men are expected to do this. Thus, they do not need to worry about being rejected. And (4) homosexual eroticism is usually available to them at parties whereas it is never available to husbands. Only the women accept the principle that human beings are intrinsically bisexual.

Despite the fact that they usually end up coming away with less than their wives (except at "intimate" parties where the sexual rewards are typically more evenly divided), the husbands pride themselves upon becoming maximally competent in all of the many facets of heterosexual eroticism. They compete with each other as well as with themselves, and their goal is to develop a reputation for being "one of the best" at their art, and hence one of the men most likely to be sought after at swinging parties. This competition also extends to their physique and all other aspects of their personal appearance. Women, too, compete with each other in keeping their appearance trim and attractive. But the competition in even this area seems to be more acute among husbands than among wives. Surprising though it might seem to some readers, personal warmth combined with a highly effective ability at pleasing a man sexually are far more important determinants of female popularity in swinging circles than is pulchritude.

As in any "sport," there is much comparing of notes among swingers in terms of what they did in any particular sexual encounter. During erotic interaction there is very little talk other than affirmative communications on the part of both partners as to what is particularly pleasing. But during the "in-between" times and before the sexual festivities actually get underway there is a good deal of talk about especially pleasing erotic maneuvers and sexual approaches they might have invented or would like to try on someone at the party. In effect, even among these highly experienced men and women there is quite a bit of teaching and learning as far as erotic techniques and approaches are concerned.

Women almost never experience anxiety in regard to sexual performance at parties. This is so despite the fact that swinging women probably assume a far more active, assertive role in lovemaking than do most American women. Women do not have to worry about the state of a highly visible sex organ. Regardless of whether they are assuming the active or the passive role they are in a better position to relax and enjoy the delights of the existential moment than men are.

None of the husbands interviewed for this study indicated that anxiety attacks over performance at swinging parties constituted a problem for them. But several of them did admit to frequently worrying about how they will do compared to other men on the scene. Surprisingly enough, the first sexual liaison of an evening usually arouses more worrisome feelings in men than sexual liaisons that occur later in the evening. If they should have erection failures later on in an evening they usually feel confident in the assumed validity of the excuse that they are "petered out" from all that they had done earlier. At large parties there are always a few men who can no longer bring themselves to have an erection after they had already had their first party orgasm of an evening. At smaller, more intimate parties the atmosphere tends to be less competitive and more relaxed. The men usually view smaller parties as imposing fewer demands on them, and they are thus less likely to view themselves as being in any kind of competition with their fellows. In any case, as soon as a husband learns that one or more of the other men at a party can no longer manage an erection, his own level of anxiety about performance diminishes and he often finds himself performing in his second liaison of an evening even more competently than he performed the first time around.

Another factor which served to reduce the sexual performance anxiety of many of the men was their detailed knowledge of non-coital techniques for bringing women to orgasm, some of which many of the women claimed to enjoy even better than regular sexual intercourse. As swingers and as experts on sexual technique and the art, science and competitive challenge of pleasing many different women, the husbands were highly effective at oral-genital techniques and at scores of body massage and hand-genital techniques of sexual arousal. In addition, 7 percent of the men *frequently* brought in dildos, vibrators, penis aids, petroleum jelly, and various other kinds of creams and lotions, after they found themselves no longer capable of gaining an erection. Indeed, an additional 25 percent of the husbands similarly did this on at least an occasional basis. Those who were able to bring in these aids with a humorous, joking spontaneity usually managed to remain quite undaunted by their erection failures. Corollatively, a good sense of humor was one of the attributes most frequently mentioned by the wives as being highly valued in their swinging husbands. For as long as the men could remain undaunted by various plans going wrong, the female partners could similarly remain unbothered: they could "relax and enjoy it."

Despite occasional worries about erection failures and the heavy accent upon competence and performance, almost all of the swinging husbands interviewed for this study insisted that they continued to enjoy swinging very much and that they looked forward to many more years of it. Even those men who preferred attending fewer swinging parties than their wives felt that they derived enough fun, gratification, and friendly comradeship from their involvement in swinging to make continued participation in it highly worthwhile for them.

SOME CONCLUDING THOUGHTS

I separately asked each swinging husband and wife the following question: "If you had to move away from southern California, thereby losing contact with your swinging friends, would you make a serious effort to find new swinging friends in your new location?" Only 1 percent of the swinging husbands said "no" and just 8 percent indicated that they were "uncertain." Among the wives just 5 percent said "no" and 15 percent said that they were "uncertain." In other words, in spite of any anxieties or worries about performance which their involvement in sexual mate sharing may have imposed upon them, fully 91 percent of the swinging husbands would seek out new swinging friends if they were forced to move to another geographic area. And among the wives 80 percent would similarly choose to seek out new swinging friends if they were forced to move. Figures such as these strongly suggest that most swingers derive a very substantial reward value out of their brand of recreational nonconformity, and that problems inherent in the swinging way of life tend not to be debilitating enough to be perceived as discouraging.

Corroboration for this view can be seen in the swingers' responses to the question: "At this point, would you say becoming a swinger was worth whatever difficulties it may have involved?" Only 5 percent of the swinging husbands and wives interviewed said "no."

In recent years many clinical and psychiatric writers have suggested that there is psychotherapeutic value in group nudity involving both men and women. Some have further suggested that when such coeducational nudity is combined with erotic freedom it becomes even more strongly therapeutic and that it renders even very withdrawn people highly sociable and outgoing, sometimes for the first time in their lives.

Sex has long been viewed as *an affirmation of life* by many of the best-known philosophers and psychologists. While none of the swingers seem to have ever been withdrawn psychologically, perhaps like their preliterate ancestors of 2,500 years ago the underlying purpose of their nonconformist recreational style is simply to celebrate and to affirm life.

A small handful of "avant-garde" psychologists have tried to scientifically test the therapeutic value of group sex. A few years ago a German psychiatrist provided for group sexual intercourse in a mental hospital where he had been employed. The late great psychiatrist (and disciple in his early years of Sigmund Freud) Wilhelm Reich similarly tried a number of experiments involving coeducational nudity and eroticism. But these and many other courageous thinkers got themselves into severe legal difficulties as a result of their unusual empirical efforts. In the Western world most people are still too fearful of the joys of sex to permit anyone to systematically investigate the potential properties that heterosexual eroticism might have for emancipating the human spirit.

Nevertheless, San Diego psychologist Paul Bindrim (1969) and southern California social worker Carolyn Symonds (1971b) have achieved an impressive amount of success with various types of nude psychotherapy. To be sure, not everyone would seek help from someone whose techniques include "nude psychotherapy." Hence, it is not possible to suggest at this point that coeducational nudity or eroticism would be of help to most people with personal problems. But for people who *are* able to accept social nudity as a therapeutic approach, its use along with the various optional techniques of erotic massage and sex play appears to have proven itself profoundly beneficial.

So perhaps the swinging party or get-together can be viewed as a kind of "psychotherapeutic encounter group" that is being run by psychiatric non-professionals for their own benefit. Generally speaking, people usually have an intuitive knowledge or "feel" as to what is truly best for themselves, and they gravitate toward those activities. When the activity is no longer perceived as beneficial they discard it. But as long as it continues to provide rewarding interaction with fellow human beings and continues to make them feel good about themselves, they remain with it. All people want to grow, and most people will eventually take whatever risks may be necessary in order to "see and feel" themselves becoming whatever they want to become. Thus, non-professional though it might be, the swinging party may be providing a kind of psychotherapy to its devotees that is rewarding and highly gratifying. And highly controversial though it may indeed be, the same might well be said for the various "love groups" for teenagers that are sponsored by some of the swinging parents (see Chapter 11).

Of the many psycho-emotional afflictions that plague man in the modern world, shyness has been about the most refractory to psychotherapeutic help. Yet this is the very affliction for which various techniques of nude psychotherapy *including* sexual intercourse may eventually prove to be most beneficial. Teenagers and young adults of high school and college age who are too shy to date or to enjoy any kind of a social life may eventually be swiftly healed of their problems by placing them into coeducational nude encounter groups with age-mates where they could be encouraged to enjoy sexual intercourse as well as a wide variety of techniques of erotic and body massage. (See the work of Philip Zimbardo, 1977, for a good coverage of the prevalence and prolonged severe social and psychological consequences of shyness here in America.)

Chapter 11

Sex and the Swingers' Children

Eighty-two percent of the swingers studied were parents. It is therefore evident that being a swinger does not in and of itself militate against the having of children. Most swingers do have children and feel that they would have been quite uncomfortable and disappointed with themselves and life if they had not been able to have any. Among the non-swinging couples 88 percent were parents.

Up to now no one has had anything much to say about the children in swinging families and about how they are reared. And yet, when I give lectures on swingers and their sexual spouse-sharing activities I usually receive more questions from the audience about the children of swingers than about almost any other topic. People are curious about how swingers manage to integrate their deviant recreation with their child-rearing responsibilities. For this reason I devoted quite a bit of my research time and attention to this topic. This chapter will deal with the approaches swingers use for integrating their parenting roles with their nonconformist sexual life styles. Chapter 13 will focus upon techniques and philosophies of child-rearing among swingers.

At the outset it is important that the reader be reminded that *only half* of the teenaged young people interviewed for this study were the offspring of the original 100 swinging couples. Because I wanted a more complete picture of the personal and sexual lives of these youngsters it was necessary for me to interview an additional 24 swinging families, all of which had teenaged children, and some of which also had children in older and/or younger age groups. These additional swinging families were very similar to the 100 swinging families upon which the bulk of this research focused.

Should the Children Know?

I asked the swinging couples whether they expected to ever advise their children about their spouse-sharing recreation. Among the couples with children 81 percent indicated that they would so advise them. But what was really surprising was the fact that 65 percent of these couples indicated that their children *already* knew. One couple in their mid-twenties went so far as to assert that their two-year-old daughter already knew "that her mommy and daddy enjoy making love to a lot of different people," and that they believed that this made them capable of loving her even more strongly than they otherwise would. This couple along with five other couples interviewed allowed their pre-school toddlers to roam about the house freely while open sexual activities were going on. All of these couples ran comparatively small parties with seldom more than four couples present. All of the participants would be nude throughout much of their parties and any children present would be likewise. These couples were all just getting started in their careers and did not have much money available for baby sitters. Often they would cope with this problem by simply "bringing their children along." One young woman commented that at first she felt somewhat guilty and uneasy about this. But after the end of the second sex party with her four-year-old son along she claimed that all feelings of guilt that she might be an "inadequate" mother seemed to leave her. She and her 26-year-old husband stalwartly maintained that their little son was getting the best possible sex education and that he seemed to them to be the happiest and best-adjusted little boy in their neighborhood.

In short, while bringing the children along often started out as an economic necessity for many of these young couples, within a few weeks a self-justifying ideology developed within their minds. This ideology often led them to bring their children along even after baby sitting services became readily available.

However, swingers are not all cut out of the same mold, and a small percentage of them go to the other extreme. Nineteen percent of the swinging couples believed that they would never tell their children about their deviant recreation. In three of these cases the children were already over 18 years of age and living away from home. But apart from their children's ages, fully 14 percent of the couples told me that they would be significantly disturbed and very upset if their children did somehow find out.

Because this research involved the detailed study of only 100 swinging couples, caution must be exercised in the making of generalizations. But it does seem safe to conclude that these more conservative swingers tend to be both older and less experienced in the world of comarital sex. In this study all of them were at least 42 years of age or older, and none of them had been involved in the swinging movement for more than 18 months. Nevertheless, most of the swinging couples interviewed did know of at least one husband and wife in the swinging movement who continued to harbor quite conventional child-rearing attitudes and values, and some of these people were believed to be still in their early thirties. Female swingers were more likely than their husbands to cling to conventional views on how children should be reared. But wives as well as husbands tended to undergo a transformation of attitude if they had been involved in the swinging world for more than three or four years. This was particularly true for those who had also engaged in many non-sexual forms of recreation with their swinging colleagues.

Perhaps the most crucial test of the degree and extent to which these couples had managed to fully integrate their sexual life style into their framework of values is whether or nor they could register agreement with this simple statement: "I would be quite happy about it if my own children became swingers when they grow up." Only 15 percent of the swinging couples with children indicated "no" to this statement and another 12 percent were "uncertain." On the other hand, fully 54 percent of the couples checked "emphatically yes" and the remaining 19 percent indicated "mostly yes." In addition, parents of daughters were equally as likely as parents of sons to say "yes."

In effect, almost three-quarters of the swinging parents saw their spouse-sharing behavior as being so conducive to happiness and the good life that even the idea of their own children later becoming involved in this presently quite deviant practice failed to arouse any marked feelings of apprehension. The swingers spent a good deal of time talking about their plans and aspirations for their children. Like almost all parents they want their children to lead happy and productive lives. And their comments to this effect seemed every bit as sincere as did those of the non-swinging mothers and fathers. However, some of the swingers did qualify their support of future comarital sexual involvement for their children. Many of them reiterated their earlier comments about the danger of becoming involved with the wrong kind of people, about the necessity of exercising great care and caution in "getting started" as swingers, and about the necessity of a husband and wife both viewing the relationship between sex and marriage in the same libertarian, proswinging manner.

Almost all of the couples interviewed made it clear, however, that any decisions would have to be left entirely to their son or daughter and his or her future spouse. Twenty-two percent of the couples did plan to openly discuss with their children "at the proper time" what they saw as being the benefits of comarital sexual activity, and some of the parents (especially some of those with teenaged children) had already done this. But the idea of using any "hard-sell" techniques "turned off" even the most militant of the swinging couples interviewed. As one 41-year old sales executive put it, "If you are fortunate enough to have a really great relationship with your kids as my wife and I do, they [your children] will naturally tend to model their behavior after yours." And indeed, many of the swinging couples studied did have very close, ongoing social relationships with their children.

One factor which more than 80 percent of the swinging parents had in common was a strong belief in letting their children learn things and find things out for themselves, even when this requires the child to suffer some pain as a consequence of his mistakes. Swinging parents in contrast to the non-swinging parents tended to permit their children a high degree of autonomy. They allowed them to make most of their own decisions considerably earlier in life than was true for most of the non-swinging parents.

This emotional differentiation of parents from their children occasionally manifested itself during the interviews, in what most Americans would view as very extremist statements. One 35-year-old mother, for example, told me (husband present) that she wouldn't mind it if her 8-year-old daughter became a prostitute when she grows up. "Why should I mind it?" she said. "The average prostitute is only 25 years old when she decides to give up the business. And during the time she is involved she has a hell of a good time and makes a hell of a lot of money. I mean, the whole thing is temporary, so why get so damned keyed up about it! If she's wise she'll put a lot of that money away and she may never have to work again, especially if she's attractive. A lot of those girls have college degrees and get very good business jobs after they decide to give it up."

This woman who, by the way, I found to be very attractive and unusually well groomed, revealed these feelings with a straight face and calm demeanor. Her husband, similarly calm, remained silent but nodded his head at several points. It seemed to me that for him what his wife was saying could be taken as a "given" of life and hardly worth commenting on.

A clear illustration of the difference in sentiments between the swinging couples and those of the non-swingers can be seen in the way in which they responded to the question: "Do you think your children will someday have premarital sex relations?" Ninety-six percent of the swinging couples indicated that it was "highly probable" that their children would do so, and the remaining 4 percent thought that it was "moderately probable." Among the non-swinging couples, on the other hand, almost 40 percent felt convinced that their children probably would not do so. And among those who felt that premarital sex was probable for their children only one-third felt impelled to check "highly probable" as opposed to "moderately probable."

Most people would say that findings such as these are to be expected. Yet they do reveal a considerably higher degree of realism among the swinging parents than among the non-swinging parents. Most child-rearing experts view realism with children as a virtue. When the swingers' children reach adolescence they are likely to be far less reticent than the non-swingers' children about discussing sex and dating with their parents. The data obtained for this study from the parents of teenaged children strongly suggested that this is so.

To the extent that there is meaningful communication between parents and children, to that extent there can be meaningful influence. When children are reticent about discussing certain topics the probability that they will be effectively influenced by their parents' views on these topics is minimized. Few of the non-swinging parents would want their children to be influenced by the swinging perspective. However, swinging parents *do* have a patterned system of values, deviant though it indeed is. And many of the swingers' children are exposed to this well-structured pattern of sex values, and in some cases they are exposed to it quite early in life. Unfortunately, the children of conventional parents very often end up with little or no pattern of sexual values because they lack meaningful communication with their elders in regard to these topics. They recognize their parents' unspoken or seldom spoken values as unrealistic and as not adaptable to their current lives. The children of "straight" parents are hence quite often forced to depend heavily upon peers for the development of a structured system of values. On the other hand, most of the swingers' children seem to emerge into adolescence with much greater feelings of confidence as far as the sexual side of themselves is concerned.

The foregoing should not be interpreted as supporting the swingers' perspective. The point is that no matter what a parent's philosophy or personal morality is in regard to sex, he stands a far greater chance of effectively influencing his children to the extent that he keeps open the lines of meaningful communication between himself and his children. Fear and apprehension are poison to ongoing parent-child communication about any subject.

Experiments in Adolescent Sexuality

Some social commentators have viewed swinging as a kind of social movement. If so, it is a very quiet one. Swingers do not march around or engage in demonstrations in order to attract attention to themselves and their ideas. New members to the fold are recruited quietly and slowly. Virtually all of the swingers with whom I spoke are desirous of keeping things quiet and "non-political." But this does not mean that some of the experiments currently going on within their ranks may not eventually come to have formidable social and political significance.

A comparatively small minority of swingers with teen-aged children have taken steps to introduce these children to group sexual activities. Technically, in California at least, these parents are taking a formidable legal gamble:

if their actions were ever made public they could be arrested for "endangering the morals of minors," and might even be declared "unfit" as parents. The fact that swingers have a very different concept of morality and of what is "moral" than the rest of society makes virtually no difference at all as far as the law is concerned. This is so despite the fact that America is doubtless the most pluralistic of any democracy in the world. Although we may have more philosophies, ideologies, and religions within our borders than can be found anywhere else in the world, the amount and degree of tolerance for sexual nonconformity, particularly to the extent that it involves children, remains very low. Parents may freely expose their children to whatever philosophies they might wish, but when ideas give rise to actual behavior serious legal difficulties become and remain a constant risk.

Despite such sobering considerations, 46 percent of the swinging couples I interviewed had heard of the practice among their associates of introducing teenaged children to group sex. And 6 percent of the couples had themselves been involved in this practice. All six of these couples were *currently* involved at the time of the study.

But before we probe this issue further, it might be illuminating to survey the results of an attitude question presented to the 100 swinging couples investigated for this study:

> "A few cases have been reported in which groups of swingers, all with adolescent children, have introduced their own children to the fun and to each other. While the adults are having their sex party the kids hold their own in a nearby house and under the supervision of one of the wives who happens to be menstruating. What are your feelings about this?"

Fully 31 percent of the couples interviewed registered approval of the practice. The other 69 percent disapproved, and only 21 of the 69 who disapproved did so strongly.

While 31 percent is not an enormously high figure, it

does represent almost one-third of a slowly increasing nonconformist minority in this country. And the activities of that portion of this deviant minority that is actualizing their views in real behavior may well constitute what eventually turns out to be an important social experiment in human relations.

The above item had been developed during the pilot phase of the study. During the course of interviewing it became apparent that the teenaged sex parties were seldom held in "a nearby house and under the supervision of one of the wives who happened to be menstruating." Rather, the parties were normally held in the same private residence as the adult couples' party, but in another part of the house—quite commonly the basement. And menstruating wives rarely decline invitations to swinging parties that include their closest friends.

Inasmuch as swingers do not get along as well with kin outside of their own immediate nuclear families as most people do, their swinging groups often take the place of normal kin family networks. And so it is with the teenagers involved in the sex parties. Most of these young people had known each other since early childhood from trips that they had made to nearby nudist resorts. And I think it is significant that all six of the couples currently involving their children in group sex recreation had been involved for varying lengths of time in the social nudist movement. None of these couples were associated with conventional nudist resorts at the time of the interviews, but all were at least casually associated with the more liberal nudist and sexual freedom groups such as Elysium of Topanga Canyon.

Do love relationships ever develop out of such adolescent group sex contacts? According to the data I collected at least 60 percent of the teenagers involved did view themselves as "being in love" with a fellow group member of the opposite sex, and all of them viewed the opposite-sexed members of their group with a noteworthy degree of possessive in-group loyalty.

I interviewed eighteen teenagers involved in such groups—nine boys and nine girls—and none of them discounted the possibility that they might later fall in love with and marry one of their fellow group members. In addition, all of these young people voiced a group privacy ethic with a seriousness that made them seem quite mature for their years. They made it clear that any discussion at all of their activities outside of the group could never be tolerated, and that "the worst sin of all," to quote one young man's terminology, would be for a group member to brag publicly about how "easy a make" a particular girl in his group might be.

Some of the most stunningly memorable of my experiences while interviewing for this study involved my interactions with members of parent-supervised, high-school-aged sex groups. These young people conveyed the impression of being more naturally spontaneous even than their parents. And this is saying something, because the parents of these teenagers struck me as being the most attractive and naturally outgoing of all the people I interviewed, with the possible exception of some of the swingers still in their early or mid-twenties. These teenagers had the highest regard for their parents. And these positive feelings were revealed in many unsolicited, positive statements made during the course of the interviews.

As an example of one of the seemingly "unreal" (for our society) families from which I collected data, the Simmonses had three children: a boy of 17, a girl of 14, and a pre-teen boy of 9. The father runs his own business from his home and is usually around when the children come home from school. I began interviewing Tom and Lisa Simmons one afternoon at about 3:30. And when I got around to the questions dealing with children both Tom and his wife enthusiastically volunteered an avalanche of information about the "love group" of which both their 14-year-old and 17-year-old were a part. The 17-year-old boy happened to be home that afternoon; he was in his bedroom playing records with his 16-year-old sweetheart and classmate who also happened to be a member of the "love group."

Tom called his son in, telling him that a sociology professor was there trying to learn something about the family lives of swingers. As a somewhat naive interviewer I was almost shocked when the son and his girl both came dashing into the living room stark naked. Like their parents, both children were quite attractive—indeed, considerably more so than most of the other people I interviewed. Neither Tom nor his wife Lisa seemed at all undaunted or surprised by the young people's nudity. In fact, they nodded approvingly at almost everything the young people said.

Parenthetically, this was not the only occasion during which some of my respondents were nude. About two-thirds of the swinging families *frequently* go nude around the house, and among those with teenaged children involved in sex groups virtually all of them do. One couple even asked me at the start of an interview whether it would bother me if they removed their clothes, explaining that they seldom wear anything around the house, and that if I wanted to gain a valid picture and "feeling" for what swinging homes are like it might be in my best interests if they did shed their clothes. In this particular case there wasn't even very much to shed. Neither the husband nor the wife had on anything more than very lush, expensive-appearing bath robes. And when I indicated my approval these were rapidly removed. This couple also had teenaged children, and after about two hours of conversation with their parents they also entered the room fully nude. (This family had an 18-year-old girl, 16-year-old twin boys, and a 14-year-old girl.)

As the reader might well imagine, it was virtually impossible to stick to a pre-arranged interview schedule while talking with people like this. And I think it clearly would have been to the detriment of the study had I endeavored to do so. I think it is worth repeating here that the written questionnaires which each individual husband

and wife filled out separately served to effectively satisfy the need to obtain at least some data amenable to statistical analysis. The fact that the written questionnaires were an integral part of the study similarly served to free me as an interviewer to respond with some degree of spontaneity and naturalness to each situation and facet of conversation as it arose.

In the case of the Simmons family I asked the teenaged couple whether they copulated regularly. The girl responded laughingly that they hadn't done anything sexual yet that afternoon, but that they probably would before she went home for the night. Tom, the father, interjected the thought that he believed they had been having sex at least once per day. In response to this, and all four people were laughing at this point, the boy indicated that this was true and that the night before last he and the girl had done it three times. She immediately added in a quiet, smiling tone: "And you actually got an 'A' on your trig test the next morning!" Following this there was a ten minute discussion about the son's outstanding academic performance. He had already been accepted by UCLA and had plans of entering medicine. The girl's grades were somewhat lower, but still impressive. She boasted that since grade school she had never received anything lower than a "B".

In regard to grades I was unfortunately not able to obtain objective data from all of the teenagers involved in these groups. Feedback from the parents, however, revealed that only five out of the eighteen youngsters with whom I talked were performing below what was considered to be their ability levels. For a group comprised of eighteen youngsters this might be an expected or "chance" figure. Just as the parents regarded their own sexual spouse-sharing as a kind of hobby and recreation, they similarly regarded it as such for their adolescent children. "Taking part in after-school recreation is no excuse for poor grades" is a comment that I heard over and over again from the swinging mothers and fathers. And I would have to assume that contained within that comment is an integral component of the swingers' working philosophy and ideology. This seems to be particularly true in regard to swingers whose teenaged children were involved in the "love groups." After all, if these people had to admit to themselves that their children were not performing up to par, it would throw a damper on their own feelings of confidence about the validity and workability of their nonconformist sex-family philosophy of life. I got the feeling that some of these parents were trying to prove something to themselves and to others. This may be one key reason why after I succeeded in earning their trust they were so exceedingly cooperative during the interview sessions.

Author Robert H. Rimmer (1966) is an extremely important model to a good many of the people I interviewed who assume a liberal stance in regard to the sexual behavior of their teenaged children. Of particular importance is Rimmer's pedagogic novel *The Harrad Experiment*, which depicts a closely knit group of undergraduate student couples living together unmarried on a college campus. *The Harrad Experiment* has become a kind of Bible of sorts for many of these families. Some of them even have copies of the hardbound first edition lying around in conspicuous places such as on the coffee table, the mantelpiece, or the kitchen counter.

> "One of the things that really bugs me about our society is that the love and romance needs of people are so often confused with their sex needs. I believe that all adolescents, girls as well as boys, have very strong sex needs—probably stronger than they ever will be for their entire lives. I believe our society is all screwed up when it tries to get our kids to repress these drives. Now, don't get me wrong! The last thing I'd want to see is any of these nice kids getting hurt either physically or psychologically. In fact, we've worked out a number of policies and procedures to assure us that that won't happen. We

don't let our kids do anything and everything sexually that they might have an impulse to do. But then, we as adults don't do everyting we've a mind to do either. We all have certain rules of good behavior and conduct. But the important thing for you to know for the book you're trying to write is that all of our rules are rational. We've tried to develop a set of rules and regulations in our family and in our swinging groups which are in harmony with the needs and nature of all the people involved. We would never be satisfied with a rule unless everyone in the family affected by that rule gave unanimous assent to it—and that includes all the kids. A lot of people forget that kids are people too! I think a lot of our problems with young people today would no longer exist if we would all just start respecting our kids and started treating them with simple dignity. People have to be treated as people if they are going to behave in a human way." (40-year-old swinging father.)

Another husband explained his support of the adolescent "love groups" by insisting that normative systems governing adolescent sexuality, if they are to remain workable and viable, must be in reasonable harmony with the needs and nature of human beings during their teen-aged years. When norms are out of harmony with people's needs and natures various kinds of unrest begin to occur. People either tend to develop various kinds of internal emotional "hangups" or they begin to create problems for those around them.

"One of the main problems is that most people today have been programmed to think very negatively about human nature. In fact, after Vietnam and Watergate and the Nazi regime I'm convinced that most people my age at least are convinced that man's inborn nature isn't worth a shit. They just don't trust it anymore. And they certainly aren't ready to trust it in inexperienced teenaged kids. That's why I and three of my closest friends got

together and decided to create our own insulated
world for our kids, so to speak. We know that our
kids were born intrinsically good and that they are
still good, and that the only way they are ever going
to become anything less than good is for their
minds to be contaminated by the kind of negative
thinking bullshit that is constantly fed to us in all of
the media and throughout society. We are trying to
immunize ourselves and our children against that.
And we think our love groups have enabled us to
take a giant step in that direction. Anyway, neither
we adults or the kids spend all that much time in
purely sexual activity—not even when we hold sex
parties. But sexual activities are nevertheless in
there. They are enjoyed along with many other fun
activities by both the kids and by us adults." (49-
year-old swinging father.)

A common theme in the conversations of many swinging
parents is that a conceptual distinction must be drawn
between the need for sex and the need for love and romance. Some of the swingers discussed this theme with
the erudite sophistication of an experienced behavioral
scientist while others kept their conversations basic. But I
think it is fair to say that the sex/love distinction has become a central component of the swingers' self-
legitimating ideology. Typical were the comments of one
44-year-old father:

It can be disastrous when a 16- or 17-year-old kid
blindly sells himself a bill of goods that he must fall
in love in order to get laid. Sure, every once in a
while there is a situation where a 17-year-old really
does make it with someone who is near perfect for
him and with whom he will be able to enjoy a successful life-long marriage. Some people are very
lucky. I have a friend who married his next-door
neighbor. I mean, he had been playing with this girl
everyday after school from the time he was in the
first grade. By the time the two of them got through
junior high school they one day realized that they

were in love—whatever that means. Anyway, they married at the age of 18. Both finished college in spite of their early start in life. And today, over twenty years later, they raised a beautiful family and are still getting along great. I really envy them. But I think they are the exception. Most people don't meet the right person while they are still teenagers, much less when they are still toddlers in elementary school. Most people have to play the field a little bit. They have to find out who the hell they are and what they want out of life. And sometimes even after they think they found out who they are they find out a few months later that they are no longer the person they first thought they were. Life is crazy, mixed up, complicated. And for most people it takes some amount of exploration of alternatives before a truly wise and judicious decision can be made. This applies to careers and I think it certainly applies to the husband-wife relationship. Now the structured sexual freedom we allow for our teenaged sons and daughters allows them to satisfy their basic biological sex drives and experience the total personality of a lot of different people of the opposite sex without having to commit themselves to any one person until the time is ripe for them to do so." (44-year-old swinging husband.)

I pointed out during several of the interviews that social scientists and clergymen often worry that people used to a good deal of sexual freedom from an early age may grow up emotionally incapable of making a final marriage commitment. Only time will tell whether these youngsters will eventually find it difficult to make a commitment to their future spouses and children. But it should be pointed out that many preliterate societies in which divorce is either very rare or unknown provide their citizens with a great deal of *pre*marital sexual freedom. In essence, premarital sexual freedom either in the modern world or in the primitive world may not be a sufficient condition in and of itself to effectively program a person to be emotionally incapable of making a commitment for most of his adult life. Indeed, it seems most likely that the only young men and women who may in fact be incapable of making a genuine commitment are those who continue a lifestyle of casual sex and of "playing the field" for more than eight or nine years after they leave high school. Controlled experiments in adolescent sexual freedom may not augur poorly at all for later marital commitments, particularly if the young people involved are programmed with the notion that their "love groups" are merely there as temporary learning experiences valuable in their own time and in their own place. But just as a person would not find it satisfying to remain a high school student throughout his life, so it is that he would not find it very gratifying at a deep emotional level to remain an adolescent "love group" member throughout his life. Young citizens of the Trobriand Islands lose a great deal of sexual freedom when they marry. Yet all Trobrianders eagerly look forward to their own marriages.

It could be argued that swingers have remained members of "adolescent love groups" of their own creation. In fact, some of them may have indeed done this. But as a social scientist I was impressed that a sizable proportion of the swingers truly believe in their often-stressed conceptual distinctions between (1) committed love and noncommitted love, (2) between person-centered sex and body-centered sex, (3) between "faithful" and "nonfaithful" adultery, and (4) between emotional/residential monogamy and sexual monogamy. To the extent that these ingredients of the swingers' self-legitimating idea system are truly absorbed by the teenaged offspring, to that extent we might expect these young people to be fully capable of making genuinely committed attachments leading to permanent, emotionally monogamous relationships. Only time will tell whether this hope is justified. Hopefully the future will lead to some appropriate research efforts on this point.

This research did reveal a key point suggesting that there is hope for these teenagers as far as their eventual experiencing of committed love is concerned. Almost two-thirds of them reported that they were "in love" with an opposite-sexed "love group" member. In fact, only two of the teenagers with whom I talked reported not being "in love." All of the others were "in love" with an opposite-sexed friend whom they had met at school. This finding provides some modicum of support for the theory that the need for love and romance is basic in all human beings of both sexes and that this need is conceptually distinct from the need for sex. It may be that just as the need for love often leads to sexual release in young people from conventional homes, it may also be that sexual intercourse itself will normally work to facilitate the development of emotional love feelings for the partner involved.

Swingers have rejected the "double standard" morality more vehemently than virtually any other group in society, with the possible exception of "women's lib." Throughout the years I worked on this research I never once heard the child of a swinger use a term such as "easy lay." In fact, such terms appear to be used far less by swingers than by the majority of non-swingers of the same ages.

One of the especially interesting insights which my interviews with the swingers' teenaged children revealed is that a strong need for a variety of sexual partners may not run in families. For even when the opportunity for the experiencing of a variety of sexual partners is given to happy, well-adjusted young people on the proverbial "silver platter," not all of them or even most of them take the fullest possible advantage of their privilege.

I found that the amount of sexual activity that went on at swinger-sponsored teenaged "love group" meetings was actually somewhat less than that which went on among the elders holding their party in the same house at the same time. And it was a good deal more monogamous. But the teenagers would be nude throughout most of their party evenings together. And they would be encouraged, particularly by their fathers, to "play the field" and gain as much self-confidence in dealing with other people of both sexes as they possibly could. But few of the young people typically took this advice. Moreover, they simply did not have the inner set of complex psycho-emotional needs to take advantage of this advice. The psychological needs of these teenagers were doubtless a good deal different than those which affected their parents during adolescence. The swinging parents had had strong unfulfilled needs for which their deviant recreation may have provided an effective solution. Perhaps for a complex set of reasons they became fixated on these needs. The point, however, is that their own children were unique individuals just as they themselves were unique people, with a unique constellation of inborn temperaments and learned personalities.

The adolescents conveyed the impression of being unusually happy, spontaneous people. Yet despite this their "love groups" served as a source of considerable frustration to many of their swinging fathers—particularly to the fathers of teenagers with strong love relationships. For these teenagers were using the "love group" opportunity to copulate and to learn sexual skills. But they were doing so in a monogamous manner that was frustrating to the fathers.

Not surprisingly, it was the fathers who collectively engineered the adolescent "love groups." The fathers had expected that the young people would model their behavior after that of their swinging elders. But they did not do this. Rather they evolved their own party atmosphere, an atmosphere that was considerably quieter and less frenzied and competitive than that of their swinging mothers and fathers.

I do not want to convey the impression that these young people were not unusually sexually active for their ages and socioeconomic status and culture. In point of fact they were *highly* active. But their activity was primarily monogamous. It is important to stress that this monogamy had not been brought about by any norms created by the young people themselves. None of the "love groups" that I either studied or heard about entailed any norms restricting frequent partner selection and change. Occasionally a group member would suggest that monogamy norms be initiated, but despite their own sexual monogamy or near-monogamy such suggestions have been consistently voted down by the young people. The adults with whom I spoke did not expect that their young people would ever develop any sexual monogamy rules for their groups. The young people's attitude seemed on the most part to be that each person should be free to choose for himself or herself. But since most of the members of each group practiced a kind of de facto sexual monogamy there was little opportunity for the other members to do differently.

The sex ratios of the groups were kept even. In engineering the various details for the development of these groups the husbands had taken special pains to rule out problems that might be created by uneven sex ratios. They decided that surplus members of either sex would simply not be admitted, and that monitoring would be carried out at the front door by the same person who greeted and screened the adult guests. As it turned out, youths with close monogamous romantic relationships always arrived together as couples, presumably to avoid any potential embarrassment to themselves that might accrue from their "love mate" not being admitted to the teenaged sex gathering.

The young people's parties, like those of their parents, were usually small. Four or five boys and four or five girls was about as large as any party ever became, and this tended to be the case for their parents' sex parties as well. The mothers and fathers of each youth did not need to be present at the married adults' party going on at the same time. But care was always taken to make sure that each youth present was in fact the son or daughter of an accepted and respected swinging couple. Hence, while the young people handled their own inviting, this had to be done within certain limits that had been set down by the parents sponsoring the "love group" parties.

Despite their parents' liberal views on such matters, the teenagers were not permitted to have marijuana or other drugs at their parties. Alcoholic beverages (usually wine) were available to the young people. But they were not permitted to drink these outside of the adults' party area, and they were expected to limit their number of drinks to two per party. Some of the swingers had a fear of being "busted" by the law. But this seems to never occur as far as small to medium sized parties held in private residences are concerned. Throughout my years of researching this subject I never heard of a private residence being "busted."

The issue of birth control and contraception for these teenagers is a particularly important and fascinating one. It will be dealt with quite fully in Chapter 12.

Venereal diseases constitute only a very minor worry as far as these teenagers are concerned. The swinging parents take the same approach with their children as they use among themselves in dealing with VD prevention. In short, they (1) prohibit any non-members from attending the sex parties; and (2) they continually stress to their children the importance of keeping their copulations strictly within the group. Some families have excused their children from abiding by this second rule. But in all such cases the young person involved had been going with a particular opposite-sexed friend for at least three months. In cases where a child had been involved in an exclusive, monogamous relationship with someone outside of swinging circles and that "sweetheart" was believed to be "faithful" (sexually monogamous), the young person was allowed to continue his or her sexual relationship with that individual. Some of the teenagers had been involved in such steady love relationships at the time their fathers had initiated the teenaged "love groups." And some of these young people actually had to be sold on the benefits of joining the "love group."

It is worth repeating here that an indispensable prerequisite for the contracting of any venereal disease is that of sexual contact with an already infected person. As long as such contact can be avoided there is no way a person can become afflicted with a venereal disease germ no matter how many times he might copulate with non-infected people. Theoretically, a person could engage in rampant promiscuity with a pool of 1,000 or more people of the other sex, and as long as none of those 1,000 or more people were infected, there would be *"zero"* risk of venereal disease.

Like their elders, the young people engage in many different kinds of activities during the course of a typical five-hour sex party. Ordinarily the young people arrive a half-hour to an hour earlier than their parents, although a few of them come to a party with their parents. Most adolescent parties start around 8:00 P.M. of a Friday or a Saturday night.

Upon arrival the youngsters are often encouraged to shed their clothes and take a swim in the heated pool if there is one on the premises (and there almost always is). The youngsters remain in and around the pool area for the first 90 to 120 minutes of their party, but they are not confined there. They are often seen walking in and out of the kitchen during the course of a party. Bathrooms and basement bedrooms are another popular destination for the young people. The young people make frequent use of bathroom and basement showers during the first two hours of their party.

For the first hour or so not all of the people invited are likely to have as yet arrived. And the swimming pool and shower fun serve as effective "ice breakers" during this time period. All of the teenagers quickly acclimate to swimming pool nudity.

The showers are commonly used by couples who already have a sex and/or love-romance interest in each other. But they are also the scene of fairly frequent group horseplay; such activity facilitates efforts toward getting to know one another (when newcomers are there) or in breaking the ice for a particular evening. Couples will normally use upstairs bathroom showers. Most swingers' homes possess large, non-slippery basement showers which permit simultaneous usage by five or six people, and these are used by those desirous of horseplay and by those who do not have a "sweetheart" present.

Normally by 9:30 or 10:00 P.M. the young people will all gather in a basement area that has been assigned to them. Here they will normally start engaging in a variety of group games. All are likely to be nude at this point, but none are likely to be engaged in any "deep" sexual activity. For some of the young people "deep" sexual activity might well have occurred earlier in the evening during the "shower/swimming pool" stage. During the time that the youths are all together in the same room there is no pressure to engage in any standardized activity. In fact, it is not at all unusual for some youths to be stretched out on the floor watching television with each other. One thing that does matter, however, is that no one be observed "doing his thing" alone. Watching television is considered acceptable so long as there is an opposite-sexed partner lying alongside a person perhaps massaging him or her, or gently holding him or her in some type of embrace. These youngsters are taught the art of non-verbal communication by their parents in the course of everyday life, and most of them are quite good at it. In some ways these parties resemble "encounter groups" inasmuch as intellectual responses are frowned upon both by the young people and by the adults. Verbal and nonverbal responses are geared toward the effective expression of feeling and emotion. And if there is any type of status hierarchy among these young people it has a lot to do with their effectiveness at verbal and nonverbal communication of what is true feeling and emotion.

All of the groups that I had either studied or heard about had strong unofficial norms against adults walking in on the young people and against young people walking in on the adults. Frank and confidential exchanges of informa-

tion were reserved for family conferences which were regularly held in these homes. And it was upon such occasions that most of the pedogogic instruction went on.

Fondling and massaging are both important activities
at these teenaged sex parties, and while coitus and highly
intimate sexual conduct tends to be reserved (by those "in
love") for "sweethearts," the fondling and massaging activities are not so reserved. Indeed, this may well be one
key reason why these groups tend to develop very tight,
strong feelings of "in-groupness" and loyalty. Ordinarily
the young people take turns at each meeting with the role
of group facilitator. Some of the young people are better at
this role than others. But all are schooled in it by their
parents during the family conferences. Each group
member will ordinarily massage and fondle each
opposite-sexed member on several occasions during the
course of an evening. The fondling that does not involve
the "sweetheart," however, will always occur inside of a
group context. Sometimes it will also occur at the swimming pool or in the shower, but always there are others
present.

The young people have all received encouragement from
their parents to engage in some fondling of same-sexed
peers. And such activity does go on at the parties, but, as
with the adults, the young girls seem to be far better able
to fondle and massage each other than the teenaged boys
are, and they often do it outside of the party context. But
unlike the swinging wives, the teenaged girls often razz
the boys present if they do not massage each other while
they (the girls) are massaging each other. As pointed out
earlier, the adult men often step aside and watch the wives
fondle each other; they believe that they derive a sexual
recharging from this voyeuristic activity. But this type of
male voyeuristic activity tends to be discouraged among
the adolescents.

Music is an important component of all these teenagers'
interest patterns. And much of the time during the course
of a typical evening is spent dancing and in just simply

lying on the floor listening with a chosen love partner to a favorite album on the stereo. Musical taste among these teenagers tend to be fairly typical for their age group and they tend to vary somewhat from youngster to youngster. The young men I found to be somewhat more interested in hard rock than the girls. All were interested in country and western, and occasionally an album of standard love ballads would be played, usually upon the insistence of one of the young women present.

During the course of a typical five-hour party each teenager experiences sexual intercourse an average of 2.74 times. My data indicated that this figure applies for the young men as well as for the young women. The reader will recall that among the parents the mothers are normally likely to enjoy a higher sexual activity rate at a typical party than the fathers. But like their elders these young people experience orgasms in more ways than just through copulation. Mutual masturbation as well as oral-genital lovemaking are both extremely common.

During the course of a typical party each teenager spends an average of about two hours engaged in activities that could be considered erotic. This includes the fondling and massaging referred to earlier, which usually goes on in a kind of encounter group setting. The coitus, mutual masturbation and oral-genital behavior tends to occur both in private as well as in a group context. As with the adults, some of these young people are more naturally outgoing than others, and some of them tend to be more introspective and private in terms of temperament. But naturally outgoing or otherwise, seeing their friends engaged in intimate sexual embraces has a potent psychological effect. Sociologists refer to this as *social facilitation*. It is through social facilitation that even the less naturally outgoing members of the group feel much freer than they ordinarily would about initiating the same sort of behavior. Social facilitation also very frequently precipitates sexually quite assertive behavior on the part of the young women vis-à-vis their young men.

Upon becoming "turned on" some of the couples are likely to leave the group and head for a bedroom or a private corner if an unoccupied bedroom cannot be found. Others, on the other hand, become intimately involved in erotic embraces right there on the floor of the main encounter room. Comparative newcomers to the adolescent "love groups" can normally be expected to opt for comparative privacy, although even this does not always apply. Nor is there any particular regularity in what any one couple or individual will do. The couple who on one occasion opt for privacy will on another occasion choose to copulate quite openly. Since most of these young people get to copulate with each other quite often on a private basis during the week, at the parties they are very likely to remain in the group for much if not all of their sexual activity. This is particularly true once the adults' party gets fully underway as the young people often feel strongly embarrassed upon encountering the adults, and perhaps one of their parents, upon searching for an unoccupied bedroom or bathroom. None of the teenagers with whom I spoke admitted to watching their friends copulate for more than a few seconds at a time. In essence, while each teenager may have sex quite publicly, in the course of doing it each is in point of fact wrapped up in his or her own private world.

One of the commonest reasons given by the swinging parents to justify the adolescent "love groups" is that the sexual experiences that they offer provide young people with a high degree of genuine self-confidence that will serve to help them in all sectors of their lives, not just the boy-girl sector. The same thing is often asserted to be a significant benefit of social nudist participation for teens. Because the swingers' self-justifying ideology places a strong and consistent emphasis upon the expectation that increased self-confidence and friendly assertiveness will accrue to those who take an active part in swinging activities, I included several questions pertinent to this matter in my interviews with the eighteen young people.

While it should be kept in mind that eighteen is a comparatively small number of people, the interview data
strongly supports the view that participation in the "love
groups" develops and strongly supports a strong, friendly,
relaxed self-confidence. It does this for both sexes, but the
effect appears to be particularly strong for boys. Without
exception, all of the teenaged boys interviewed stressed
(with a noticeable degree of enthusiasm) that a heightened
self-confidence was the main and most valuable thing they
had been able to get out of their affiliation with their "love
group." Four of the young men went on to extol the virtues
of their earlier childhood participation in conventional,
non-erotic social nudism. This, they claim, had made it
easier for them to shed their clothes in mixed company
and to feel at least reasonably secure when they attended
their first "love group" party.

The girls also talked about a heightened self-confidence
accruing to them from their "love group" participation.
But in general the girls tended to talk more than the boys
about learning to feel better about themselves and about
their bodies. In spite of women's lib, young women are
still not expected or encouraged by the culture of the
wider community to assume the assertive role in approaching boys to ask for first dates. The fact that boys
have always been expected to assume the assertive role
not only in asking for first dates but also in initiating petting and erotic love-play may partially explain why they
sensed somewhat more of an increase in self-confidence
than the girls did.

My own subjective impression was that six out of the
nine girls I interviewed were very attractive, and in some
ways surprisingly so. Two of the girls, on the other hand,
were physically rather plain. Yet I was amazed that it was
just these individuals and their less than handsome male
counterparts who extolled the virtues of the "love groups"
the most. One of these girls had found a steady
"sweetheart" in the group, a boy who appeared to be considerably more attractive than she; yet the boy frequently

praised the girl's warmth, sincerity, and skill as a lover. The other girl had developed into a sought-after "love-partner" at the parties.

The swinging adults claimed that physical appearance means very little to them compared to the virtues of sexual skill as well as basic human warmth, sincerity, and relaxed friendliness. Many of them insisted that only the beginner looks for physical attractiveness in the other sex at parties and in life in general. The people whom many of these swinging adults liked best were not conspicuously attractive on the surface, and they credited swinging as sensitizing them to the importance of getting to know the whole person.

I think it is significant that these sympathies were often voiced by the young people as well, and it may partially explain why they all felt confident in themselves and happy. In fact, on a five-point scale ranging from "very happy" to "very unhappy," fourteen of these youngsters saw themselves as being generally "very happy" with their lives. The other four saw themselves as being "happy." Anyone who has studied adolescent psychology knows that such a distribution of responses on a happiness question for contemporary American adolescents is very rare. Most American teenagers are not particularly happy people.

Most teenagers tend to be quite concerned about such superficialities as breast development and penis length. None of the swingers' children with whom I talked made any reference at all to these topics. When asked directly about them they revealed a serene confidence regarding their own physical characteristics. This was true even for those with small or slowly developing breasts or penises. One boy had a curved penis that brought forth a considerable amount of razzing from his peers in his high school gym class. He claimed to feel no insecurity or inferiority about this. He had an attractive girl friend with whom he was "making it" both at parties and in his and her bedroom after school. And he viewed himself as being "very happy and fortunate." Like many of the swingers' children he boasted an "A–" average in his high school studies.

Of course, not all swingers feel comfortable about the idea of introducing their children to the "love groups." One swinging father of a 19-year-old son perceived him as being too shy and inhibited. I did not interview this young man, but reports from several people suggested that he suffered from a severe case of shyness with the opposite sex. At 19 he had allegedly only been out on three dates, and these had all been arranged for him by his parents and close relatives. And in each case he had been too fearful about picking up the phone and calling for a second date. Interestingly, his mother objected strenuously to the idea of introducing him to a teenaged "love group."

But, being a swinger, his father eventually decided to take him into Hollywood to be sexually initiated by an attractive call girl. Several of his friends both in and out of swinging had done this for their own sons, and they were only too happy to recommend several high-level, professional call girls. Many swingers feel a good deal more comfortable and secure about this type of an approach than about the adolescent "love groups," although there is evidence that the latter are slowly beginning to win favor.

This particular father paid $250 to a call girl for spending an entire night with his son at a cabin he owned in the San Bernardino Mountains. The son had originally balked at the idea of going to a room at an expensive hotel. The father decided to spend $250 in order to motivate the girl to accept the idea of a trip out to the mountains where the young man would feel more secure.

Not all swingers demonstrate this kind of deep interest in the sex lives and social lives of their children. As is true among conventional people, some swingers feel threatened by the real or imagined shortcomings of their offspring. But most of them are too preoccupied with their own lives to feel particularly interested in what is happening with their children.

The young man allegedly emerged quite happy from his

evening with his father's hand-picked call girl. Unlike many such sexual initiations, which turn out to be absolute emotional disasters for the young men involved, this young man had copulated with the girl three times over a 14-hour period. Taking into account the fact that he was a virgin when the evening began it would seem that the experience had been an unmitigated success for him as well as for his father.

But it wasn't! The young man did confidently know after the experience that he was capable of having and enjoying sexual intercourse. But sexual skills and *social* skills are *not* the same thing. And learning how to experience sexual intercourse and please a woman have little to do with enabling a person to rid himself of a low interpersonal anxiety threshold and with providing him with the kind of social skills that might enable him to initiate and effectively carry on informal conversations with female age-mates whom he might desire to bring into his personal life. The young man's confidence in himself and in his abilities had improved in some important particulars as a result of his experience. But the positive outcomes sought by his father had not been attained. This was so because sexual intercourse is not a magic wand that can automatically dissipate the interpersonal anxiety problems from which many people suffer. The father had failed to realize what the *real* problem was. Fortunately some friends of the family did size up the situation more accurately. They convinced the parents to allow their son to spend a weekend with them at the Elysium Resort (a libertarian nudist resort in the Topanga Canyon area of Los Angeles). Through these family friends and presumably through learning how to relax nude with age-mates of the other sex this young man finally gained the social skills necessary for commencing an active social life. Today he is reputedly about to join a "love group"—a move to which his parents had long objected.

The ages of the eighteen "love group" youths whom I interviewed ranged from 14 to 20. Of course, additional research will be necessary to determine the typicality of this age distribution. But the data I obtained suggested that youths in excess of 19-years of age seldom endeavor to join these groups. None of the "love groups" I had heard about had been in existence for more than twenty-six months at the time of the interviews. Thus it seems likely that swinging mothers and fathers have only recently become confident and fearless enough to initiate the development of these groups for their children. Only time will tell what will happen as far as the future in-flow and out-flow of members is concerned.

That forming such a group was in large measure a matter of confidence and guts was strongly suggested to me by one 40-year-old real estate salesman father who claimed to have been envisioning such a scheme for well over twenty years.

> "I was in the military at the time. I was stationed near Norfolk, Virginia, and during my leave time I would go into town with the guys and try to find some fun things to do. I remember I picked up a magazine off the stands one time. I don't even remember now what the name of the magazine was. I can tell you that the pictures in it were very tame by today's standards. But there was this article in it about swingers—they called them 'wife-swappers' in those days, you know. Anyway, this article was about swingers who made a kind of family thing out of it. If I remember right there were these three families and they felt guilty about not sharing their fun with their kids. So they went ahead and educated them on birth control, you know, and they let them hold swinging parties whenever they wanted, like after school, Friday nights, and so forth. They even got to the point where brothers and sisters were "making it' with one another. But they didn't care. Hell, if there aren't going to be any babies the whole thing about incest doesn't make any difference either. The only thing the parents insisted on was that some adult be around to supervise during

party time and to protect the kids against the intrusion of any uninvited guest and shit like that . . . Anyway, that article really set my mind on fire with enthusiasm. A lot of my friends told me it was just a bunch of bullshit and that I should forget it. I couldn't understand their attitude. I mean, a lot of those guys were a lot more sexually active than I was at the time. I know that for a fact. Anyway, the whole idea remained in the back of my mind for all these years. And when my wife and I became swingers five years ago I got together with my best friend, who is an attorney. And we constructed what we felt was a foolproof plan for giving our kids what we felt was one of the most beautiful presents any parents could ever give to their teenagers. I'll be perfectly frank. I was scared shitless for more than two years about putting the plan into effect. It got to the point where my wife was teasing me about it and my friend was really pushing me. Laurie, my oldest kid, had just turned 16, and she had been dating boys anyway for at least three years before that. So I finally decided to take the plunge. It's been two years now and I don't know what the fuck I was so scared of. No one has bothered us and things have gone just great. All the parents of the kids in our 'love group' are our closest friends. We're doing something with at least one of those people every day."

Comparatively few of my respondents had children who were over twenty years of age. And among those who did none reported their young people as having any noticeable trouble in making friends with the other sex. Thus, as the current "love group" members grow older they might remain in their groups until they marry. If they do the age distribution for the groups will grow wider than it is now. Another possibility is that a cutting point will be placed between the ages of 19 and 20, and that some of the "love groups" will bifurcate into two separate groups, one for those 19 and younger and the other for youths 20 and over. Several of the adults suggested that they planned to push for this. The young people themselves, however, were strongly opposed to any such plan. Their feeling was that nature would take its course in the selection of "love partners," and that a breaking up of a group in terms of age would break up some of their strong, pre-existing "emotionally monogamous" unions.

The issue may not be as real as some of the adults imagine it to be. I learned of three 18-year-olds who had dropped out of various "love groups" in order to go away to college. And I learned of a 19-year-old boy and a 17-year-old girl (one of the emotionally monogamous love unions) who dropped out because they felt that they had "outgrown" their need for their "love group." In another case a boy of 16 dropped out because he was no longer interested in the activities of the group. This particular boy was the son of a highly gregarious and vivacious swinging couple. The boy was not without his love interests; he had been going for quite some time with a girl he had met at school. The girl's parents were as far from being swingers as anyone could get. Her father was a bishop in a nearby ward of the Latter-Day Saints Church, and the boy had recently taken part in various religious activities with her. From a clinical standpoint this case nicely illustrates the psychological differentiation from parents which most psychologists believe all teenagers must undergo. It is usually spoken of in terms of young people becoming more liberal than their parents. But it can and sometimes does go the other way too.

None of the people with whom I spoke knew of anyone who had ever been forced to resign his or her membership in a "love group." Just one love group member had ever become pregnant as a result of teenaged sex activities. Possible reasons for the contraceptive success of the love groups will be discussed in Chapter 12. Bad behavior of a type that might endanger the well-being of a "love group" or of any of its members was also unknown among the people whom I interviewed.

The strongest "group norm" that applied to virtually all

of the "love groups" was that of secrecy. Unintentional violation of the secrecy norm by the teenagers at their schools has remained a constant worry among the swinging parents. But the teenagers themselves don't worry about it. Several of the young people mentioned that on a number of occasions they had felt a strong urge to talk about their "love groups" with their non-swinging friends, especially since they frequently experience an emotional "high" as a result of attending each group meeting. And there is a natural tendency to want to share "peak expexiences" with friends. A few young people mentioned that they had experienced some feelings of uneasiness on a few occasions when they had to explain why they did not want to attend a Friday night party, movie, or basketball game with some conventional teens. But up until the time of the interviews everyone concerned had successfully resisted the temptation to discuss the "love groups" with the wrong people. At the time of writing this book no such teenaged "love group" had ever been publically exposed in any way.

The case regarding the boy who was on the verge of joining the Latter-Day Saints Church again raises the question of the strength of adolescent sex needs as opposed to adolescent love and romance needs. In and out of the "love groups" many teens are able to effectively combine sex with love. Some have even combined sex with a strong feeling of emotional commitment. But not all human beings are the same. Making predictions about human behavior is never easy. As a scientist I would hazard the guess that the need for love is probably stronger in *both* males and females than the need for sexual release. But when it is possible for a person to experience both without the necessity of having to pay a price, that person will almost always do so in preference to having to choose between sex and love. The "love groups" provide a means through which a teenager can have both—until or unless that teenager falls in love with a non-group member. There are many factors that can lead a person to fall in love with someone from outside the group. But it is worth repeating that *most* of the teenagers involved in the "love groups" *did* fall in love with an in-group member. Whether they will stay in love and how long they will stay in love are both important questions. But unfortunately they are beyond the scope of the present investigation.

Pre-Teen Children

By virtue of an informal consensus a child must be at least a teenager before he can be considered for admission to a "love group." Most of the groups require that a youngster be at least 14 years of age and at least one group I heard of will not admit teenagers until they are 16 for boys and 13 for girls. No group whose existence came to my attention will accept youngsters of either sex who are not at least 13 years of age.

Pre-teens might not *need* any manner of sexual release. But anthropologists have clearly documented over the past generation that need is in large measure determined by the cultural programming of people's minds. A small number of known societies have sustained very permissive (by American standards) norms that neither encourage nor discourage preadolescent sexuality. In some of these societies, such as the Muria and the Trobriand Islanders, it is not at all unusual for children as young as five or six years old to be seen engaging in penile-vaginal sex play including intercourse. Even though it is true that a boy cannot ejaculate semen until he becomes pubescent, it is also true that erections are possible in sheer infants, and that orgasms as well as erections and penetration of the vagina by the penis are possible in very young children.

As mentioned earlier, six of the especially young swinging couples allowed their pre-verbal toddlers to toddle around amid the sexual festivities during parties. These children would usually fall asleep somewhere on the floor when they were sufficiently tired. Upon seeing one of the children asleep, one of the parents would simply pick it up and tuck it into its bed. Whether these couples will continue to permit their children to "have the run" of swinging get-togethers as they grow older is a moot question. They say that they want to, but even among very relaxed, liberal couples there is a clear feeling that pre-teenage children ought not to be around the home when comarital sexual festivities are going on. And if they are home the belief is that such young children should be asleep. It therefore seems likely that these very liberal young couples will eventually bow to the informal pressure of their swinging peer groups as their children get to be 3, 4, and 5 years old.

I found that most couples usually send their pre-teenaged children off to the homes of relatives or friends for the duration of party nights. The services of grandparents are frequently used when they reside within an hour's driving distance; this is so even though most of the swingers got along rather poorly with their parents. Also very common is for the children to attend an all-night "pajama party" in the home of one of their friends. Most of these friends came from non-swinging families—a fact which necessitated a willingness to reciprocate. Several swinging couples spoke of occasionally having to turn down invitations to swinging parties because they owed a "pajama party" to the parents of one of their children's friends.

Swingers involved in the "love group" movement usually allow their pre-teen youngsters to remain home. In fact, some of their guests who are also parents of pre-teen youngsters bring these children along to some of the parties. These pre-teen children may eventually form the nucleus of a "love group" of their own. But presently these children do not seem to be engaging in any erotic activity at the parties. Such younger children are usually sent to a separate room of the party house where they will watch television and play various games.

I obtained a substantial portion of my information from the eighteen "love group" teenagers. But it must be realized that these young people cannot be considered typical of the swingers' offspring. As long as it is realized that they come from families that are a good deal more unconventional and adventuresome than most swinging families are, it will be possible to view their comments in the proper perspective.

Eleven of the eighteen young people claimed to have had their first full copulation prior to their thirteenth birthday, and four of these eleven claimed to have first experienced sexual intercourse prior to the age of ten. Of course, it is possible that some of these youngsters may have felt motivated to exaggerate their sexual histories. Suffice it to say that their discussions with me seemed dispassionate and serious, particularly as far as their own and their siblings' pasts were concerned.

One 18-year-old "love group" member discussed his initial sexual intercourse:

> "I was in the fourth grade at the time. Mom and Dad were attending some convention together up in Vancouver. We kids had the whole house to ourselves. Mom had arranged to have one of the neighbors look in on us on occasion. But we told them we didn't need any babysitters. We knew how to fix dinner and all that. Anyway, I had this girl friend Peggy. She was in the third grade and I used to like to help her with her homework. (A lot of the guys used to tease me about spending so much time with her, but I didn't care. I used to tell the guys that they were babies because they didn't want to have any girl friend play with them.)
>
> Anyway, I invited Peggy to come home after school when my mom and dad were away. She had been to my place a lot of times. Mom didn't care; she never said anything about us playing and talking in my bedroom. Anyway, we were sitting on the bed and listening to some records when suddenly she broke out into hysterical laughter. I couldn't get her to tell me what she was laughing about. So I put my arm around her head and started petting her back.

I don't know what made me do it. But she looked up and started to kiss me. She said she liked what I was doing and she said that I should continue rubbing some more. So I did, and I also started undoing her blouse. She didn't say anything but she began laughing again. After a couple of minutes she asked me why I didn't take my shirt off too, and that she would give me a nice rubdown if I did it. So I started unbuttoning and then she started unbuttoning my shirt too. We both started lying on our sides and fondling each other. She didn't have any breasts yet, but I still found her very pretty and nice.

I don't know what made us do it, but inside of a few minutes we were both removing each other's clothes. She said she was curious about what I looked like and that she wanted me to take my pants off just for a minute. I told her I was also curious about what she looked like and that it would be fun to give each other a nice rub and then maybe take a bath together. After we both had our clothes off, though, we started kissing again. And after about five minutes or so I started to get a very strong feeling that I had never felt before. I didn't have the foggiest notion about what was happening. I mean, I guess I knew the basic facts about sex but I guess I didn't associate anything I knew with what was happening to me. All I know was that I felt this extremely strong feeling and after a minute I had an overwhelming urge to get on top of Peggy. And as I did it became stronger and stronger. All she kept saying was 'that feels good—that feels good.' And without thinking about anything at all I started pushing my penis, which was then quite hard, against her vaginal opening. I don't think it was another minute before I had completely penetrated her.

She started crying real softly, but she didn't pull away. I remember I asked her if I was hurting her and she said 'no.' Looking back on it now I don't know why she didn't pull away. I don't know. I mean, I knew she liked me. Maybe she was feeling something nice too. Anyway, I had an orgasm, and I still think it was one of the strongest I ever experienced.

Anyway, after it was all over I noticed that Peggy was bleeding all over the blankets. I thought something was wrong, but she said she was fine. I was really worried about her bleeding, but the next day at school she told me she was fine and that she wanted to eat lunch with me.

Peggy's father got a job in Houston two years later, and I felt really bad when she moved away. We kept writing to each other for over a year. I still have her letters somewhere up in our attic. Anyway, between the first time when I was in the fourth grade and when she moved away we had sexual intercourse four other times, and we fondled each other without any clothes on I guess about a dozen times."

This young man, now 18, had two older sisters. He was the youngest of three children and had enjoyed quite a bit of freedom and autonomy while growing up. Despite the unconventional character of his past he enjoys a high degree of popularity with his same-sexed friends, and he achieved some outstanding scores on his college entrance examinations. At the time he was interviewed he had already been accepted by the University of California at Berkeley, but planned to turn it down in order to attend UCLA. He wanted to remain close to his friends.

The foregoing case can be considered typical of how swingers' children become involved in prepubescent copulation. But let us consider another case. Lisa, now 15, had experienced her first copulation at the age of 11. She has been "going strong" since that time even though she claims to have had only three partners. One of these three partners was her 17-year-old brother, although she did not have intercourse with him until three months after she joined her "love group."

> "Well, it was a nice hot, dry summer day. According to the radio it was over a hundred degrees, I remember. All four of us were home and we were fooling around with the water hoses and the swimming pool. I had on a light bikini bathing suit and I was on some kind of a teasing jag, like I usually am—ha, ha. I just couldn't leave Carl [her brother] alone, and we were running all over throwing water and food and soda pop and everything else at each other. Mom and Dad kept yelling at us to cut the shit. I kept screaming back that I didn't want to dirty the knife! Anyway, about halfway through the afternoon we saw Nat and Sarah pull up in front of our house. Nat and Sarah are Mom and Dad's best swinging chums. I don't think Mom and Dad had been expecting anyone that afternoon, but Mom had them come in the house. They said they wanted to get away from us crazy kids for a while. Neither Carl nor I felt like going anywhere. So we chased each other down the basement where we have a nice big guestroom and a beautiful sexy bathroom. You know, you interviewed Mom and Dad there last time you were over to our place . . . Anyway, Mom and Dad forgot us pretty fast when we went down there . . . We ended up in the shower together and pretty soon we ended up in bed together! It was all pretty weird. I mean, I never planned to fuck around with my brother. But there we were! We were doing it and I was really enjoying it! Brothers and sisters sometimes massage each other at our parties. I guess you already know that. But I don't think too many of us would even dream of fucking with a brother or sister. Even though we like each other we just wouldn't! I don't think Carl or I will ever forget what we did that hot summer afternoon. It was great. But neither of us would ever want to do it again."

Lisa was 14 when the foregoing incident occurred, and

her brother Carl was 16. But Lisa had had her first sexual experience at the age of 11. At that time her swinging parents were not getting along very well. Their relationship had allegedly improved a very great deal since the time of the following:

"I've always been a bit closer to my dad than to my mother. And I think sometimes my mom used to resent me for all the time and attention he gave me. Like five summers ago my dad decided to take us up to Zion National Park for a vacation of horseback riding and camping out. I was really overjoyed. But mom hates camping out. So dad decided to compromise. The idea was that we would spend ten days at Zion and ten days at Las Vegas, which is a place I really hate because it's so hot and it's only for adults. Everything went beautifully until we were supposed to leave Zion and head for Las Vegas. Our car broke down. Dad and Carl and I always take minor crises of this kind with a sense of humor—but not my mother. She was mad as hell, and things really went bad when we found out that it would take two more days before the car could be fixed. Dad left Mom behind in the motel room in the park and took Carl and me off on a two-day horseback trip. When we got back Mom created such a scene that one of the park rangers had to restrain her. She was screaming at us and throwing things and it was really embarrassing, especially for Dad.

Anyway, the next morning Dad took us aside and told us that he was afraid for his marriage and that the rest of the time would have to be spent doing the things that Mom wanted to do. So we headed for Las Vegas and registered there for a whole week at some motel. Carl took a Greyhound back to LA because he wanted to be with his friends back home.

Well, let me tell you, that was the most boring week I ever spent in my life. Mom and Dad left me alone at that motel for almost the whole, entire week. They felt I should be happy because the place had a nice swimming pool. But most of the time it was too hot to be outside swimming in it.

Anyway, on the third day I met this kid, Robby. He was in the same predicament I was in. He was also eleven and I found out that he lived only a few miles from where I lived. We hit it off real well together. For five full days and most of five nights we were constant companions. Most of the time we spent either in his motel room or in mine because it was just too damn hot to enjoy the pool. We played a lot of different games, and before you know it we were in the shower together. By the time we had spent three full days together we were experimenting sexually with each other. And before long we had sexual intercourse. In fact, we did it twice during the time we were together. I didn't feel like stopping him. I mean, we were having the best time we could together, and even though it was kinda crazy I really enjoyed a lot of the sexy things we did to each other. Anyway, I knew that he couldn't get me pregnant and I was enjoying what we were doing. So I figured, what the hell!"

I did not interview any families where preadolescent copulation or sex play was an everyday occurrence. But few swinging parents go to any pains to discourage either prepubescent or adolescent sexuality. The fact that swingers' children do not devote a great deal of their time to sexual activities would have to be attributed to factors other than parental authority. Children of any age do not and cannot live in a normative vacuum. They are affected and influenced by several different normative systems. Of far greater significance than norms which proscribe the open expression of sexuality in children and in young teenagers, is the far stronger complex of norms which *prescribes* competence and competitive activity in a range of endeavors such as sports, academic study, the playing of musical instruments, reading, motion picture attendance, and hobbies of all sorts. In short, the swingers' children have a wide variety of interests and activities that compete for their time and psychological energy. In this regard they do not appear to be any different than any other group of American youngsters.

I did observe that the children and teenagers of swinging parents do tend to spend a conspicuously greater amount of their free time in *mixed* peer groups. Their hobbies and their sports and games tend to be supportive of participation by both girls and boys. I also noticed that the swingers' daughters tend to be considerably more assertive, aggressive, and (especially in the younger ages) tomboyish than the daughters of non-swingers. And I noticed that even very young elementary school-aged boys wanted girls to be part of their play groups. But the range of interests displayed by these children and teenagers struck me as being as good and probably even better than that which is usually manifested by similar-aged children from conventional middle-class homes.

The interview data did clearly establish the point that the swingers' teenaged offspring do engage in significantly more boy-girl sexual activity than the non-swingers' teenaged offspring do. But in no case does sexuality appear to dominate the lives of any of these youngsters. A small amount of time is devoted to enjoying sex; but they enjoy and become competent at many other activities as well. Writer Neil Elliott (1970) in his recent book *Sensuality in Scandinavia* wrote of how the average girl in contemporary Iceland is only 13 years old when she first enjoys sexual intercourse with a boy; and in most cases Icelandic parents tend to be quite supportive of their teenagers' sexuality. In this perspective much of the sexual behavior of the Los Angeles area swingers' children cannot even be considered unprecedented as far as Western civilization is concerned.

The Teenagers' Sexual Monogamy

Important as they are to study and to understand, the "love groups" were comparatively uncommon among the ranks of the swinging families studied. Far more common was the practice of teenagers establishing sexually monogamous relationships with school friends of the other sex. Some of these relationships appeared to have lasted for an extended period of time while others were of comparatively short duration. But all of these romantic sex-love relationships involved regular premarital sexual intercourse in the private bedrooms of the youngsters concerned. In most cases the swingers' children established such strong, intimate relationships with age-mates from ordinary, non-swinging homes. And as might be expected, the bedroom of the swingers' son or daughter tended to be the one that was used most of the time. However, many of the young people involved in such relationships employed the bedroom of the partner from the non-swinging family on at least an occasional basis.

Most swinging parents tend to maintain an air of detachment as far as the personal lives of their teenaged offspring are concerned. When questioned they usually say that they do not want to interfere in their young people's lives in any way (apart from contraception) that has to do with sex. Most swinging parents are interested primarily in pleasuring themselves. This is a key reason why they become swingers in the first place and why they go to the sometimes formidable amount of trouble necessary to sustain membership in swinging cliques. To them, their children have their own lives and they do not feel that it is their business to interfere. Egotistical (and some recreational) swingers are especially likely to display this attitude; they angrily scoff at the thought of some of their fellows setting up "love groups" and helping their children to get started with the other sex. Many of them claimed that they do not even like to swing with such people because they are "too possessive" or because they are "clinging vines." "They don't seem to realize that all

we really want when we go out is two or three good fucks,"
one 36-year-old mother asserted; "They want to befriend
you and then they want you to help them reform the
world! Shit! We don't want to reform anything! All we
want is a good time. And we already have all the friends
we need. We don't want to make close friends with the
people we swing with. Who needs it!"

But just as this "hands off" attitude keeps these mothers
and fathers from helping their children get started with
the other sex, it also keeps them from interfering in any
major way with their children's sometimes very unconventional (by contemporary suburban middle-class standards) lives.

On the positive side, the swinging mothers and fathers
provide their children with a model of active and effective
sociability. Shyness and inhibition seem to be quite uncommon among young people who grow up in swinging
families. Two exceptions to this were found, and both of
these youngsters were only children of the male sex. The
often very self-centered attitude of swinging parents usually results in their children developing a high degree of
self-sufficiency very early in life. In cases where there is
some degree of dependency it tends to be on brothers,
sisters and friends, rather than upon parents or upon
adults in general. It is often said that swingers' children
stick together; my data tend to support that judgment.

I studied a total of 95 swingers' children who, at the
time of the interviews, were between the ages of 13 and 19.
Out of this number only 23 had "lived together unmarried" in their own bedroom (and/or in the bedroom of the
love partner) with a friend of the opposite sex. Just 16 of
the young people were "living together" at the time of the
interviews. With one exception, all of the teenagers who
had ever "lived together" had done so with a love partner
who was also the son or daughter of swinging parents.

However, 24 of the swingers' children investigated for
this study were 20 or more years of age at the time the
interviews were conducted, and 19 of these young people

had also "lived together." But among the 17 of this older group that were "living together" at the time of the study, only three were doing so with the son or daughter of another swinging family. All of the others were living with a "love mate" who had grown up in a more conventional family situation. Only two of the young people "living together" with a partner who had *not* grown up in a swinging family were doing so within their parents' domicile. One of these was a 24-year-old male graduate student in biology who was "living together" in his parents' home with a 21-year-old undergraduate college girl whose parents and family lived in Richmond, Indiana, some 2,400 miles away. The other case involved a 20-year-old swingers' daughter who was "living together" in her parents' home with a 21-year-old fellow college student whose family resided in Stamford, Connecticut, some 3,000 miles away. All of the others who were cohabiting with someone who did not hail from a swinging family were doing so in their own apartment or living quarters.

About half of the swingers' teenagers had never spent much time around people of their own age who had also grown up in swinging families. On the other hand some of the swingers' children frequently interacted after school with age-mates of similar background who resided within a nine or ten mile radius of their own home. Nine of these youngsters struck up romantic friendships that eventuated in cohabitation. It should be emphasized that I am referring here to teenagers who had never been affiliated with the "love groups."

Sociologists have pointed out for many years that in order for a person to sustain an ongoing, viable friendship the two people involved in that friendship must have many opportunities for being around each other. This is probably why most of the romances experienced by the swingers' children tended to be with age-mates who were attending the same school, whom they saw everyday and with whom they shared various extracurricular activities and academic classes. As might be expected, these romances did not involve people who had grown up in swinging homes.

But just as the teenagers who were dating fellow swingers' children tended to gravitate toward wanting to "live together," so it was with the teenagers who had fallen in love with a boy or girl of a non-swinging household. It quickly became apparent to these young people that they would not be able to "live together" as long as one of the partners in a relationship was the son or daughter of parents who would not accept this type of life style for high school-aged offspring. It became apparent to them that other arrangements for satisfying their needs and fantasies would have to be worked out. Unlike most teenagers in today's society these teenagers only had to deal with one, not two pairs of objecting parents. They might not be able to live with their girlfriend or boyfriend but they could engage in all the sex they wanted with that boy or girl without having to worry about any adults getting in the way.

Some of the swinging mothers mentioned that they often worried about being "found out" by the parents of the boy or girl their own son or daughter was seeing. The usual rejoinder to this worry was that they could always convincingly claim ignorance of any teenage sexual activity if anyone accused them of permitting or sponsoring any such activity in their home. The swinging fathers seemed to worry less about this matter than the swinging mothers, although both would commonly reassure the other that the teenagers had been fully educated as to birth control and that their sexual behavior was something that the parents couldn't do anything about anyway.

Listening to remarks such as these constituted what to me, the interviewer, was one of the most strange yet strikingly memorable experiences of this whole research effort. Here were middle-class mothers and fathers sitting on expensive sofas in expensive houses located in what were very often extremely attractive suburban neighborhoods telling a social scientist in all seriousness that the sexual activity of their adolescent daughters and sons was not really the parents' business—not even when such sexual activity was occurring on a day-to-day basis in their own domiciles. To be sure, the spontaneous nudity that accompanied some of the interviews was also very striking. But the swinging parents' attitudes with respect to their own children's sexual behavior was in many ways even more noteworthy.

Out of the 77 swingers' teenaged children who were not affiliated with any of the "love groups," 52 had had close friends of the opposite sex with whom they enjoyed premarital sexual intercourse. All 52 of these young people had used their own private bedrooms for lovemaking, and 27 of them had at least occasionally used the private bedrooms of their girl friend or boy friend who was not a member of a swinging household. At the time of the interviews 45 of the swingers' teenaged children were involved in such ongoing sex-love relationships, and all but four of these claimed to be having sexual intercourse an average of between five and seven times per week.

Given the life style of the swinging parents and the freedom they accorded their adolescent children, I think it could be considered both remarkable and significant that none of the children involved in this study used their bedrooms of their homes for "promiscuous" sexual behavior. Promiscuous sexual behavior can be defined as sexual behavior, without regard to any criteria of partner selection, and characteristically involves the frequent changing of sexual partners as well as the absence of any effort to get to know any of the partners on a meaningful psycho-emotional level. None of the teenagers with whom I spoke indicated that they had ever been involved in this type of sexual behavior. Moreover, some of the parents indicated amazement that their children were not sexually "playing the field" and "getting it all out of their systems now." About half of the young people had had two sexual partners thus far in their short lives, and twenty of them claimed to have had as many as three or four partners. But none of the

young people had ever had more than one sex-love relationship going on at the same time.

Sixty-eight percent of the swinging parents interviewed
for this study had an accepting attitude toward adolescent
young people "living together," and a similar percentage
approved the idea of teenagers using their own bedrooms
for premarital coitus. I asked the swinging couples
numerous questions about this subject. One of these read
as follows: "A small minority of parents here in southern
California permit their adolescent sons and daughters to
use their own bedrooms for premarital coitus. They do
this with the view that negative consequences are very
unlikely to occur as a result of sexual intercourse when
parents provide their children with both warm emotional
support and keen sympathetic interest in their needs. Do
you agree with this perspective?"

Only 21 percent of the swinging mothers and 14 percent
of the swinging fathers indicated disagreement, and 13
percent of the swinging mothers and 18 percent of the
swinging fathers were "uncertain." Only two of the swinging couples had a punitive attitude toward teenagers "living together." Nevertheless, twelve of the couples believed
that young people should not be permitted to "live together" in their parents' home.

To give the reader some feeling for how "different" the
swinging mothers and fathers are from their non-swinging
next-door neighbors, only 15 percent of the non-swinging
fathers and 6 percent of the non-swinging mothers could
accept the idea of their adolescent children using their
own bedrooms for premarital coitus. In addition, 43 percent of the non-swinging husbands and 46 percent of the
non-swinging wives indicated that they would assume a
punitive attitude toward even a 20-year-old son or daughter who was "living together" while away at school. *None*
of the swinging mothers and fathers held so negative an
attitude.

Whereas only 23 of the 95 teenaged children of this
study had *actually* "lived together" with an opposite-sexed

love partner, a much greater number than this *initially* indicated that they had "lived together." Because the meaning of the term "living together" has become increasingly ambiguous and amorphous over the past few years it became apparent quite early in the interviews with the swingers' children that I would have to establish a definition for the concept that could be consistently applied. I therefore decided that a young person would be considered to have "lived together" with someone of the other sex if he or she had shared a private bedroom with his or her lover for a minimum of four nights per week over a period of at least one month. This definition is admittedly somewhat loose. But since we are dealing here with high-school-aged adolescents I decided that a looser than usual definition was in order.

While the lack of a clear-cut meaning for the concept of "living together" poses some problems for the serious researcher in this area, I believe that the widespread tendency among swingers' children to identify themselves with the concept serves to underscore the increasing acceptance and affinity toward "living together" within this group. If the idea were an unpopular one, then young people who had simply engaged in premarital sex with their loved one while on a camping trip or while watching television with no one else at home would be quite disinclined to label themselves as having ever been in the "living together" category.

However, seeing each other each day after school and spending a great deal of time with each other tended to be perceived by many of these young people as being the same as "living together."

> "Jack and I would be living together if we didn't have to worry about what his parents might think. We both have to depend on our parents for food, clothing, shelter, money, and all kinds of other stuff. So we might as well go along with some of the things they want. I really like Jack's mom and dad anyway. I don't see any point in pissing them off

whcn we already have almost everything we want right now the way things are. Sure, we don't sleep through the night with each other. But we probably have more sex together than most married people the way things are right now. Like we take showers together, we play games in the nude, we do our homework together almost every night, and if we feel like having sex we do it. So, I'm satisfied and I think Jack is too. He usually leaves our house around 11 o'clock each night, and when he goes I think he's ready to go. Sure, I miss him, but still I enjoy having a few minutes of privacy before I go to bed. I think even if we were married I'd want to be alone at least once in a while. So as far as I'm concerned we're like living together ... like we see a lot more of each other than my mom and dad see of each other." (Vivian, a 17-year-old high school senior.)

The tendency of some of these young people to see their behavior as "living together" unmarried is further demonstrated in the comments of Reed, an unusually large and mature-looking 16-year old.

"Kathy and I started living together two months ago. Yeah, I know you wouldn't consider what we're doing to be living together. But to us that's what it is. Sure, we never actually spent a whole night together except once last summer when we went on a camping trip up in the Sierras. Ha! Her mom and dad took me along on the trip ... We slept right next to each other three nights in a row. But we were both in our own sleeping bags so we couldn't fuck around at all. I think her old man or her brother Bill would have killed me if I'd tried anything. I was so fuckin' horny after that weekend I almost flipped right out of my skin! Shit! Anyway, we haven't *slept* next to each other since that time. But I bet we've fucked each other more times than the average husband in this country fucks his wife in a whole year! And she loves it! Shit, man, the way I feel now I wouldn't part with this fuckin' arrangement I've got if you paid me a million dollars!"

Like their parents, the swingers' children tended to become romantically interested in the opposite sex very early in life, although in no case did they do this to the exclusion of other interests. This early interest and involvement is certainly not difficult to understand inasmuch as the swinging parents in almost all cases tended to be quite demonstrative. They frequently kissed and petted their spouse while the children were around and they frequently went about their daily routine household chores nude and often encouraged their children to do the same. In short, they presented to their children a strong and effective model exalting the joys of heterosexuality in all of its major ramifications.

Several of the young people mentioned the fact that they perceive their parents as "different" from most other parents, but that they had not really begun to view their parents as "different" until they were 14 or 15 years of age. Daughters tended to sense that their parents were different" earlier than sons, although even they seldom became strongly conscious of this "difference" prior to the age of 13. But more importantly, none of the young people discussed their parents' peccadillos in a disparaging way. Most of them thought their parents were "neat" but wished that they would give them more time and personal attention.

It is worth repeating here that few swinging parents give their children as much conversational time and attention as non-swinging parents devote to their children. But my analysis also made it clear that even in non-swinging families with a lot of informal parent-child communication, very little is ever said about sex, birth control, or even about the everyday matters of dating and courtship. The swingers talked comparatively little with their children, but when there was talk there was little if any avoidance of open discussion of personal matters such as sex and courtship.

Since the swingers' children had never been programmed to feel reticent about discussing personal sex matters with their parents they doubtless were influenced by their parents in this area to a far greater extent than were the non-swingers' children. This influence manifested itself as this particular study was concerned in (1) *no* cases of venereal disease reported by either the parents or by the young people themselves, and (2) only two reported cases of unplanned pregnancy. Both the young people and their parents reported on the same two cases of unplanned pregnancy. Given the unusually extensive amount of heterosexual copulation that had been taking place among these adolescents these findings would have to be considered most impressive.

Despite the swingers' often expressed disinterest in their children's sexual lives, some of them volunteered comments suggesting that they enjoyed watching their children's heterosexual behavior, particularly when it occurred at home. The following quote from a 42-year-old swinging mother exemplifies this:

> "Oh my Jimmy has the cutest little girl friend. He brings her home almost everyday after school, and I can't tell you how much their presence brightens up my day. It's just so beautiful! Yesterday I was watching them skinny dipping in our swimming pool. I didn't want them to know that I was watching them. But I ran and got my movie camera. It was so beautiful watching them. I just couldn't resist it. Especially when they kiss or when they were rubbing suntan lotion on each other. It was really precious watching them. I just had to get a movie of them together like that. Love is so beautiful, it just has to be preserved. What's more beautiful than two adorable ninth graders in love with each other like that? I watch them whenever I can do it without their knowing it. I look forward everyday to seeing their cute little happy faces together."

Another 46-year old swinging mother expressed it this way:

"Well, when I first found out that they were doing it it blew my mind. I had just returned from the grocery store and I hear strange squealing sounds coming from my son's bedroom. I went to open the door and it was locked. He had his goddam dog in there and as soon as he heard me he started barking and scratching his nails against the door. Now I don't mind him having his door locked. But I couldn't take the barking, so I got my spare key and opened it just to let the dog out and stop all that racket. Well, I saw the two of them laying there in the nude and I almost died. I was too dumbfounded to even know what to say. So I didn't say anything and I took the dog out for a long walk so I could do some serious thinking about how I would handle the situation . . . I suddenly realized that I was only 15 myself when I started doing it—and in those days you had to use the back seat of a car. You wouldn't dare do it in your parents' home. But my son was a high school senior. He was older than I was when I started . . . Anyway, my husband and I had a talk with the two of them that night. And we decided that we'd let them do what they wanted so long as they used something. I mean, I didn't want him to get her pregnant . . . Well, I guess they must have really been in love because they were together at the house almost all the time. Tommy and Becky [her younger children] were really being given quite a sex education by what was going on and I was a bit concerned. But after a couple of weeks Sam [her husband] and I actually began looking forward to seeing Max and his girl friend at the house. It got to the point where we didn't even mind the added expense. And it was an expense! She ate a lot of meals over at our place and her family very seldom reciprocated. They seemed to want to spend their time at our place, and you don't have to be too bright to be able to understand why. But Sam and I came to the realization that we weren't being taken advantage of. Having those two kids around made the both of us feel younger.

They were more fun than any television show ever could be! So we permitted it because we were enjoying it ourselves." (This young couple was still together at the time of the interviews. They were college sophomores and "living together" unmarried in their own apartment.)

The fact that this mother was a swinger herself no doubt helped to make it comparatively easy for her to adjust to her son's behavior. In many ways she could even "relax and enjoy it." However, it was often even easier for the teenagers themselves to get their swinging mothers and fathers to accept the idea of premarital sex. As one 48-year-old swinging father expressed it:

"He [the teenaged son] just came to me one day and nonchalantly announced that he had been having sex in his bedroom with his girl friend. I knew by the way he approached me and by the tone of his voice that he didn't expect any kind of a disapproving reaction from me. He just wanted to share his experience with someone older. At least that's what he said. My first impulse was to raise hell with him. But something stopped me before I could say a word. I mean, I couldn't see myself becoming any goddam hypocrite. You know, once a person gets started having sex they usually don't stop. So me and my wife—we just figured that he's less likely to get into any kind of trouble if he does it right here at home. At least we know who he's seeing and he's not afraid to approach us about any problems he's been having. Up to now I don't think our son has had any fears or qualms at all about talking over his problems with either me or his mother. I don't always have time for him. But at least he known he's not going to get put down."

The active sexuality of teenaged daughters did not seem to stir up any stronger feelings of apprehension in these swinging parents than did the active sexuality of the sons. Dora M's daughter Suzie was only 15 when it became apparent that she was using her bedroom for premarital coitus.

"I came home from work one day to find Peggy [the 8-year-old sister] doing her homework on the kitchen table. I asked her what she was doing with her crap all over my kitchen table and she says that old Suzie-goozie had temporarily evicted her from her bedroom. Suzie and Peggy have to share a bedroom and up to that time they never seemed to have any big fights. So I went to see what was going on. Suzie had the door locked, but she opened it right away. And I want to tell you I was shocked to find her in there half-dressed with a boy. He was fully dressed but she only had on her underdrawers and a light blouse with nothing on underneath. The boy was obviously nervous. But my daughter very brazenly announced to me that they had been swinging that afternoon just like my husband and I do. Then she showed me a vaginal foam container and a condom that they had been using. And before I had a chance to even open my mouth she said she hoped I wasn't going to be upset. Well, my husband came home shortly after that and all four of us had a long talk. Little Peggy was also there listening in, and I wasn't very happy about that. But we decided that something like this couldn't be hidden and that things usually work out better when the cards are honestly laid out on the table for everyone to see . . . It was finally decided that Suzie and her boyfriend could use the bedroom as long as they continued to take proper birth control precautions and as long as Peggy could continue to have her fair share of time in her room. And believe me, for the past couple of months the two of them have really taken advantage of their privilege. For a while I felt like something of an ass for letting my daughter have her way so easily. But I've really been surprised at how many of the people we swing with allow the same thing. As long as the kids are protected against having any babies of their own, sex among teenagers seems to be the accepted thing in

the crowd we go with." (40-year-old swinging
mother.)

Many of the teenagers simply announced to their parents that they were "swinging" too, or that they too had
begun having sex and that they would like to have the
convenience of using their own bedrooms instead of having to go somewhere else. In many instances the teenagers
asked permission beforehand, but many others just took
the initiative upon themselves and let their parents react
to the situation upon discovering it. A few of the teenagers
let their parents in on the "secret" only after they had
been using their bedrooms after school for a lengthy
period of time. In no case, however, did the parents' "discovery" develop into any kind of a major family crisis.

In most non-swinging families such a discovery would
probably develop into a major crisis. This is especially so
inasmuch as we are talking here about mere teenagers,
some of whom were as young as 13 or 14. But what is
experienced as a crisis is always related to the socially
programmed beliefs and perceptions of the beholder.
America is moving in a liberal direction as far as the acceptance of premarital sex among college students and
young adults is concerned. But this increased acceptance
seldom extends to high school aged youth or to the young
person's use of his own bedroom in his parent's home, an
acceptance which virtually symbolizes full parental approval and psychological serenity about the idea of teenaged heterosexuality.

One of the most interesting teenaged sex-love relationships encountered by this research involved Sylvia, a 15-
year-old girl who had run away from home. Sylvia had
grown up in Dallas, Texas, and had allegedly been beaten
by both her father and mother on a daily basis. Her parents had subscribed to a very strict, fundamentalistic
Southern Baptist philosophy of life. And when Sylvia was
even so much as suspected of deviating from the many
rules they had laid down they beat her, usually by tying
her up nude, gagging her, and beating her with hoses and

razor straps. One day Sylvia secretly pawned $300 worth of her mother's property, boarded a Greyhound bus and headed for Los Angeles.

For about six weeks she worked as a prostitute. When she was caught by the police she refused to discuss anything about her family and background. As the authorities had no way of ascertaining where she came from they placed her in a foster home in the San Fernando Valley. It was at her new school there that she met Mickey, the 15-year-old son of swinging parents.

Mickey's older brother was already involved in a stable, on-going, afternoon sexual relationship in his bedroom. Mickey was very attached to his brother and tended to emulate him in every way possible. He found himself strongly attracted to Sylvia. But he couldn't understand why so "pretty" a girl often was so poorly dressed and so lonely and withdrawn. Nevertheless, he made friends with her and within a short time he invited her to his home.

Mickey's swinging parents were as delighted with Sylvia as they were with his older brother's girl friend. But they too were confused by Sylvia's passivity and often unkempt appearance. Sylvia and Mickey became virtually inseparable and often had sex after school in his bedroom. But one day she came to Mickey's home in tears and told the full story of her past, indicating that her present foster mother could not take care of her anymore and that the state was going to place her elsewhere.

Quite remarkably, these swinging parents promptly contacted the state officials and asked to serve as Sylvia's new foster parents. Even though this family had an annual income in excess of $40,000, I think it is particularly significant that on behalf of the son's wishes they volunteered to take the girl on a permanent basis. The state accepted the arrangement as it permitted Sylvia to continue on at the same school. Sylvia and Mickey had been sharing the same bed for four months at the time I talked to them and they were getting along very well. Needless to say, the state social workers had no idea of the arrangement. The older brother was continuing to see his girl friend each day after school as well as on weekends. And a family situation which most American social scientists would doubtless view as highly improbable continues to function in a manner deemed by each of its members as smooth and harmonious.

While most swingers' children appear to be quite dauntless in their ability and willingness to discuss personal sex matters with their parents, I uncovered five teenaged sex-love relationships in which the sex part had remained hidden from the parents. Bob and Rachel, now 18 and 17 respectively, had been using their home bedrooms for lovemaking for over a year and a half. Despite the fact that Rachel's parents are very active recreational swingers she just doesn't feel comfortable about telling them what is going on. And she feels that it isn't even necessary:

> "Both my parents work and my brother is attending college out of state. So he's never home. I have the whole house to myself when I come home from school as well as most evenings. So Bob and I just make ourselves comfortable there whenever we want to. We've been seeing each other now for almost two years and we love each other very much. We don't feel as though we're doing anything wrong. A lot of the time we just study together. Neither of us drink and we haven't taken any drugs—not even marijuana. Gee, I think we're tame in comparison to some of the stuff that goes on at our school. I don't want to ruin my life and neither does Bob. I feel we're both very level-headed compared to most of the kids we know at school. Sure, we have sex a lot. But I think that's only natural. I mean, we enjoy it and I know I've grown so much in just the past year that I'm a totally different person . . . I guess my mom and dad would eventually accept what we're doing if we let them find out. But the way I figure—why get their bowels in an uproar when it isn't necessary. Sex is a personal thing, right? Why bring Mom and Dad into it when it isn't

necessary? Like they say, what you don't know can't bother you."

The True "Living Together" Style

As pointed out earlier, only 23 of the swingers' teenagers had *actually* "lived together" unmarried. Fourteen of these young people had lived together with the son or daughter of a fellow "love group" member. Eight of them had "lived together" with the son or daughter of another swinging household, and one of them "lived together" with someone who had not originated in a swinging household. The latter case involved the runaway girl discussed earlier.

When a son or daughter "lives together" with his or her lover in his or her parents' domicile the family must necessarily undergo a transformation of both structure and function. This is so regardless of whether the young couple is married or unmarried. If they are unmarried and especially if they are of high school age the larger family system of which they have become a part necessarily becomes quite nonconformist within the larger perspective of suburban American families generally. This nonconformist status is bound to affect the interaction patterns of family members even though within the smaller perspective of swinging families the idea of teenagers "living together" unmarried can hardly be considered seriously deviant.

Yet in spite of certain problems most such families continued to function with a degree of harmony that probably exceeded that of a normal, non-swinging suburban household. One of the reasons for the success was probably that the parents viewed their teenaged children as children despite the fact that they were enjoying the "adult privilege" of regular sex and intimate heterosexual companionship. In effect, these teenagers were not expected to make any economic contribution to the household of which they were a part. They *were* expected to keep their rooms neat, to respect their elders for the privileges they allowed, and to respect the rights of their younger brothers and sisters.

Additionally, many of them were expected to play an active role in the performing of routine household chores. But it must be reemphasized that none of these expectations conferred any responsibilities of economic support upon the teenagers. All were regular students in local public high schools, and outside of their homes all were living lives that would have to be regarded as normal and typical for American teenagers.

Another factor that was strongly credited for the tranquility of the cohabiting teenagers' home life was the dedicated willingness of the swinging parents involved to cooperate with each other. For each cohabiting couple two pairs of parents had to be sufficiently committed to the success of their teenagers' consensual union to provide necessary financial and psycho-emotional support. The following case exemplifies the way style problems were commonly worked out by the swinging parents:

> "We've been swinging with Madge and Gus for the past five years and we love them as though they were a part of our own family. Now our daughter Cindy and their son Russ have been cohabiting for almost a year and a half now and we think it has gone beautifully. None of the neighbors suspect anything and I know that all the teachers at school view Cindy as just another happy teenaged girl. In the beginning we really weren't sure how the six of us were going to work things out. For the first six months or so Cindy and Russ simply rotated houses. One night they would sleep here and the next night they would sleep over in Madge's house. That worked for a while. At least we didn't have to end up with another mouth to feed. At first we were really worried about that because that kid Russ can really eat anybody out of house and home! By having them rotate houses every night we were able to share expenses pretty nearly equally ... But the kids soon got tired of the rigidity in that kind of schedule. Some nights they didn't even want to be together and some nights they wanted to be at the other person's house. So we finally decided to let

them do what they want. I keep track of the amount
of food Russ eats and Madge keeps track of what
Cindy consumes and dirties over at her place.
Things have evened themselves out. We just let it
all hang loose and everyone gets along real well."
(45-year-old swinging mother.)

Sometimes the "keeping track" of who uses what becomes a bit difficult. Many of the cohabiting couples in
this sample were strongly attached emotionally. And despite their very young ages they did not want to separate
even for a few weeks of summertime travel. Some of these
same couples would casually decide to spend some nights
sleeping alone. Yet if the prospect arose of a three or four
week separation they tended to rebel at the thought. In the
case just cited, Madge and Gus took their family on a four
week vacation to the Canadian Rockies. Neither they nor
Cindy's parents were at first very comfortable about the
matter; but Cindy ended up going along on the trip so that
she could continue being with Russ.

Further complications can arise when a cohabiting boy
and girl belong to different school districts. The fathers of
Jeff and Becky were ardent supporters of the teenaged
"love groups," and at first they were not too keen on their
children's stubborn emotional-love fixation on one
another. But the mothers were evidently "in love" with
the young couple with whom they spent much time talking and observing. They did not have to work very hard in
order to convince their husbands to be supportive of the
children's cohabiting relationship. Nevertheless, Jeff and
Becky were kept to a rigid schedule. Every two weeks they
were required to change houses. In the morning, either the
father or the mother with whom they were living had to
drive one of the two lovers to a high school some seven
miles away. The fact that at the time they were interviewed these four parents had been living with this inconvenience for seven months strongly suggests that they
were deriving some sort of gratification for themselves out
of their offspring's love affair.

One of the parents claimed that his own marriage had grown even better since the young couple had started cohabiting. The wife extolled the joys of knowing where her teenager was "hanging out" most of the time. It is difficult to accept the notion that these homes can go month after month without serious friction, especially since they are most atypical families by American standards. But the data obtained by this research suggest that they do just that.

Some of the cohabiting couples did spend all or a majority of their nights in just one domicile. The tendency was for the girl's house to be selected, and for the boy's expenses to be borne by his own father and mother. Few of the couples in this category spent every single night together. But I could find no case where a couple's temporary separation had been precipitated by or insisted upon by the parents. Temporary separations normally lasted for from one to three consecutive nights and most of the couples had at least one such separation every two weeks. Couples who were cohabiting in just one domicile tended to experience at least one such separation every week. Both the parents and the young people themselves agreed that the separations were usually brought on by an occasional desire for privacy or by a desire to spend time with brothers, sisters, parents, or personal friends. Boys were about equally likely as girls to precipitate such temporary separations. However, there seemed to be no indication at all in this sample that the couples who took such temporary "vacations" from each other were getting along any less well than those who seldom or never slept apart.

Such separations seldom caused major arguments. The cohabiting couples tended to gravitate toward these occasional separations as naturally and as casually as they had initially gravitated toward "living together." Nevertheless, arguments occasionally did arise in regard to spending too much time with same-sexed peers. The feeling on the part of one partner that he or she was not receiving enough attention from the other also tended to precipitate arguments, particularly on school nights. But the parents saw their cohabiting sons and daughters as being *less* argumentative *overall* than they themselves had been prior to marriage. And parents of boys, in particular, tended to praise what they saw as the beneficial effect of cohabitation on academic performance. (The effect upon the girls' academic performance appeared to be nil.)

Seven of the 23 teenaged cohabitation relationships had broken up at some point within one year of the completion of the interviews for this study. This represents a 30 percent "failure" rate. Since these couples were not followed up on a long-term basis it should be clear that 30 percent represents only a part of the eventual story.

Of course, some degree of hardship and emotional turmoil is a part of the breakup of any close, emotional relationship whether it involves legal marriage, cohabitation, or just plain steady dating. Indeed, even the forced separation of same-sexed friends can cause temporary depression and adjustment problems. But as the swinging adults and many of the teenagers kept hammering home to me, learning how to cope intelligently with such emotional pains is a part of life and of healthy growth. The seven who had suffered breakups all were working out constructive adjustments in their lives. But more significantly, none of the seven young people regretted having "lived together" with their opposite-sexed roommate.

> "Why should I regret it? To me it was a great learning experience. I learned a lot about myself and about guys. Jack and I are still good friends, but I could see that it wasn't doing me any good to continue on with him. At least not as roommates. I know Jack isn't the kind of guy I'd want for a husband. But I don't fault him for anything. I'm sure there are a lot of girls he would be really great for . . . I broke up with him because he was spending too much time with his friends. I started to get lonely and, well, I wouldn't have minded it so much if his interests had been more like mine. Jack is a very athletic guy and I'm not. I think it got to the

point where we were both holding each other back.
We just finally realized that we didn't have enough
in common and that we would just be kidding ourselves if we continued to live together."

Unfortunately, seven is far too few cases to permit the
making of reliable generalizations. But focusing on individual cases may provide some tentative insights. Only
one of the seven cases seemed to have involved a marked
degree of emotional pain. And it involved a 17-year-old
boy who had cohabited for four months with a 16-year-old
girl. Unlike the case just cited, the decision to separate had
been made entirely by the girl. The boy had been strongly
desirous of sustaining the relationship, and it took him
three months after the breakup before he became desirous
of dating again. This young man had been strongly encouraged by both parents and friends to have sex with
other girls after the break up of his love relationship. At
the time of my last interview with him he had begun dating another girl, but he was still far from the point of
wanting to recommence his sex life with anyone.

"Well, see, I was really in love with her and I guess I
thought we were getting along real well. I don't
know. Maybe we were getting along. Maybe she
just needed more elbow room. Some people do.
Like she kept complaining before we broke up that
she felt cramped. Like I have this friend who is into
astrology. He told me that our relationship never
had a chance because she is a Leo and I'm a Taurus.
Shit. I know there's no simple answers. But like I
was hurting pretty bad for a while. I think I'm beginning to get over it now. But I still would like it
better if I could somehow get back with her again!"

As I have pointed out, six out of the seven cohabitation
relationships that broke up did so largely on the basis of
mutual desire. All of these young people indicated to me
that they were grateful for having had the opportunity to
"live together," and that they looked forward to the opportunity of finding another partner and commencing

another love relationship that would also involve cohabitation. By the way, this was also true for the young man discussed above. The attitudes of the parents of these young people were quite similar. As one swinging mother expressed it:

> "It's only natural for a broken love affair to cause some hurt. But believe me, the people who avoid close relationships in order to avoid pain are the very same ones whose attitude also causes them to avoid pleasure. People who can't or won't take risks may avoid some pain but they always end up leading dull lives without any intense pleasure."

Some of the swinging parents harbored very pragmatic attitudes toward unmarried cohabitation.

> "Shit! You tell me that there's a 40 percent breakup rate among couples living together. And some people say that's bad! Well, in my opinion I think the breakup rate ought to be a hell of a lot higher than 40 percent! What the hell good does a trial marriage do for society if everyone involved in such trial marriages eventually marries? It seems to me that the whole idea behind so-called trial marriages is to screen out weak or ill-suited unions before they manage to get as far as the altar or that fuckin' legal document we've come to call marriage. If every young kid who gets it in his head to start cohabiting with his lover eventually marries that lover, what the hell is the point? If that happens we won't have accomplished anything and the society will not have grown. In my opinion I'd say that at least 70 percent of all consensual unions should fail. If that happened we wouldn't be having all this divorce. The quality of legal marriage would be improved and family life would be sharply upgraded. If I had anything to say about it I'd require every young couple contemplating marriage to live together for at least one year before allowing them to tie the *legal* knot and begin having children. It's the only way a couple can really get to

know each other and what being together day-in and day-out is actually like. It's the only way people can look at their situation free from the damned rosy-colored smokescreen we've come to call love. Now I'm certainly not opposed to love! But you've got to be able to see things beyond the smokescreens of love and passion if you're going to be able to make intelligent decisions about things that affect your whole life." (40-year-old swinging husband.)

The idea of requiring couples to live together for at least one year prior to legal marriage is not new. In fact, over one hundred years ago in what is now Scotland, the Presbyterian Church sustained a custom that went by the name of "handfasting." Under this custom no minister would be permitted to marry a couple that had not "lived together" for a minimum of at least one year.

Like the Scotch of a century ago, most preliterate societies have viewed marriage as existing only for the purpose of legitimating and stabilizing the institution of parenthood. According to this classic view marriage has nothing to do with legitimating cohabitation or with legitimating sexual intercourse. However, in order to survive all societies have always been concerned about the propitious growth and development of their new offspring. Today it is widely believed by contemporary anthropologists that all societies originally invented the institution of marriage in response to this universal concern about the proper care and socialization of children. In essence, the marriage ceremony legitimates two specific people, i.e., a man and a woman, for playing the socially prescribed roles of father and mother.

It is quite popular today for some people to view cohabitation among the unmarried as being competitive with legal marriage. However, as long as such unions remain uninvolved in the procreation of children they clearly constitute a part of the *courtship* institution, and hence cannot logically be considered competitive with marriage and family institutions. The major functions served by the courtship institution are those of recruiting young people for the stable, long-term roles of husband-father and wife-mother. If the evolving middle-class custom of "living together" does this better than the old-fashioned American courtship system did, then "living together," rather than being competitive with legal marriage, will eventually be shown to be a facilitator of strong marriage and family systems. The Scotch Presbyterian ministers of a century ago continued to see it this way until the Victorian ethic forced them to revise their church laws in a sexually ascetic direction.

Unfortunately it is still far too early for social scientists to try to determine the effects on legal marriage of unmarried cohabitation. The social context within which most American young people are forced to function is still too conservative in regard to sexual norms. The presence of such conservative norms is bound to adversely affect the thoroughness with which young people are going to be able to internalize the new norms emotionally and cognitively. For this reason a fair test of the beneficial effect of cohabitation experience upon legal marriage and parenting is not yet feasible. As a social scientist I would suggest that a fair test could be made in any social setting in America in which *a minimum of 80 percent* of all parents have socially programmed their children into viewing premarital coitus and unmarried cohabitation as morally correct and proper under a specified range of circumstances. Presumably mutual love, respect, and contraceptive responsibility would lie at the heart of the specified range of "moral" circumstances. At the present time few American parents are this liberal. As a consequence, most young men and women are forced to work out a viable and realistic morality on their own. As such, even among cohabiting couples marriage and/or pregnancy sometimes occur too soon. Again, lovers must *fully* accept premarital sex as morally right for themselves *before* they can serenely talk with each other about their sex life and their contracepting responsibilities.

One of the most frequent criticisms of "living together" voiced by the non-swinging husbands and wives I interviewed was that couples who cohabit are "emotionally incapable of making a commitment." It may indeed be that a small minority of cohabiting couples are incapable of making a commitment. But for the majority of cohabiting couples the idea of being incapable of making a commitment defies common sense. In most cases if any of these couples married they would immediately be accused (and probably by the same people) of marrying prematurely and with excessive haste. Many cohabiting couples (both among the swingers' children reported on in this book and among college-age young people from non-swinging homes) have known each other for only two or three months before moving in with each other. In many cases they have only known each other for just a few weeks. To accuse a cohabiting young man or woman of being emotionally incapable of making a commitment because they have not married when they have only known each other for just a few months simply does not make sense. Many of these young couples may be far *more* prone toward making commitments than non-cohabiting couples of the same ages. Perhaps this is one reason why they find greater satisfaction in cohabiting than in "playing the field." In addition, particularly among the swingers' children reported on here, the very young chronological ages would certainly argue strongly against the judiciousness of legal marriage for them at this time. To the extent that their cohabitation reduces their desire for "tying the knot" while still in high school, it is probably doing society a very formidable service.

An additional objection very often brought up by well-meaning, conscientious people is that teenagers are seldom *emotionally prepared* for entering into sexual relationships. One of the points which this research made very clear was that emotional readiness is always strongly affected by the *social context* in which a child lives. Thirty-six percent of the swingers' children had had their first copulation prior to the age of 13, and almost all of the children had had sexual intercourse prior to their 16th birthday. In fact, for the sons of swinging parents 14.6 was the median age for first sexual intercourse; for the daughters of swingers the median age for loss of virginity was 14.3. In essence, these children were all living in families that were highly charged with an atmosphere of sex, nudity, and eroticism. Most of them learned very early that sex and erotic play are activities which are recreational and highly enjoyable. Unlike the conventional non-swinging families that existed throughout their neighborhoods of residence, these children received almost no messages from their parents suggesting to them that sex is a very delicate business for which something as (to the children) esoteric as "emotional readiness" ought to exist as a precondition for enjoying it. In this regard I believe that the preadolescent and teenaged children of American swingers constitute a very unique microcosm that might offer us some useful insights as to how children in a large number of preliterate societies manage to engage in a very large amount of *unusually early* premarital sex without experiencing any apparent ill effects.

Two of the many societies in which *pre*adolescent sexual intercourse has always been the common order of the day are (1) the Muria, which were studied by anthropologist V. Elwin (1947), and (2) the Trobriand Islanders who were studied by anthropologist B. Malinowski (1930). Most Muria children are only four or five years old when they first begin regular penile-vaginal intercourse. Trobriand children normally begin their sexual lives at about the ages of seven or eight. Of course, boys this young cannot ejaculate semen; but they can and do experience orgasms as do their female counterparts. The female children are able to experience orgasms this young because they have never been exposed by their mothers and fathers to any ascetic social programming that would inhibit a natural sexual response.

The emotional unreadiness for sex which is commonly talked about as existing in American children and teenagers is essentially a socially programmed response. This socially programmed response is indoctrinated into children in a whole host of subtle and not-too-subtle ways. from babyhood on. This is not to say such social programming is "good" or "bad." It *is* to say that it *is* responsible for children and young teenagers in America being indeed "emotionally non-prepared" for handling sexual intercourse while their brothers in preliterate societies and in swinging families in American suburbs are fully prepared at such early ages. Whether or not a youth is emotionally prepared for sex is a function of that youth's social and cultural background, *not* of his chronological age or psycho-physiological level of development.

Unplanned Pregnancies

The main form of contraception prevalent among the swingers' teenagers will be dealt with in the next chapter. At this point it should be pointed out that only two of the 95 teenagers studied for this research had ever suffered an unplanned pregnancy. None of the 24 swingers' children over 19 years of age had ever experienced an unplanned pregnancy.

One of the girls who had become pregnant was a "love group" member and was also cohabiting with her boyfriend. The other girl had been engaging in monogamous premarital sex after school with her boyfriend. The first girl saw her pregnancy through to term while the second one secured an abortion. At the time they became pregnant neither of these girls had been engaging in very frequent sexual intercourse. The significance of this point will become clear in the next chapter.

Until about two months before she became pregnant the then 17-year-old Amy had been copulating with her roommate and fellow "love group" member on an almost daily basis. However, summer vacation came and she used this time to travel to Hawaii in order to work at a concession run by her uncle. She had been very anxious to spend the summer in Hawaii, but her time there resulted in a lengthy separation from her "love mate" back in California. Upon her return home in September she was quite slow to recommence her heavy sexual involvement with her partner. In fact, it was mid-November before he had moved back in with her. And it was shortly after that time that she discovered that she was pregnant. She had copulated with him upon her return home; but her sexual encounters had been scarcely more frequent than once per fortnight until the date of her resumed cohabitation.

> "Oh Christ! I was shocked and dumbfounded when I found out! I just didn't know what to do. Jim [her "love mate"] was very upset too when I told him. But he wanted me to get an abortion. His dad knows a doctor who is supposed to be very good. I didn't have any fears about going to my parents. I mean, they had always supported us in what we were doing. Parents who are into this sexual freedom thing, you know, I guess it would be hard for them to gripe, even when their kid gets pregnant. Anyway, we started discussing whether or not I wanted to have the child. I had always assumed, you know, that if I got pregnant I would be taken right away to a doctor who would give me an abortion. But a couple of days later when I came home from school my mother introduced me to this lady who turned out to be the sister of one of my mom and dad's closest swinging friends. She was 34 years old but she had never been able to have a child even though she wanted one very badly. She had been to all these adoption agencies but never had any luck. Well, anyway, she told me that she and her husband would pay me $20,000 plus all my medical bills if I would be their baby factory and let them take care of the baby after it's born. She said that I could visit the baby as often as I wanted, but that I would have to agree to let them raise it."

Within just a few days Amy had not only accepted the plan but was actually extremely enthusiastic about it. She had been given $4,000 as a preliminary down-payment on the nine month service she had agreed to perform, and she and Jim were soon excitedly poring over European travel folders in anticipation of a trip they would take together that summer after the child's birth, due in June.

Of course, Amy was forced to put up with a considerable amount of inconvenience to her life that year. Her major hardship was that she had to spend from January until graduation of her senior year of high school attending classes in Long Beach, some 50 miles away. It had been decided that it would not be in anyone's best interest for her to continue attending school where she was known. So she was sent to live with some very close friends of her parents who were also swingers. During this period she returned to her parents' home on weekends, and her boyfriend often drove the 100 miles round trip to see her during the week.

I talked with Amy and Jim just four months after their return from Europe. Her childbirth had gone smoothly and she had not been asked to give the baby over to her mother's friend until three weeks after delivering it. Two days after that she and Jim were in Europe together.

Perhaps it was in some measure due to the pleasant and challenging distraction of her trip. But Amy claimed that she did not miss her baby very strongly during the period she had been away. However, upon her arrival home she was extremely anxious to see it. Interestingly enough, the woman had no apparent objection to Amy presenting herself to the baby as "Mommy." Whether Amy's easy acceptance will continue for very long into the future is a question of particular interest to me and to virtually everyone else connected with this case.

The strong quasi-kin group ties which swingers commonly have with their fellows was commented upon at length in Chapter 5. Such close ties represent what most sociologists would regard as an extremely powerful form of social control. This social control may not have any *legal* clout; but it should be realized that most people comply with the major norms not out of fear of violating laws and being arrested but out of fear of violating conscience and disappointing friends and loved ones. It is this very close attachment to people that guarantees the very deep and thorough internalization of normative beliefs in the first place, regardless of whether such beliefs are conformist (in the eyes of the larger society) or highly deviant. Similarly, it is the close attachment to people that guarantees order rather than chaos within the context of any subculture, whether that subculture is one that is highly nonconformist or one that is quite ordinary.

One of the swinging mothers mentioned to me that she had a swinging friend in Chicago who literally took over her daughter's child and was raising it as her own. This woman believed that her daughter was simply not yet ready to assume the role of a mother. She and her husband were able to accept the daughter's sexual activity but they were not willing to accept the idea of her assuming the role of a parent. The girl and the boyfriend in this case had been opposed to the idea of an abortion.

When this case was presented to me I immediately thought of some demographic data that has recently been collected in Iceland. Iceland has been found to be the most permissive of all literate, urban-industrial nations as far as sexual norms affecting unmarried teenagers are concerned. The average Icelandic girl has her first sexual intercourse by the age of 13, and the average Icelandic boy has it by the age of 14. Unlike the children of American swingers, however, the tremendous amount of coitus among Icelandic teenagers *does* give rise to quite a bit of unintended pregnancy. Another key difference is that swinging and virtually all other forms of adultery are virtually unheard of in Iceland. Like the other Scandinavian nations, Icelanders tend to be very hostile to the idea of adultery despite their liberality when it comes to premarital sex.

As researcher Neil Elliott (1970) and numerous other scholars exploring Icelandic customs have pointed out, the Icelandic family has evolved a system for smoothly handling the large numbers of unplanned pregnancies among unmarried teenaged girls. This system simply prescribes that the firstborn child of any teenaged girl be reared by that girl's mother. In essence, the child's maternal grandmother becomes its "social mother" and guardian. The real or biological mother, if she is under the age of 18 or 19, is almost universally regarded by Icelanders as being too young and immature for the role of mother. Hence, she plays the role of "older sister" and playmate to her own child. (This same system has prevailed in many parts of the lower-class black culture in America as well.) However, in Iceland the biological mother's firstborn child is seldom returned to her when she does become of age and/or legally married. The maternal grandmother keeps the child as her own. This is what is expected by all people involved and it is also what everyone involved views as "natural" and "normal." Again, they view it as natural and normal because that is the way they have been socially and culturally programmed by their loved ones to view it.

This system has had one consequence which many Americans and certainly all swingers would view as undesirable: Many Icelandic teenagers do not begin to take the idea of birth control seriously until they have had their first child.

Abortion is the most common way of resolving the unplanned pregnancy problem when it occurs among the sexually active teenagers of swinging parents. And indeed, the only other girl in my sample who suffered an unplanned pregnancy ended it in that way. This girl was only 15 when she became pregnant. But neither she nor her parents indicated that she had been very disturbed about it. In fact, the boyfriend was the only person who had displayed any marked degree of upset. The parents' main concern was that their daughter become contraceptively more sophisticated so that unplanned pregnancy would not happen to her again. They promptly took her to a gynecologist after the pregnancy was discovered, and an uneventful abortion was performed. The cost of this abortion was borne equally by the girl's parents and the boy's parents. Less than one week later the girl was back copulating with her boyfriend again—and with her parents' blessings. However, for the next few months her mother did cross-examine her and the boyfriend about their birth control preparedness.

CONCLUSIONS

While most swinging parents are adult centered and do not pal around a very great deal with their children, they do tend to enjoy harmonious parent-child relationships. The swinging parents studied for this research tended to make premarital coitus easily available to their children, and many of them maintained a very sexually charged atmosphere in their homes. The swingers' children tended to grow very used to this atmosphere and tended to view it as natural and normal. In fact, many of them viewed the homes of their school chums as unnatural and "up tight."

Some of the swinging parents commented that they would have felt guilty and hypocritical had they not made provision for their teenagers to initiate sexual lives of their own. As one father put it, "Teenagers are supposed to be at the height of their sexual drives. Right? Well, how can me and my wife lead orgiastically rich, swinging lives as long as our kids living in this same house with us are forced to live monastic, sexually up-tight lives? I'm not going to be a goddam hypocrite and I don't want to go around feeling guilty about making my kids feel guilty about one of the best things in life!"

It is too early to say whether the children reported on here will themselves grow up to be swingers. Doubtless many of them will. But it is likely that the majority of them will not. Despite a wealth of opportunities for highly casual promiscuity, the vast majority of the teenagers and young adults studied maintained quite monogamous heterosexual love relationships which nevertheless did involve a lot of copulation. This tendency among these young people to stick with just one love partner at a time (often in the face of parental pressure to "play the field," "sow wild oats," and enjoy many sexual partners) provides further support for the view that the basic human need for psycho-emotional and residential monogamy is far stronger than the need for sexual variety.

As far as the experiencing of premarital sex itself was concerned the swingers' children chose to abide by the norms of their nonconformist parents rather than by the norms of their communities. But as far as keeping their relationships *monogamous* (sexually as well as emotionally) was concerned they clearly tended to follow the patterns of their local *communities* to a far greater extent than those set by their parents.

Finally, regarding abortion, many swingers and their teenaged offspring hold that if the universal cosmic consciousness or God-mind (see chapter 6) intends for a particular soul to be born onto the earth plane, that soul will inevitably and inexorably gravitate toward an appropriate fetus and be born regardless of whatever abortion or abortions might take place. By this perspective, the fetus is only a *potential* vehicle for a soul. To the materialist the human body (or fetus) is commonly equated with the soul The (increasingly popular with swinging families) metaphysical perspective holds that the physical body can be destroyed and annihilated but that the soul, along with its true purpose and destiny at any given point in time, is *fundamentally indestructible.*

Chapter 12

The Method of
Frequent Ejaculation

The purpose of this chapter is to present a systematic overview of what was the most widely used method of birth control among the swingers' sexually active young people. All of the teenagers who were involved in the "love groups" at the time of the study were using the method which will be detailed here. In addition, over 60 percent of the sexually active swingers' children outside of the "love groups" were also using the method.

The method, which is more accurately describable as a method of birth control than as a method of contraception, can appropriately be labeled the *"method of frequent ejaculation."* It is a method which places the major responsibility upon the *male*. And it is a method which preliminary data suggest is 100 percent effective against pregnancy *when used with sincere and conscientious attention to the directions for its practice*. But it is a method that requires complete openness and honesty between partners as well as an easy ability to talk about all aspects of sex. People who do not honestly accept premarital coitus as morally valid for themselves and who cannot serenely, comfortably and guiltlessly discuss sex with their love partner will not be able to practice the method.

As pointed out in Chapter 11, two of the teenagers studied did become pregnant. However, neither of their respective boyfriends had been practicing the method at the time. Also, most people today are especially concerned about the health side effects of the chemical methods of contraception such as the pill. The method discussed in this chapter entails no adverse side effects from the standpoint of personal health.

The Method

Most of the major scientific breakthroughs that have greatly benefited man have been arrived at by the sweat of the scientist's brow. But the history of science is replete with cases of very meaningful and important discoveries being made purely by chance. Scientists are so used to working hard to arrive at significant findings that they sometimes display an irrational distrust of what seem on the surface to be easy answers, even when such answers can be empirically verified.

Several years ago a San Francisco newspaper ran an article about a college girl who had very much wanted to become pregnant. While most undergraduates try as hard as they can to avoid pregnancy this particular woman and her husband had a very strong desire for a child. They tried desperately for many months to bring their dreams to fruition. Virtually every morning they had sexual intercourse almost as soon as they woke up. In the evenings they sometimes made love as often as three times before finally going to sleep. In fact, so determined were they that they even returned to their apartment during their lunch hour in order to enjoy sexual intercourse together for dessert!

After about six months of this the couple naturally became very worried about the possibility that one of them might be infertile. They reluctantly went to see a physician about their problem. The doctor took a sperm count for the young man and thoroughly checked out the wife.

Everything proved normal. There seemed to be no reason why the couple should be having difficulty in conceiving. That is, there did not seem to be any reason until the couple very worriedly advised the doctor of the very frequent sexual intercourse that they had been having.

The doctor immediately advised the couple to cut down their coital frequency from three or more times per day to a maximum of once every three days. The couple acted upon this advice, and to their great surprise and relief, within just four weeks the doctor pronounced the wife pregnant!

In 1973 I was introduced to a group of young swingers in the San Francisco area who had heard about this case and who had been successfully governing the birth control norms of their group (which was composed of twelve couples) in accordance with it for the prior two years. The jist of their rules was that all husbands had to either masturbate or copulate with their wives within four hours of the start of any sex party. The age range within this group of swingers was from 20 to 29. In the three years during which I kept track of this group, *none* of the members became pregnant.

During the past decade the "method of frequent ejaculation" has been fleetingly alluded to by two quite different kinds of experts. First, medical researchers Masters and Johnson have pointed out that for most men at least thirty hours is required after an ejaculation before an amount of sperm sufficient to permit fertilization is again accumulated. This is so despite the fact that only one sperm is required to cause a pregnancy. It would appear that individual sperm cells cannot function properly unless they are contained in a huge gestalt with many hundreds of millions of other sperm cells. In fact, this gestalt also seems to require the presence of a certain optimum quantity of seminal fluid as well. This too has been found to require about thirty hours to accumulate.

Anthropologists constitute a second group of scientists who have alluded to the "method of frequent ejaculation."

Ashley Montagu has pointed out how only one to four percent of the teenagers in sexually very permissive societies ever become pregnant before they are expected to, which is after the time of their socially recognized marriages. As indicated in Chapter 11, the Muria is one of the most sexually permissive societies on earth as far as the *pre*marriage period is concerned. But unmarried Muria teenagers never seem to get pregnant. Muria boys and girls begin having sexual intercourse at the age of five or six. In fact, after their fourth birthday they no longer sleep in their parents' hut. All Muria children are expected to sleep with their age mates in the "ghotul," which is a coeducational bachelor house. By the time these children reach adolescence most of them are experiencing coitus at least once per day. Again, the ejaculation of semen cannot occur prior to pubescence. But the ecstasy of orgasm can be experienced by everyone including even one-day-old infants.

The Trobriand Islanders are another group that sanctions sexual intercourse for preadolescent boys and girls. But like Elwin who studied the Muria, Malinowski found very little unplanned pregnancy among the Trobrianders. In fact, the Trobrianders did not even believe that intercourse leads to pregnancy! To them pregnancy was brought about by a visit from a discarnate spirit. The spirit, however, would seldom visit a girl until after she had been formally married. The purpose of marriage for the Trobrianders was to legitimate and regulate parenthood, *not* sexual intercourse or cohabitation. Most of the teenaged Trobrianders enjoyed sexual intercourse even more frequently than their married elders!

Given these facts, how can we account for the quite considerable amount of unplanned pregnancy among American adolescents? In order to answer this question we must examine the ways in which the sexual patterns of American teenagers differ from those of such permissive societies as the Muria and the Trobriand Islanders. It is often contended that the superior nutrition enjoyed by American teenagers makes them mature faster and renders them more vulnerable to pregnancy. But this is only a very small part of the full story.

It surprises many people to learn that every year in the United States there are ten to fifteen cases of virginal impregnation, almost all of which involve junior or senior high school aged girls. These girls are typically very conservative and "up tight" in their feelings about sex. The effect of their parents' antisexual programming is still very strong for them and they believe that it is wrong to experience premarital sex, especially at their age. Their belief makes it very difficult for them to discuss contraception or even to learn about it when they find themselves in a situation with their boyfriends where coitus might become a likely possibility.

High school aged boys are believed by many medical scholars to be at the apex of their sexual drives. The average 16-year-old boy, once aroused, may have an even more urgently strong need for sexual release than his 20-year-old college age brother. And just as his girl friend is likely to be very "hung up" about the idea of having sex or discussing contraception, he is likely to be extremely uncomfortable about the idea of masturbating by himself.

When an American boy of 15 or 16 has an ejaculation with his girl friend it is likely to have been many weeks and possibly months since the time of his last ejaculation. Occasionally a girl will try to appease her boyfriend by permitting him to insert his penis between her thighs. Even though her thighs will usually be bare during this process, she will usually be wearing an undergarment. When the ejaculation occurs the amount of seminal fluid and the number of sperm cells contained therein is likely to be extremely huge due to the boy's long period of abstinence. Because of the unusually large and powerful outpouring of sperm, some of it on rare occasions seeps through the tiny holes of the girl's undergarment fabric. When this happens some of the sperm can and occasionally do enter the vagina.

If the girl was sexually aroused during this process of

interfemoral, penile lovemaking, the surface of her vagina will very likely be heavily alkaline. This provides the optimum set of conditions for the sperm that escaped through the undergarment into the vagina to swiftly find their way up to the ovum. This is true in light of recent findings indicating that young women tend to be *maximally arousable* during the *center* of their menstrual cycle just when pregnancy is *most* likely to occur.

The reason why the adolescent boy in such cases proves to be so highly fertile as to impregnate his sweetheart even without intercourse is simply that he has abstained from *any* kind of sexual outlet for many weeks or months. In societies such as the Trobriand Islanders and the Muria no adolescent boy is likely to abstain for more than the 30-hour period pinpointed by Masters and Johnson as being necessary for an amount of sperm sufficient to permit fertilization to again build up. It is for this reason that premarital pregnancy tends to be so common among American teenagers who have not as yet thrown off the shackles of their parents' anti-sexual programming. A person must first accept sex on an *emotional* as well as on an intellectual level if he is to be able to comfortably masturbate or discuss copulation and contraceptive precautions with his lover. In fact, sociologist Frank Furstenburg found non-acceptance of premarital sex to be the single most important determinant of premarital pregnancy among sexually active teenagers.

Of course, there is a good deal more to the "method of frequent ejaculation" than simply ejaculating every 24 to 30 hours. But before examining some of the other details I think it is important to take a closer look at the apparent biological necessity for sperm cells to function in the immediate company of millions of other sperm cells as a prerequisite for one of them fertilizing an ovum.

For about a half-century medical researchers have been working on artificial insemination. A key fact which this work has made clear is that for a man to ejaculate healthy sperm cells into the uterus of a completely healthy and aroused woman is never sufficient by itself to permit pregnancy. The findings have shown that a man can ejaculate 180 million perfectly healthy sperm cells per cubic millimeter, time and time again over months and even years of time. Yet despite the health of his wife this effort alone will consistently fail to produce a pregnancy.

Now, 180 million per cubic millimeter would certainly seem to be an exceedingly huge number. This is especially so in light of the often quoted truism that only one sperm is required to fertilize an ovum. But scientists have ascertained that 200 to 300 million sperm cells per cubic millimeter are the absolute minimum of healthy sperm cells necessary to give rise to a pregnancy. The reasons why so many are needed when only one does the actual fertilizing have not been determined. Suffice it to say that some half-century of research has made it clear that the sperm cell that accomplishes the eventual fertilizing requires the close companionship of many millions of others in order for it to do its job. Most healthy men ejaculate 700 million to 800 million sperm per cubic millimeter. And a man's sperm count needs to be somewhere in that area in order for the probability of pregnancy to be reasonably high.

The Technique Itself and How it is Practiced

The basic thesis of the "method of frequent ejaculation" is simply that if a man ejaculates within a 24-hour period prior to any given copulation, the probability is *zero* that that copulation will give rise to a pregnancy. While the many sexually liberated people who practice this technique tend to be very confident of its basic validity, most of them apply some additional procedures in order to make their minds one hundred percent sure and serene. Shortening the time period between ejaculations from 24 to 30 hours down to 6 to 15 hours is very popular among swinging couples and their sexually active teenaged youngsters. But many couples dependent upon the "method of frequent ejaculation" for birth control back up their use of the method with either an aerosol vaginal foam or a condom.

An unmarried man does not need to ejaculate each and every day in order to satisfy the requirements of the "method of frequent ejaculation." Were he to do so he would be going to a great deal of needless trouble. Single men usually have no way of knowing beforehand whether or not they are going to have sexual intercourse on a particular night. This is particularly true for men who are playing the field. But even if a man is involved in a warm and steady, potentially permanent relationship he cannot be entirely certain that his sweetheart will be in the mood for sex on a particular occasion.

One of the beauties of the "method of frequent ejaculation" is that a man can ejaculate by way of masturbation a few hours before going out on a date which he believes might eventuate in sexual intercourse. For example, if a young man believes that coitus might be likely some time around midnight, he can masturbate some time around 6:00 P.M. That would leave only six hours between ejaculations. This six-hour period would constitute only one-fifth of the time specified by Masters and Johnson as being necessary to permit the build-up of a supply of sperm cells and seminal fluid sufficient to cause pregnancy.

Spouse-sharing husbands in lieu of masturbating tend to have sexual intercourse with their wives prior to attending a swinging party. Many swinging couples allow a 10 to 15 hour time period between their own pre-party copulation as husband and wife and the first one they expect to have extramaritally at a party. However, at least a few swingers deal with the birth control issue by making their first party orgasm an oral-genital affair rather than a penile-vaginal one.

But when it comes to advising their own sexually active teenagers most swingers tend to be a good deal more cautious. They usually counsel their children to make sure that the male partner masturbates no earlier than 6:00 P.M. on the night of the date when a copulation is believed to be a realistic possibility. They tend to discourage their children from starting their sexual lovemaking with an oral-genital or interfemoral orgasm because of a fear that

the youths in their passion might lose control and commence regular sexual intercourse. The swingers' teenagers
seldom rebel at such counsel. They seem to get along very
well with their parents because of the almost total lack of
social distance in the parent-child communication system.

Along with confining the period between ejaculations to
just six hours the teenaged children of the swingers often
employed one of the better aerosol vaginal foams as a supplement to the "method of frequent ejaculation." The various foams also tend to be used by some spouse-sharing
swingers as part of their foreplay procedures. Taken by
themselves the foams have been found in numerous research studies to be highly effective spermicidal contraceptives. When used strictly in accordance with in-
structions the aerosol foam has been found to be over 98
percent as effective as "the pill."

When the "method of frequent ejaculation" is combined
with an aerosol vaginal foam we have two different birth
control methods that are being used simultaneously. My
own observations of more than 300 people using it have
convinced me that the "method of frequent ejaculation" is
at least as effective as "the pill," and it is a very great deal
safer from a health standpoint. Simultaneous use of an
aerosol foam merely serves as added insurance. It insures
by killing the relatively small number of sperm that are
ejaculated in a copulation over which there is concern
about protection from pregnancy.

Even though it is not necessary to take any further precautions with the "method of frequent ejaculation," a very
small number of nervous, sexually active young people
combine their use of the method with use of an aerosol
foam or condoms plus the rhythm method. In other words,
on top of everything else they abstain from intercourse
(but not oral-genital sex) during the nine or ten "least
safe" days of the female partner's cycle.

One of the chief problems concerning the use of the "safe
period" as a method of birth control is that most women
tend to be *least* arousable during this period. It used to be
believed that women were maximally arousable during

their "safe period" because studies conducted several decades ago indicated that women preferred coitus during this period. However, during the past few years some very important research conducted at the University of North Carolina, under the direction of J. Richard Udry, has shown that both human women and menstruating monkeys tend to be maximally arousable at the *center* of their cycle just when pregnancy is *most* likely to occur and when the amount of estrogen contained in their bloodstream is at its highest. Udry's findings strongly suggest that the rhythm method is not in the best interests of sexual gratification. Its use is definitely not indicated for couples who correctly practice the "method of frequent ejaculation."

By now it should be clear that a man need not ejaculate "frequently" in order to correctly and effectively practice the "method of frequent ejaculation." In fact, a man could abstain for seven weeks and then masturbate an hour before going out with his girl. Such a man would be correctly practicing the method. But he would be doing so with maximal safety and effectiveness if he also used a condom or if his partner used an aerosol vaginal foam.

For couples who are involved in stable, on-going love relationships the menstrual period need not interfere in any way with the "method of frequent ejaculation." A couple can abstain from coitus for as many days as they wish. As long as the man either masturbates to ejaculation a few hours prior to the recommencement of coitus or he and his girl make their first lovemaking session following the period of abstinence an oral-genital (or a mutual masturbation to orgasm) affair, the couple will be correctly and effectively practicing the method.

Metaphysical Visualization, Meditation, and Affirmations

An additional adjunct to the "method of frequent ejaculation" that was used by a sizable minority of the swingers and their sexually active teenagers was *metaphysical vis-*

ualization. In Chapter 6 I showed that over one-third of the swinging husbands and wives had been substantially influenced by metaphysics, and that it had taken the place of conventional organized religion for many of these people.

A major tenet of metaphysical teachings is that illnesses of all sorts can be arrested and cured through a disciplined program of daily meditation and visualization. Just a few years ago the majority of American physicians viewed this tenet as amounting to little more than a bunch of occult nonsense. But today the burgeoning medical subfield of "holistic medicine" is deeply rooted in metaphysical and occult philosophy. Texas physician O. Carl Simonton is perhaps the best known disciple of this new approach. Simonton and his wife Stephanie have been able to cure hundreds of cancer patients who had been originally adjudged as terminally ill. The main thrust of their approach has been to get their patients to *visualize* the ill part of their body as being perfectly healthy and free of any pain; additional visualization might take the form of motivating the patient to mentally "see" a hungry polar bear eating away and fully removing all cancerous tissue. In addition to curing cancer this way, numerous physicians have achieved remarkable success in curing or greatly alleviating such diseases as hypertension, ulcers, arthritis, bursitis, asthma, back pains, migraine headaches, insomnia, and many other human maladies both serious and minor. (If interested, see Kenneth Pelletier's book *Mind as Healer, Mind as Slayer.* It is listed in the bibliography.)

Those wives who applied this philosophy to their birth control simply visualized themselves as remaining completely free from pregnancy, and a hungry tiger as eating up any and all sperm that might be inside of themselves. They did this between two and three times daily while in the course of their regular meditation. Their husbands and children backed up the effort by similarly visualizing the wife-mother as free from pregnancy. In some of the families in which a teenaged daughter was sexually active the same visualization exercise was practiced in regard to "seeing" that daughter free from unwanted pregnancy.

One of the key tenets of metaphysics is that human thought affects and creates form, and that all forms of matter are merely energy fields that are temporarily holding still. Metaphysical practitioners believe that whenever two or more people concentrate their thought energies upon one specific visualized goal, that that goal will be actualized in conformance with the faith and belief of those doing the visualizing. In essence, they believe that the combined thought of several minds constitutes an immense power, provided that each mind (or person) has complete faith that what he or she is visualizing has indeed already come to pass.

Many of the families incorporated metaphysical affirmations into their daily meditation programs. An affirmation is a prayer, but unlike conventional prayer it does not beg or beseech. Instead it affirms. Each affirmation is rooted in a deeply felt confidence that every human being has a "higher mind," and that God exists throughout all of nature and within the "higher mind" of each and every human being everywhere. The "higher mind" is contacted through the process of meditation. Once a person feels that she is in a deep enough state of meditation she might state something like this: "Through the power of the universal God-mind within me, I affirm that I am completely free of any chance of pregnancy, and that I shall continue to remain so for the next three years. And for this realization I give thanks. And so it is." In making the affirmation the person *strongly feels, believes,* and *visualizes* that which he or she affirms.

Some Non-Contraceptive Functions of the Method

Birth control is obviously the main reason and purpose for the "method of frequent ejaculation." But the method usually does some other very good things for a couple as well. In fact, the non-contraceptive functions of the method serve as an exceedingly strong advertisement for its frequent use.

One of the key non-contraceptive functions of the method is that it seems to serve as a very useful coital (sexual skills) training device, particularly for young and relatively inexperienced men. Many young men suffer from premature ejaculation, and many others "come" a great deal sooner than either they or their partners would like. In our society it usually requires a good deal longer to properly arouse a woman than it does a man. So anything that can effectively serve to postpone the occurrence of the man's ejaculation can be seen as a welcome boon toward helping couples get to know each other better and to more thoroughly enjoy each other sexually.

If a man has ejaculated six or seven hours before he makes love to his sweetheart he is necessarily going to have to "work" harder to become aroused to the point of orgasm than he otherwise would. In effect, he is going to have to take longer, and probably a good deal longer, to "come." However, this does *not* mean that he is likely to develop any vulnerability to impotence. Men who do not have a history of sexual performance problems are highly unlikely to develop any such problems as a result of using this new method of birth control. Most young men can easily manage as many as four or five ejaculations in the course of an evening. In fact, I interviewed swingers in their forties who were able to manage even more than that.

A key point is that the additional time required by the male partner to become aroused to the point of ejaculation can serve to significantly lengthen the period of sexual pleasure for both partners. It can enable them to get to know each other better physically, emotionally, and spiritually. The added time can also serve to greatly increase the probability that the woman will have an orgasm and maybe even more than one. This is especially true if the man uses the time to bring pleasurable friction to his woman's clitoral area. In fact, most swingers recommend that the male partner bring the woman to at least one orgasm before commencing regular sexual intercourse. As indicated in Chapter 10, swingers use many techniques of manual massage and oral-genital sex in order to accomplish this.

A second non-contraceptive function of the "method of frequent ejaculation" is that its use tends to make sexual intercourse a far more intensely pleasurable experience for both partners. Some medical doctors have been inclined to debate this point. But all of the student users and mate sharing couples I studied reported that it does make sexual intercourse seem on a subjective level to be much more intense than normal. With each copulation of an evening the sexual pleasure sensations for most people tend to become progressively more intense. The second copulation is perceived as being more intense than the first, the third more intense than the second, and so on. This may be one of the essential rewards that many people reap from attendance at swinging parties. The sexual pleasure for most of those who are sexually active at such parties tends to expand and increase as an evening progresses.

From an objective standpoint medical researchers might be able to show that what happens during a second copulation is basically the same as what happens to the same couple during the first copulation of an evening. But if that couple *subjectively perceives* a more intense pleasure the second time, then that couple's subjective feelings must be considered real for them. What a lab report may indicate constitutes an irrelevant consideration from the standpoint of a couple's feelings. This same principle also applies in regard to the relationship between sex and marijuana. Objectively, marijuana may indeed do nothing to prolong the joy of intercourse or of the orgasm experience. But if a person or couple perceive a more intense ecstasy, then that perception must be considered real for that person or couple.

For many years now men have been talking about how the second copulation of an evening seemed to them to be more intense than the first. One of the most interesting findings of my own research is the extent to which women are now claiming the same thing. As the leaders of the women's liberation movement have been telling us, there are far fewer differences between the sexes than many of us had been led to believe.

A third function of the "method of frequent ejaculation" is that its use increases the amount of intimate conversation that can take place between two lovers. This is especially true for lovers who are living together or who are involved with each other on an exclusive basis. It has long been known that pleasant social interaction between people leads to an increase in their liking for one another and to an increased similarity in their attitudes, values, hopes, desires, dreams, etc. Just as mutual liking and loving can lead to sexual intercourse between two people, sexual intercourse can also lead to an increased love between two people. Love leads to sex and sex leads to love. Lovers practicing the "method of frequent ejaculation" can be expected to grow increasingly close and emotionally attuned to each other.

For couples who are living together the "method of frequent ejaculation" can very easily become the "method of frequent *intercourse*." By enjoying intercourse together at least once per day a couple can experience the joy of growing closer while at the same time practicing a foolproof method of birth control. Any time they might wish to abstain for a few days they can always do so simply by resorting to mutual masturbation or oral-genital sex a few hours prior to the recommencement of their regular sexual intercourse.

A fourth non-contraceptive function of the "method of frequent ejaculation" was alluded to in Chapter 10: it can help those who practice it keep in shape. Properly performed, each copulation burns up a minimum of 150 to 250 calories. Prolonged intercourse with its concomitant sexual excitement burns up a great deal more than 250 calories. In short, frequent intercourse can be a boon to health and to physical appearance in addition to provid-

ing a couple with great fun, emotional closeness and release.

Frequent Ejaculation as Birth Control

Most of the enormous progress that has been made in
contraceptive technology over the past twenty years has
benefited women who have completed their child-bearing
to a far greater extent than it has benefited anyone else.
Couples who do not wish to have any more children and
couples who are interested in spacing the births of their
offspring now have several good methods available to
them. But contraceptive research has almost totally ignored the needs of sexually active young people who have
not as yet begun having children and who have no desire
to begin doing so for quite some time into the future.

In most respects the vasectomy is the best birth control
method available. But it obviously is not a viable alternative for the young man who wishes to eventually have
children. Next to the vasectomy, the contraceptive pill
possesses more of the earmarks of perfection than any
other conventional method. But for the unmarried girl
who has no idea as to when or whether she will want to
engage in sexual intercourse on a regular basis, its use
presents an unwarranted hassle and burden. Even among
married swingers its long-term use is both feared and
strongly discouraged because of mounting evidence
suggesting a causal link between such long-term use and
cancer.

In contrast, the "method of frequent ejaculation" does
not require people to purchase or to place any potentially
dangerous chemical into their bodies. It does not entail
any undue inconvenience to those using it. And it is in
conformance with the values of the women's liberation
movement because it does not place the burden of contraceptive purchase and use upon women.

The "method of frequent ejaculation" is an especially
ideal birth control approach for unmarried teenagers and

young adults. It quite clearly emancipates them from having to confront medical doctors and pharmacists about prescriptions for pills or diaphragms. And even though it is preferable for users of the method to supplement it with a condom or a non-prescription aerosol vaginal foam, it even emancipates teenagers from that inasmuch as there is very good reason to believe that an ejaculation within six or seven hours of a copulation quite totally obviates any possibility of pregnancy.

But such non-prescription tools as condoms and aerosol vaginal foams can now be obtained by teenagers anywhere in the United States or Canada through mail order firms. *Penthouse, Playboy, Psychology Today,* and many other major mass media publications today contain numerous advertisements for non-prescription foams and condoms which can be obtained by mail.

In addition to serving as a great boon to teenaged lovers desirous of enjoying sexual intercourse, the spread of education regarding the "method of frequent ejaculation" should serve to greatly reduce unwanted pregnancy and abortion. Knowledge of the method should in time take care of the needs of young people who are too reticent about approaching doctors or pharmacists about contraception. The same can be said about the many mail order advertisements which have become available to teens over the past few years.

Drawbacks to the Method

There are only three very minor drawbacks to the "method of frequent ejaculation." The first of these is that for some people it entails too much regimentation. It has already been shown that it is not necessary for a man to copulate or even to ejaculate every day in order to successfully practice the method. But the fact that the man is required to masturbate within six to fifteen hours of his first copulation following more than a day's abstinence tends to be seen by many as imposing too much structure and restriction upon highly personal behavior.

A second very minor drawback is that the method is suitable primarily for men under the age of 35. Even married swingers do not regard the method as appropriate for men over 40, although some swingers beyond that age do use it on an occasional basis. Swinging groups comprised primarily of people over the age of 38 tend to view vasectomy as the ideal method of birth control. The pill, the various intrauterine devices, and even the diaphragm, were all developed primarily for purposes of helping couples who had either completed their desired level of fertility or who wanted to space their children. With all of these methods readily available older people already have many contraceptive alternatives.

The third drawback presents a much more difficult problem. In the United States both men and women are made to feel extremely uncomfortable about masturbation. Researchers have pointed out how most housewives can far more easily and comfortably discuss the intimate details of their conjugal lovemaking than they can discuss the subject of masturbatory activities. It was recently found that only one-half of all contemporary college girls even know where their own clitoris is located! This is especially sad in light of evidence that clitoral friction, whether it occurs in coitus or in masturbation, is a precondition for a woman experiencing orgasm. Women who masturbate during their teenage years are far more likely to easily achieve orgasms with their mates later on than women without masturbatory experience.

The situation is not much better among young men. Even though most of the old myths about how masturbation leads to insanity, imbecility, acne, chronic lethargy, etc., have died out, many high school aged boys are still programmed by their parents into feeling that masturbation is an emasculating and degrading activity.

Young men who will not masturbate for any reason can still practice the "method of frequent ejaculation" by engaging in oral-genital sex or by petting to orgasm a few hours prior to engaging in sexual intercourse. However, it seems clear that those who have an accepting attitude towards masturbation are going to be able to practice the method far more easily than those who do not have such an attitude.

On the hopeful side, attitudes toward masturbation have been improving and there is every reason to believe that they will continue to do so. The increased ability of young women to experience orgasms and to enjoy sex has been attributed, at least in part, to this trend. It is likely that through exposure to discussions of the "method of frequent ejaculation" and of masturbation, both men and women can be led toward a more realistic, positive attitude regarding sexual self-stimulation.

Finally, a *potential* drawback of the "method of frequent ejaculation" is that its use requires the female partner to *trust* her male partner. For couples with emotionally close, loving relationships this poses little problem. Swingers similarly seem to be able to trust one another as far as contraceptive responsibilities are concerned. On the other hand, single women living in areas where the "double standard" is still strong or who are involved in relationships with men in which deception is a likely possibility obviously need to exercise care, caution and discretion.

Chapter 13

Parenting Attitudes
and Behaviors

This chapter will concern itself with the swingers' philosophy of child rearing and discipline. It will focus on the kinds of rules and policies that are commonly found in the swingers' homes and on the techniques used to enforce these rules and policies. Data on the family lives of the *non-swinging* parents and their children will be frequently cited in order to afford the reader a clear basis of comparison between the swinging and the non-swinging families.

Despite the highly non-conformist nature of swinging homes, I found that the parent-child relationships in such homes tended to be a good deal more harmonious that the parent-child relationships in the non-swinging homes. My data were secured from four sources: (1) my own subjective impressions while visiting the homes and observing interaction patterns; (2) interviews with the swinging and the non-swinging parents; (3) interviews with the swingers' children; and (4) interviews with the children in the "normal" non-swinging homes. Like all of my findings, the statements reported in this chapter should not be taken as conclusive. Very little has been written up to now on parent-child relationships in swinging homes. And nothing up to now has been written that contrasts such relationships with those between parents and children in non-swinging homes. Only time will tell how valid and reliable the data reported in this book are.

One of the most noticeable differences between the swinging and the non-swinging parents is that the former tended to relate to their children in much the same way as they would to adults. Even elementary school children in swinging homes were often related to by their parents in a manner that might be thought of by some as befitting adults or older adolescents. The swinging parents studied for this research tended to trust their children to take care of most of their own needs. For example, seven- and eight-year-olds were often trusted to buy their own clothes, to use the buses without an accompanying adult, to supervise themselves in lieu of babysitters, and to decide their own bedtimes even on school nights.

To some extent this early thrust toward independence was inspired and facilitated by the swingers' adult-centeredness. Many of the swingers were simply not interested in the world of children but, at the same time, were not about to punish childish behavior unless it interfered in a tangible way with their own adult behavior and needs. As a case in point, the swingers' children were normally allowed to fight their own battles. Angry fist fights between siblings that surely would have been stopped in most non-swinging households were allowed by most swinging parents to come to a natural conclusion. Yet if that fist fight disturbed a swinging parent's reading or sleep or telephone conversation, the siblings involved would very likely be punished for "interfering with the parents' rights," *not* for the fighting behavior. The idea was that they were to work out their own disagreements and not bring the parents into their conflicts. Some of the better educated swinging fathers mentioned that they often tried to show their children how solutions to conflicts could be worked out through techniques of compromise such that "neither would lose and both would win." But even in these cases it was always made clear to the children that in the final analysis *they* were to be "responsible for their own shit."

This very widespread attitude among the swinging parents harks back to their own childhood relationships with their own parents. As was pointed out in Chapter 1, most of the swingers had come from homes where the approach to discipline had been either authoritarian or "laissez-faire." Both authoritarian and "laissez-faire" parents tend to be disinterested in the personal needs, wants, and egos of their children. The "laissez-faire" parent displays his indifference by not even trying to come to any understanding with his children about proper and desirable behavior. Both types of parents want to escape from situations that will involve meaningful communication with their children. They do not have the skills for effective and rewarding communication with children and so they both fear and avoid it.

A massive amount of research evidence has made it clear that no single variable better predicts how a person will rear his own children than the way he himself had been reared. In essence, parent-child interaction patterns tend to be picked up and absorbed by children during their formative years. These parent-child interaction patterns tend, on the most part, to remain latent in the young person's mind until he or she becomes a parent. Then such interaction patterns become manifested anew. This is why most studies of the "battered child" have shown that abused children almost without exception had been abused on many occasions themselves as they were growing up.

The swingers of this study had not been understood by their own parents as they were growing up. So like their own parents they tended to fear and to avoid frequent communication with their elementary school-aged children. But their avoidance did not go as far as it had gone in their own relationships as children with their own parents. Only three of the swingers who had been reared in an authoritarian climate replicated that climate with their own children. Those who had come from authoritarian homes *and* those who had come from "laissez-faire" homes *both* tended to gravitate toward the "laissez-faire," seemingly highly permissive child-rearing approach.

In addition, most of the swingers found themselves communicating more and more frequently with their children as their children grew into their teenaged years. As highly self-sufficient for their age as most of the swingers' children were, none of them revealed any noteworthy degree of disenchantment with their parents. None of them had any desires to run away from home, and none of them seemed to dislike their parents. As was documented in Chapter 4, the swinging mothers and fathers tended to be quite negative toward their own parents and they tended to retain this negativity over the years. In spite of this, the following quote was typical of the feelings of the swingers' own children:

> "My parents are weird! Sometimes I just don't understand them. My mother especially—I mean, one minute she's down in the dumps and the next minute she's on top of the world and she wants to go out and party ... But in a way I feel lucky to have my parents. Like my girl friends are always complaining about the things their parents won't let them do. My mom and dad usually want to know where I'm going to be. But they leave me alone. I mean, they don't bug me. We sometimes fight, but it's never about anything really important. And they don't punish me just because I don't always go along with their ways of doing things. I guess my parents are real unusual in a lot of ways. But I wouldn't trade them for any other parents I know."
> (13-year-old daughter of swinging parents.)

Walt C., a 32-year-old father of two children, exemplifies quite well the type of swinging father who himself had grown up in an authoritarian environment, but who is presently gravitating toward the "laissez-faire" approach with his own offspring. The following quote illustrates very well some of the conflicts he is having within himself—conflicts which do *not* tend to be common among non-swinging parents who had been reared in strict environments.

"Ahhhhhhhhhh, sometimes I just feel a fucking strong impulse to just kick the shit out of my kids, especially Gary, my three year old. He comes in here and tugs on my newspaper when I'm trying to read. He gets his filthy hands all over my clothes, and he constantly asks all these dumb, fuckin' questions. I shout my mouth off at him all the time, but so far something grabs hold of me and I just can't hit him. Cathy [his wife] spanked him a few times, but I've never laid a hand on him. Frankly, I think I scare the shit out of him and I'm really concerned about that. Shit! I don't want to raise a freaky kid. I think a father should be close to his son. But sometimes I get this urge for quiet and I sometimes feel I could kill anyone who bothers me when I'm in that kind of mood . . . My parents used to beat the shit out of me all the time when I was a kid—both of them. My fuckin' mother was just as bad as my old man. She used to come at me with a strap. My earliest memories of my old lady are of her beating me with a strap. Shit! I don't know. But I will tell you this. When Gary was born I just made up my mind I wasn't going to hurt him no matter what he did. My wife has been a big help. I think she's a lot more comfortable with kids than I am anyway. But, the way I figure, I'd rather have my kid remember me as an asshole than as a fuckin' sadist."

Frank G. is another example of a man who originated in an uncomfortable home. Today he views himself as very happy and well adjusted. Unlike Walt C., he enjoys a good relationship with his children, although most contemporary Americans would probably view him as inordinately "permissive." Commenting on his past and its relationship to his current philosophy of parenting he said:

"Christ! When I was 13 and 14 years old I was afraid to even come home at night. My kids will never have to be afraid to come home. I don't like all the things that they do but at least they're not afraid to talk to me. I think I've had a constructive

influence on them. They usually come to me when
they have something bugging them. They talk it
over and they know I'm not going to chew them out
if they don't follow my advice. I only wish I had
someone to turn to like that when I was a kid. My
parents had no control over me and I did a lot of
really stupid things that I don't think I would have
done if I'd only had a mom or a dad I could talk to.
My dad had his own ideas of right and wrong and
you didn't dare challenge anything he hàd to say or
he'd beat the shit out of you. Even when I was 17
years old. He didn't give a shit. My mother was a
deeply religious woman and you couldn't challenge
her ideas of right either. That's why I got the hell
out of there as soon as I graduated high school. I
suffered some bad, lean years after that. But nothing could ever get bad enough to make me move
back with my folks. They live back east in Mil-
waukee and I haven't even seen them in thirteen
years. I just don't give a shit about them." (31-
year-old swinging father.)

Due in part to the unhappy character of many of their
own backgrounds, most of the swinging parents had an
uncomfortable feeling about rules—*any* rules. Virtually all
of them readily admitted that rules governed the swinging
clubs and social organizations of which they were a part.
But they tended to avoid making house rules for their
children, preferring instead to deal with each situation as
it came up. At such times the children almost always had a
significant role in determining policies affecting them.
Decisions were often made in the swinging homes amidst
shouting and confusion. But in spite of themselves the
swingers tended to *unintentionally* heed the widespread
counsel of contemporary child psychologists that parents
should not arbitrarily impose their own unilaterally arrived at rules.

One of the statements to which I obtained the reactions
of both the swinging and non-swinging parents was:
"Children should have an active part in the making and

revising of those family rules that affect them." The swinging parents were more than three times as likely as the non-swinging parents to *strongly agree* with this statement. But most of the swinging parents saw themselves as maintaining very few family rules for their children anyway, whereas close to 50 percent of the non-swinging parents saw themselves as maintaining a good many rules.

The non-swingers' children saw their parents as sustaining a lot of family rules and many of them complained about being treated as "babies" by their parents. Interestingly, the non-swingers' children were highly likely to see themselves as being subjected to many family rules and regulations regardless of whether or not their parents similarly indicated that they were so subjected. In contrast, the swingers' children tended to agree with their parents that there were few rules. Only 8 percent of the swingers' children I interviewed saw themselves as being subjected to many rules and regulations by their parents.

I asked all of the parents I interviewed to indicate their level of agreement with the statement: "Children who are subjected to firm rules grow up to be the best adults." Only 20 percent of the swinging parents indicated any agreement at all. In contrast, 43 percent of the non-swinging parents agreed, and about half of these indicated strong agreement. Even though most of the remaining 57 percent of non-swinging parents did not sustain long lists of rules for their children, they clearly indicated by the nature of their child-rearing discussions with me a much stronger preoccupation with discipline than that which was held by the swinging parents. Indeed, only about one-third of the non-swinging parents seemed to be able to truly relax and enjoy their children on a sustained day-in, day-out basis. In contrast, about 70 percent of the swinging parents seemed to have this ability.

> "Well, I think people very often confuse the need among children for caring and concern with some kind of an alleged need for discipline. Children don't want discipline any more than adults want

discipline. But everyone wants to know that someone gives a damn about them." (38-year-old swinging mother.)

Preoccupation with discipline is a characteristic that is
quite common among American parents. In a study involving Danish and American high school students
sociologists Kandel and Lesser (1969; 1972) found that the
average Danish 14-year-old is subjected to significantly
fewer rules in his home than the average American 18-
year-old. American parents to a much greater extent than
Scandinavian parents tend to be bent upon prolonging the
childhood of their children for the greatest possible
amount of time. As a result of this they usually get along
less well with their children than Danish parents do. But
more importantly, as a result of strained communication
within the home American parents commonly wield less
influence over their children than Danish parents do with
theirs. Again, *the strongest social control is that which is
least felt.* In order to influence someone you must be able to
enjoy casual, relaxed communication with that person.
People who utilize fear and threats of coercion seldom
influence their children in any meaningful way. The children "behave themselves" only as long as the authority
figure remains in sight.

"Respect"

When I was a student in junior and senior high school I
observed that a certain few teachers had 90 percent or
more of the "discipline problems." For a time this amazed
me because all of the teachers had to deal with the *exact
same students.* Parents are no different than teachers in
this regard. Because of their temperaments some parents
and some teachers have developed a preoccupation with
discipline. They come to *expect* discipline problems. And
because they come to expect it they are seldom disappointed. They constantly holler and punish whereas their
colleagues in the same types of situations manage to re-

tain their "cool" and communicate in a meaningful way with their charges.

Part of the difficulty is that many people have somehow been programmed to believe that *respect* is a *one-way street*. They believe that children must *first* respect them. And if the children do display respect they will give back a modicum of respect in return. Unfortunately for people who harbor this viewpoint, respect and love are two virtues that can only be *inspired* and *earned;* they can never be obtained through coercion. Parents *precede* children into the world by virtue of the fact that they were born before them. As such, it is the parents who must make the *first* move in manifesting true and genuine respect (as well as love) for their children. When they do this they invariably find that the child respects them in return. I strongly suspect that this is one key reason why some of the teachers in my secondary schools enjoyed a degree of success with their students that far surpassed that of their discipline-preoccupied colleagues. By their actions, tone of voice and style of conversation they displayed a natural, easygoing respect for their students. The students, in turn, had no other alternative but to respect them in return. Many American parents tend to view their children as something *less than people.* As a case in point, many adults make derogatory and insulting remarks to children that they would never dream of making to people of their own age.

I asked all of the couples in this research to react to the following statement: "Adult authority figures who do not respect youth cannot legitimately expect youth to respect them." The non-swinging parents were more than five times as likely as the swinging parents to *disagree* with this statement. In contrast to the swinging parents they were far more likely to believe that respect is something that must be earned by the child. This may be one key reason why the swinging parents, in spite of themselves, tended to enjoy more harmonious parent-child relationships than the non-swinging parents.

Protectiveness

One of the most noticeable differences between the swinging and the non-swinging parents was that of *protectiveness*. Many of the non-swinging parents regarded their children in very much the same way as one might regard pet dogs and cats. They saw themselves as owning the body, mind and spirit of their children. Most of these parents believed that children should be thoroughly exposed to the "three Rs" but that controversial material should be kept away from them. They believed that their offspring should live and play as immature children and that anything that might hasten their maturity should be regarded with suspicion. Despite advances made by the women's liberation movement in recent years most of these parents had rather rigid ideas as to what constitutes proper "boy behavior" and proper "girl behavior." They tended to believe that boys should play with boys, and that girls should play with girls. The coeducational peer group was regarded by most of these people as being especially undesirable for boys, and just barely tolerable during only the "tomboy stage" for girls.

A good illustration of the non-swinging parents' protectiveness can be seen in their attitudes toward the motion picture rating codes and their enforcement. Two questions on this subject were posed to all parents in the study. The first simply asked them to react to the statement: "Teenagers should *not* be prevented by motion picture rating codes from seeing the films they wish to see." Three-quarters of the swinging parents agreed with this statement compared to only 23 percent of the non-swinging parents. Fathers in both groups tended to be somewhat more liberal than mothers. But whether one focuses on the difference between the two groups of mothers or that between the two groups of fathers, it is clear that the difference between the swinging and the non-swinging parents on this issue is immense.

The second item yielded more permissive responses

from most of the non-swinging parents. But the differences between the two groups of parents were still substantial. The question read: "A new film with excellent reviews from the majority of critics opens at a nearby theatre. Your 15-year-old daughter who is very interested in good drama has been extremely anxious to see it. An announcement outside the theatre, however, indicates that persons under 18 cannot be admitted unless accompanied by a parent. Would you take your daughter to see it?" In this case 71 percent of the non-swinging parents indicated that they would take their daughter to see the film. The analogous figure for the swinging parents was 97 percent.

In practical everyday reality the problem for teenagers is that they almost invariably prefer to attend the theatre with their *peers* or opposite-sexed friend, NOT with their parents. Secondly, even among non-swinging parents I found that the mothers and fathers were ordinarily too busy with their own social affairs to give up a Friday or a Saturday night in order to humor a son or daughter in regard to attendance at an "R" rated movie. The upshot is that most of the teenagers in *both* groups managed to find ways of getting into "R" rated movies *without* the presence of their mothers or fathers. Drive-in film theatres were most commonly used by teenagers desirous of seeing "R" rated films because they are easier to sneak into than walk-in theatres usually are. But most of the teenagers, with whom I spoke, particularly the swingers' teenagers, tended to know of walk-in theatres with permissive policies. Fifteen- and sixteen-year-old teenagers would often travel as much as twenty miles in order to attend one of these theatres.

One of the most widely accepted truisms in all of psychology is that *felt deprivation leads to preoccupation.* When a person is deprived of something he truly wants he tends to become distracted and preoccupied with fantasies of the object or experience he is prevented from having. It is here that we find a very interesting paradox. For it appears that the motion picture rating code defeats the very purpose for which it was originally established. Rather than decreasing the interest and preoccupation of teenagers with sex and four-letter swear words it tends to *increase* this interest and preoccupation. In fact, many of the things that teenagers privately fantasize about films they are not permitted to see (but strongly wish to see) are far, far more extreme than anything that actually appears in these films.

Exacerbating the situation further is the fact that since the motion picture rating code was first initiated most of the most critically acclaimed films have been "R" rated. A brief overview of all of the Academy Award nominations made since 1968 should swiftly convince any reader that this is so. The result of this situation is that teenagers are often made to feel like second class citizens, thus increasing their feelings of alienation from parents and other adult authority figures.

To be sure, not all teenagers do feel deprived by the motion picture rating code or by any other adult imposed system of rules. Better than half of the *non-swingers' daughters* with whom I talked did *not feel* deprived by the motion picture rating code; and they could not understand the feelings of their brothers and friends who *did feel* deprived. While it is true that some people have been programmed in such a way that they are willing to go along with almost any restriction, this does *not* appear to be the case with the majority of teenagers—particularly *boys*. Of course, in order for deprivation to lead to preoccupation that deprivation must be *felt* deprivation. If a person does not feel deprived she is in no danger of becoming preoccupied. But on the other hand, once a deprived person becomes preoccupied he cannot easily be talked out of that preoccupation. The only cure is the experiencing of that which he has been deprived of having.

The non-swinging parents seemed more concerned about protecting their children from sexual knowledge and experience than about protecting them from virtually anything else with the possible exception of drugs. Support of the motion picture rating system was based almost entirely upon the fear of arousing sexual interests and desires in their children. The near-unanimous opposition to the motion picture rating code system among the swinging parents could similarly be understood in terms of the latter's full and complete acceptance of their children and teenagers as sexual beings.

Many of the non-swinging parents found it extremely difficult to view their children as human beings with sexual natures. This can be seen in the attitudes of these parents toward masturbation. I posed the following question to both groups of parents: "Ideally, should unmarried boys be able to obtain sexual relief at all other than through nocturnal emissions?" Fully 36 percent of the non-swinging mothers and 21 percent of the non-swinging fathers said "no." None of the swinging parents said "no" to this question.

An additional item yielding strong data pointing to a very punitive attitude among the non-swingers toward youthful sexual behavior was the following: "A very good student academically is caught one Saturday night quietly engaging in sexual intercourse with his girl friend in his dormitory bedroom. Do you believe that there should be a penalty? And if so, what?"

Most of the swinging parents indicated that their own children would never reside in dormitories in the first place. The swingers tended to view college dormitories as very depressing, monastic environments that do more to distract their residents from the drive to study than to facilitate a true enthusiasm for academic inquiry. In line with these liberal attitudes, none of the swingers recommended that the copulating student be given anything more than a token warning, and only three of them recommended that much. In contrast, only 27 percent of the non-swinging fathers and 21 percent of the non-swinging mothers recommended that the hypothetical student receive no penalty. Almost one-fifth of the non-swinging parents would have suspended the student from the university and most of the others would have placed him on a strict probation.

Today coeducational dormitories for college students are becoming increasingly prevalent. In California as of the year 1976, about half of the public and private colleges and universities permit unrestricted boy-girl visitation in the dormitories. The non-swinging parents tended to be very worried about this trend. Most of them believed that 18 years of age is not old enough for "children" to be permitted to determine their own personal life styles. In fact, many of the parents would sooner deprive a child (even their own child) of a college education than allow that child the freedom to choose a life style of his or her own. To many of these parents the *traditional*, sex-segregated dormitory is the best way of prolonging the emotional and financial dependency of their sons and daughters. In stark contrast, most of the swinging parents believed in promoting the psychological differentiation and personal self-sufficiency of their sons and daughters even as early as the second or third grade of elementary school.

One of the best illustrations of the difference in philosophy of child-rearing between the swinging and non-swinging parents can be seen in the pattern of reactions to the statement: "Curfew laws which restrict all persons below a certain age rather than just those who are disruptive, disorderly and inconsiderate, constitute a violation of teenagers' constitutional rights as free citizens." Seventy-two percent of the swinging parents endorsed this statement compared to only 31 percent of the non-swinging parents. In essence, the non-swingers were even willing to enlist the coercive help of the law in their efforts to retain a firm hold on the body, mind and spirit of their adolescent offspring. In contrast, the swingers wanted the loyalty and the occasional companionship of their children. But they constantly made their children aware of the fact that they (the children) were to be their own masters and would have to assume responsibility for their own destiny. In fact, many of the swingers assumed this attitude while their children were still in the early years of elementary school.

The swingers also tended to be somewhat less protective of their children in regard to alcoholic beverage use. For example, only 13 percent of the swinging parents felt that young people should *not* be permitted to purchase beer at 18. In contrast, three times as many of the non-swinging parents (39 percent) felt the same way. Despite the fact that California has long been in the vanguard of the rest of the nation as far as most social issues are concerned, its alcoholic beverage laws for 18- to 20-year-olds remain more restrictive than those of many American states and Canadian provinces. Whereas a majority of even the non-swinging parents of the present study supported the idea of making beer and wine available to 18-year-olds, the California state legislature has continued year after year to vote against such a measure.

In a similar question I asked the respondents to react to the following: "In order to discourage unhealthy curiosity, parents should permit their children to taste alcoholic beverages under their supervision even prior to the age of 12." This statement is not as extreme as it may at first appear. Most Jewish parents permit their children to *taste* small amounts of wine at family dinners. Irish and Italian Roman Catholic parents similarly tend to permit their prepubescent children to at least taste diluted wine and sometimes light beer on the occasion of major holiday dinners. In Europe, French and Italian parents typically expose their young children to quite a bit of wine tasting, even at ordinary meals. But despite the seeming permissiveness of such parents and cultures, the incidence of alcoholism and problem drinking among such groups has long remained substantially lower than that among most groups of Americans.

Sixty-five percent of the non-swingers, compared to 81 percent of the swingers, registered agreement with the above statement. Hence, whereas the non-swinging parents did tend to be somewhat more protective of their children than the swinging parents on alcohol related matters, the differences between the two groups were obviously far less substantial than they were on matters pertinent to sexual expression.

But as pointed out in Chapter 6, the differences between the two groups of parents were quite considerable in regard to marijuana. Only 11 percent of the non-swinging parents, compared to 33 percent of the swingers, favored no restrictions on the availability of marijuana. Fifty-two percent of the swingers felt that marijuana should be as available to the public as liquor. Only 22 percent of the non-swingers felt this way.

Despite their more liberal stance on marijuana, many of the swingers appeared quite nervous about the idea of their children using it or keeping it around the house. Almost two-thirds of the swinging parents mentioned having frequent discussions with their children about the marijuana issue, the major objective being to convince their children not to bring any of it around the house. In all of the swinging families that held regular family conferences the children allegedly voted along with their parents not to keep marijuana or any other illegal drugs on the premises. In this regard the swingers seemed far more worried about having marijuana around the house than about their children experimenting with it.

In point of fact, 74 percent of the swingers' teenagers had tried marijuana at least once, but only 18 percent indicated that they used it on an average of once or more per month. Most of these young people had used it at parties and other social gatherings with their non-swinging school chums. The analogous data for the non-swingers' teenagers may be less reliable. But 52 percent of those I interviewed indicated that they had tried marijuana at least once, and 23 percent indicated that they were using it once or more per month. In both groups the use of pot seemed to be exclusively confined to the peer group. No one admitted to ever using it by themselves. The following comment by 17-year-old Mark is typical:

"Well, sometimes like when I'm at a party with
school friends I mess around a little bit with it.
Personally I've never purchased any of it myself.
But if I'm around where everyone else is doing it I
wouldn't feel right not doing it too. Anyway, it's not
harmful and I know I'm not going to develop any
addiction to it. The reason why I know that . . . see,
I've never had any craving for it when I'm not
around where it's at."

Sixteen-year-old Margie claimed to enjoy the "high"
marijuana gave her. But she too claimed that she never
had any desire to use pot on a frequent basis:

"My mom and dad always told me that life is
meant to be lived! I enjoy getting high on pot when
I'm with my friends and they're doing it too. If
they're not smoking it and there isn't any around I
don't even think to ask for any. If it's there and my
friends are doing it I figure why shouldn't I! I enjoy
sex a lot more, though. And I wouldn't dream of
bringing any of that stuff into the house. We have a
lot of sex parties here and if we should ever get
busted I don't want the police to find any of that
stuff around. If it were something really important
to me it would be different. But for me I can take it
or leave it. And I think the other swinging kids will
tell you the same thing."

Finally, the non-swinging parents were *less* protective
than the swinging parents in regard to the unplanned
pregnancy and forced marriage issues. Fully 46 percent of
the non-swinging mothers felt that an unmarried college
girl should be required to see her unplanned pregnancy
through to term, whereas only 6 percent of the swinging
mothers felt the same way. Most of the non-swinging parents believed that what they regarded as sexual transgressions should be punished.

Enjoyment and Satisfaction with Family Roles

Parenthood is the only important role in society that is

left to amateurs. Yet in spite of the lack of formal training for parenting responsibilities, most American families seem to provide their members with a considerable amount of emotional satisfaction and psychic rewards. I was especially interested in ascertaining whether the swinging parents of this study were as satisfied with their parental roles as the non-swinging parents were. I was also interested in determining whether the swingers' offspring were as satisfied and happy with their roles as children as were the young people who were growing up in the more conventional, non-swinging households. I succeeded in obtaining some fascinating data pertinent to these points.

First, the swinging and non-swinging parents did not differ from one another in terms of their perceived enjoyment of parental roles. Only 6 percent of the parents in each group felt that they did not enjoy their roles as mothers and fathers. The fathers were no more likely than the mothers to feel dissatisfied or unhappy about being expected by society to play their parental roles. Even more heartening is the fact that in both samples the large majority of the children who had not yet attained their 13th birthday also viewed themselves as being satisfied with their roles as their parents' sons or daughters. Only 16 percent of the preadolescents in the swinging sample and 18 percent of those in the non-swinging sample viewed themselves as being less than happy with their current roles as their parents' children. Of course, both of these figures are higher than the 6 percent figure for the parents—a fact which may reflect an easier ability on the part of children to give frank replies and to be less concerned than their elders with presenting a "fake" image of happiness and satisfaction with family life because it is the "socially desirable" thing to do.

The picture that emerged for the teenagers and young adults still living with their parents was quite different. The swingers' teenagers were significantly more likely than those of the non-swingers to view themselves as happy and satisfied with life in their parents' home. Only 4 percent of the teenagers living in swinging families expressed unhappiness and dissatisfaction with their family lives. In contrast, 37 percent of the non-swingers' teenaged offspring expressed unhappiness and dissatisfaction. It should be pointed out, however, that more of the sons than of the daughters in the non-swinging homes felt dissatisfied. Specifically, only 28 percent of the teenaged daughters felt dissatisfied compared to 46 percent of the teenaged sons.

In essence, while the large majority of the adults tended to enjoy their parental roles (or at least felt impelled to say that they did), almost two-fifths of the teenaged offspring of conventional, non-swinging households did not enjoy their roles as their parents' children. Only 36 percent of the non-swingers' teenagers said that they enjoy spending a good deal of time with their parents, and only 41 percent indicated that they frequently go to their parents for advice about their problems. Yet despite their unconventionality, the swinging parents fared much better in the eyes of their teenaged children. Seventy-six percent of the swingers' teenagers indicated that they frequently seek advice from their parents and/or discuss their personal problems with their parents. In addition, 62 percent of these young people indicated that they enjoy spending time with their parents. In fact, a good 15 percent wished that their parents would spend *more* time with them. *None* of the teenagers in the non-swinging households wished their parents would give them *more* time.

All of this suggests that at the time of the study the swinging parents were exerting a greater influence over their teenaged children than the non-swinging parents were. If we assume the validity of the proposition that a prerequisite for effective social influence is mutually enjoyable social interaction, then such would virtually have to be the case.

Nevertheless, the non-swinging parents evidently were in reasonable, mutual rapport with their preadolescent youngsters. Perhaps a major reason why this was so is simply that the pattern of expectations they held for their children was easier for younger aged children (and daughters) to live up to than for teenagers (or boys). With the onset of adolescence usually comes a strong internal pressure for psychological differentiation from parents. A teenager wants to become his own independent, autonomous person; he wants to be in charge of his own life. And in most American families this may not be particularly easy to accomplish. Many adults have an unconscious desire to keep their offspring in the roles of young, dependent children. A related problem is what scientists often refer to as *perceptual constancy*. Since parents see their children everyday they often fail to perceive the fact that their child is not the same person as he or she was three or four years ago. In essence, parents are often quite blind to the growth and maturation in their children that is very evident to outsiders.

Sources of potential family disharmony were uncovered in the pattern of responses I received to many of the parental attitude questions. For example, I asked all of the adults to react to the following: "The age at which a young girl should begin dating is ideally the age at which she personally wishes to begin." Only 22 percent of the non-swinging parents agreed with this statement compared to 74 percent of the swinging parents. In a similar question I asked each of the parents to react to the statement: "After a girl has reached the age of 18 her parents should no longer require her to return home at any particular hour from a date." Here again, 84 percent of the swinging parents agreed compared to only 23 percent of the non-swinging parents. At the time the data for this study were collected California had already lowered the age of majority to 18 for all privileges and responsibilities except the consumption of alcoholic beverages. Yet most ordinary suburban American parents remain emotionally unprepared to allow their 18-year-olds the full range of normal adult freedoms and privileges. This may be one reason why so many young people from attractive suburban neighborhoods leave home as soon as they are able to do so. The lack of willingness of many American parents to trust their adolescents and to provide the type of guidelines that might be in reasonable harmony with teenagers' basic needs and natures is also apparent in the above findings.

One of the major problems with the discouraging of early dating and emotionally close boy-girl relationships is that it is very difficult to discourage these things without also at the same time discouraging *love* and its manifold emotional expressions. Paradoxically, the discouraging of "steady" boy-girl love relationships may be tantamount to discouraging psycho-emotional *monogamy* in addition to love. The 25-year-old woman who finds it very difficult to be demonstrative and loving toward her husband very often has a history of having had demonstrative heterosexuality discouraged and punished by parents.

I asked the adult respondents to react to the following:

> "If a 9th grade boy and girl prefer each other's steady companionship to the 'best friend' companionship of persons of *their own* sex, their relationship should be *neither* encouraged *nor* discouraged by their parents. (Assume that the couple studies together almost every night and earns grades in the A− to B+ range.)"

Only 11 percent of the non-swinging parents found themselves able to register *strong* agreement with this statement compared to a full 52 percent of the swinging parents. On the other hand, 32 percent of the non-swinging parents *disagreed* compared to just 5 percent of the swinging parents.

One of the major problems of life in modern America is that a very great many people lack communication skills. Even within highly educated groups it is not necessary to look far in order to find the person who can communicate effectively on an intellectual level in impersonal situations, but who is totally lacking in an ability to make his ideas and feelings known on a deeper, more meaningful emotional level. Probably at least half of our society is incapable of communicating adequately *with the other sex* in a manner that is emotionally meaningful and mutually rewarding. Almost all social scientists agree that this is a major reason behind the burgeoning divorce rate in America today. Almost all would similarly concur that a key reason for communication problems between men and women is that boys and girls are strongly encouraged by their parents and teachers to play, grow and develop within the context of *sex-segregated peer groups*. Cultural anthropologists have made it clear that it is *not* natural for preadolescent children to gravitate exclusively toward members of their own sex for play activities. The coeducational peer group is the natural and normal state of affairs; and so is the development of strong, emotional love interests and involvements between girls and boys throughout their preadolescent years.

I found the swinging parents to be far more sensitive than the non-swinging parents were to the negative consequences of sex-segregated play groups during the childhood years. Many of the swingers mentioned that the main reason why most men think and react to things differently than women is simply because they are socialized in the context of a completely different peer group subculture. Simply put, the female peer group differs in a host of ways from the male peer group; and this is something that holds true at all age levels. Similarity of interests, feelings and values can come about only when men and women share a similar background of informal play activities in coeducational peer groups. The ability to communicate with and to fully understand the feelings and needs of the other sex can similarly come about only through a history of informal interaction with members of the other sex from early childhood onward.

A few of my swinging respondents felt that the ability to

relate to the other sex on an emotionally meaningful level is something with which all of us are born. Several of the couples took the position that customary modes of socialization in American society *take away* certain highly desirable natural abilities that exist in all people at the very beginning of life. Supporting this position are recent studies showing that 10 percent of all graduating college seniors have never in their lives had a date or an informal relationship with an opposite-sexed age-mate, and that 25 percent had averaged only one date or less per year over their four years of undergraduate college life. These same studies have indicated that only very few of the inactive individuals had ever had any homosexual inclinations or desires. Most had always been fully heterosexual men who had always been very shy and had simply never learned how to communicate with female age-mates in a relaxed, mutually enjoyable manner.

Shyness is a far more widespread problem in American society than its opposite. And as most of the very limited amount of work into it has shown, most of its sufferers are men. Women can do without men a great deal more easily and successfully than heterosexual men can do without women. School and college administrators up to now have chosen to ignore the problem because shy people "suffer quietly" and because effectively remedying the situation would require that the development of sex-segregated peer groups no longer be encouraged in the elementary schools and at all other levels. It would require that the natural inborn ability of people to relate meaningfully with the other sex *not* be "temporarily" suspended.

Some of the younger couples I interviewed advised me that they had taken steps to assure that their children always retain an easy ability to relate with and to enjoy the company of the other sex. Gail and Doug, both 32, did most of their swinging with another young couple who also had young children. Gail's comments here are especially interesting:

"We put up that big fence in our backyard just so our kids could play nude in the pool without being disturbed by any outsiders. Hank and Carol's kids come over here a lot. They still live in an apartment and their kids don't have access to any pool. Doug and I love them. We've been swinging with them now for five years and their kids have always been the perfect companions for our kids. The boys and girls always play together. I've never seen them segregate themselves sexually. Once Bobby asked me why the kids at school always seem to divide themselves up according to sex. He couldn't understand that because for him it has always been completely natural to play in mixed groups. When I was growing up I always preferred mixed company myself. I think you have to learn to want to play with only people of your own sex. One of my neighbors came here last week and tried to talk me into having Jimmy join the Cub Scouts so that he could get away from all these girls. I told her that he had Bobby to play with and that he enjoyed playing with the girls as much as he enjoys playing with the boys. She just couldn't understand that. She said she didn't think it was natural. I think her way is the way that is not natural!"

The swingers' children were far more likely than the non-swingers' children to play in coeducational peer groups both at home and at the schools they were attending. Their initial proclivity to play in mixed groups can probably be attributed to a combination of two factors: (1) coeducational play may indeed be more natural than sex-segregated play unless a person has been socially programmed to believe the opposite; and (2) the children's swinging parents had always provided a strong model glorifying the joys of heterosexual interaction and making it seem more natural and desirable than sex-segregated interaction. As was documented in Chapter 7, the swinging mothers and fathers had always been prone from the time of their own earliest years to prefer the coeducational peer group. As the reader will recall, many of them had sustained this preference in spite of efforts on the part of their parents, teachers, and same-sex peers to discourage it.

Conservative thinkers often take the position that people ought to have well-developed feelings of personal identity and of self-awareness *before* they begin to have relationships with the other sex. On the other hand, George Herbert Mead (one of the founding fathers of modern social science), pointed out that informal play with other children is the most important means through which human beings of both sexes develop a sense of selfhood and of personal identity. Today psychologists agree that informal play is not only indispensable to the formation of a healthy personal identity, but that the nature and type of the informal play that is experienced during the formative years determines a person's later ability as an adult to relate to others in a satisfying and meaningful manner.

Eleanor Macklin (1974), who has done the best work up to now on the subject of college students "living together" unmarried, is among the many who have pointed out that the development of a strong feeling of self-awareness and personal identity is one of the main benefits of such activity. Well over 80 percent of Macklin's hundreds of cohabiting students claimed that being with a person of the other sex on an emotionally intimate basis on a day after day basis taught them things about themselves that they had never before known and about which they probably could not have learned in any other way. In fact, even the people who had broken up with their lovers tended to feel this way and tended to regard the "living together" experience as having been worthwhile for just self-awareness reasons alone. All of them viewed having an opposite-sexed roommate as being far more natural and comfortable than the usual pattern for college students of same-sexed roommates. Conservative thinkers often fear that early informal heterosexual interaction will lead to premature

marriages. The "living together" unmarried courtship option would appear to be an answer to this fear that is well
worth very serious consideration.

Some of my findings suggested that most conventional
non-swinging parents were also a good deal more prone
than the swingers to discourage close heterosexual interaction even among older college age offspring. More
specifically, they even appeared to be more likely to discourage *legal marriage* than the swinging couples were. For
example, I asked all of the respondents to register their
level of agreement with the following statement:

> "When an undergraduate college student marries,
> his parents should continue to provide him with
> *equally as much* tuition, and room and board
> money for *equally as much* time as he would have
> received it had he not married."

Only 28 percent of the swinging husbands and 32 percent
of the swinging wives *disagreed* with this statement. In
contrast, fully 46 percent of the non-swinging husbands
and 53 percent of the non-swinging wives saw fit to *disagree*.

In short, many of the non-swinging parents were bent on
discouraging the joys of youthful sexuality regardless of
the circumstances under which it might occur. Many of
the swingers expressed the view that they would prefer
their children to "live together" unmarried while they are
still students. But these same people indicated that if their
children felt determined to legally marry, such *legal* "living together" should not be financially penalized.

A greater tendency among many of the non-swinging
parents to believe in certain old myths might also partially explain their comparatively strong opposition to
college marriages. For example, the non-swinging parents
were almost three times more likely than the swinging
parents to agree with the statement: "If college students
could have all the sexual freedom they wanted it would
interfere with their school work." In point of fact, most

pertinent studies have shown that, age for age, college students with regular sex lives earn considerably *better* grades than those who do not have a heterosexual love life. Male students in particular seem to benefit very substantially from having a regular sexual life.

Children and Contraception

I asked all of my respondents to indicate their level of agreement with the following statement:

> "Ideally, teenagers should have a thorough knowledge of contraception and should be free to obtain it through medical sources without parental knowledge if and when they decide to engage in premarital intercourse."

Among the swinging parents 92 percent of the fathers and 85 percent of the mothers registered agreement. Among the non-swinging parents only 51 percent of the fathers and 38 percent of the mothers registered agreement. The differences between the two groups of parents were clearly very substantial on this issue, and they reflect the more highly "protective" posture of the non-swinging parents that was referred to earlier in this chapter.

Of course, the question as to what is "protective" in terms of whether or not teenagers should have contraception freely available to them is a matter of individual interpretation. The non-swinging parents preferred the traditional interpretation that freely available contraception would "encourage" teenagers to have sex and that it would increase the already high rates of unplanned pregnancy and of venereal diseases. On the other hand, the swinging parents saw freely available contraceptive supplies as insuring and "protecting" against pregnancy and venereal disease. They also viewed the easy availability of such supplies to teenagers as promoting sexual responsibility.

A most crucial issue is that of whether or not parents are able to accept the idea of their teenagers enjoying sexual intercourse. One of the most painstaking and thorough studies to date on teenagers' use of contraception was conducted in the Baltimore area by Frank Furstenberg. Furstenberg found that the single most important determinant of whether a teenaged couple would use contraception was the extent to which the two people genuinely viewed premarital sex as morally appropriate and acceptable for themselves. Corollatively, it can safely be said that the single most important variable determining whether a young couple is likely to remain free from unwanted pregnancy is simply their degree of acceptance of premarital coitus for their own lives. In other words, guilt over premarital coitus is the main reason why teenagers and other young people do not take contraceptive precautions or take them haphazardly. Similarly, it is the main reason why many teenaged lovers do not discuss either sexual technique or contraception before engaging in the sex act. For such people it is far easier to engage in sex than it is to talk about it with the love partner.

The practical implications of these truths became particularly obvious in my own research findings. The non-swingers had had just as many teenaged children as did the swingers, and the ages of the two groups of teenaged young people were essentially the same. Yet in spite of what appeared to be a far greater amount of active teenaged sexual expression among the swingers' youngsters, *only two* of them had ever been involved in an unwanted or unplanned pregnancy. In contrast, *at least eight* of the non-swingers' daughters studied for this research had experienced unwanted pregnancies. I am less certain about the validity of my data for the teenaged boys; but here again, none of the swingers' sons admitted to impregnating anyone. In contrast, seven of the non-swingers' sons admitted to having impregnated someone; and five of them appeared quite boastful about having done so.

Most non-swinging parents in our society continue to make their children feel very guilty about the mere idea of premarital sexual intercourse. Many convey this negative idea to their children simply by remaining silent on matters pertaining to sex. Others combine silence with a good many remarks that make teenaged girls in particular feel "sinful" or disloyal to their parents by engaging in premarital sexual intercourse, or even by talking about it with a boy of their age. This is why as a social scientist I frequently feel compelled to predict that until at least 80 percent of all American parents accept non-promiscuous premarital coitus as morally right and good (under such conditions as mutual love and respect, but not necessarily any commitment in regard to marriage), the rate of unplanned teenaged pregnancy will continue to remain high. It is *not* enough for parents merely to "condone" premarital sex. The word "condone" carries a negative, disparaging connotation and denotation. The proper word is "accept." Parents must *accept* the idea of responsible and loving premarital sex for their teenaged young people. If they do not accept, then teenagers are not likely to communicate. And if there is no mutually enjoyable communication on this issue, then there cannot be any positive or constructive influence, and responsible contraceptive use becomes less likely.

Comparing the swinging with the non-swinging parents, one of the most conspicuous differences was the former's *realistic* acceptance of *what is*. Until people accept the true facts of a situation they are never likely to be in a position to take constructive action in regard to those facts. According to official government statistics about 50 percent of all young people today between the ages of 13 and 19 *are sexually active.* Of course, not all are equally sexually active. For some, sex is experienced very rarely and sporadically. But those who experience it rarely or sporadically are, for reasons that were made clear in the previous chapter, very often the ones who are the prime candidates for unwanted pregnancy and venereal disease. The fact that so many young people *are* to a greater or lesser extent sexually active would appear to be a very strong argument in and of itself for making contraceptive information and

supplies easily and readily available in drugstores, medical clinics and schools. It would also appear to be a very
strong argument for modifying our socialization procedures with teenagers in such a way that we as parents and
teachers no longer make them feel guilty or "sinful" about
engaging in premarital sexual intercourse.

As a final illustration of the great difference in
philosophy between the swinging and the non-swinging
respondents as far as teenagers and birth control are concerned, let us consider the following questionnaire item to
which I asked all of the respondents to register their
agreement or disagreement:

> "The first and foremost goal of all sex education
> ought to be to encourage children to intellectually
> and emotionally separate in their minds the idea of
> sex from the idea of reproduction."

Fully 74 percent of the swingers agreed with this statement compared to only 34 percent of the non-swingers.
Many of the respondents spontaneously mentioned the
importance of "love," and others stressed the idea of responsibility. There can be no question about the importance of these virtues. The question, however, is whether
such virtues are in any way threatened by programming
young people with the idea that they ought not become
involved with the business of procreating new life until
both they and their partners are ready to do so financially,
emotionally, and educationally. Reproduction is always
going to be a necessary endeavor. But the expression of
love and the satisfaction of basic human needs should
never be sacrificed merely because sex potentially can
lead to babies.

As I have shown, the emotions are a far stronger determinant of behavior for most people than the intellect. This
is particularly true as far as the behavior of teenagers is
concerned. Simply put, having contraceptives available
and knowing how to use them is not enough to assure that
a person will use them or use them properly. The ability to

emotionally *as well as* intellectually accept and use birth control requires a home atmosphere that is very *relaxed* and *accepting* as far as premarital sex and birth control are concerned. Keeping non-prescription contraceptives conspicuously available on drug store shelves would also help out a very great deal in terms of enabling teenagers to integrate sex into their emotional as well as into their intellectual makeups. And it would increase the likelihood that sexually active people would buy and use such materials.

Punishment

One of the questions people most frequently ask me is that of whether or not swinging parents ever spank their children. Preoccupation with force and violence is quite common in the United States. Both children and adults alike tend to be suspicious as to whether it is realistically feasible to discourage undesirable behavior without fear or the threat of coercion and physical pain hanging over one's head. Most Americans tend to view spanking as a necessary part of proper socialization. And several sociologists have recently found that even high school seniors are far from immune from the physical assaults of their angry parents. In Straus's (1974) New Hampshire study 46 percent of the young people interviewed had received parent-inflicted corporal punishment at least once during their senior year of high school. Straus also found that 81 percent of the parents he surveyed had resorted to corporal punishment at some time during the past year.

Up to now, researchers have not bothered to *operationalize* the concept of "spanking." Spanking, like the seemingly more general term "corporal punishment," can mean anything from cuffing a child once with the bare hand over the clothed buttocks to the types of severe beatings with chains, razor straps, hoses, wooden rods, etc., that often eventuate in what has come to be called the "battered child syndrome." As the term "spanking" means so many different things to so many different people under so many different circumstances, it is bound to be associated with many different sorts of consequences.

I tried to deal with this problem in the present study by asking parents *when* and *how* they "spanked," and whether they used any implements other than their own bare hands. I similarly asked the children to discuss the style and techniques of discipline and punishment within their homes.

Most studies have shown that more than two-thirds of American parents spank their children. More specifically, about one-third of all parents depend very heavily upon corporal punishment as a punitive approach, and most of this group tends to be very severe and pain-oriented; that is, they try to cause a maximum of pain without inflicting any injury or scar upon the child's body. The second one-third of all parents tend to use physical punishment primarily as a last resort. Some of the parents in this group are quite severe when they apply physical punishment; others tend to be quite mild. Only about 25 percent of all American parents seldom or never resort to corporal punishment.

My own data parallel very closely the above general trends. More specifically, I found that 28 percent of the non-swinging parents and 34 percent of the swinging parents never resort to the use of corporal punishment in the disciplining of their children. This difference is not very great. It suggests that swinging parents do not differ much from non-swinging parents in terms of their general predisposition to employ physical punishment. It also suggests that both the swinging and the non-swinging parents studied tend to be quite similar to American parents generally in terms of the use of corporal punishment.

On the other hand, there were some strong and noteworthy differences between the swinging and the non-swinging parents in terms of their use of physical punishment. For example, I found that the swinging parents

tended to be considerably more impulsive and spontaneous than the non-swinging parents when it came to disciplining their children. When their children angered them
about half of the swinging parents tended to be highly
overt and uninhibited in showing this anger. This easy and
overt display of anger very often extended to smacking or
hitting the child. Preadolescent children were more vulnerable in swinging homes to this type of punishment
than were teenaged children, and girls were not less vulnerable than boys. The immediate objective of the angry
parents was to show their anger and purge themselves of
their pentup tensions. Several of these people hastened to
point out to me that they were often sorry afterward for
having smacked their child and that their actions were
often caused by a lack of adequate control on their part.
But they also made clear to me their belief that anger
should be openly, frankly, and immediately expressed
whenever it is felt.

For the approximately one-half of the swinging parents
who seldom or never used corporal punishment there
seemed to be an easy ability to relieve tensions through
hollering and shouting their displeasure at some act (or
omission of an act) by the child. Only about 15 percent of
the swinging parents adhered to any intellectual justification for corporal punishment. To most swingers corporal
punishment was merely an adjunct or byproduct of their
anger—an adjunct easy to display on the grounds that the
offender was *their child* rather than a fellow adult or
somebody else's child. In stark contrast to this, 58 percent
of the non-swinging parents held strongly felt belief systems morally justifying (to them) the use of physical
punishment in certain instances.

Despite the fact that some of the swingers' children occasionally caught the brunt of their parents' anger, painful
"spankings," beatings, whippings, etc., were almost unheard of in swinging families. For example, only 12 percent of the swinging parents had ever used any object
other than their bare hands in spanking their children,

and most of the spankings were over the child's full array of clothing. The only major exception to this was the fairly frequent use of facial slaps. In contrast, 62 percent of the non-swinging parents admitted to at least an occasional use of such implements as belts, hairbrushes, razor straps, paddles, birch rods, dog leashes, ropes, etc. In addition, the non-swinging parents were also far more likely than the swinging parents to plan out in advance their method and severity of corporal punishment. I encountered several cases where the time lag from the time of a child's transgression to the time of a severe beating was as much as two days. However, usually the time lag was between ten minutes and an hour in length. But among the swinging families there was almost never any time lag.

Delegation of the authority to administer corporal punishment was nonexistent among the swinging families I studied. Among the non-swinging families 32 percent of the mothers had on occasion delegated what they deemed the "necessary" task of spanking to their husbands.

Disciplinary action was most likely to be taken by swinging parents when their children interfered with their freedom or frustrated their plans and activities. In essence, the range of circumstances under which a swinging parent was likely to take disciplinary action against his child was considerably narrower than the range of conditions under which a non-swinging parent was likely to take disciplinary action.

The non-swingers displayed a noticeably higher level of personal ego involvement in what they saw as being the propitious growth and development of their offspring. When a non-swinging parent perceived a shortcoming in his child he was far more likely than a swinging parent to regard that perceived shortcoming as a negative reflection upon himself. He was similarly more likely to worry about "what the neighbors might think" if he left his child's behavior unchecked. And he was more likely than the swinging parent to worry about the possibility of the child continuing the undesired behavior long into the future. He was less likely than the swinging parent to perceive children as capable of naturally outgrowing undesirable behavior on their own without punitive action on the part of parents. The non-swinging parent had a strong confidence in punishment and fear as effective teachers and motivators for desirable behavior. On the other hand, most of the swingers revealed a far greater confidence than the non-swinging parents in the instinctual ability of their children to "evolve" and grow up in a desirable manner.

The foregoing can be illustrated by the way the two groups of parents would react to such nonconformity as (1) coming home late for dinner; (2) not doing homework; (3) staying up all hours of the night on a school night; (4) bringing home a poor report card; (5) watching too much television; (6) not getting up early enough to be on time for school; and (7) maintaining a slovenly appearance. All of these behaviors would tend to be regarded as "transgressions" by most non-swinging parents. And in fact, most of the non-swinging parents I interviewed would have punished such behaviors.

On the other hand, the swingers tended to view such behaviors as posing potential problems to the child but *not* to themselves. Thus they seldom punished such behaviors; in fact, they usually ignored them. Sometimes they would advise a child that he might encounter difficulties from outsiders if he did not assume a more mature degree of responsibility for this behavior. But in such cases it was always made clear to the child that the responsibility belonged to him and not to his parents.

For example, if a child came home late for dinner it was his responsibility to fix his own food and to clean up afterward. If he failed to clean up adequately the swinging parent perceived his own freedom as being threatened and he would rouse the child from whatever he was doing and insist that the mess be properly cleaned up. The non-swinging parent, on the other hand, tended to view not coming home on time as a "moral infraction." Normally it would be punished by denying the child dinner or by deprivation of some set of privileges. Frequent repetition of the behavior would typically be dealt with via corporal punishment, even if the "child" was of high school age.

Such behaviors as not doing homework, being late to school, bringing home a poor report card, etc., were not punished at all by swinging parents. Non-swinging parents tended to view propitious performance in these areas as being as much their responsibility as that of their child.

Swinging parents tended to be quite open about their dependence on children's peer groups for such matters as teaching proper table manners, appropriate dress and appearance, etc. The swinging parents were far less likely than the non-swingers to complain about such matters as the personal appearance of their children or long hair on boys. Long hair and personal appearance was one of the most frequent sources of major argumentation in the non-swinging homes. In contrast, I could find only three swinging homes where either long hair or the personal appearance of teenagers was a major source of family friction.

Behaviors such as watching an excessive amount of television or staying up too late were only punished by swinging parents when such behaviors interfered with their own lives. Having the television or the stereo on too loudly would very frequently (but not always) be reacted to by swinging parents in a punitive manner. But if the children pursued these pleasures well into the night without distracting the parents in any way they were tolerated and not punished in any way. The non-swinging parents were as inconsistent as the swinging parents when it came to punishing the playing of the stereo or television too loudly. But in contrast to the swinging parents they were very consistent about punishing what they viewed as an excessive amount of self-indulgent behavior. In short, watching television or listening to records well into the night was seldom tolerated by the non-swinging parents no matter how quietly their children did these things.

Just as the swinging parents were less likely than the

non-swinging parents to punish certain behaviors they were similarly less likely than the non-swinging parents to *reward* many behaviors. The non-swinging parents were far more likely than the swinging parents to reward good grades in school with money. Again, the attitude of the swingers was that the children have their own lives, and if they do well they are doing well for and on behalf of themselves, *not* their parents.

Self-Sufficiency

The swinging parents tended to be less generous than the non-swinging parents in terms of allowances, particularly as far as their high school aged youngsters were concerned. Forty-two percent of the swingers' children worked at least some of the time after school and/or on weekends during the regular school year. In contrast, only 21 percent of the non-swingers' children worked after school or on weekends with any degree of regularity.

Most of the jobs which the swingers' offspring held were entrepreneurial in nature. Few of these young people were regular employees of any firm. They earned their money on their own initiative by soliciting a wide variety of odd jobs among the residents of their suburban communities.

The early tendency on the part of the swingers' youngsters to earn much of their own money can be seen as being in harmony with the strong value most of their parents placed upon self-sufficiency and early autonomy. In line with this, most of the swingers' teenagers appeared considerably more confident and self-assured than the non-swingers' teenagers.

To be sure, not all of the entrepreneurial activities of the swingers' children would be met with approval by most Americans. Children from five of the swinging families were involved in the making of pornographic films and magazines, and six of the children from these families were under 13 years of age. Eight others were between the ages of 13 and 19. At the time this book was being written several demonstrations were held in various parts of the United States against the use of minor children by the pornography industry. When the data for this study were being collected this issue had not yet surfaced into the public spotlight. At that time pornographers were only beginning to employ preadolescent children for the production of their photographic materials. Of course, children had been a part of the pictorial content of nudist magazines for over twenty-five years. But posing for nudist magazines had never been a financially lucrative enterprise. And when hard-core sex publications began to become available during the late 1960s most of the nudist publications were forced out of business.

As pointed out in Chapter 10, most swingers never buy pornography, and those who do, purchase it very seldom. Nevertheless, swingers recognize pornography as a financially lucrative industry. Sixteen percent of the swinging couples I interviewed occasionally posed for pornographic magazine or film producers in order to earn extra income. None of the couples or individuals I interviewed had ever engaged in such work on a full-time basis. However, 31 percent had posed for such publications or films at least once at some time in the past. And 16 percent were still active at it.

Five of these sixteen still-active couples decided to introduce their children to the work because they saw it as an easy way for them to earn a substantial amount of money. In fact, all five of these couples indicated that their children made a good deal more at it than they themselves did.

> "All three of our kids are doing it. They go down there maybe every other Saturday or Sunday, and for just a few hours' work they bring home quite a bundle. Shit! They don't even pay tax on it. They don't report the fuckin' income to Uncle Sam and neither do we. Hell, Cindy [their 11-year-old daughter]brought home $600 last Saturday! I'd say that's pretty fuckin' good money for a day's work,

wouldn't you? Shit! She wasn't even there for a day. She worked only six hours according to Bobby [the 13-year-old son]. Bobby worked 3½ hours and brought home $225. I don't know how they pay them. All I know is at the rate they're going they'll be able to earn enough to buy brand new sports cars for themselves when they come of age. Shit! They'll even be able to pay for their fuckin' insurance and their college expenses on top of that!" (A 37-year-old swinging father.)

I asked each of these couples whether they ever worried about their children suffering at all as a result of working for pornographers. None of the couples revealed any feelings of worry or apprehension about the matter. Here are the remarks of one mother, four of whose children were actively involved in the pornography industry:

"What do you mean? I don't think it's been more than forty or fifty years since kids were forced to work in coal mines. And that's really cruel ... Do you mean that they might later be recognized by people on the street? I don't think there's any chance of that. Kids grow up and their appearance changes a lot as they grow up. As for right now, they never walk the streets alone when they're in the city anyway. They look like any other kids their age. I think that's one reason why they're picked [to work] so often! I don't think any of the creeps who read that stuff would have the balls to stop one of our kids on the street anyway. Most of 'em are just a bunch of fags anyway. Huh. I guess I really shouldn't say that. I mean, even if they are fags they are fags with a lot of money. So we're kinda grateful!"

I asked this mother whether she ever worried about possible adverse psychological consequences that her children's work might eventually create:

"Listen, we're tired of hearing about bullshit like adverse psychological consequences! There's nothing to fear but fear itself! You know who said that? Listen, when you're afraid of something, that usually causes the thing you're most afraid of to happen. Our kids are afraid of nothing! They're healthy kids and nobody's going to make them afraid of nothing! Our kids know the kind of kooks who'll be looking at their pictures. They're sorry for them! I think they have a very mature perspective about what they're doing! They also have a mature perspective about the money they're making! They're making more now than some college educated adults are making! They know that and they feel damn good about themselves! Jay and I will see to it that no one hurts them and that they stay happy. Do you understand?"

I should hasten to add that most of the swingers held quite negative views about those among their fellows who introduced their children to the pornography business. Also significant is the fact that more than a third of the swinging couples I interviewed claimed ignorance of the pornography industry and of any involvement in it by swingers' children.

"I think they're a bunch of nuts who are out to give swinging a bad name. We wouldn't want to have anything to do with such people. Children have their own lives and adults have no right to screw them up. . . . If children want to fool around sexually with each other, well that's another matter. I've always seen to it that my children are prepared for any sexual encounters they might have. But for grown adults to be fooling around with children—ugh—that disgusts me." (40-year-old swinging mother.)

Another swinging parent indicated the following:

"Yes, I know that some of our people have been getting their kids involved in that sort of thing. I feel kind of uncomfortable about it myself. I know the money's good. But I just wouldn't fool around with it ... I just have this feeling in my gut that it's wrong and I wouldn't want my kids to have anything to do with it. I don't fault those who let their kids do it. I just think they're wrong, that's all."

I talked with each of the swingers' offspring who were employed by the pornography business. All appeared to be quite happy and unusually articulate for their ages. None of them seemed to have any fear of adverse parental reaction that might accrue to them if they quit the business. Sixteen-year-old Jerry had this to say about his experiences:

"I've been doing it for two years now. My mom and dad introduced me to the business and at first I thought it was silly. But now I kinda like it and I like the money that I get paid. Most of the time I just pose for them. Sometimes I pose alone, but most of the time they set me up with a girl or sometimes with a bunch of kids my age. Usually they just have me make out in lots of different ways with some girl. .... Everything is done all naked like and sometimes a lot of sexual excitement is involved, especially if they have me work with some girl who really turns me on."

However, some of the children occasionally are asked to do some bizarre posing. A 12-year-old girl, for example, was required to do a lot of sexual posing with a large Great Dane dog. She claimed to have been quite upset by the situation at the time that it occurred. But when I talked with her about it she was all giggles. The fact that two of her siblings were in the studio with her at the time may have served to substantially mitigate whatever anxieties she might have felt. Parenthetically, she was paid $300 for her sexual scenes with the dog.

It was evident in my conversations with these children that most of the photographers and directors know how to handle them in a friendly, cordial manner. While high wages may inspire some of the children to overlook some amount of shoddy treatment, I think it is significant that none of those with whom I spoke complained about foul treatment that might have occurred while they were on the job. Nevertheless, all of the children did complain about the "silliness" of some of the things they were required to do before the camera.

Of course, it is impossible to say at this time whether such highly deviant employment among children will ever be found to be associated with the later development of psychiatric pathology. It is interesting and perhaps quite meaningful that none of the children I interviewed ever read the publications that they themselves had had an important part in making. In fact, most of the children viewed with either pity or contempt the men who purchase pornographic films and picture magazines. But then this is the attitude with which most of their parents had conditioned them.

SUMMARY

The main purpose of this chapter was to summarize the main differences in child-rearing attitudes, values, disciplinary techniques, philosophy and style, between the swinging and the non-swinging parents.

The swinging families tended to maintain significantly fewer rules for their children than the non-swinging families did. However, the rules they did maintain were enforced as often as were the rules in non-swinging homes. The rules in swinging families were put into effect primarily to assure that the rights and freedoms of the parents would not be encroached upon by the children. The swingers were a good deal less child-centered as parents than were the non-swingers. But they were as likely as the non-swinging parents to see themselves as enjoying the roles of parenthood. And their children were more likely to communicate with them frequently about meaningful issues.

In terms of philosophy the swinging parents are more likely than the non-swinging parents to agree with such statements as:

1. Children should have an active role in the making and revising of those family rules that affect them.

2. A child has a right to his own point of view and a right to express it.

3. Children should be permitted to disagree with their parents if they feel their own ideas are better.

4. There is no reason parents should have their way all the time, any more than children should have their way all the time.

The non-swinging parents were far more likely than the swingers to view their children as being very much akin to personal property. They viewed their children as being extensions of themselves, and they saw their children's public behavior as reflecting upon the personal quality of themselves as people and as parents. Because of this the non-swinging parents supervised their children more closely and were far less likely than the swinging parents to leave such matters as personal appearance, long hair, etc., to their children's discretion. This restrictive philosophy tended not to disrupt family harmony very much as far as preadolescent children were concerned. However, the non-swinging parents were far more likely than the swingers to complain that their teenaged children were incomprehensible or that they would not communicate in a meaningful way.

The non-swingers were a great deal more protective of their children than the swingers were. The swingers were far more open to the idea of their sons and daughters exploring such things as sexuality, birth control, beer and wine, and even marijuana. They were also much less likely than the non-swingers to sustain rules regarding such matters as bedtimes, eating habits, television, etc. All in all, they were much more trusting of their children than the conventional parents were. Perhaps many people would regard them as far too trusting.

Summarizing the great differences between the two groups of parents on matters related to sex and romantic love relationships among young people was the pattern of responses to the following two statements:

> a. A teenager should normally be free to entertain guests of the opposite sex in his bedroom without being encumbered by parental supervision.

> b. A 22-year-old living at home should normally be free to entertain guests of the opposite sex in his bedroom without being encumbered by parental supervision.

Fully 100 percent of the swinging husbands and wives registered agreement with the second statement, and 97 percent of them registered agreement with the first. On the other hand, among the non-swingers only 22 percent of the fathers and 17 percent of the mothers registered agreement with the first statement. Even as far as 22-year-old *adult* offspring were concerned, only 47 percent of the non-swinging fathers and 39 percent of the non-swinging mothers would permit unsupervised boy-girl visitation in their son's or daughter's private bedroom.

The swinging parents were *more* demanding than the non-swingers in the area of personal autonomy and self-sufficiency. Their children were expected to perform certain chores around the house, and they were a good deal more likely than the non-swingers' children to hold part-time jobs. Most of the jobs of the swingers' children were quite entrepreneurial in nature and required quite a bit of independent initiative and assertiveness. And judging by their behavior during the interviews, the swingers' children were indeed more friendly, outgoing, outspoken, articulate and assertive (some might even say "fresh"), than the non-swingers' children were.

Chapter 14

Perversions and Other Unusual Behavior in Swinging Families

Sexual perversions have long been a source of endless fascination to some people and of great disgust and revulsion to many others. Still other people, probably the majority, tend to perceive themselves as being indifferent to and just plain uninterested in the phenomena.

Despite the intrinsically controversial nature of this topic, social scientists and those in the helping professions are beginning to become interested in systematically exploring it. This is so because the many perversions found in any given subculture, such as suburban middle-class America, point up more clearly than could few other topics the incredibly wide range of variation that is possible in human sexual attitudes, fantasies, and behavior. There is little evidence suggesting that anyone is ever born with a proclivity toward the kinds of behavior to be discussed in this chapter. Such behavior patterns can emerge only through a process of social learning and conditioning. Probably few if any families intentionally condition their offspring into developing an interest or psychological fixation on unusual forms of sexual behavior. However, such behavior can be seen as an unintended byproduct of the overall atmosphere and learning experiences which the homes of some middle-class suburbanites provide. Some evidence to support this assertion will be presented in this chapter.

To be sure, what most young Americans think of as "perversions" tend to be very uncommon among suburban swinging couples. Among the 100 sexual mate-sharing couples from whom most of the basic data for this study were obtained, only 7 percent had ever had any experience with the "perversions," and only 3 percent gave any evidence of being fixated upon (or psychologically identified with) any of them. Lengthy conversations with these three couples provided most of the data upon which this chapter is based.

While 3 percent does not appear at first glance to be a very large figure, in terms of concrete numbers of American couples involved in the perversions it is quite huge. For example, there are roughly fifty million married couples in the United States today. Hunt's (1974) recent research and that of Gebhard (at Indiana University's Kinsey Institute for Sex Research) suggested that about 2 percent of these couples at some time in their married lives had practiced sexual mate-sharing behavior. Two percent of fifty million couples means that about one million American couples are practicing or have practiced some form of comarital sex behavior. Three percent of this latter figure mean that an estimated 30,000 married couples throughout the United States either are now or in the past have been involved in what most people would view as sexually "perverted" behavior.

It must be made clear at the outset that just because a sexual behavior is nonconformist does not necessarily mean that it is "perverted." Indeed, millions of people would consider swingers to be perverts. But many millions of others, including many millions who themselves would never even dream of practicing swinging, would disagree. At various times in our very conservative, "uptight" history of sexuality such activities as masturbation, fellatio and cunnilingus (oral-genital sex), use of dildos and various types of vibrators, etc., were all considered to be perverted. Today, these and other sexual behaviors are often recommended to people by health professionals. There is a continuing debate as to whether or not homosexuality, bisexuality, and lesbianism, are "perverted" activities. A large professional association of heterosexual psychiatrists recently voted that such activities are *not* "perverted." In essence, there is little consensus today regarding (1) what kinds of sexual behaviors *are* "perverted," (2) how the word "perversion" should be defined, and (3) whether *any* sex act that does not hurt another can be "perverted."

In this chapter I shall deal only with sexual activities which more than three-fourths of the American public would view as "perverted." It will not be my intention to condemn these activities or those who practice them. But I do think they need to be discussed. Hopefully, in the not-too-distant future it will become possible to develop a research design that will enable scientists to shed some real light on the practitioners of sexually unusual and bizarre behavior. The data which I collected permit only some educated speculations.

Swinging with Animals

Several couples in the course of my interviews with them spontaneously mentioned sexual behavior with dogs, cats, snakes, sheep, goats, pigs, and other animals. Only two of the couples in my study had actually practiced these behaviors themselves. But a good many of the respondents were able to recount incidents which had involved swinging acquaintances they had known.

For example, in one of the swinging clubs several of the women derived a great deal of delight out of putting raw hamburger meat into their vaginas and letting their dogs or cats suck it out. Sometimes they would do this at the parties, and they would glow with childish excitement as their husbands and non-participating wives would gather around and watch them. All kinds of dogs, both large and small, were used for this. But there did tend to be somewhat of a preference for the terriers. One woman had a wire-haired fox terrier that exuberantly refused to stop licking and sucking from all of the vaginas at a party until all of the meat was out.

One woman I spoke with said that she preferred cats for this activity, but that it was first necessary to clip their nails and to keep the stubs as rounded and dull as possible. This woman seldom went through the routine at parties, but when alone in her house with all of her children at school and her husband away at work she would meticulously put together a taste treat which she knew her hungry cat could not refuse. She would then go to her bedroom, show the food to the cat and then shove it into her vagina. The cat would then lick and gnaw at her vaginal area as would a dog. But it would also scratch at her clitoris and labia minora with its dullened nails. And this allegedly brought the woman to many orgasms.

Dogs were similarly used at home in private as well as at the parties. One woman was alleged to soothe her loneliness by having her large Irish setter suck and gnaw the food out of her vagina for hour after hour. Just as the dog gave notice that he was satisfied that he had licked out every last bit of food she would immediately grab another fistful of raw hamburger meat and cram it into her vagina for another round. This woman, by the way, lived in a beautiful $90,000 home and had a husband whose job as a sales executive for a major television network required him to do a great deal of traveling and to be away from home occasionally for weeks at a time. When he was at home their sexual relationship together was believed to be good. The overall marital relationship of this couple, however, was seen as being only fair due to their frequent arguments about his prolonged absences.

Dogs also tend to be used by some swingers as sexual love objects, although I did not hear of anyone who had actually gone so far as to have had sex with a dog at a party. I think it is especially interesting that among married swingers it is almost always the wife and virtually never the husband who goes to bed with the dog. Presumably this is due to some extent to the kinds of roles the two sexes play in society. Husbands usually leave the home everyday in order to pursue their work roles which they can segregate in a variety of ways from the awareness of their wives. None of the women involved in these sexual activities with animals held jobs of their own. This takes on greater meaning when we recall my earlier finding that swinging wives were almost twice as likely as the non-swinging wives to hold jobs of their own outside the home. Also of interest is the fact that these women were not believed to belong to any clubs or recreational organizations (aside from their swinging clubs)—again quite unlike swinging wives generally.

Many of the swingers I interviewed mentioned that dogs are a frequent feature of the social scene at swinging get-togethers. People fondle them and play with them and, in general, derive minor delight out of the dogs poking them with their wet noses in various parts of their nude bodies. Dogs are also seen by some swingers as providing a needed alarm system, as they do bark whenever anyone approaches the door from outside.

Among the wives who do occasionally go to bed with their dogs, large animals are almost always preferred for specifically sexual activities—other than those involving the licking of meat out of the vagina. One of the wives I was informed about had an anxiety about germs and the possibility of contracting an illness from her dog during the course of her sexual activities with it. This dog was a large male collie that had already won at least two prizes for her at dog shows. She kept the dog immaculate and never let it outdoors except when she walked it on a leash.

Prior to this woman's sex sessions with her dog, which were always conducted when she was alone in her house, she would scrub the dog's teeth with a strong toothpaste and toothbrush. Then she would squirt several good-sized portions of mouth wash into the dog's mouth. She would then take it to bed and rub her body against that of the dog. This gave her a very great feeling of sexual excitement although she usually had a considerable amount of difficulty in keeping the dog under the covers for very long. Before long the dog would pant very rapidly for want of oxygen. And while this was doubtless very distressing to the dog, she found that it aroused her sexual passion all the more strongly.

One of the couples with whom I spoke owned a small boa constrictor snake, which had been caught at a summer camp by the couple's 9-year-old son. One Sunday morning the boy arose quite early. It was about 5:30 A.M. and the father and mother were still asleep. The boy had always enjoyed playing practical jokes on people, and he immediately recognized the opportunity which the snake together with his sleeping parents provided.

The boy sneaked into his parents' bedroom and deposited the snake underneath the covers at the foot of the double bed on the mother's side. About ten minutes later loud screams filled the quiet morning air. The snake had slithered up between the thighs of the mother. She had awakened and upon discovering the snake screamed out in terror. In fact, she was so terrified that she had an orgasm, one of the strongest and most intense she had allegedly ever experienced.

Since that fateful morning the husband and the son on various occasions teased the wife by bringing the snake into her presence. Gradually the extreme fear reaction became weaker and weaker until she no longer felt any fear when confronted by the snake. Behavior therapists will recognize this as the "extinction" effect. In other words, the original fear response was gradually diminished with each occasion that the snake was brought into the wife's presence.

But whereas the response of fear was extinguished, the response of sexual pleasure for some reason continued to take place. So consistently did this happen that the husband began taking the snake to bed as a tool for sexually arousing his wife. Indeed, so ecstatic was this couple with their newfound source of sexual arousal and pleasure that they began taking the snake to their sexual mate sharing parties, where their colleagues delighted in looking on while the wife and some man other than her husband engaged in a host of erotic activities together. Very often in the midst of passion the wife would ask one of the observers to place the live snake more evenly between her thighs or on her buttocks, etc.

If the reader regards the foregoing as especially "far out," he might be surprised to learn that this couple went even farther than this before their fascination with snakes began to subside. The couple, with the aid of their young son, caught about twenty small green garter snakes. And one evening they excitedly put them all under the covers of their bed. As the little creatures hurriedly slithered in and around the fissures of each of their bodies a feeling of sexual ecstasy mounted very quickly for both. In fact, for the next several months these little snakes allegedly brought so much pleasure to this couple that their attendance at swinging get-togethers actually diminished quite substantially.

At this time the couple no longer continues to sustain the sexual preoccupation with snakes that they once had. However, on occasions when the wife does not feel particularly in the mood for erotic activities her husband can still successfully arouse at least some sexual interest in her by bringing in a live snake. And according to reports, he does this with considerable frequency.

In Woody Allen's recent comic film *Everything You Always Wanted to Know About Sex But Were Afraid to Ask,* there was a skit in which a man became sexually infatuated with a sheep. Comic though it may have appeared, a sexual interest in animals of this type does occasionally happen in real life. One of the couples interviewed for this study was once invited to a farm that was owned and managed by a very wealthy swinging couple. And while the usual range of sexual activities took place at this couple's party which happened to be a very large one and which lasted for a whole weekend, at one point the host came in with three sheep, a goat and a pig, and asked his guests quite seriously if they would like to sexually experiment with some of the animals.

Parenthetically, this particular man at no time gave any indication of preferring sexual behavior with animals to that with female human beings. But during the course of his party it became clear that he and his wife derived quite a bit of sensual delight out of rolling around nude on the floor with the sheep. This was particularly true after he had already experienced a few orgasms without the aid of his animals.

Of special interest is the fact that the man and his wife seemed to display no inhibitions or qualms of any sort about interpolating the farm animals into their erotic party routine. In effect, their unusual behavior did not seem to embarrass them at all. Rather, like swinging itself, they tried to encourage their guests to savor some of the sensual pleasures they saw themselves as deriving from the animals, and particularly from the sheep. They would wrestle with these animals on the soft carpet of their living room floor while encouraging other attractive people to do the same. Their usual rationale, which they frequently stated, was, "You never know whether you'll like something until you try it." After they became aroused to a certain point they would often reach for what they believed to be an interested and willing human sexual partner and resume normal heterosexual erotic activity with him or her.

Encouraging guest couples to savor this quite nonconformist type of erotic activity seemed to be viewed by this couple in much the same way as a more conventional couple might view the encouraging of their friends to try various exotic foods. Each cook tends to inject his own flavor and style into his food, and among swingers each one has his own style for managing parties. Occasionally, although not very often, the style becomes markedly atypical as in the case of this farm couple. On the surface my informing couple found the goings-on at this party to be exceedingly hilarious. But they did not feel comfortable enough to accept a second invitation from the couple.

Still, this farm couple allegedly continues to enjoy a reputation for throwing outstanding swinging parties, and they evidently do not have any difficulty in attracting sexual mate sharing couples to their home. Indeed, couples come from all over California just to see what their parties are like.

Swinging and Sadomasochism

Sadomasochism is in many respects the most anamolous and difficult to understand of all the perversions. It becomes even more difficult to understand when it is realized that some of the devotees of this form of behavior are swingers. None of the couples interviewed for this study indicated that they had any predilections for sadistic or masochistic activities. But six of the couples did indicate that at one time or another they had been forced to participate in such activities against their will. In all such cases such participation occurred within the first two months of the couples' initial involvement in the swinging world.

Swinging places a great premium upon hedonistic behavior—upon the savoring of sexual pleasure for its own sake. How then does the experiencing of pain become mixed in with such hedonistic activities? The answer to this seems to lie with the families in which sadomasochists grew up. All six of the couples who had tasted this form of behavior pointed out how so-called "spankers" and "discipline lovers" invariably enjoy discussing how they see themselves as having benefited from their own parents' tough hand. All of these people had received a great deal of corporal punishment from their own mothers and fathers, and all seemed to have learned to associate a feeling of sexual pleasure with pain.

Of particular interest is the fact that all of the sadomasochists had parents who had taken a strong interest in the technology of producing pain. It was not enough to merely spank their children in preference to using other forms of discipline. These parents were remembered as having made a systematic study of the various ways of producing different degrees of physical pain. As we shall see shortly, the sadomasochists continue this approach with their own children. And they delight in heaping self-congratulatory praise upon themselves in the course of their conversations.

It was pointed out earlier that people desirous of meeting swingers are often counseled in swingers' literature against making dates with any couple before interacting informally with the prospective couple in a safe, neutral setting such as a bar or a restaurant. The remarks of the people I interviewed made it very clear that those who follow this advice are unlikely to ever find themselves locked in with the wrong people. People who do not follow it are highly likely to be novices wanting to get started in sexual mate sharing but having little if any knowledge as to how to go about doing so.

One of my interviewees who unknowingly violated this advice had participated with his wife in three large swinging parties over the preceding month. This couple was very excited about swinging, but they wanted to zero in on just one or two other couples with whom they could become emotionally close.

In their efforts to accomplish this goal they responded to several ads that had been placed by alleged swingers in an underground newspaper. Usually sadomasochists will employ such terms as "discipline," "English culture," "bondage," or "spanking," in their ads in order to properly identify their sexual style. Unfortunately, this couple, whom I shall call Bob and Jenny, made arrangements to meet with a sadomasochistic pair whose ad did not identify their style.

Bob and Jenny wrote the couple a letter which was

quickly responded to with a brief note requesting a telephone call. Jenny called and was delighted that she and her husband were to come to a "small party" to be held that Friday evening.

The sadomasochistic couple, whom I shall call Jay and Cynthia, resided in a very attractive suburban neighborhood. In driving up to their home Bob and Jenny had little reason to feel nervous, particularly since they had experienced several good-sized swinging parties with total strangers. However, upon arriving at the door they discovered that Jay and Cynthia were the only couple there.

All four sat down to what Bob and Jenny in retrospect recall as having been pleasant, introductory "chit-chat." However, after about a half-hour Cynthia announced that she was getting very warm. She quickly shed all of her clothing in front of the other three and walked into the kitchen. She emerged five minutes later with two ice cube trays that were filled with her frozen urine. Bob and Jenny thought this was quite strange, and they looked on in amazement as Cynthia took several of the cubes and pressed them all over her own body and that of her husband who, in the meantime, had been undressing.

Bob and Jenny promptly announced that they were not interested in participating in this type of behavior and were leaving. But at this juncture Jay's manner changed abruptly. He angrily grabbed Bob and handcuffed him to the couch. He and his wife then grabbed Jenny who by this time was screaming loudly. Jay slapped Jenny to the floor while Cynthia announced that if the attention of the police was attracted they would all be equally vulnerable to prosecution for "lewd and immoral" behavior. Bob feared for his job and his reputation in his community. The result was that he and his wife passively submitted to an hour of bizarre physical torment. Usually sadomasochists will not find any pleasure in a completely passive, non-sexual response in their victims. Their "fantasy" is to find others who will delight in the same kinds of unusual behavior in which they themselves find great pleasure. When evidence of this delight is not forthcoming after a certain amount of laborious effort, interest very often tends to be lost.

In their efforts to "arouse" Bob and Jenny, this sadomasochistic couple performed several maneuvers in quick succession. First, they tied Jenny to a bed, face up. Cynthia then climbed over Jenny's body and rubbed her vulva over Jenny's thighs, chest and face. At that point she proceeded to urinate over Jenny's mouth, breathing sighs of pleasure as she did this. Meanwhile, Bob was forced to watch as this was going on.

Then both Jenny and Bob were tied and handcuffed to the bed, face down. Cynthia and Jay then emerged with razor straps, hairbrushes, leather belts, ropes, and other objects which would be used to "discipline" the couple. The bed that was used, by the way, was located in the basement; there were no windows and the room was alleged to be soundproof.

After both Bob and Jenny had received a quite considerable amount of torture, they were asked if they would like to return the "favors." At this point Jay tied his own wife to the bed, face down, and released Jenny. Holding Jenny firmly by a dog leash (the collar of which had been placed around her neck), he commanded her to begin lashing Cynthia with a razor strap. Bob, during this period, remained tied to the other side of the bed, this time facing up so that he could watch.

Ultimately, the lack of enthusiasm of the imprisoned couple resulted in their being cursed at by the sadomasochists and almost literally thrown out of the house by way of the back door. And as this was done they were again warned about what would happen if they reported to the police what had happened to them.

Most of the people who unwittingly become involved with sadomasochists probably do not suffer at their hands quite as much as did Bob and Jenny. More frequently they will be invited and sometimes strongly encouraged to spank and be spanked. Because many swingers have the "try anything once" attitude their initial resistance to being roped in may in some cases be quite mild. Indeed, we've already seen that this tends to be the case with regard to animal-human sexual behavior.

There is good reason to believe that many would-be swingers become alienated for life from sexual mate sharing because of having experienced an unintended confrontation with another couple that enjoys spanking or "discipline." But it is not entirely unheard of for a victimized couple to find out that they actually enjoy some degree of "spanking" as an integral part of their regular sexual activity. To be sure, this does not happen very often. But several of my informants were able to recount instances of it.

About three-quarters of American parents at one time or another use some degree of physical punishment in the disciplining of their children, and about one-third of all parents depend heavily upon physical punishment and its accompanying fear as their chief means of controlling their children. Since spanking and other forms of harsh physical discipline are what they had grown up to perceive as being appropriate parenting behavior, it can hardly be considered surprising that spankers and other sadomasochists invariably received quite a bit of physical punishment when they themselves were children. Indeed, it is even less surprising that these people invariably tend to be dedicated to the use of physical punishment as a means of disciplining their own children.

The scientific reasons why physical punishment is not a desirable means for disciplining children are beyond the scope of this volume. Here I merely wish to illustrate how sadomasochists tend to enjoy studying pain, and how they often gravitate toward use of their children as subjects (or victims) for their perverted research endeavors.

In one case, a 17-year-old girl came home late from a date and made what was viewed by the parents as a "fresh" remark. When the girl was asleep the parents grabbed her, gagged her, undressed her and carried her into the bathroom where a tub full of hot water was waiting. They dropped her in and held her down for several minutes. Then they tied her feet together and tied her hands to an overhead shower curtain bar which was about 6½ feet above the floor. They then took turns for about a half-hour in beating her with razor straps, leather belts, birch rods, and other implements of pain that they had collected.

The object of the hot water was to open the pores of the skin; this serves to increase the pain. The welts of the straps, hoses and belts were received by the girl in an untimed, non-rhythmical fashion—again because when the victim does not know when to brace for the blow the severity of the pain is increased. And one of the cardinal rules that these parents seem to have is that blows must not draw blood. This is to prevent the attention of outsiders from being drawn to the parents' mode of "discipline" (or child abuse). In addition, enemas are often administered to compound the pain.

Situations such as the foregoing are happening all the time in the homes of sadomasochistic parents. And these people very much enjoy discussing their exploits with others of like mind. Not only do they discuss it extensively at their parties, but they also have two or three pornographic publications of their own which contain many personal advertisements and "letters to the editor" columns that often run for a dozen or more pages in each issue. In these columns they castigate so-called "permissive" modes of child-rearing and they congratulate each other for their "toughness" with their children. Their letters as well as their conversations are fraught with references to their own tough-minded parents whom they "love" but usually don't see anymore. In more specifically sociological terms, the publications of these people are filled with ideological articles which serve to *normalize* harsh disciplinary techniques and make them seem fitting, proper, and normal.

Sadomasochism, particularly when it involves children,

is probably one of the very few kinds of unusual sexual behavior which clearly does involve victims and which appears to be intrinsically socially deleterious. However, it is very difficult to enforce laws against this kind of people because their children almost always become extremely docile, submissive, and fearful of their parents' threatened reactions were they to discuss their problems outside the home. Moreover, there continues to be a tendency in the United States for the law to operate under the assumption that parents own their children and that they have a right to "discipline" them as they see fit. With the increasing concern in medical circles over the "battered child" it is possible that one day we shall find ways of spotting the abused *older* child and of taking the appropriate corrective action.

Parenthetically, one informant did advise me of a child whose eventual behavior did not turn out to be so docile. This child, after having been beaten severely by his sadomasochistic sexual mate-sharing parents, quietly got up out of bed at three o'clock one morning and proceeded to the garage of a friend where he had several gallon cans of gasoline hidden away. He quietly spilled the gasoline over everything and set his parents' house on fire. Both of his parents and three of his five brothers and sisters were killed in this fire.

Swinging Along with Various Substances and Gadgets

Because of their strong recreational interest in sex, many swingers are constantly on the alert for things that might add to their sensual pleasure with themselves and with each other. This generalization applies only to some swingers, not to all. But it does apply to enough of them for the topic to be accorded some attention in a book about sexual mate sharing.

For example, one swinging woman became so excited about what she thought was the sexual potential of vaseline (petroleum jelly) that she purchased $1,200 worth of it. She filled her children's rubber swim tank with it, climbed in and wriggled around in sexual ecstasy for hours. When her husband arrived home from work she undressed him and pulled him in. For a long time the couple used the swim tank loaded with vaseline as their swinging trademark. They were often referred to as "crazy" by other swinging couples, but they continued to throw popular parties in spite of their unusual peccadillo. In time they had to throw all the vaseline away because it became too dirty. But according to reliable reports they went on to replace it three times during the course of the past two years.

Another couple became excited over the sexual potential of grape jelly. The man in this case had been punished quite often for sloppiness as a child. And he still had what he regarded as sexual fantasies about getting sticky jelly all over his hair, face, hands, feet, etc. In addition to that, he wanted to copulate in a huge bowl of grape jelly along with his wife and other attractive women.

Again, extravagant as it may sound to outsiders, he and his wife invested several hundred dollars for the amount of grape jelly necessary to fill a huge vat they had constructed in their basement. For a few weeks they had an ecstatic time swimming and copulating in grape jelly. Unlike their friends with the vaseline, however, they had to throw their grape jelly away within a few short weeks because it had begun to go stale.

Another couple who was part of this same group tried Jergens hand lotion. Still another tried peanut butter. And another tried whipped cream. The latter, by the way, is often used by more "normal" or typical swinging couples as part of their oral-genital lovemaking. Whipped cream and sometimes chocolate or butterscotch syrup is squirted on the bodies of people at parties from an aerosol can. And when alone at home it is not unheard of for a woman to spread some substance on her body which she knows her dog likes, and she will take delight as the dog licks it off.

Sexual gadgets are also occasionally employed at swinging parties. Gadgets such as dildos and vibrators can hardly be considered indicative of "perversion" inasmuch as their use is beginning to pervade American culture. But there are certain other kinds of more unusual devices which some swinging groups occasionally use for laughs and sometimes for the sexual pleasure which such gadgets provide for certain group members.

Perhaps the most amusing of these is the rectal vibrator. This device is inserted into the rectum of a person and then a mild electrical current is turned on. The vibrating sensation is believed by some of the devotees of this gadget to be extremely intense and ecstatic. But on most of the very few occasions during which it turns up at parties it is used primarily for laughs and to add variety to the endless round of sexual activities.

The artificial vagina is another gadget which occasionally turns up as a laugh facilitator. None of the people with whom I spoke had ever heard of a swinging husband actually using this as a means of obtaining sexual pleasure or relief. But on rare occasion at a party it will be brought out by someone and, perhaps, tied around a post of some kind. The person who wishes to make a joke of his behavior will then insert his penis into it and commence coital thrusting. Such behavior, however, seems never to be done to the point of orgasm.

A small number of swinging husbands own very expensive, soft rubber mannequins of attractive women. Evidently there is a factory in Frankfort, Germany, which constructs these to order and ships them to American swingers for a fee ranging from $800 to $1,500. These mannequins are to scale. They look like very beautiful women, and each one contains an artificial vagina that is quite realistic in appearance and is large enough to easily accommodate an erect penis. The more expensive models can be plugged into a regular 120 volt AC outlet; when this is done the mannequin warms up and the artificial vagina begins pulsating in a rhythmical fashion. Men who have copulated with these very expensive mannequins claim that it is "quite an experience" though not in any way comparable to a real, live woman. But those who have invested the sizable purchase price for one of the mannequins sometimes enjoy using them as an easy excuse to "show off" at a party.

Incest and the Swinger

In almost all societies throughout history incest has been regarded as a perversion and as a seriously reprehensible behavior. The only historical exception of any importance occurred during the Roman period of ancient Egypt when men were encouraged to marry and procreate children by their blood sisters. And, according to a report by sociologist-historian Russel Middleton (1962), about half of them did just that.

Whereas incest means to have sexual intercourse with one's blood sister, brother, mother or father, the behavior takes on particularly crucial social significance when this intercourse results in the procreation of children. And until quite recently in historical terms, pregnancy always had to be looked upon as a viable possibility in reference to any particular copulation that might take place. For this reason, it is not difficult to understand why strong norms against incest came about.

A very small number of swinging husbands and wives have been known to practice incest. Usually such behavior will come about as a result of the married children in the family wanting to become involved in a swinging group of their own similar to that of their parents. When this happens and the sister and brother both join the same group, incest becomes a slight but realistic possibility. Only one of my informants knew of a case where this had occurred.

On the other hand, incestuous behavior among the teenaged children of swinging couples may be somewhat more common. In Chapter 11, I presented in some detail the case of Lisa and her brother Carl. They were aged 14 and

16 respectively, at the time their incest had taken place. They contended that they did not feel guilty about their behavior. But at the same time it is important to recognize that they did not continue their sexual behavior together even though they apparently had the freedom to do so.

In the very few rare cases where incest does take place among swingers or among their children, it appears that the incestuous sex is defined and viewed by the partners involved in it as *recreational*, body-centered sex. In other words, they define the behavior in essentially the same manner in which they define regular spouse sharing behavior. They don't see it as being competitive with their husband-wife, person-centered love relationship. On the other hand, it appears very clear that it requires a much more unusual person to be able to disassociate guilt feelings from the idea of incestuous sex than it does to disassociate guilt feelings from the idea of regular comarital sexual behavior. From a purely intellectual standpoint a person could argue that these guilt feelings are irrational provided that contraceptive precautions are taken. But they are nevertheless very real and they appear to be powerful enough to keep even highly permissive people from experimenting with incestuous sex even on a purely "body-centered" as opposed to a "person-centered" basis.

CONCLUSIONS

Even within the context of middle and upper middle-class America a minority of people tend to pick up some very unusual sexual behavior patterns. Unless we want to speculate on a person's karma or astrological signs, etc., it seems fairly clear that most of the sexual anamolies that were considered in this chapter are picked up by people through a process of social learning.

Given that the perversions discussed in this chapter are more deviant than regular sexual mate sharing, it might be predicted that the amount of psychological autonomy from parents necessary to permit their practice is probably greater than the amount of psychological autonomy necessary to permit the practice of conventional mate sharing. My analysis of the limited data at my disposal leads me to conclude that the people involved in the kinds of behavior discussed in this chapter tend to interact with relatives and kin even less often than regular swingers do. And as children their relationships with their parents had been even less emotionally satisfying than those experienced by the regular swingers had been.

In order for a person to engage in a highly deviant form of behavior on a regular basis he would have to be pretty far removed from conventional social forces, and he certainly could not feel emotionally close to such people as relatives and kin when such people represent (as they usually do) conventional or traditional social forces. Interestingly, even the "spankers" and "discipline" lovers who so enthusiastically praise their parents for having been tough with them tend not to see their parents very often now that they are emancipated and have families of their own.

Finally, it would appear that some of the perversions might under certain circumstances be able to coexist with happiness while others probably could never do so. The farm couple who enjoyed inviting sheep into the sexual act were seen by their friends as being very happy. Of course, that couple might have been putting on a good act. But none of the people who knew them suspected them of this. On the other hand, many of the women who had to have their dogs attend to their sexual needs when they were alone in their homes may indeed have been suffering from a real sense of unhappiness and lack of fulfillment. But the moralist must realize that their sexual attachment to their dogs was not the *cause* of their unhappiness. It was instead an *effect*. It may indeed be sad that such women find it necessary to do what they do. But I think it is sadder still that they have no one around to help them out of their rut—to give them the loving attention which every human being needs, and to provide them with some interesting and constructive things with which to become emotionally involved.

In other words, instead of strongly discouraging bizarre sexual behavior and making people feel guilty about such behavior, the moralist would be on safer and more socially constructive ground if he were to work out ways of providing deviant individuals with the love and stimulating activity that they need. To be sure, some such persons might still occasionally engage in their bizarre behavior. But they would do so only because they *want* to and not in order to find an escape hatch from their "hang-ups."

Most of my informants regarded the sadomasochists that they knew as being uniformly high strung, tense and unhappy. The sadomasochists' children were also seen as being inhibited, retiring and docile. Yet in their docility these children were quietly picking up habit patterns which are likely to govern how they will deal with their own future children. These destructive habit patterns are likely to effectively perpetuate the perverted view of "discipline" from one generation to another. Of the various perversions discussed in this chapter, sadomasochism is the only one for which strong law enforcement would appear to be in order.

Chapter 15

Summary,
Conclusions, and
Implications

The purpose of this final chapter is to tie together some of the major findings presented in the previous chapters against the background of what is known about deviance in general. I shall also suggest implications which the findings seem to have for swinging and for traditional marriage within the wider society.

The Major Causes of Swinging

The swingers studied for this research were found to be a great deal more alienated from their parents and kin than the non-swingers were. In fact, even among respondents who were living within the same metropolitan area as their relatives, the swinging husbands and wives were still found to interact informally with their relatives a great deal less often than the non-swingers. These findings were particularly strong for the wives. Normally husbands interact less with relatives than wives do anyway. Inasmuch as women are ordinarily more closely tied to the family system then men, these findings must be considered particularly noteworthy.

The findings further revealed that swingers tend to regard their relatives as being a great deal less important in their overall scheme of things than most people do. In line with this it was found that they viewed their friends as being a great deal more important to them personally than their relatives. And as might be expected, they interacted with their chosen friends substantially more frequently than the non-swingers interacted with their chosen friends. Neighbors living next door and in nearby and adjacent houses were also seen a good deal less often by the swinging husbands and wives than by the non-swinging husbands and wives.

In general, the swingers were found to have had less happy childhood and adolescent periods than the non-swingers. Their relationships with their parents while living in their families of orientation tended to have been distant and cool. For example, in comparison with the non-swingers, the swingers had engaged in relatively little meaningful communication with their mothers and fathers. In addition, the swingers remembered themselves as having been considerably less satisfied (than the non-swingers recalled themselves as having been) with the amount of freedom and autonomy their parents had permitted them during their later adolescent years.

The child-rearing approaches of the swingers' parents tended to have been primarily either "laissez-faire" (a "couldn't care less" brand of extreme permissiveness) or authoritarian. They were less likely than the parents of the non-swingers to have involved their children in any family decision-making or in the development or revising of family rules and regulations. It was suggested earlier that "laissez-faire" parents have certain key points in common with authoritarian parents despite the fact that in some ways these two child-rearing approaches are polar opposites. Neither "laissez-faire" parents nor authoritarian parents manifest much care, respect, or compassionate concern for or about the feelings, needs, or unique individuality of their children. One kind of parent displays his indifference by arbitrarily imposing his regulations and standards upon the child while the other shows his indifference by ignoring the child. People who have had the experience of growing up under either kind of regime tend to recall having felt unfree during their adolescent years. They further feel that as children their parents did not accord them a sufficient amount of freedom. Such was found to have been the case for most of the swingers who were researched for this study.

The findings strongly suggested that the emotional dependency which prevails between most children and their parents never became very firmly established in the families of orientation of most of the swinging husbands and wives studied. It is because of this strong emotional bond between individuals and their families that the family system for most people is an extremely powerful social control agent. Since that bond did not effectively develop in the case of most of the swingers, the foundation tended to be laid down very early in their lives for fostering a sense of personal freedom permitting the exploration of a wide variety of alternative life styles and philosophies. Because of their pattern of deeply internalized norms most people tend to be strongly affected by their parents' attitudes and perspectives in ways of which they are scarcely even aware. A close emotional bond greatly facilitates the degree and thoroughness with which norms are internalized. Social influence tends to be strongest and most thorough in *mutually enjoyable* social situations characterized by warmth and kinship. It is in this manner that the range of behavioral alternatives for most people becomes effectively narrowed. This is not to suggest that people on very good terms with their parents never deviate from any of their parents' normative ideas and values. They are, however, likely to deviate from far fewer of them (and to a lesser degree) than people who are not on such good terms with their parents.

Involvement in comarital sex was found to be more strongly associated with estrangement from relatives and kin for the wives than it was for the husbands. It is likely that the key reason for this is that sexual mate sharing, while deviant for both sexes, can probably be regarded as a good deal more deviant for wives than for husbands, due to the double standard. Generally speaking, the more deviant a person's behavior is as viewed from the standpoint of the dominant norms within a given community, the greater the need for estrangement from the kin network that person is likely to require in order to comfortably pursue his or her form of deviance.

In essence, the swingers were found to be less closely tied emotionally to their parents during both their childhood and their teenaged years as well as presently as married adults. This weak emotional tie was reflected in the lower kin visitation rates for swingers as contrasted with the non-swingers. It was also reflected in a substantially lower tendency on the part of the swingers as compared to the non-swingers to feel that they presently agree with their parents regarding their ideas and opinions about the things they consider to be really important in life. There was also a marked tendency, particularly among the wives, for the swingers as adults to feel less emotionally close to their mothers than was the case for the non-swingers.

The swingers recalled communicating far less often with their parents as teenagers than did the non-swingers. They were also much less likely than the non-swingers to feel that their parents had always respected them. Given these findings, it cannot be considered surprising that the swingers, in comparison to the non-swingers, recalled having been less happy during both their childhood and their adolescent years.

A further point of considerable interest regarding the swingers is that they were found to have been more than three times as likely as the non-swingers to have come from homes that had been broken by divorce. In fact, it was further found that even among the respondents whose parents had never been divorced, the swingers were substantially more likely than the non-swingers to rate their parents' marriages as having been less than happy.

Presumably because of the relatively cool and emotionally aloof home life to which the swingers had grown accustomed as children, they had good reason for being strongly motivated to turn from an early age to their peer group of age-mates for most of their emotional gratification. Despite their shortcomings as parents, the mothers and fathers of the swinging respondents were recalled as always having been quite sociable. They were commonly recalled as having been deeply involved in their own social affairs with their own adult friends. Given these tendencies among the swingers' parents, the young swingers-to-be had seldom if ever been without good sociability models upon whom to pattern their own behavior. It was suggested that the presence of such effective sociability models served to militate against the selection of any of the many forms of deviance which tend to be practiced alone.

Some of the strongest, most impressive findings in this study pertained to dating, courtship, and sex play during the years prior to marriage. As a group the swingers, in comparison to the non-swingers, recalled having developed strong romantic interests in the opposite sex a good deal earlier in life. Dating, going steady, and erotic behavior similarly started earlier for the swingers than for the non-swingers. It would thus seem that the swingers learned early in life that many of life's greatest pleasures and adventures could be experienced through heterosexual involvements. It therefore cannot be considered surprising that when the swingers were attracted toward deviant life styles these styles came to entail deviance in the heterosexual area. Indeed, the strong tendency on the part of the swingers to agree with the statement that at the age of 20 they could not have gone for long without being involved with the other sex and still have remained basically happy and secure, further testifies to the very strong orientation the swingers had had throughout virtually their entire lives to social heterosexual involvement.

Is the need for the romantic companionship of an

opposite-sexed age-mate among some very young, pre-teenaged children *inborn* or is it *socially learned?* The fact that love and romance needs affect *some* preadolescent children so strongly (even in some situations where boy-girl interaction is discouraged by elementary school teachers, parents and same-sexed peers), suggests that the need for heterosexual companionship may have nothing to do with the need for sex and eroticism, which does not begin to burgeon until after the onset of adolescence.

Carlfred Broderick's study of socio-sexual development among preadolescents revealed that the earlier children became romantically interested in the other sex the sooner they tended to begin dating and to pass through the other heterosexual stages normally considered antecedent to marriage in our culture. Three of his other findings are of special pertinence to the research data on swingers discussed in this book: (1) children who were successfully involved socially with the other sex early in life tended to be quite popular with their own sex and involved in numerous peer-related activities; and (2) children who felt close to their parents and who admired them as model couples were found to be significantly less likely to have a romantic attachment during their pre-teenaged years than those children who were less close or who were critical of their parents' marriages (57 percent versus 85 percent). Broderick suggested that even among preadolescents romance probably competes to a considerably greater extent with parent-child ties than it does with peer ties. Thirdly, preadolescent romances were found to be far more prevalent among middle-class youngsters than among those of the lower class. As was pointed out in Chapter 2, swinging similarly tends to be very uncommon among the economically disadvantaged.

It was suggested that the relatively non-satisfying quality of the parent-child relationship served as a strong motivator inspiring the child to seek out age-mates for most of his emotional satisfactions. Since the parents of the swingers were neither overprotective toward their children nor nonsociable with their own age-mates, they presented their children with an optimum situation for early peer group involvement and for early emotional emancipation from the family.

Now, even among some pre-teenagers same-sex peers may not be able to adequately satisfy the full range of normal psycho-emotional needs. Indeed, the mass media and other cultural forms of the middle-class serve to heighten these psycho-emotional needs among children and to direct them along heterosexual-social channels. For children who truly feel emotionally close to their families, it may be that opposite-sexed parents and siblings take care of many of these needs for a considerable period of time. Where intrafamily relationships are cool, however, there may be an unusually early impetus among most children so affected to seek out opposite-sexed companions in their own age group to fill the gap.

As Broderick's data pointed out, the most socially successful children are the ones who are likely to be romantically involved in both fact and fantasy during their pre-adolescent years. In line with this, very few of the swinging husbands and wives gave any indication at all of being lonely or in any sense socially isolated either now as adults or during their formative years. Rather, from all indications, both the swinging husbands and their wives seemed to have thrived to an above-average extent on the stimulation which comes with continued social interaction with peers. In short, whereas the swingers were found to be much less socially involved with relatives and kin than the non-swingers, they were involved with chosen friends to a much greater extent than were the non-swingers.

The foregoing may contain some important clues as to why the particular type of deviance, that of sexual mate sharing, was arrived at. If the swingers of this sample are reasonably typical of American swingers generally, it would certainly appear that (1) long-term alienation from the family system, and (2) an early and sustained tendency to view heterosexual-social interaction as providing strong emotional gratifications, combined with (3) the availability of a literature (fictionalized or otherwise) and services providing direction and ideological supports for becoming involved, together do much to push middle-class couples toward the specific deviance of comarital sex rather than toward some other kind of deviance. The fact that such literature and services exist was amply documented in Chapters 2 and 8. If a person had not learned to associate great feelings of satisfaction with heterosexual interaction (or if heterosexual interaction had never been viewed by the person as easy or easier than same-sex interaction), and if this satisfying interaction had not continued for the person throughout his formative years, then it is not likely that comarital sex would have been the mode of adaptation (deviance) chosen.

Thus it can be said that when swinging behavior is learned, the learning includes (a) the techniques of practicing comarital sex (including techniques for becoming involved); and (b) the specific direction of motives, drives, rationalizations and attitudes. The advertisements, the swinging literature, and the experienced swingers, all provide the novice with this service. Without them, the potential swinger would very likely never even become aware of comarital sexual behavior and would be forced to arrive on his own at some other kind of adaptation to the stresses and strains of everyday life. In this sense, then, swingers' magazines, advertisements, and clubs can be considered necessary "career contingencies" for active comarital sexual involvement.

People with rich premarital dating and sexual histories, as most of the swingers of this study definitely had, are doubtless especially prone to be attracted to erotic literature and/or to libertarian-humanistic publications such as the *Los Angeles Free Press*, where advertisements for swinging organizations are commonly carried. Such people are also likely to have long viewed love, romance, and sex as highly desirable and richly satisfying ends in and of themselves, quite apart from such conventional and

normative considerations as marriage and family formation. Before a person can move toward comarital sexual
involvement there must first be an autonomous state of
mind (freedom from the usual controls) and a strong, autonomous heterosexual interest, in addition to the literature and the advertisements which show the way.

The Characteristics of Swingers

A large amount of fascinating data were accumulated
during the course of this study on the demographic
background attributes, the personal and social adjustment characteristics, the political and social attitudes,
and the child-rearing attitudes of the swingers as compared to the non-swingers.

All of the respondents resided in the middle and upper
middle-class suburbs of the city of Los Angeles. In addition, most of them had lived their formative years in suburban neighborhoods. However, the non-swingers were a
great deal more likely than the swingers to have lived all
or most of their lives in the suburbs. The swingers were
more likely to have lived their early adulthood lives in
attractive urban apartments; their movement back to the
suburbs had been comparatively recent. But for most of
the swingers it was not a comparatively lower level of
financial affluence that kept them close to the central city
for so long. Most of them wanted to get away from their
parents and relatives, and they preferred the atmosphere,
excitement and stimulation which life close to the central
city provided. Their move back to the suburbs had been
brought about primarily by (1) consideration for their
children, and (2) a desire to invest in real estate. In addition, many of them were lured by the greater privacy and
indoor space that suburban life provides.

The swingers were more likely than the non-swingers to
have grown up in major metropolitan areas such as Los
Angeles, New York, San Francisco, and Chicago. The non-
swingers were more likely to have originated in the Mid-

west and South. However, many of them hailed from smaller cities in all sections of the country.

The swingers were not found to differ from the non-swingers in terms of upward or downward social mobility. In other words, the occupations of the swingers were equally as likely as those of the non-swingers to be better than those of their fathers. Very few people in either group gave any indication of having been downwardly mobile. But it should be borne in mind that the swinging wives contributed far more to total family income than the non-swinging wives did. Fully 62 percent of the swinging wives were employed outside the home compared to only 33 percent of the non-swinging wives. Yet, despite their higher incidence of employment outside the home, only 15 percent of the employed swinging wives indicated that if they had their choice they would prefer not to work. In contrast, 44 percent of the employed non-swinging wives indicated that they would really prefer not to work. (Curiously, this 44 percent included several women who said they enjoyed their work and that they derived a lot of personal satisfaction from it.)

Whereas the swingers had *not* been either more or less *socially* mobile than the non-swingers, they *had been* a very great deal more *geographically* mobile than the non-swingers. In other words, the swingers had changed residences and had moved around the country (and even around the state and city) a great deal more often than the non-swingers had. This high rate of geographic mobility had continued for the swingers well into their married years.

The swingers had grown up in smaller families than the non-swingers, and they tended to have had fewer siblings *of their own sex* than the non-swingers.

For readers interested in astrology, some fascinating and thought-provoking data were collected pertinent to birth dates. The non-swingers' birth dates were equally distributed across each of the twelve sun signs. But certain birth (sun) signs were definitely overrepresented among the ranks of the swingers, particularly for the husbands. These were: Leo, Gemini, Sagittarius, Aquarius, and Aries, *in that order*. Signs *underrepresented* among the swingers were: Cancer, Pisces, Capricorn, Scorpio, and Virgo. Again, these data were weaker for the wives than for the husbands. But they were *not* weaker for the wives who had *already* been swingers (single swingers) at the time when they met their current husbands. The reader should further bear in mind that these data pertain only to sun signs. Anyone not versed in astrology needs to be advised that it would require the passage of 25,000 years before someone with his personal horoscope could again be born. In essence, there are *millions* of possible horoscopes in astrology, *not* just twelve!

Because swinging is a nonconformist pastime there has been a good deal of speculation by both psychiatrists and moralists regarding the personal and social adjustment characteristics of men and women who engage in it. Most of this speculation has been far from flattering to swingers. But the data obtained for this study revealed few differences in adjustment between the swingers and the non-swingers. And the few comparatively small differences between the two groups that were found tended to favor the swingers! More specifically, the swingers were not found to be any more likely than the non-swingers to be suffering from feelings of personal unhappiness. And their self-images (levels of self-esteem) were actually somewhat higher than those of the non-swingers. None of the swingers viewed themselves as being in any way shy or inhibited, while more than two-fifths of the non-swinging husbands and wives viewed themselves as being to at least some extent afflicted with this problem. And while almost 80 percent of the swingers rated their physical health as "excellent," this was true of only slightly more than one-half of the non-swinging husbands and wives. (The distribution of ages among the swingers was the same as that among the non-swingers.)

On the basis of these findings it would certainly appear

that the swingers had adequately worked through their
feelings about their sexual nonconformity by the time the
data for this study were obtained from them. These data,
as well as data collected by anthropologists studying life
in other societies, strongly suggest that swinging cannot
by itself cause guilt or a diminished sense of self-respect.
Such negative feelings as low self-esteem, guilt, or unhappiness, can come about only through violation of one's
pattern of internalized norms. When these internalized
norms are permissive (regarding sex) for a person, or when
they are in the process of moving toward permissiveness,
guilt, low self-esteem, unhappiness, and similar outcomes
cannot come about for that person. If a person's behavior
is in reasonable harmony with his value system, his serenity cannot be undermined, even when that behavior tends
to be viewed by the dominant majority as highly unconventional.

On the basis of the data of this research, it appears that
swingers might tend to be less stable and content than
most people during the first twenty-five or so years of their
lives. But after they have lived through this period and
successfully grappled with its problems they tend to
emerge with a sense of personal happiness and adjustment
to life which at the very least seems to be no different than
that which ordinary people at the same social level enjoy.

Like the kin family network, conventional organized religion constitutes another agent of social control for most
people in American society. Not unexpectedly, the
swingers at the time of the interviews were found to be a
very great deal less involved in conventional religion than
the non-swingers. But on the other hand they tended to be
a great deal *more* involved in the *less* conventional religious philosophies such as metaphysics, the occult,
spiritualism, pantheism, psychic phenomena, etc.

Most of the swingers admitted that they had spiritual
needs, but they did not wish to involve either themselves
or their children in a religion that might tell them how to
lead their lives or make them feel guilty about certain

behaviors that do not in and of themselves involve a victim. Quite a few of the swingers revealed strong feelings of hostility toward conventional organized religion.

Yet at the age of 15 the swingers studied for this research had attended organized religious services every bit as frequently as did the non-swingers! This suggests that the swingers' peer groups of chosen friends may have been far more conventional during their early teen years than they are now. It also suggests that the swingers' parents were not substantially less likely than the parents of the non-swingers to have required them to attend religious services. Of course, not being as closely tied emotionally to their parents as the non-swingers were, the parents' stated normative expectations regarding religion were less likely to have been internalized. When the swingers came of age and began to leave home it thus became much easier for them to drift away from conventional religion than it had been for the non-swingers. The continued greater importance to them of peers as opposed to relatives and kin as key reference group figures could also be seen as facilitating a continued movement away from participation in organized religion. It must be remembered that religiously based values are mediated primarily by parental authority figures.

Some of the most fascinating data revealed by this research pertained to the social and political beliefs of the swingers. As a case in point, the swingers were found to be a great deal more likely than the non-swingers to identify themselves as being either "independent" or as "uncommitted and not interested in politics." But by the same token they were *also* a great deal more likely than the non-swingers to view themselves as politically liberal. In fact, their views on virtually all political and social issues they were asked about revealed far more liberal, socially compassionate opinions than was the case for the non-swingers. For example, the swingers were more sympathetic toward hippies, long-haired students, black people, and other minority or nonconformist individuals and groups. They were also far more likely than the non-swingers to be strongly "pro-women's liberation." The swingers were a great deal less likely than the non-swingers to accept such propositions as "a woman's place is still in the home" and "duties are more important than rights." They were also much less likely than the non-swingers to identify with either of the two major political parties—or with *any* political party for that matter. Unlike the non-swingers, the swingers did not consider themselves to be a part of the "silent majority."

The child-rearing attitudes of the swingers were also far more permissive and liberal than were those of the non-swingers. However, like their own parents the swingers tended not to be very child-centered. The main focus of their attention during their non-working hours was on enjoying themselves; and usually this meant being with their chosen friends and age-mates. This attitude led to the swingers' children enjoying far more freedom to pursue their own interests than most children of their age in American society enjoy. None of the more than 250 swingers' children interviewed for this study indicated that they disliked or were uncomfortable around their parents. Most of the children enjoyed very good relationships with their swinging mothers and fathers and communicated freely with them when they were present.

Whether these good parent-child relationships will continue indefinitely on into the future is a question only another research study can answer—namely a study that would follow up a large group of children and their swinging parents over an extended period of time. Suffice it to say here that the non-swingers' children appeared less happy and satisfied with their parents and with their family lives than did the swingers' children. I found the differences between the two groups to be very small and almost imperceptible as far as preadolescent children were concerned. But among the teenagers the differences between the two groups were very marked and noticeable indeed. And while they were noticeable for both sexes they tended to be more noticeable for boys than for girls. It would thus appear that teenaged boys benefit the most from having swinging parents.

Seventy-three percent of the swinging mothers and fathers indicated that they would be quite happy about it if their own children became swingers when they grow up. This strongly suggests that the swingers studied have truly accepted and internalized the ideology of their sexual spouse-sharing groups. Indeed, the swingers were also found to be a great deal more likely than the non-swingers to accept the idea of premarital coitus among their own children. Despite being parents, most of the swinging couples displayed what for American society would have to be considered highly permissive attitudes towards teenagers' sexual behavior and contraceptive use. Almost all of the swingers' teenaged children either were involved or had been involved in premarital sexual relationships. But the really important point is that most of this premarital sex was carried on in the teenagers' own bedrooms and under the indirect supervision of the swinging mothers and fathers.

Swinging and Other Forms of Deviance

Hundreds of studies have been published on the causes of criminal and non-criminal forms of deviance. In surveying the findings of these many studies it has become clear that certain common denominators exist in the backgrounds of almost all people who choose to behave over long periods of time in ways that are conspicuously or markedly nonconformist. Swingers share some of these common denominators, and their backgrounds also contain some ingredients that are unique to them.

First of all, deviants of almost all kinds tend to be on very cool terms with their parents and with other major relatives of the kin family network. In the case of the swingers the childhood and adolescent backgrounds tended to be comparatively unhappy. The swingers' parents had never developed either the capacity or the inclination to *listen* to their children. Instead they tended to be so wrapped up in their own adult affairs and interests that their children had to find ways of taking care of their own major emotional needs.

The backgrounds of many different kinds of criminals have similarly been found to be characterized by this same coolness and aloofness from parents. In addition, frequent geographic mobility is another trait common among criminals and also a major earmark in the backgrounds of the swingers. Detachment from, disinterest in, and disenchantment with such major social institutions as conventional, organized religion and politics can also be cited as a major common denominator in the backgrounds of deviants.

On the other hand, some of the major characteristics common to swingers but *not* common to most criminals and nonconformists include: (1) very early and sustained romantic interest in and desire to interact socially with the opposite sex; (2) middle and upper middle-class socioeconomic status; and (3) a lifelong tendency to skillfully interact on a frequent basis with people, particularly chosen friends. Fourthly, swingers tend to value education and job success.

A high degree of emotional detachment and alienation from such major social institutions as the family, religion and politics, provides people with a strong sense of *emotional autonomy*. Emotional autonomy frees an individual to select deviant or nonconformist paths when everyday stresses and strains overtake him. If a person becomes emotionally autonomous very early in life it becomes all the easier for him to thoroughly learn the inroads of effective adaptation to a nonconformist life style. After all, the family and conventional religion or politics never provided the pre-deviant with the warm emotional nurturance, sincere caring and love that he or she needed. Such conventional institutions never *listened* in any sincere or caring manner to the expressed needs of the pre-deviant.

To be sure, such conventional institutions *do* adequately listen and respond to children who will *not* turn toward gross forms of deviance and nonconformity; but they *do not* pay sufficient attention to the deep emotional needs of the pre-deviant individual. Hence, the pre-deviant does not have any kind of true vested interest for conforming to the ostensible belief systems of conventional institutions, including the family.

On the other hand, since most swingers grow up in middle-class homes, attend middle-class schools and reside in middle-class neighborhoods, it stands to reason that the forms of deviance selected by swingers would have to be such as to *not* stand in the way of their successful pursuit of such middle-class goals as a good job, good salary, education, house in the suburbs, etc. In spite of the fact that most Americans regard swinging as one of the more undesirable forms of deviance, it is quite clear that its practice does not stop people from attaining many goals that are well respected in middle-class society. Moreover, like most forms of heterosexual deviance swinging can be camouflaged; being a swinger does not necessitate broadcasting the fact.

Finally, no treatment of deviance could be complete without some attention being given to the issue of *relativism*. Social scientists have often had to confront this issue. This is so because research findings often vary a great deal by the social context in which they were obtained. For example, in a conservative social context premarital coitus tends to be associated with many different negative consequences while in liberal social contexts (i.e., those permissive toward premarital sex) it tends to be associated with positive or neutral consequences.

Whereas the *substance of what deviance is* varies greatly from setting to setting, the correlates of deviance tend to be the same *regardless* of setting. Hence, in a setting where premarital sex is widely defined as appropriate and expected behavior for young people, *those abstaining tend to be the ones with the weak kin ties, the emotional detachment from religion, politics, etc.* Those conforming, i.e., those who are actively involved in premarital sexual lovemaking, tend to be the ones with good, strong kin family ties.

The same thing can be said for social settings where the "double standard" continues to be popular. In these social settings young men who are sexually active before marriage tend to have always enjoyed good, strong relationships with their relatives and kin. Young men abstaining in such settings, on the other hand, tend not to get along so well with their families. In contrast, unmarried women who are sexually active in these same "double standard" settings tended to be on poor terms with their family and kin while those who abstain tend to be on good terms.

In American society wives usually interact with relatives more frequently than their husbands. Yet among the swinging couples the husbands actually saw their relatives somewhat more often than their wives saw theirs. Swinging is considered more deviant for married women than it is for married men. Inasmuch as it is seen as somewhat less deviant for married men, somewhat less psychological autonomy and psychological differentiation from relatives and kin is required of them than is the case for their swinging wives.

In sum, involvement in a behavior cannot in and of itself be associated with or be caused by poor kin or family relationships. The norms prevalent in the community (social setting) in question as well as the norms of a particular family must always be taken into account in assessing what the probable antecedents and consequences of a particular form of deviance are likely to be.

The Marital Consequences of Swinging

One of the key findings of this study was that the swinging men had contracted their *first* marriages at ages that are unusually early for middle-class Americans. And judging by the responses made in the interviews, they often initially married girls to whom they had felt strongly attracted on a physical level, and they often accomplished this before any kind of adequately comprehensive knowledge and appreciation of the values and personal attributes of the girl could be realized at a rational, intellectual level. Much of the research on courtship behavior has shown that "love" during the early months of a relationship tends to serve as a smokescreen blinding the "lovers" to many of the most essential personal attributes of each other. This element, combined with the weak social control of the family and the strong psychological autonomy of pre-swinging men all doubtless functioned as a powerful force pressing toward early marriage.

Marriage is often perceived by teenagers as constituting a major indicator of adulthood status. And the status of independent, fully autonomous adult is one which the pre-swinging men tended to crave unusually early in their youth. A quite common outcome of these first marriages was that the men (and women) gradually began to find their partners "too conventional" for them. Usually within from one to three years of the marriage a clash of values between the pre-swingers and their first spouses gave rise to great conflict, alienation, and unhealable cleavages.

Upon being divorced, and often before, the pre-swinger began hanging around politically liberal and/or socially unconventional groups of young people. "Swinging singles" groups and sexual freedom organizations in particular tended to be frequented on a fairly regular basis. In fact, fully 38 percent of the swinging couples in this study claimed that they actually met their present spouse at "swinging singles" gatherings. In short, for many of the couples studied, swinging actually preceded the current marriage.

This point is of considerable significance, for it provides us with a viable explanation as to why the swinging couples were as happy, and in some respects even happier with each other than the non-swingers were, even though as a group they were far more likely to have experienced at least one divorce in their lifetime. It would appear that when the swingers chose their second spouse they were much more careful than they had been the first time around about selecting someone whose major life values, outlooks on life, recreational interests, and personal understandings were reasonably similar to their own. Virtually all social scientists are agreed on the point that a reasonable amount of similarity of major life values, goals, etc., between a husband and wife is a major precondition of marital success and happiness. Among the many swingers who had experienced a divorce, the first marriage did not entail such homogeneity while the second one did. Of course, only a very expensive type of study that would follow couples up over many years could ascertain the degree to which the swinging couples of today remain legally married to each other throughout their lifetimes.

Many people find it hard to believe that a couple could swing and still remain happily married. The answer to this seeming mystery probably lies in the relative degree of congruence of temperaments and of deeply held value systems between a husband and wife. If both a husband and a wife share essentially the same pattern of expectations with regard to their marital relationship together and if they actually live honestly in accordance with these expectations, it is difficult to see how their relationship could falter.

Of course, people do change over time, and this change often occurs at a different pace in each spouse, a situation which can lead to difficulties. However, there is no evidence to suggest that swingers are likely to encounter greater difficulty than non-swingers on the issue of differential rates of personal change. Indeed, the fact that they tend to share more of their social and recreational activities, with their spouses than the non-swingers do suggests that they should prove somewhat less likely than most couples to grow and develop in divergent directions.

Despite the extramarital sex implicit in swinging activities, the swinging husband and wives copulated with each other *inside* of their legal marriages a great deal more frequently than did the non-swinging husbands and wives. In addition, the swinging husbands and wives claimed to derive greater emotional satisfaction from coitus than the non-swinging spouses claimed to derive. In sum, the marital happiness and satisfaction of the swingers studied compared favorably with that of the non-swingers.

Effects of Swinging on the Marriage and Family Institutions

What about the effects of swinging on the institution of marriage in society as a whole? One of the liveliest areas of debate among social scientists at the present time is that of whether or not such phenomena as sexual mate sharing, living together unmarried, urban communes, group marriage, the burgeoning divorce rate, the comparatively easy availability (for many) of premarital and conventional extramarital sex, augur poorly for the safety and viability of the family system as we know it. Many laymen and some scholars see the family as being on extremely shaky ground at the present time. Others see the various changes that seem to be occurring as posing no serious threats to the family system. Still others view some of the ongoing social changes as holding a strong potential for eventually benefiting the family system.

It is my position that in a highly pluralistic society such as the United States there are numerous ways in which family life can be effectively organized on a viable basis. The traditional system of marriage has long served for many people to render adult sexuality orderly, predictable, and stable. But whereas the traditional system of monogamy has served to structure and order the sexual cravings of most adults, it is difficult to study comarital sex participants for very long without also discerning a marked pattern to their sexual involvement as well. There are undoubtedly *many* ways of patterning human sexuality. Sexual monogamy confined to the marital institution would appear to be only one such way. Furthermore, as I have shown throughout this book, psychological or emotional monogamy and residential monogamy can and often do successfully exist over long periods of time in the absence of *sexual* monogamy.

From the standpoint of psycho-emotional (and residential) commitment, all of the couples studied for this research would have to be considered "monogamous." All wanted to continue living in their own independent suburban dwellings. This was as much the case for the more liberal younger swingers who preferred confining their sexual mate sharing to close friends as it was for the more impersonal "recreational" and "egotistical" swingers.

The swingers did not want their sexual mate sharing activities to dominate their entire lives. Rather they wanted these activities to be compartmentalized. The degree of compartmentalization desired varied from swinger to swinger. But everyone interviewed was highly averse to the idea of establishing a more open or communistic type of family system simply because he or she occasionally enjoyed engaging in sexual spouse sharing behavior.

If swinging were to be competitive with marital and family institutions it would probably need to take up considerably more time than it does. Most swinging couples attend an average of little more than one swinging get-together per fortnight; few average more than one such get-together per week. From a purely temporal standpoint, swinging does not appear to dominate the lives or the marriages of its participants anymore than golf or tennis or watching football or basketball games on television would appear to dominate the lives or the marriages of those who prefer those more conventional sorts of recreation. Again, it is important to recall that swinging is a recreational form that is engaged in on a joint (shared) as opposed to a sex-segregated basis, a fact which may of itself serve to diminish the potential of emotional estrangement developing between spouses.

In fact, several of the findings of this research indicated

that swinging tends to be associated with more frequent husband-wife conversation, more frequent conjugal sex, greater satisfaction with the amount of attention and affection spontaneously received from the spouse around the house, etc. This is not to imply that swinging "caused" these results. But for the couples who were studied, becoming a swinger was found to be associated with these outcomes.

It may well be that in suburban America swinging may be good for some couples and very bad for others. With the range of data presently at our disposal it should now be possible to predict with a high degree of accuracy just what kinds of couples for whom swinging would be quite likely to be bad and which ones for whom it might be good, or at least neutral in its effect. It seems clear that swinging cannot in and of itself precipitate negative consequences for any couple or person. The consequences of swinging depend on the social and cultural context within which it occurs. A husband and wife who are not particularly happy with each other and/or whose normative perceptions of social reality—especially as those perceptions relate to mate sharing—tend to be markedly disparate, would be well advised to steer clear of this form of nonconformist recreation as it would be highly likely to precipitate relationship-deteriorating, self-esteem-diminishing consequences.

Finally, in connection with the impact of swinging on the family as an institution, it should be emphasized that there is no indication of any kind that sexual mate sharing is likely to expand appreciably in popularity over the coming decades. In the context of American culture it requires a certain kind of personality, set of background factors, homogeneity of values between husband and wife, etc., for someone to want to become a swinger in the first place. Indeed, even among the sexually active teenaged youngsters of swinging parents there was evident a strong predilection for sexual monogamy. And this sexually monogamous tendency often greatly baffled the swinging parents!

But even if its popularity does increase slightly, swinging does not appear to discourage family formation. Almost as many of the swinging couples as of the non-swinging couples (82 percent as against 88 percent) had children. And all of these children were living within the context of a psycho-emotionally and residentially monogamous family life.

And like their parents, these children tended to favor the increasingly popular courtship custom of "living together unmarried" *only* as an *antecedent* to marriage, *not* as a *substitute* for marriage. Like the teenagers of numerous sexually permissive preliterate societies, all of the swingers' children seemed to look forward to their own future marriages.

But the most important reason for doubting that swinging will ever increase in popularity above and beyond two percent of the married population is that most Americans simply do not have an interest in sex that is overpowering enough for them to want to make it a veritable avocation and recreational hobby. Swingers' interest in sex is extremely strong. Swingers believe that they need very frequent sexual gratification and they are willing to go out of their way to a very considerable and sometimes amazing extent in order to get it. The vast majority of the American population simply does not have the inclination to go to this bother. Most Americans satisfy their needs for sexual variety through fantasy and sometimes through expanding their sexual versatility with their own spouse. There is little reason to expect that this will change. Even though for some people fantasy may frequently be unsatisfactory, the high level of motivation necessary for becoming involved in the recreation of sexual mate sharing simply is not there for the vast majority of the population.

What about the effects of swinging on children? There are stable societies in various parts of the world in which some variation of mate exchange is fully institutionalized and regularly practiced. The children in these societies do not appear to suffer from any handicaps due to their parents' erotic behavior. However, we need to be concerned about the possible effects which comarital sex might have upon children right here within the social context of America suburbia. Pluralistic though America may be, the typical middle-class child even today continues to come into regular contact with sentiments that are strongly negative toward such activities as mate exchange. For this reason, some time during the course of growing up swingers' children are faced with the problem of resolving in their own minds the plethora of negative, hostile attitudes with the libertarian sexual behavior patterns of their mothers and fathers. For some children this may not always be very easy or comfortable to do.

Nevertheless, almost all of the swingers' children interviewed for this study appeared quite natural, spontaneous, outspoken and happy. And none of them appeared confused or upset about their situation. In fact, if my impressions are accurate I think it can be confidently asserted that at least at the present time the swingers' children as a group are psychologically healthier and happier than the children of the non-swinging couples.

The swingers tended to rear their children a great deal more permissively than the non-swingers. It thus appears highly probable that the swingers' children will grow up to be far more sexually experienced premaritally and far more free of guilt about such experiences than the vast majority of young people of their social class. Whether or not they will gravitate toward swinging themselves once they are married is an interesting question that is well deserving of exploration in future research.

In review, comarital sex may be viewed as an alternative albeit unconventional way of patterning and ordering the sexual drive of adult members of society. Less than 2 percent of all American married couples today ever choose comarital sex as a life style, and it seems highly unlikely that the figure will ever surpass 2 percent. However, if comarital sex participants all share similar definitions and expectations as far as their behavior vis-a-vis each other is concerned, there is no reason why their behavior should not be able to exist side by side with stable, satisfying family systems.

Bibliography

Bartell, Gilbert D. *Group Sex.* New York: Peter H. Wyden, Inc., 1971.

Bell, Robert R. "Swinging: The Sexual Exchange of Marriage Partners," *Sexual Behavior* 1 (May 1971): 70–79.

Bernard, Jessie. "Infidelity: Some Moral and Social Issues," in Roger W. Libby and Robert N. Whitehurst (eds.), *Marriage and Alternatives.* Glenview, Illinois: Scott, Foresman and Company, 1977, 131–146.

Bernstein, Morey. *The Search for Bridey Murphy.* Garden City, New York: Doubleday and Company, 1956.

Bernscheid, Ellen, and Jack Fei. "Romantic Love and Sexual Jealousy," in Gordon Clanton and Lynn G. Smith (eds.), *Jealousy.* Englewood Cliffs, New Jersey: Prentice-Hall, 1977, 101–109.

Bindrim, Paul. "Nudity as a Quick Grab for Intimacy in Group Therapy," *Psychology Today* 3 (June 1969): 24–28.

Brecher, Edward M. *The Sex Researchers.* Boston: Little, Brown, 1969.

Broderick, Carlfred B. "Socio-Sexual Development in a Suburban Community," *Journal of Sex Research* 2 (April 1966): 1–24.

———, "Children's Romances," *Sexual Behavior* 2 (May 1972): 16–21.

———, and Stanley Fowler. "New Patterns of Relationships Between the Sexes Among Preadolescents," *Journal of Marriage and the Family* 23 (February 1961): 27–30.

Byrne, Donn. "A Pregnant Pause in the Sexual Revolution," *Psychology Today* 11 (July 1977): 67–68.

Christensen, Harold T. "Normative Theory Derived from Cross-Cultural Family Research," *Journal of Marriage and the Family* 31 (May 1969): 209–222.

————, and C. F. Gregg. "Changing Sex Norms in America and Scandinavia," *Journal of Marriage and the Family* 32 (November 1970): 616–627.

Colton, Helen. "Teenage Sex at Home," *Penthouse Forum* 6 (June 1977): 22–26.

Coopersmith, Stanley. *The Antecedents of Self-Esteem.* San Francisco: W. H. Freeman, 1967.

Cressey, Donald R. *Delinquency, Crime and Differential Association.* The Hague, Netherlands: Martinus Nijhoff, 1964.

Crookall, Robert. *The Supreme Adventure.* London: James Clarke, 1961.

————. *The Study and Practice of Astral Projection.* New Hyde Park, New York: University Books, 1966.

————. *Out-of-the-Body Experiences: A Fourth Analysis.* New Hyde Park, New York: University Books, 1970.

Cuber, John F., and Peggy B. Harroff. *The Significant Americans.* New York: Appleton-Century, 1965.

Denfeld, Duane. "Dropouts from Swinging: The Marriage Counselor as Informant," in James R. Smith and Lynn G. Smith (eds.), *Beyond Monogamy.* Baltimore: Johns Hopkins University Press, 1974, 260–267.

————, and Michael Gordon. "The Sociology of Mate Swapping: Or the Family that Swings Together Clings Together," in James R. Smith and Lynn G. Smith (eds.), *Beyond Monogamy.* Baltimore: Johns Hopkins University Press, 1974, 68–83.

Elliott, Neil. *Sensuality in Scandinavia.* New York: Weybright and Talley, 1970.

Elwin, Verrier. *The Muria and Their Ghotul.* London: Oxford University Press, 1947.

Eysenck, Hans J. "Introverts, Extroverts and Sex," *Psychology Today* 4 (January, 1971): 14–19.

Ford, Clelland S., and Frank A. Beach. *Patterns of Sexual Behavior.* New York: Harper and Brothers, 1951.

Freedman, Jonathan N., and Anthony Doob. *Deviancy: The Psychology of Being Different.* New York: Academic Press, 1968.

Furstenberg, Jr., Frank F. "Preventing Unwanted Pregnancies Among Adolescents," *Journal of Health and Social Behavior* 12 (December 1971):340–347.

Galant, Matt and Kathleen. *Sex Rebels.* San Diego: Publishers Export Company, 1966a.

———. *The Swinging Bisexuals.* Cleveland: Century Books, 1966b.

———. *Wife Swapping: The People.* San Diego: Publishers Export Company, 1967.

Gilmartin, Brian G. "Relationship of Traits Measured by the 'California Psychological Inventory' to Premarital Sexual Standards and Behaviors." Unpublished Masters Thesis. Salt Lake City: University of Utah, 1965.

———. "Premarital Coitus and its Differential Social Consequences," *Sexology* 32 (October 1965): 198–200.

———. "Some Personal and Social Characteristics of Mate-Sharing Swingers," in Roger W. Libby and Robert N. Whitehurst (eds.), *Renovating Marriage.* Danville, California: Consensus Publishers, Inc., 1973, 146–165.

———. "Sexual Deviance and Social Networks," in James R. Smith and Lynn G. Smith (eds.), *Beyond Monogamy.* Baltimore: Johns Hopkins University Press, 1974, 291–323.

———. "That Swinging Couple Down the Block," *Psychology Today* 8 (February 1975): 54–58.

———. "The Social Antecedents and Correlates of Comarital Sexual Behavior." Unpublished Doctoral Dissertation. Iowa City: University of Iowa, 1976.

———. "Swinging: Who Gets Involved and How?" in Roger W. Libby and Robert N. Whitehurst (eds.), *Marriage and Alternatives.* Glenview, Illinois: Scott, Foresman and Company, 1977, 161–185.

———. "Jealousy Among the Swingers," *Penthouse Forum* 6 (June 1977): 27–31.

Goode, William J. *World Revolution and Family Patterns.* New York: The Free Press of Glencoe, 1963.

Goodson, Alice. "Experiments in Nude Psychotherapy," *Ankh* 1 (Summer 1967): 20–41.

Greenhouse, Herbert B. *The Astral Journey.* Garden City, New York: Doubleday and Company, 1974.

Henriquez, Fernando. *Love In Action: The Sociology of Sex.* New York: Dutton, 1959.

Hunt, Morton. *The Affair.* New York: World Publishing, 1969.

———. *Sexual Behavior in the 1970s.* Chicago: Playboy Press, 1974.

Kandel, Denise B., and Gerald S. Lesser. "Parent-Adolescent Relationships and Adolescent Independence in the United States and Denmark," *Journal of Marriage and the Family* 31 (May 1969): 348–358.

———. *Youth in Two Worlds.* San Francisco: Jossey-Bass, 1972.

Kinsey, Alfred C., et. al. *Sexual Behavior in the Human Male.* Philadelphia: W. B. Saunders, 1948.

———. *Sexual Behavior in the Human Female.* Philadelphia: W. B. Saunders, 1953.

Knapp, Jacquelyn J., and Robert N. Whitehurst. "Sexually Open Marriage and Relationships: Issues and Prospects," in Roger W. Libby and Robert N. Whitehurst (eds.), *Marriage and Alternatives.* Glenview, Illinois: Scott, Foresman and Company, 1977, 147–160.

Lewis, Robert W. "The Swingers," *Playboy* 16 (April 1969): 149–228.

Libby, Roger W. "Extramarital and Comarital Sex: A Critique of the Literature," in Roger W. Libby and Robert N. Whitehurst (eds.), *Marriage and Alternatives.* Glenview, Illinois: Scott, Foresman and Company, 1977, 80–111.

Lipton, Lawrence. *The Erotic Revolution.* Los Angeles: Sherbourne Press, 1965.

Macklin, Eleanor. "Living Together Unmarried," *Psychology Today* 8 (November 1974): 32–40.

Malinowski, Bronislaw. *The Sexual Life of Savages in North-Western Melanesia.* New York: Harcourt Brace Jovanovich, 1929.

Martin, R. M., and F. L. Marcuse. "Characteristics of Volunteers and Nonvolunteers for Hypnosis," *Journal of Clinical and Experimental Hypnosis* 5 (October 1957): 176–179.

Maslow, Abraham H., and J. M. Sakoda. "Volunteer-Error in the Kinsey Study," in Jerome Himelhoch and Sylvia F. Fava (eds.), *Sexual Behavior in American Society.* New York: Norton, 1955, 119–125.

Masters, William H., and Virginia E. Johnson. "Playboy Interview," *Playboy* 15 (May 1968): 67–202.

Matson, Archie. *Afterlife: Reports from the Threshhold of Death.* New York: Harper and Row, 1975.

McClosky, H., and J. H. Schaar. "Psychological Dimensions of Anomie," *American Sociological Review* 30 (February 1965): 14–40.

Merton, Robert K. *Social Theory and Social Structure.* New York: The Free Press of Glencoe, 1957.

Middleton, Russell. "Brother-Sister and Father-Daughter Marriage in Ancient Egypt," *American Sociological Review* 27 (October 1962): 603–611.

Moody, Jr., Raymond. *Life After Life.* Atlanta, Georgia: Mockingbird Books, 1975.

———. *Reflections on Life After Life.* New York: Bantam Books, 1977.

Murdock, George P. *Social Structure.* New York: Macmillan, 1949.

Neubeck, Gerhard. *Extramarital Relations.* Englewood Cliffs, New Jersey: Prentice-Hall, 1969.

O'Neill, George C. and Nena. "Patterns in Group Sexual Activity," *Journal of Sex Research* 6 (May 1970): 101–112.

———. "Open Marriage: A Conceptual Framework," in James R. Smith and Lynn G. Smith (eds.), *Beyond Monogamy.* Baltimore: Johns Hopkins University Press, 1974, 56–67.

Palson, C. and R. "Swinging in Wedlock," *Society* 9 (February 1972): 28–37.

Pelletier, Kenneth R. *Mind as Healer, Mind as Slayer.* New York: Delta Books, 1977.

Phillips, Derek L. "Rejection: A Possible Consequence of Seeking Help for Mental Disorders," *American Sociological Review* 28 (October 1963): 963–972.

———. "Mental Health Status, Social Participation, and Happiness," *Journal of Health and Social Behavior* 8 (December 1967): 285–291.

Reiss, Ira L. *The Social Context of Premarital Sexual Permissiveness.* New York: Holt, Rinehart and Winston, 1967.

———. *Family Systems in America.* Hinsdale, Illinois: Dryden Press, 1976.

Renne, Karen S. "Correlates of Dissatisfaction in Marriage," *Journal of Marriage and the Family* 32 (February 1970): 54–67.

Reuben, David. *Everything You Have Always Wanted to Know About Sex But Were Afraid to Ask.* New York: David McKay, 1970.

Rimmer, Robert H. *The Harrad Experiment.* Los Angeles: Sherbourne Press, 1966.

Roberts, Jane. *The Seth Material.* New York: Bantam Books, 1970.

———. *Seth Speaks.* New York: Bantam Books, 1972.

Rodman, Hyman. "The Lower-Class Value Stretch," *Social Forces* 42 (December 1963): 205–215.

Rubenstein, Paul, and Herbert F. Margolis. *The Groupsex Tapes.* New York: David McKay, 1971.

Sherman, Harold. *How to Make ESP Work for You.* Santa Monica, California: DeVorss, 1966.

Simonton, O. Carl and Stephanie M. *Psychological Factors, Stress and Cancer.* Fort Worth, Texas: Cancer Counseling and Research Center (1413 8th Avenue), 1976.

Smith, James R., and Lynn G. Smith "Comarital Sex and the Sexual Freedom Movement," *Journal of Sex Research* 6 (May 1970): 131–142.

———. "Comarital Sex: The Incorporation of Extramarital Sex into the Marriage Relationship." Unpublished Paper Presented at the Symposium of the American Psychopathological Association on "Critical Issues in Contemporary Sexual Behavior." New York, February, 1971.

———. "Introduction" and "Comarital Sex," in James R. Smith and Lynn G. Smith (eds.), *Beyond Monogamy.* Baltimore: Johns Hopkins University Press, 1974, 1–45, 84–102.

Steiger, Brad. *The Enigma of Reincarnation: We Have Lived Before.* New York: Ace Books, 1967.

———. *The Mind Travellers.* New York: Award Books, 1968.

Stevenson, Ian. *Twenty Cases Suggestive of Reincarnation.* Charlottesville: University of Virginia Press, 1966.

Straus, Murray A., and Suzanne K. Steinmetz. *Violence in the Family.* New York: Dodd, Mead and Company, 1974.

Symonds, Carolyn. "Sexual Mate Swapping and the Swingers," *Marriage Counseling Quarterly* 6 (Spring 1971a): 1–12.

———. "A Nude Touchy-Feely Group," *Journal of Sex Research* 7 (May 1971b): 126–133.

———. "Sexual Mate Swapping: Violation of Norms and Reconciliation of Guilt," in James M. Henslin (ed.), *Studies in the Sociology of Sex.* New York: Appleton-Century, 1971c, 81–109.

Tec, Nechama. "Family and Differential Involvement with Marijuana: A Study of Suburban Teenagers," *Journal of Marriage and the Family* 32 (November 1970): 656–664.

Twichell, Jon. "Sexual Liberality and Personality: A Pilot Study," in James R. Smith and Lynn G. Smith (eds.), *Beyond Monogamy.* Baltimore: Johns Hopkins University Press, 1974, 230–245.

Udry, J. Richard. *The Social Context of Marriage.* Philadelphia: J. B. Lippincott, 1974.

Varni, Charles A. "Participant Observer Study of Sexual Mate Exchange Among Married Couples." Unpublished Masters Thesis. San Diego: San Diego State University, 1970.

———. "Contexts of Conversion: The Case of Swinging," in Roger W. Libby and Robert N. Whitehurst (eds.), *Renovating Marriage.* Danville, California: Consensus Publishers, 1973, 166–181.

———. "An Exploratory Study of Spouse Swapping," in James R. Smith and Lynn G. Smith (eds.), *Beyond Monogamy.* Baltimore: Johns Hopkins University Press, 1974, 246–259.

Walshok, Mary L. "The Emergence of Middle-Class Deviant Subcultures: The Case of Swingers," *Social Problems* 18 (Spring 1971): 488–495.

Wambach, Helen. "Past Life Recall," *Psychic* 7 (November-December 1976): 56–61.

———. "Life Before Life," *Psychic* 7 (January-February 1977): 8–13.

Weinberg, Martin S. "Becoming a Nudist," *Psychiatry* 29 (February 1966): 21–33.

Wheeler, David R. *Journey to the Other Side.* New York: Ace Books, 1976.

Whitehurst, Robert N. "The Monogamous Ideal and Sexual Realities," in Roger W. Libby and Robert N. Whitehurst (eds.), *Marriage and Alternatives.* Glenview, Illinois: Scott, Foresman and Company, 1977, 14–21.

Wilson, Thomas J. B., and Everett Meyers. *Wife Swapping: A Complete Eight Year Survey of Morals in North America.* New York: Volitant Press, 1965.

Wolf, Karl H. (ed.) *The Sociology of Georg Simmel.* New York: The Free Press of Glencoe, 1950.

Zimbardo, Philip G. *Shyness.* Reading, Massachusetts: Addison-Wesley, 1977.

Index